OUTSMARTING

IQ

The Emerging Science
of Learnable Intelligence

by DAVID PERKINS

THE FREE PRESS

New York   London   Toronto   Sydney   Tokyo   Singapore

The Free Press
A Division of Simon & Schuster Inc.
1230 Avenue of the Americas, New York, N.Y. 10020

Printed in the United States of America

printing number

1 2 3 4 5 6 7 8 9 0

Library of Congress Cataloging-in-Publication Data

Perkins, David N.
    Outsmarting IQ: the emerging science of learnable intelligence/
David N. Perkins.
        p.   cm.
    Includes bibliographical references.
    ISBN 0-02-925212-1
    1. Intellect.   2. Intelligence levels—Social aspects.   3. Nature
and nurture.   4. Learning, Psychology of.   I. Title.
BF431.P365   1995
153.9—dc20   94-45954
                                                            CIP

Illustrations on pages 48 and 71 are reprinted with the permission of The Free Press, an imprint of Simon & Schuster, from *Bias in Mental Testing,* by Arthur R. Jensen. Copyright © 1980 by Arthur R. Jensen.

Illustration on page 186 is reprinted with the permission of Reuven Feuerstein from his book *Instrumental Enrichment: An Intervention Program for Cognitive Modifiability,* University Park Press, Baltimore. Copyright © 1980 by Reuven Feuerstein.

Illustration on page 303 is reprinted with the permission of Blackwell Publishers, Oxford, from *Intelligence and Development: A Cognitive Theory,* by Mike Anderson. Copyright © 1992 by Blackwell Publishers.

To the memory of

PAUL KOLERS
(1926–1986)

mentor, colleague, and friend,

who introduced me to

cognitive psychology

Contents

Acknowledgments

Many years of pondering the mysteries of intelligence in general and learnable intelligence in particular lie behind this book. The ideas have been long in the making and no doubt would not have emerged at all without crucial help from a number of sources. My colleagues and I have benefitted from research support for investigations of thinking and its cultivation. The John D. and Catherine T. MacArthur Foundation has been especially generous in this regard. Important resources also have come from the Spencer Foundation, the Getty Center for Education in the Arts, and the Pew Charitable Trusts. I much appreciate their faith and commitment.

In the course of the years I have sought ideas, counsel, and feedback from many colleagues who have been gracious and forthcoming with their thoughts and suggestions. I recall many valuable conversations with my wife Ann Perkins, my sons Theodore and Thomas Perkins, and my colleagues Beatriz Capdevielle, Allan Collins, Catalina Laserna, Abigail Lipson, Raymond Nickerson, Stellan Ohlsson, Gavriel Salomon, Rebecca Simmons, Robert Swartz, Shari Tishman, and Carlos Vasco. My thanks to others whom a ragged memory does not let me list here.

As to the book itself, Diane Downs conducted invaluable background work for several chapters. Dorothy MacGillivray did background research, assembled the bibliography, and helped with many other facets of getting the book in order. My long-time colleague Shari Tishman and my editor at The Free Press Susan Arellano offered insightful section-by-section commentary on drafts. Howard Gardner, Emma Policastro, and Robert Swartz read drafts and contributed a number of helpful suggestions.

My final thanks go to a colleague who will never read these words. Paul Kolers was a research associate and lecturer at the Massachusetts Institute of Technology when I was pursuing my doctoral degree there. I sat in on his course about cognitive psychology and found it fascinating. We struck up an acquaintance, he employed me one summer and introduced me to Nelson Goodman, who was then forming Project Zero at the Harvard Graduate School of Education, the research and development group that has become my life's work. We argued endlessly in the best of spirits about how the mind worked. In the years 1970–1986, while he was a professor in the Department of Psychology at the University of Toronto, we kept in touch and continued to collaborate, coauthoring a couple of papers. His untimely death in 1986 at the age of 59 was a blow. His sharp mind, wicked humor, and commitment to understanding human cognition are all missed.

1

Telescopes and Intelligence

When I was a child, my family lived in a large sprawling house in a small town in Maine, a former schoolhouse in fact, with a couple of the blackboards still in place. There was a flat roof over part of the house, where my mother hung the laundry to billow and dry on clear days. But the flat roof meant more to me during clear nights. I would sometimes go out with a pillow to rest my head, lie on the roof, and stargaze for an hour or so.

Later, I bought a cheap reflecting telescope. I picked out craters on the Moon, scrutinized the red sphere of Mars, located Saturn, marveling at the tiny image of the planet with its delicate rings. I was caught up by the magnitude of creation and our diminutive place in it, an experience innumerable human beings have had, albeit far fewer human beings than there are stars of which to stand in awe.

Although I was not very educated when I went stargazing on the laundry roof, I had the benefit of some knowledge. I knew that the earth circled around the sun, the moon around the earth. I knew that the other planets circled around the sun. I knew that the stars were way out there, our sun but one of countless hydrogen sparks wending their firefly ways through a vastness without compass. My father told me about such things, and I had read about some of them in books.

So, between 10 and 11 PM up there on the laundry roof, that's how the universe looked to me. Scanning the sweep of the Milky Way, our own galaxy, I often felt I was no more than a speck of rust on the fragile spokes of gravity that made that awesome wheel go round.

I was harvesting the heritage of human intelligence. For thousands of years, priests and scientists, magicians and navigators, astrologers and philosophers had been looking at the sky and wondering, making up stories, proposing theories, building conceptions—a motley team of human intelligences at work, stirred by every concern from the most cosmic to the most pragmatic.

We think of the telescope as our instrument of inquiry for the heavens. Even more fundamental is the instrument behind the instrument, the resource of human intelligence. Every one of those stargazers drew upon it to make sense of what they were seeing.

An Apple Cart Waiting to Be Upset

Whatever I knew about astronomy at the time, there was another matter of which I knew nothing: how hard-won was that look of infinite reach in the sky, what a work of intelligence it was, what a revolution it took—a conceptual revolution that changed the universe, by changing what people took the universe to be.

Children, grandfathers, and everyone in between have been looking up at the stars for a long time—something like 2 million years, if one counts as human the tool-using hominids who once lived and hunted in the environs of the Olduvai Gorge of the Serengeti. It would be easy to assume that what we see today is not much different today than it has been for millennia.

Easy to assume, but quite false. While the physical pattern of the stars has not changed much, what we see has. The look of the stars depends not only the light that tickles our retinas but on our conceptions, on what we think things out there are really like. Five centuries before, a young ancestor of mine somewhere in the British Isles might have spent that same hour between 10 and 11 lying in a field to watch the heavenly pageant march around the earth. He would not have felt like a mote in an infinite universe. Believing something very different, he would see something quite different, the stars parading for his benefit.

The neat cosmology of Aristotle and the Catholic church had put the universe into a satisfying order and served it up in a form pleasing to most everyone concerned. The earth lay at the center of the universe. Around the earth circled the sun, the moon, the fixed stars, and the planets, all ordered on crystalline spheres at various distances from our planet.

Make no mistake: This was magnificently intelligent in its time. It solved the problems of its day. It certainly made my ancestor happy. He could be proud of his position on the reviewing stand, enjoying the parade of stars, because in the dogma of his day it was all there for him and his fellow human beings, lords of creation every one. But reviewing stand it actually was not. More of an apple cart, just waiting to be upset.

No one then knew that the planets were whole worlds in themselves, like the earth. They were just more lights in the sky like the stars, but with a difference. A half-dozen aberrant points of light wandered around against the background of the innumerable "fixed" stars over periods of months and years. They came to be called planets—wanderers—from the Greek verb *planasthai*, to wander.

The planets became a problem for an idealized earth-centered picture of the universe. As far back as the time of Christ, those who studied the stars had looked upward with better and better instrumentation. They saw the planets, night after night and season after season, tracing their paths against the backdrop of the fixed stars. They measured those paths with some precision. They tried to fit what they found to the theory that the planets were making circles around the earth, but the paths did not quite match. The circles did not quite work.

What to do? When a theory has a leak, patch it! The great patchmaker was the Egyptian astronomer Ptolemy, who lived from about 100 to 170 A.D. Ptolemy made his observations in Alexandria, Egypt, during the period 127–151 A.D. He wanted to preserve the notion that heavenly objects moved in circles, an idea precious to the philosophy of the times. So Ptolemy proposed that each planet not only made a great circle around the earth but also continuously made little circles within that big circle—epicycles, they were called. These epicycles accounted for the mismatch between a circle-around-the-earth theory and the data on the positions of the planets in the sky. And best of all, they kept the planets moving around the earth and things moving in circles generally.

Ptolemy rescued the whole notion of an earth-centered universe with his epicycles, a brilliant albeit mistaken act of intelligence. Aristotle before him was no fool either, nor the others of those times who looked at, pondered, and wrote about the sky. Intelligence does not make you right, but it helps you find patterns, right or not. It's striking that we understand the optics of telescopes so much better than the true instrument of all inquiry, human intelligence.

Reconstructing the Universe

Ptolemy's patch was clever, but sooner or later the flaws were bound to show up. Copernicus, a Polish astronomer in the years 1473–1543, devoted his life to the meticulous gathering of data about the motions of the stars and planets. He pored over his measurements, compared them with the epicycles theory, and could not make epicycles work, at least not in any reasonably straightforward version. Hoping to get rid of these errors, he reviewed the older literature of the subject and found that a minority opinion had been long neglected, the heliocentric concept that placed the sun at the center of the universe.

So Copernicus bit the cosmic bullet. He mustered his intelligence and his evidence. We had it all wrong, he argued. The planets do not circle around the earth. They make circles around the sun—and so does the earth. This was his proposal in his great work, *On the Revolutions of the Celestial Spheres*, not published until well after his death around 1543.

With Copernicus's proposal began modern astronomy and cosmology, sciences that have grown tremendously over the five centuries since, sciences that, every step of the way, have expanded our conception of the scope and complexity of the universe. These same sciences have just as steadily shrunk our conception of our own importance in the scheme of things.

This was the original Copernican revolution, but not the one and only. Historians of science have borrowed the name of Copernicus for other equally fundamental shifts of theory. A *Copernican revolution* has come to mean any revolution in our scientific conception of things that upsets the apple cart, reverses old conceptions, remakes the fabric of our beliefs down to their warp and weft. There have been many such collective acts of intelligence in the rising spiral of science, for instance the dual revolutions of quantum mechanics and of relativity theory that marked the first decades of the twentieth century.

Goddard's List

This book concerns a Copernican revolution in the making, one far from cosmological and about as close to home as you can get. It concerns what I called the instrument behind the instruments, that very instrument with which you are reading these words, that very instrument with which you walk, talk, find your way to work and home again. It concerns the nature of intelligence and especially the idea that intelligence is not fixed but learnable. It asks whether you or I or most anyone can learn to behave more intelligently.

Who would not want a sharper mental edge? Yet the classic view of human intelligence takes a grudging stance on that prospect. Just as Ptolemy's epicycles gave the original Copernican revolution something to revolt against, so this classic view of intelligence does for the new Copernican revolution—it is a view to think with and think against, to test and critique, and perhaps even to come back to, if in the end the evidence insists. This severe picture of intelligence has rarely been as concisely and chillingly asserted as by H. H. Goddard in 1920.*

Goddard was one of the three major pioneers of hereditarianism in America. He popularized the Binet scale and used the scores from these tests to measure intelligence as a single, inherited entity. As director of research at the Vineland Training School for Feeble-Minded Girls and Boys in New Jersey he claimed to localize the cause of feeble-mindedness in a single gene. It was Goddard who coined the phrase *moron* for *high-grade defectives*—all people with mental ages between eight and twelve—from a Greek word meaning foolish. Here is what he said:

> Stated in its boldest form, our thesis is that the chief determiner of human conduct is a unitary mental process which we call intelligence: that this process is conditioned by a nervous mechanism which is inborn: that the degree of efficiency to be attained by that nervous mechanisms and the consequent grade of intellectual or mental level for each individual is determined by the kind of chromosomes that come together with the union of the germ cells: that it is but little affected by any later influences except such serious accidents as may destroy part of the mechanism.

*Citations for ideas and sources mentioned in the text appear in the Notes at the end of the book, which are organized by chapter and section. Full references appear in the section following the Notes.

We have good reason to resent Goddard's list. It says that we are pretty much stuck with the intelligence we are born with. According to Goddard, and such contemporaries of Goddard as psychologist Lewis M. Terman and psychometrician Charles Spearman, people can learn particular bodies of knowledge and skill, but there is not much they can do to get more of this special stuff, intelligence. Your personal allotment determines limits of insight you must live with all your life.

Of course, how angry Goddard's list makes us and how true it is are different matters. As a broad generalization, the universe has not been especially responsive to how human beings feel about things. For instance, we might have preferred that the earth stand still at the center of the universe, the mansion of humankind. However, it turned out to spin around a quite ordinary star spinning around the center of a quite ordinary galaxy adrift among billions of others. Preferences do not count for much in the face of facts. Whatever we prefer about intelligence, it simply might turn out another way.

For a long time, however, psychologists technically concerned with the nature of intelligence have found reason to challenge the claims in Goddard's list. Here are some of their reservations:

Unitary. Although Goddard wrote of intelligence as a unitary mental process, several old and new views of intelligence argue that intelligence is multiple—there are different kinds of intelligence. Rather than measuring intelligence by a single yardstick, we might find that different people have different kinds of strengths.

Inborn. Although Goddard wrote of intelligence as inborn, research suggests that most people can learn to behave considerably more intelligently. Learnable intelligence might help us all to meet better a myriad of social and personal challenges.

Nervous. Although Goddard saw the nervous system as the seat of intelligence, current science argues that intelligent behavior is only partly attributable to an efficient nervous system. When people learn to conduct themselves more intelligently, they learn how to make the most of the nervous system with which they are endowed.

Process. Although Goddard treated intelligence as a process, contemporary investigations suggest that intelligent behavior has at least as much to do with knowledge and attitudes—what you know and understand about the way your mind works, what strategies you have at your fingertips, what attitudes you hold toward the potential of your mind and toward intellectual challenges.

Goddard's list is in trouble. As in the original Copernican revolution, fundamental conceptions are at stake. What was once viewed as central—Goddard's unitary inborn nervous process—is getting pushed toward the periphery as our inner cosmology of mind undergoes reconstruction. Conceptions of intelligence today are in radical flux, with new theories asserting their rights like African bees. It is to the Copernican revolution in our ideas about intelligence that this book is dedicated.

The Revolution We Need

As a cognitive psychologist, I have good reason to be interested in this Copernican revolution. However, as a parent, a citizen, a voter, a shopper, a boss, an employee, and a player of many other roles, why should I care? Why should any of us care?

Because how intelligence really works matters in a very concrete practical way—arguably it matters much more than whether the earth circles around the sun or vice versa. We could use more intelligence. Other people do not always behave as intelligently as we would like, and neither do we ourselves, as we realize when we stand back and reflect on our behavior. If intelligence is learnable, we can hope to do something about it directly. If intelligence is not, we just have to live with the fact and work around it.

Of many sources pointing to the need for more intelligence in the form of better thinking, I was recently struck by a report from the Rand Corporation, *Global Preparedness and Human Resources: College and Corporate Perspectives*. The report examined what people from the corporate and academic sectors felt was needed to meet the escalating challenges of the times. Their answer: General cognitive skills were rated more highly than knowledge in an academic major, social skills, and personal traits. Good thinking counts most; so say some of those who have thought about it.

Another compelling appeal for better thinking and learning appears in the recent book *Thinking for a Living* by Ray Marshall and Marc Tucker. These authors turn to the educational shortfalls of U. S. students in comparison with students in several other nations. They examine the economic roots and economic consequences of the education gap. Their conclusions are cautionary: As the title of their book suggests, economic productivity and competitiveness in the world today depend on workers who are skillful thinkers and learners. This is just what U. S.

education is not producing, with certain minorities particularly suffering. Marshall and Tucker cite these statistics in illustration:

> Fewer than four in ten young adults can summarize in writing the main
> argument from a lengthy news column—one in four whites, one in four
> blacks, and two in ten Hispanics. Only twenty-five out of 100 young
> adults can use a bus schedule to select the appropriate bus for a given
> departure or arrival—three in 100 blacks and seven in 100 Hispanics.
> Only 10 percent of the total group can select the least costly product
> from a list of grocery items on the basis of unit-pricing information—
> twelve in 100 whites, one in 100 blacks, and four in 100 Hispanics.

They sum up the reality this way:

> These findings make it clear that only a tiny fraction of our workers can
> function effectively in an environment requiring strong communications
> skills and the application of sophisticated conceptual understanding to
> complex real-world problems.

Of course, one response to this concern might be that students need
more back-to-basics education, more drill and practice, more reading,
'riting, and 'rithmetic in a classic regimen. However, in terms of routine
competence—the kind built by drill and practice—U.S. students score
reasonably well. It is tasks requiring a modicum of reasoning that floor
many of them. Students need better thinking and learning skills. As I
argued in my recent book *Smart Schools,* real learning is a consequence
of thinking. People retain, understand, and make active use of knowledge through learning experiences that center on thinking both
through and with what is learned. Good thinking and good learning are
as closely tied as the hydrogen and oxygen in a molecule of water, and
they make up the drink that students need.

Not-so-intelligent behavior is a stark reality of our own lives and the
lives around us. While later chapters will turn to further evidence, let
me offer three tales by way of illustration.

> *The populist senator.* A while ago, a United States senator responded
> to concerns some had expressed that a Supreme Court nominee
> might be mediocre. His thought: "Even if he is mediocre, there
> are a lot of mediocre judges and people and lawyers. They are
> entitled to a little representation, aren't they, and a little chance?
> We can't have all Brandeises, Cardozos and Frankfurters and stuff
> like that there."

The whale movers. A while ago, a forty-five-foot eight-ton dead whale washed up on an Oregon beach. Local authorities faced the problem of getting rid of the carcass. So they decided to dynamite it, expecting it would pulverize. The pieces would be eaten by sea gulls or at least easily removed. Instead, the dynamite exploded the whale into huge chunks of blubber, one of which crushed a nearby car. Fortunately, the spectators only suffered a rain of small gobs of blubber on their heads.

The willing student. A while ago, a colleague I hadn't seen in some years passed through town, and over a cup of coffee we fell to discussing her efforts to awaken her college students to the art and craft of thinking. She told me of a student who for some time seemed not to catch on at all. But eventually he came to an insight. "Oh I see," the student said. "So in *this* class, you want us to reach our conclusions on the basis of reason and argument."

These stories catch us human beings with our intellectual pants down. Although mediocre people certainly deserve representation, they presumably do not want representation *by* a mediocre person. Although exploding a whale might work, it might go wildly wrong, so there is something to be said for a trial run on a small part like the tail. Although it's nice that the willing student seems ready to exercise reason and argument in my colleague's class, it would be even nicer if the student recognized that there was some point to reaching conclusions on the basis of reason and argument in many circumstances. To be sure, people sometimes legitimately arrive at conclusions in ways far removed from reason and argument—observation, authority, tradition, faith, intuition. What is striking about the willing student is that he viewed reasoning and argument in the classroom as somewhat exotic, a reaction that perhaps raises concerns as much about what his other classes were like as about his own thinking.

While fun, these stories are also fundamentally cautionary. They remind us that people sometimes do not think very well. They urge us to ask how often and under what conditions people think not-so-intelligently.

All too often, it seems. For a case in point, the health plan proposed by the Clinton administration in 1993 precipitated a persistent and acrimonious debate about its merits. How carefully has that debate been conducted through the media? The Annenberg Public Policy Center at the University of Pennsylvania undertook an analysis of 125 print and

73 broadcast ads drawn from both sides of the question. The analysis disclosed that about 60 percent of the broadcast ads and 30 percent of the print ads were false, misleading, or unfair. The ads tended to question the integrity and goodwill of people on the other side of the issue. The anti-Clinton ads played upon five fears: increased taxation, rationing, bureaucracy and government control, diminished choice of doctors, and massive job loss. The pro-Clinton ads tended to exaggerate the number of people harmed by present medical insurance practices and the rate of growth of medical costs, as well as suggesting that Republican programs offered people no help.

A cynical view of this would take it as no more than cutthroat politics. It is certainly that, but it also tells us something about ourselves. Political and special interest groups offer such thin and biased arguments because many people are moved by them. People of generally good character commonly simply fail to investigate or even ponder the other side of issues about which they have come to feel strongly.

Because of narrow and biased thinking, major political figures occasionally even make decisions contrary to their own best interests. The noted historian Barbara Tuchman has written an entire book about this. In her *The March of Folly*, she traces out episode after episode in history where the key players made disastrous mistakes that, she argues, they could in principle have anticipated and avoided. One of these episodes was the prolonged United States involvement in Vietnam. In Chapter 6, I discuss examples from Tuchman's work further, along with a number of other cases of faulty thinking.

If less-than-intelligent thought and action stain the world of politics, other slices of society fare no better. In the world of business, the savings and loan scandal of the late 1980s marked a clear occasion where acquisitiveness ran too far ahead of prudence. One can also ponder the Edsel and the efforts of the Coca-Cola Company to replace the old coke with a new and sweeter one. In the medical world, quackery proves to be a persistent problem as people driven by fear spend dearly on hopeless remedies. At the same time, grateful as we all must be for modern medicine, there are some valid medical malpractice suits that point up the occasionally shaky character of medical reasoning.

In the legal world, dubious evidence and argument demonstrably win the day from time to time. A case in point appears in documentary film maker Errol Morris's well-known *The Thin Blue Line*. The film focuses on the 1976 murder of a policeman by the driver of a car stopped for a minor traffic violation. In his 1988 film, made more than a decade after the event, Morris exposed the lapses of evidence and manipulation of logic involved in convicting Randall Adams, the supposed driver, and sentencing him to life imprisonment. The film led to reopening the case and setting aside Adams' conviction.

Were these avoidable errors or were people thinking absolutely as well as they could with the information they had at the time? While lack of information certainly can be a factor, shortfalls of imagination and critical insight usually seem to play a role in such circumstances. In a 1994 article in *Educational Researcher*, Keith Stanovich of the Ontario Institute for Studies in Education pointed up such concerns by proposing a label for them: *dysrationalia*. He defined the syndrome of dysrationalia as follows:

> Dysrationalia is the inability to think and behave rationally despite adequate intelligence [in the sense of IQ]. It is a general term that refers to a heterogenous group of disorders manifest by significant difficulties in belief formation, in the assessment of belief consistency, or in the determination of action to achieve one's goals. . . . The key diagnostic criterion for dysrationalia is a level of rationality, as demonstrated in thinking and behavior, that is significantly below the level of the individual's intellectual capacity.

Stanovich argues that people often think much more poorly than they can. Is this really so? Why does it happen? And can anything be done about it?

The answer developed in the following chapters comes down to this. While lapses in thinking are hearteningly rare in some circumstances, they are all too common in others. People think quite well and behave quite intelligently much of the time—so far so good. However, when faced with situations that are complex or novel or invite bias, people often think quite poorly, falling into one of several "intelligence traps." These traps figure both in the broad reach of public and political affairs and in the fine texture of everyday events. People get trapped into not-so-intelligent behavior in numerous corners of their lives—an educational opportunity missed or dismissed, a casual purchase, a hasty marriage, a job too easily abandoned, a task too stubbornly pursued, a bad risk taken, a good risk avoided. Life is peppered with such situations. They will always be there, but putting learnable intelligence to work can help to keep them at bay. We need the revolution.

An Evolutionary Double Bind

But why do we need any such revolution? Why do we find ourselves in this fix? There is something distinctly odd about not performing up to par in our day-to-day thinking, and still more so in high-stakes circumstances. We are sophisticated organisms, the product of millions of years of evolution, with intelligence our most conspicuous and powerful adaptation. How can it be, as Stanovich puts it, that we commonly function below the level of our intellectual capacity?

The answer I will develop later in this book is that we as a species are caught in an evolutionary double bind. Along with our intellectual strengths come inherent intellectual weaknesses. To preview ideas detailed later: Our minds function in a very pattern-driven way. As we go through life, puzzle out problems, and gain experience, we store up patterns that work well for us. In meeting new situations, we automatically try to make a match to what we know and select a pattern from our storehouse that might apply. This matching process gets influenced not only by what patterns we have stored up but also by our goals, prejudices, and passions.

All this works very effectively most of the time. It keeps us functioning efficiently in light of our past experience. But inherent in the process is a tendency toward rapid, stereotyped, less appropriate responses when situations are unusually complex or novel or when they evoke biases. This shortfall is built into the very nature of the way our minds work.

It may seem odd that a fundamentally adaptive system would prove self-limiting in some ways. However, this is actually quite common. The mammalian immune system provides an excellent case in point. Most people are aware that the immune system detects invasive organisms and constructs countermeasures tailored to them. It is a powerful line of defence against disease, contributing greatly to our survival. However, fewer people are aware that a number of maladies called autoimmune diseases result when a person's own white blood cells fail to recognize normal cells and attack some constituent of the body itself. These include pernicious anemia (caused by deficiency of vitamin B), thyrotoxicosis (the condition resulting from an overactivity of the thyroid gland), systemic lupus erythematosus, some types of hepatitis, many forms of arthritis, some forms of chronic liver and kidney disease, and possibly even diabetes. In other words, although fundamentally highly adaptive, the immune system is not perfect. The same can be said of the natural pattern-making proclivities of the human mind.

There is a way out of this double bind, however. Perhaps we can learn to make calculatedly better use of our own minds, not always surrendering to our quick pattern-making proclivities but sometimes working strategically against them for the sake of more critical and creative thinking.

The idea that we can learn to put our thoughts in better order is as old as Plato and Aristotle, and as new as wide-spread contemporary efforts to teach more effective thinking practices in schools and seminars. It may seem an artificial enterprise—and it is, because it works against natural proclivities. But for all its artificiality, it is no more inappropriate than people striving for a better diet or a healthier pattern of physical effort contrary to their natural leaning.

Three Mindware Questions

Basically this book is an argument for learnable intelligence. It's an argument that a revolution in our conceptions of intelligence is underway, that it's warranted, that we need it, and that we can carry it further. I want to outline a theory of learnable intelligence that says to what extent and in what ways our intelligence can be amplified.

One way to track the debate around this revolution is to use a metaphor, the idea of *mindware*. What is mindware? It is whatever people can learn that helps them to solve problems, make decisions, understand difficult concepts, and perform other intellectually demanding tasks better. To draw an analogy with computers, mindware is software for the mind—the programs you run in your mind that enable you to do useful things with data stored in your memory. Or to make a more prosaic but equally apt analogy with cooking, mindware is like kitchenware, the equipment of the mind, the pots and pans, measuring spoons and spatulas, egg beaters and corkscrews that enable people to cook up something compelling out of the information at their disposal. Or to put it yet another way, mindware is whatever knowledge, understanding, and attitudes you have that support you in making the best use of your mind.

The idea of mindware suggests three key questions about intelligence that will help us to track the arguments about its nature and progress toward an expanded view of intelligence. I will call them the mindware questions:

MWQ #1. What mechanisms underlie intelligence?
MWQ #2. Can people learn more intelligence?
MWQ #3. What aspects of intelligence especially need attention?

The first asks about the mechanisms of intelligence—the neural structures; the cognitive processes; the roles of knowledge, skill, belief, and attitude; whatever contributes to intelligent behavior. The second asks whether, in light of those mechanisms, intelligence or some aspects of intelligence can be learned. If intelligence is at least partly learnable, then the third question comes into play: What kinds or aspects or facets of intelligence most call for attention? To put it in mindware terms, what sorts of mindware do we most need?

Throughout this book, I will use the three mindware questions as a yardstick for measuring progress toward a theory of learnable intelligence. Goddard's list defines our starting point, because it suggests answers that grant nothing to the notion of learnable intelligence:

MWQ #1. What mechanisms underlie intelligence?

- The efficiency of the neural system as an information processing device, which is largely genetically determined, Goddard says.

MWQ #2. Can people learn more intelligence?

- No, because genetics determines basic intelligence.

MWQ #3. What aspects of intelligence especially need attention?

- The question is pointless, given the answer to question 2.

While those are Goddard's answers, throughout the three parts of this book I will build steadily toward a different set of answers with ample room for learnable intelligence. In particular, Part I, In Search of Intelligence, looks at the historical roots of the theory of intelligence, examines the case for Goddard's list, reviews fundamental criticisms of it, and synthesizes all this into the idea that we need to recognize three dimensions of intelligence. The first is *neural intelligence*, the contribution of neural efficiency to intelligent behavior, and a nod to Goddard's tradition. The second is *experiential intelligence*, the contribution of a storehouse of personal experience in diverse situations to intelligent behavior. The third is *reflective intelligence*, the contribution of knowl-

edge, understanding, and attitudes about how to use our minds to intelligent behavior—in other words, the contribution of mindware. The
second and third are both learnable and make up learnable intelligence.

Part II, Learnable Intelligence on Trial, focuses on the need for and
prospects of learnable intelligence, especially reflective intelligence. It
details the case for troublingly frequent shortfalls in human thinking
sketched earlier in this chapter. It provides an analysis of the evolutionary double bind that often leads us to think less effectively than our
capacities allow. Finally, it reviews some well-known efforts to teach
people better thinking—to teach them reflective intelligence—gauges
their success, and analyzes a persistent debate about whether people
can actually learn to think better.

Part III, What the Mind is Made Of, ranges beyond current theory to
introduce a new way of conceptualizing what reflective intelligence is
and how it operates. You can "know your way around" the good use of
your mind in much the same sense that you can know your way around
your neighborhood, the game of baseball, or the stock market. To
acquire such knowledge, people can "learn their way around" important
kinds of thinking, gaining concepts, beliefs, feelings, and patterns of
action that allow them to handle problem solving, decision making,
explanation, and other intellectually demanding activities better. This
view is very different from the usual emphatically process-centered view
of reflective intelligence, which sees it as a bundle of cognitive processes
that need organization and expansion. Finally, in a concluding chapter, I
explore areas of reflective intelligence that may have great social importance in the next decades.

Through twists and turns of evidence and argument, analysis and
synthesis, in the course of this book I hope to make the case that most
people can learn to function in a substantially more intelligent way. We
can beat the evolutionary double bind and its intelligence traps if we
invest our efforts in cultivating our intelligence.

Isn't the Revolution Over Yet?

But why make so much of this revolution in our conception of intelligence? Isn't it old news? Some might count this revolution as virtually
over, saying "IQ? We don't believe in that any more!" As to cultivating
better thinking, books and seminars on creative thinking are popular in
business and other settings. Several states in the United States include

thinking skills as part of their educational goals. Many textbooks have thinking-oriented questions at the end of each chapter. It looks as though people already believe in learnable intelligence and have set out to do something about it.

I cherish these signs of a thaw in our attitudes toward human intelligence. But, as a person who works professionally in this area, I have to view them more as the crocus that blooms here and there toward the end of winter than as spring itself. In point of fact, books and seminars on creative and other kinds of thinking reach relatively few people and often with rather poor models of better thinking. Very few schools mount persistent and effective efforts to cultivate students' thinking, despite the mention of thinking on state agendas. The thinking-oriented questions in textbooks by and large only make a token contribution. The idea of learnable intelligence has not penetrated our society widely and deeply.

Why not? Why is most of the revolution yet to come?

One reason is taken up in Chapter 4 and again from a different perspective in Chapter 9: Some psychologists skeptical about viewing intelligence as IQ are also skeptical about the learnability of reflective intelligence. While rejecting the idea that intelligence is mostly a matter of neural efficiency, they hold that especially intelligent behavior is a matter of learning how to think and act within innumerable particular situations, within different subject matters or professions for instance, what I call experiential intelligence. Since what is learnable about intelligence lacks generality, they say, people cannot expect to learn to be more intelligent in general, only situation by situation. I will argue later that this view is mistaken, although it has a point to make.

Another reason why the revolution is not over is that the old IQ lives! Many people believe firmly in intelligence as a fixed, genetically determined characteristic of themselves and others. Historically, many people have thought that some racial groups differ in their fundamental intellectual capacities. It is unpopular to express such a view today, but certainly the attitude persists. More broadly, a view of intelligence as fixed pervades our reasoning about human performance. For instance, when we or our children have difficulty with a demanding intellectual task, we commonly say "Well, it's just too hard. You either get it or you don't." We attribute failure to a fundamental lack of ability. Likewise, when people succeed conspicuously, we laud their talent and envy their genes. Curiously, this pattern of thinking figures much more in United

States culture than, for instance, in Japan. Research shows that Japanese parents lay much more emphasis on the role of effort in success: The way to deal with a difficult problem or a puzzling concept is to persevere systematically until you have mastered it.

Anyone who doubts that IQ has contemporary champions need only turn to *The Bell Curve*, a 1994 book by Richard Herrnstein, late professor of psychology at Harvard University, and sociologist Charles Murray, political scientist at the American Enterprise Institute. *The Bell Curve* takes IQ as the only reasonable conception of general cognitive ability and focuses on the relationship between low IQ and social ills such as poverty, unwed motherhood, crime, welfare, and the chronically unemployed. Among other things, the authors argue that racial differences in IQ are probably in part genetic and that education at present has little prospects of helping people to become more intelligent. While their position is not as stark as that of Goddard, it leans in his direction. One might almost call Herrnstein and Murray the new Goddards.

I disagree with Herrnstein and Murray on education, race, and other matters, as discussed in later chapters. Although intellectual talent is certainly a real phenomenon, I will argue that most people can learn to use whatever intellectual talents they have much better than they normally do. But whatever we make of Herrnstein's and Murray's viewpoint, its mere presence on the modern scene testifies to the continuing battle over the nature of human intelligence.

Another reason the revolution is not over is simple confusion. The public is not given a clear picture of what IQ theorists like Herrnstein and Murray say, what other scientists say about intelligence, and how it all fits together. Indeed, there is little appreciation of IQ as a construct, limited though it may be. In a recent conversation with a psychologist friend, I was startled to discover that he thought IQ was a completely discredited concept. He knew little about the basic pattern of findings behind the notion of IQ. On the contrary, IQ is probably the single most robust concept in the theory of intelligence, and any effort to expand our conception of intelligence needs to come to terms with it. In Part I of this book, I will try to make crystal clear what IQ means, what it implies, and what it does not imply.

Since the revolution is not over, perhaps to speak of a Copernican revolution is too hasty and too brash. It remains to be seen which theories will endure scientifically and empower us practically. Also, if a revolution is underway in our conceptions of intelligence, it is a leisurely one.

Challenges to what I have called the classic view of intelligence are by no means new. The first scientist to measure intelligence, the French psychologist Alfred Binet, saw intelligence as a potpourri of different abilities rather than one genetically determined essence. But researchers in the United States such as Goddard, Terman, and Spearman promoted what came to be the dominant and classic position. So, from its very inception, the notion of intelligence has been controversial.

One can argue about whether all the earmarks of a Copernican revolution concerning intelligence are apparent. But certainly the spirit is right. To speak of a Copernican revolution evokes a spirit of adventure, of worlds in the making. It captures some of the excitement that many working in this area of human intelligence feel. It honors what may emerge as a new science fundamental to our understanding of ourselves and our best use of our own mental resources.

The Affirmative Revolution

From Copernicus on down, most Copernican revolutions have diminished our human sense of centrality and power, even as they have given us more panoramic views of the universe in which we live. Copernicus taught us that we do not reside at the center of things. The Darwinian revolution taught us that we evolved from primitive stock. The Freudian revolution declared our subjugation to the dark forces of the id within us.

The revolution underway in our conceptions of intelligence is certainly more modest than any of these. It will not shake things up as much. There is no startling proposal here that porpoises or planaria or poplar trees can acquire intelligence. The claim is much more modest: Human beings, manifestly the most intelligent life form on the planet, can become even more so. From a cosmic perspective, this is no great surprise.

Although a more modest revolution, in at least one respect it strikes a happy contrast with its better known siblings in the Copernican family. Far from taxing away yet more of the power and position we thought we had, this revolution has a restorative character. It says that we are not so boxed in by our genetic heritage. On the contrary, intelligence is something that can be cultivated and acquired. People can learn to think and act more intelligently.

Although the technical debates and educational reforms underlying this revolution occur far from the conventional campaigns, polls, and maneuvering of politics, this revolution even has its political side. Luis Alberto Machado, a minister of state of Venezuela, several years ago fostered the development of nationwide programs dedicated specifically to enhancing intelligence. In doing so, he spoke and wrote of the "revolution of intelligence." Machado saw a more cultivated intelligence as a political force, an enlightened electorate as a sharpened blade that could slice through bureaucratic complexities toward a more fruitful society. Not only individually but in our collectivity we can perhaps learn to think and act more intelligently.

This news, if correct, could not come at a better time. In the transition to the next millennium, the human race faces daunting problems on a global scale—famine, overpopulation, political strife, ecological disintegration. At home, in schools, and in the workplace, people face more personal problems—violence, harassment, rivalries, discrimination—as well as the spiraling technical challenges of a complex civilization. As never before, the human race needs all the wit it can muster.

This revolution in intelligence is a revolution well-timed for the twenty-first century. At last, here is a Copernican revolution in the making that is empowering rather than disempowering, heartening rather than disheartening, the hopeful new science of learnable intelligence. May the revolution succeed, because we very much need it!

Part I

In Search of Intelligence

2

The Mind's Apple Falls

What most amazes me about Alfred Binet, director of the psychology laboratory at the Sorbonne in France during the years 1894 to 1911, was the conclusion he did not jump to, the theory he did not assert.

There was every temptation. Binet had built his career as a theoretician. He participated with vigor in the construction of theories, pondered with relish the psychological conceptions of the day, and wrote extensively on the nature of reasoning and thinking. As a result of his work with the famous neurologist Jean Charcot, Binet became interested in abnormal psychology as his primary field. In 1886 and 1887 he published books on hypnotism and subconscious thought, and works on personality and experimental psychology followed.

Who would have a better right to jump to a theoretical conclusion about human intelligence? Who would have a better right to say that intelligence was one pure essence, some psychological stuff that some people enjoy more of and some less of? After all, Alfred Binet thrived on theory, and he was "the father of IQ," the man whose work led to the notion of the Intelligence Quotient.

Yet, in 1904, when Binet was asked by the minister of public education of France to develop a way to detect school children in need of special help, he proceeded with a remarkable pragmatism. He figured out a way to measure intelligence. However, he held back from the obvious

23

conclusion—intelligence as a pure *essence* measured out more to some people and less to others. He left the door open for learnable intelligence. He focused simply on how one could put a number to a phenomenon—the phenomenon of intelligent behavior.

Everyone has heard the apocryphal tale of Isaac Newton under the apple tree. Hit on the head by an apple, Newton thought to ask, "*Why* does the apple fall?" He began to puzzle over the mysteries of gravity. As people have always sat among apple trees, people have always wandered amidst the orchard of human intelligence. The manifestations of intelligence are all around us, in our everyday puzzling and pondering, our efforts to communicate and work with others, our successes and failures. But because the phenomenon of intelligence is there does not mean it is recognized and articulated. The nineteenth century German philosopher Schopenhauer put the matter nicely when he said, ". . . the task is not so much to see what no one yet has seen, but to think what nobody yet has thought about that which everybody sees."

Enter Alfred Binet. Whereas for Newton, gravity's apple fell, for Binet, the mind's apple fell. While we all notice intelligent behavior in passing as part of everyday life, Binet paid particular attention. He saw intelligence as a distinctive phenomenon and sought to measure and understand it.

It is this posture of Binet's that I want to highlight in this chapter. I want to celebrate his wisdom in emphasizing the phenomenon of intelligent behavior. I will touch on how Binet put a number to intelligence and how that is done today. However, the fact of the matter is that all too often the numbers and theories about them have masked the phenomenon as we find it around us in the world in all its iridescent diversity. So this chapter is dedicated to freshening our images of intelligent behavior.

A Number for the Mind

As most people know, IQ is an acronym for intelligence quotient, one's mental age divided by one's physical age and multiplied by 100. An IQ score supposedly reflects a person's general level of intellectual functioning. People with higher IQs are presumably more able to learn, solve problems, sift evidence, and so on.

In fact, IQ as calculated today is not a quotient at all—and how well it represents a person's intellectual functioning is controversial. Nonetheless, it is important to understand the notion of IQ to grasp current debates about the nature of intelligence, and learnable intelligence in particular.

Binet's Ark

If I can mix apples and arks, Binet's approach to probing intelligence also puts me in mind of Noah's Ark. Just as Noah strove to gather not four or five species but all of them, so Binet looked to a great variety of kinds of human behavior to gauge intelligence. He tested children every which way, and the more ways the better. So long as the task did not depend much on unusual rote knowledge or reading and writing, it was fine with Binet. The tasks reflected everyday life situations. Here is a short list:

- Distinguishing ugly from pretty faces
- Describing a picture
- Executing three commands given simultaneously
- Comparing two objects from memory
- Recognizing nine common coins
- Naming the months of the year in order
- Arranging five blocks in order of weight
- Using three given words in not more than two sentences
- Finding three rhymes for a given word in one minute

Indeed, Binet made the sprawl of his testing techniques into a point of principle, writing "One might almost say, 'It matters very little what the tests are so long as they are numerous.'"

He took this approach because he believed that intelligence, far from being one thing, was a potpourri, a mix of this ability and that ability all jumbled together. He reasoned that the best approach to measuring intelligence was to sample widely the kinds of behaviors that might count as intelligent behaviors. He viewed the act of measurement as an act of convenience that only captured in a limited way the character of a person's intelligence. Just as the sports world has found it practical to group boxers into weight classes, even though effective boxing involves a great deal more than weight, so Binet found it practical to assign numbers to intelligence, even though in his view intelligence involved a good deal more than the number captured.

From an Ark to a Yardstick

The notion of IQ grew out of Alfred Binet's cautious approach to the measurement of intelligence. Binet found that he could characterize youngsters' general intellectual level by how they performed on his ark's worth of tasks. However, someone else might use some other set of tasks, equally apt, particularly remembering Binet's dictum that any collection of tasks that did not depend on unusual rote knowledge would do. The problem became one of rating a person's intelligence in a way that did not depend on the particular ark.

The French psychologist contrived an ingenious solution, which he introduced in 1908: Measure a particular child's performance against the trend of other children. The scores of a child would imply a particular *mental age*—the age at which children typically scored at that level. For instance, a very bright ten year old might have a mental age of thirteen. A not-so-bright ten year old might have a mental age of eight. One could place a child relative to his or her peers simply by subtracting the measured mental age from the physical age—the very bright ten year old would score three years ahead of peers and the not so bright ten year old would score two years behind peers.

A few years later, in 1912, the German psychologist W. Stern introduced an improvement: The mental age should be *divided by* the actual age, not subtracted from it. Multiplied by 100, this quotient became the IQ, or intelligence quotient. Notice what this means for the above examples. The very bright ten year old would have an IQ of (thirteen years of mental age) / (ten years physical age) × 100 = 130. The not-so-bright ten year old would have an IQ of (eight years of mental age) / (ten years physical age) × 100 = 80.

Dividing was a better idea than subtracting because the quotient reflected the importance of deficits and advantages better. Compare, for instance, a two year old with a mental age of three and a ten year old with a mental age of eleven. By Binet's original measure, they both count the same: one year ahead of peers. But by the IQ measure, the two year old has a prodigious IQ of 150, the ten year old a slightly above normal IQ of 110. This is the more realistic picture, because the two year old has shown much more rapid mental development, gaining a one-year edge over peers during only two years of life. The two year old deserves the higher score.

IQ Today

While this procedure makes sense for children, it does not for adults. People are not necessarily smarter at forty-five than at thirty, especially in a general way, in contrast with areas of expertise where they may have accumulated more skill and knowledge. It would be odd to think of a thirty year old with an IQ of 150 as having the mind of a forty-five year old.

Accordingly, psychologists developed yet another way of calculating IQ, today used for children as well as adults. This approach does not use a quotient of mental age over physical age at all. Rather, it takes advantage of the well-known bell-shaped curve phenomenon. For most things about people you can measure—such as height or weight—a frequency chart of the numbers forms a bell-shaped curve with a certain mathematical formula, more technically called a normal curve. Most common are heights or weights near the average; therefore they form the crest of the curve. The curve tapers off in both directions from the crest, roughly in the shape of a bell, so that numbers far from the average are very rare, as in the figure that follows.

By starting with the original scores on any intellectually demanding task and doing some addition and multiplication, one can rescale the

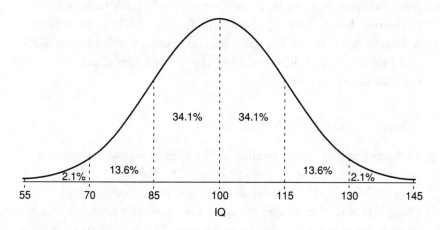

A bell-shaped curve ("normal curve") with an average of 100 and standard deviation of 15, the curve on which by convention IQ scores are represented.

scores to fit them onto a normal curve with any desired average and standard deviation, for instance an average of 100 and a standard deviation of 15, just as in the figure. (Standard deviation is a statistical measure of the spread of a distribution; the larger the standard deviation, the wider the flare of the bell.) This rescaling does not change anything about who or how many people scored high or low but simply maps the scores onto a standardized scale. That is exactly what is done today with scores from same-age children, or with adults regardless of age, to convert the scores to IQ scores.

Why 100 for the average and 15 for the standard deviation? Both choices reflect tradition. The 100 harks back to Stern's notion of dividing mental age by physical age and multiplying by 100: This of course yielded an average IQ of 100 automatically, and the modern convention keeps it that way. As to the 15, when calculated Stern's way for populations of children, IQ turned out to have a standard deviation of around 15 or 16. So when the new statistical method of using the normal curve was adopted, the standard deviation was pegged at 15 to preserve continuity with the past measures. Thus, it is still true that a ten-year-old child with an IQ of 115 performs intellectually like an eleven and a half year-old child, 15 percent older, even though the IQ is no longer actually calculated as a ratio of mental age to physical age.

Besides offering a convenient convention, the normal curve provides insight into the distribution of different IQs in the population. Notice from the figure that almost 70 percent of people, more than two-thirds of the population, have IQs between 85 and 115. Only about 14 percent have IQs between 115 and 130, and about 2 percent between 130 and 145. People with IQs above 145 constitute a slim .2 percent of the population, one in every 500.

What a Number Does Not Mean

Characterizing a person's intelligence by a single number creates a great temptation to view it as a single thing. The theory that Binet might have elaborated, but instead denied, was what Goddard (quoted in chapter 1) and other psychologists did say a few years later: Intelligence was one essence, some sort of mental energy. This was the sort of tough-minded theoretical stance that would have played well—that did play well—in a scientific world hungry to reduce complex phenomena to the fewest fundamentals possible, as physics had so successfully done with its handful of basic concepts like force, mass, and velocity.

But Alfred Binet hung back. He did not want to jump from the fact that some people seemed to behave more intelligently than others to the presumption that there was one essence, a single mental resource, that some people had more of and some less. Moreover, he had remarkably modern reasons for caution. With laudable prescience, Binet anticipated some of the mischief that the concept of intelligence might do. He feared it would offer educators the excuse to ignore the plight of poorly performing students on the grounds that they lacked the intelligence to do better. It also might give educators grounds for dismissing undermotivation and behavior problems as symptoms of low intelligence. As it turned out, Binet was right about these risks.

In later chapters, I want to confront the vision of intelligence as one essence and critique it. However, in the remainder of this chapter, let us set aside this issue and begin where Binet began—with the phenomenon of intelligent behavior.

Intelligent Behavior

Intelligent—and not so intelligent—behavior is all around us, there to be seen. It is not first and foremost a technical concept but an intuitive one, part of our common experience, as much a feature of the everyday landscape as the clothes people wear.

Here is my favorite all-time example. My wife and I established our first home in a small third-floor apartment near Harvard Square in Cambridge, Massachusetts. It was a comfortable enough space, overlooking Brattle street, close to the famous Brattle theater with its reruns of Humphrey Bogart films every time exam period at Harvard came around.

Of course, there were the limitations you might expect of a first apartment. We would have liked more space. We wished the radiators were more gracefully concealed rather than hanging out like a cut-rate version of the Beaubourg. Overnight guests would of necessity end up sleeping on the couch.

This brings us to the fulcrum of the story—what couch overnight guests would end up on. As we settled into our living space, we went searching for something more sumptuous than our original hand-me-down couch, and, at one of the sleek furniture companies off Route 128 found a long blue elegant sofa with an embossed paisley print. We liked it. We bought it. We scheduled delivery for the upcoming Saturday.

We were smart shoppers for the most part. But we forgot about one thing: The sofa was much too large for the building's only elevator. The only access to our apartment was up a single staircase that made three right-angle turns on its way from each floor to the next.

This problem had not even entered our minds until the movers arrived with the sofa all wrapped in brown paper and tape. They got the sofa through the front door easily—sofas, like all furniture, are built to fit through standard-size doors. But the staircase was another matter entirely. One man in front, one man behind, they eased it up about half way to the first landing. There it stayed. They lifted and lowered, pushed and pulled, heaved and grunted. They tried twisting it about its long axis.. They tried elevating the front end much higher than the back end. They tried lifting the back end so that it was almost as high as the front end. Nothing helped.

"We can't get it up," they said. "Hey, we've given it our best shot. You better give the company a call. They'll see what they can do."

This was not good news. We had visions of the truck carting our precious acquisition away, and us out on the road again, scouring the furniture stores for another couch a foot shorter but equally endearing.

We called the dispatcher at the furniture company. "It's probly no problem at all," said the guy there. "Lemme send the specialists."

The regular movers left and an hour later two others showed up—a couple of husky guys, brimming with confidence, bounce in their heels, brass in their walk, proud, you could see, to be "the specialists." There was the couch, sitting in the middle of the lobby where the nonspecialists had left it. They looked over the couch and looked over the staircase.

One said, "We can handle this sucka!"

The specialists started off the same way as the other two—one in front, one in back, heaving the couch up the staircase. Just like the nonspecialists, about a third of the way up they got stuck. Nothing obvious worked.

So they paused and thought for a minute. "Let's try this," the one at the rear said. And, holding his end of the couch, he walked backwards.

He did not go back the way he had come, down the staircase. Instead he backed toward the corner of the landing where the stairs took a turn. His maneuver gave the front end more play. Now the front man could get it around an obstruction there. Up they went, around the difficult turn and on to the first floor corridor.

The staircase posed the same dilemma between the first and second and the second and third landings. About a third of the way up, the couch jammed. But now they had the trick. The rear man backed into the corner. The obstruction cleared, they moved the couch on up. Pretty soon we had our new couch proudly on display in our living room, the wrapping paper and tape a heap in the middle of the floor.

How did the specialists solve their problem? They displayed a pattern of thinking very basic to intelligent behavior. Instead of always pressing forward, they tried backing up. They found themselves in a cul-de-sac with the couch and guessed that by moving away from their goal, they might find a different path toward it.

This same pattern recurs over and over in other very different situations that demand intelligence—the way forward requires backing up and seeking a new path. It happens in negotiation situations where people get locked into opposing positions, in scientific inquiry when an investigator needs to question a tacit assumption, in everyday decision making when people need to reconsider an earlier decision and find a new direction, in politics when nations need to reconsider alliances, and indeed in innumerable brainteasers including the well-known Cannibals and Missionaries puzzle discussed in chapter 9.

Of course, one can question whether the specialists right at that moment actually exercised any fresh and insightful thinking. Perhaps they already knew a "backing up" trick for moving furniture. While this is certainly possible, presumably they were called the specialists because they were good at coping with difficult situations. That means figuring out new tricks as well as relying on old ones. Whatever the causes in this case, including using known tricks, the specialists behaved intelligently. I have always remembered the specialists as paragons of practical intelligence.

Visible Intelligence

The specialists provide a wonderful antidote to the impression one can get from laboratory studies that intelligence first and foremost is a technical construct related mostly to academic ability. They demonstrate that intelligent behavior is not something you look for just in laboratories or classrooms but as much in the ordinary and sometimes very physical undertakings of everyday life. The phenomenon of intelligence begins not with a test but with intelligent behavior in ordinary situations.

The all-time prize for an acidic comment about a laboratory view of intelligence probably goes to the notable psychologist Edwin Boring. In a 1923 article, he suggested with some irony that "Measurable intelligence is simply what the tests of intelligence test, until further scientific observation allows us to extend the observation."

Boring's remark warns how easily a psychological theory can become detached from the human realities that inspired it in the first place. Measurable intelligence, in the sense of IQ or other indices, is simply an effort to attach a number to the complex phenomenon of intelligent behavior. Sometimes such numbers are useful and revealing, sometimes misleading, but never are they the phenomenon itself.

Let us neglect numbers for a while longer in favor of what you might call visible intelligence. The specialists, facing the very ordinary challenge of getting a sofa up a staircase, made intelligence visible, showing us what intelligent behavior looked like. How else does intelligence appear plainly in the world around us?

Say I go back to my high school reunion twenty years later. Linda Fennimore, who edged me out for class valedictorian, is *still* smart. She has a number of considered thoughts to offer about how people will view Gorbachev and Yeltsin in twenty years and why. She shows intelligent behavior.

Or perhaps my wife takes the car to the garage. The mechanic hears my wife's report of the problem, looks under the hood, listens to the motor, test drives the car for a block, and says, "Well, you could be right. Could be the transmission. But we got to be careful. It could be X, Y, Z too. The transmission is a pricey answer. Let me check some of the other possibilities and I'll call up, give you an estimate." Like the specialists and Linda Fennimore, the mechanic acts in a visibly intelligent way. He considers possibilities instead of jumping to conclusions.

Or a neighbor, a stock-market enthusiast, explains her latest strategy. Whether or not it makes her rich, it's a sophisticated view of the way the chaos of the market works. Her intelligent behavior is visible.

Or you are watching the TV quiz show *Jeopardy*. Martha, the Certified Public Accountant from Milwaukee, is on a roll. She rips through the "The Plant Kingdom" category, telling you that it's the Dutch Elm disease that wiped out most of the elms in the United States, "belladonna" is a poisonous mushroom, and so on. She, too, is displaying intelligent behavior.

It is not hard to recognize intelligent behavior. We see it around us all the time. Moreover, intelligence researcher Robert Sternberg and his colleagues at Yale University have taken pains to investigate the everyday conception of intelligence. What do people actually think of as intelligent behavior? How do they identify intelligence in other people, and in themselves? Finally, does their conception make logical and psychological sense?

Sternberg and his colleagues approached these questions by asking people what they recognized as intelligent behavior. That is, what are the symptoms of intelligence that people would generally acknowledge? This question should be clearly separated from the question of underlying cause or measurement. Its emphasis falls on the externals, the "outside view" of intelligence. Before reading on, you might like to take a moment to review what characteristics you would take as behavioral symptoms of intelligence. What do people do that tells you they are intelligent? What trends in behavior do you look for when trying to decide whether someone is smart enough for some intellectually demanding task? You can compare your answers with what this investigation found.

The Sternberg studies reveal great consistency across different groups of people in their conceptions of intelligence. The general view is that intelligent human beings:

• Solve problems well
• Reason clearly
• Think logically
• Use a good vocabulary
• Draw on a large store of information
• Balance information
• Are goal oriented
• Show their intelligence in practical, not just academic, ways

Sternberg adds that these characteristics make up a very reasonable lay conception of intelligent behavior. Indeed, several of the features listed above are directly measured by formal measures of intelligence, such as IQ. To be sure, in another culture or in different subcultures, one might find a somewhat different emphasis. But there is nothing bizarre about the everyday concept of intelligence. It makes good sense.

Sternberg also discovered that when lay people are asked to estimate their overall intelligence, presumably using criteria like the above, their estimates relate moderately well to their performance on tests that pose intellectual challenges. Apparently people have considerable awareness of how well they solve problems, how clearly they reason, and so on. Our intelligence is fairly visible even to ourselves.

The Fundamental Experiment

Restaurant critics and scientists alike have to be concerned with the consistency of phenomena. The critic setting out to review Peking Gardens wants to know not just whether the mu shi is good today but whether it is good next week and the week after, and not just whether the mu shi is good but whether the egg drop soup and other dishes are good as well, meal after meal, dish after dish. So the critic visits more than once, samples the menu widely, and looks for a pattern.

Although intelligence is often visible in people's behavior, psychologists, like the restaurant critic, have to ask about the consistency of intelligent behavior. Is the person who behaves intelligently today likely to behave intelligently tomorrow? Is the person who behaves intelligently in one activity likely to behave intelligently in another? At stake is the notion of intelligence as a personal trait, something repeatable and reliable. If there is no consistency, there are episodes of intelligent behavior, yes, but no stable personal trait of intelligence.

Our intuitive answer to the question of consistency, based on everyday experience, is assuredly yes. To a considerable extent, people do seem to behave more intelligently or less intelligently "meal after meal, dish after dish." In the earlier discussion of Binet and the origins of the concept of IQ, I took this for granted. But of course informal impressions often can mislead us. The question of consistency is one of the most fundamental to investigations of intelligence. To answer it with more confidence, psychologists devised a standard experimental procedure. In fact, it can be called the fundamental experiment.

All versions of the fundamental experiment work pretty much as follows. An investigator devises a series of intellectually challenging tasks on the face of it rather different from one another. The investigator administers the tasks to a number of people. The investigator re-administers the same set of tasks on another occasion—or, perhaps, a similar set of tasks, so that people will not simply repeat their answers from the first set.

Such testing puts the investigator in a position to ask two crucial questions. The first question is: Are people consistent within a task? That is, does a person who scores high in comparison with others on Task 1 during the first round also tend to score high on Task 1 during the second round? The same query also applies to tasks 2, 3, 4, and so on. The second question is: Are people consistent across tasks? That is, does a person who scores high on any one of the tasks also tend to score high on the others?

Some Typical Tasks

Historically, psychologists have employed a great diversity of puzzle-like tasks to make these judgments. Let us look at some characteristic examples. One of the most familiar problems is the verbal analogy. Here is a typical question:

Hens are to feathers as sheep are to what? (A) Lambs; (B) Wool; (C) Ewes; (D) Farms.

The correct answer is B, Wool, the protective covering of sheep, just as feathers are for hens.

Another common intellectual challenge on tests of intelligence is the number series. Consider this example, for instance:

Here are the first five numbers in a series: 1, 3, 6, 10, 15. What is the next number: (A) 20; (B) 21; (C) 23; (D) 25.

Here, the answer is B, 21. The second number in the series is 2 larger than the first, the third number is 3 larger than the second, and so on. So the sixth number should be 6 larger than the previous.

A very different kind of task is simply the vocabulary test. For example:

The word "anemic" is closest in meaning to: (A) Enemy; (B) Pompous; (C) Thin blooded; (D) Slothlike.

Here the answer is C, Thin blooded, anemic referring to anemia, a blood condition involving a reduced quantity of blood cells.

Although such tasks are commonly used to measure intelligence, they also serve to investigate the phenomenon of intelligence. They offer a way of exploring the question of consistency: Do people who score well on verbal analogies tasks today do so next week and also score well on number series and vocabulary tasks?

The Finding of a "Positive Manifold"

Over a long history of investigation, the results for experiments in this form have proved startlingly robust. Again and again, a pattern of consistency both *within* and *across* tasks has emerged. As to *within*, a person who handles a particular task better or worse the first time tends to do so the second time. This within-task consistency is hardly surprising, although it is important to note.

The more telling finding is that a person who handles a particular task better or worse in comparison to other people also tends to handle other tasks better or worse. In other words, there is an overarching performance trend on intellectual tasks, regardless of their variety.

To get a more precise idea of what this means, we need a well-known concept from statistics—the correlation coefficient. This is a number used to gauge how much two different measures vary in lock-step with one another. The correlation coefficient ranges between –1 and +1, with its exact value signaling different patterns of relationship. A positive correlation coefficient means that the two measures tend to vary in tandem with one another. For instance, taller people tend to be heavier, so there would be a positive correlation coefficient between height and weight, not 1, which would indicate a perfect lock-step relationship but perhaps something around .6. A negative correlation coefficient means that two measures tend to vary in opposite directions to one another, as with, for instance, temperature and snowfall: the higher the temperature, the lower the snowfall. A zero correlation coefficient means that the two measures are unrelated: One cannot be predicted from the other even in trend.

In statistical terms, the fundamental finding that people tend to perform better or worse across different tasks means that the correlation coefficients between scores on different tasks all tend to be positive—if a person scores better on one task, the person tends to score better on another. This does not mean that people good at one thing are good at almost everything. That would imply an almost perfect trend and correlation coefficients around .9. More typically, between intellectual tasks, the correlation coefficients range around .2 to .5.

The table below offers an example, the correlation coefficients between some subtests of the Thurstone Primary Mental Abilities test. As the headings show, these subtests have a rather different character from one another. Even so, as the table shows, how people score on one echoes how they score on another. The correlation coefficients indicate how Task 1

	Correlation with Test No.					
Test No.	1	2	3	4	5	6
1. Number		.46	.38	.18	.54	.25
2. Word Fluency	.46		.51	.39	.48	.17
3. Verbal Meaning	.38	.51		.39	.54	.16
4. Memory	.18	.39	.39		.38	.14
5. Reasoning	.54	.48	.54	.38		.38
6. Space	.25	.17	.16	.14	.38	

relates to Task 2, Task 2 to Task 3, and so on. Notice how all the entries are positive. Psychometricians call this a finding of a *positive manifold,* the earmark of moderate consistency in intelligent behavior across tasks.

Are the Tasks Too Narrow?

Number, word fluency, verbal meaning—such tasks seem a far cry from the gritty intelligence of the specialists who moved that couch up a winding staircase. They appear dry and intellectual, not sampling a very broad spectrum of human endeavor. Indeed, they seem much narrower than the potpourri of tasks that Binet liked to use. A critic might say, "Although these tasks look different, they are not different enough. They are all rather verbal in character. They all depend on a certain amount of schooling. Perhaps the consistency of performance from task to task is an illusion resulting from selecting a narrow range of tasks."

The critic is right. A range of tasks such as these really is not enough to make the case. But psychologists have taken such concerns seriously and investigated a great variety of tasks that intuitively seem to demand intellectual effort. If the fundamental experiment is repeated with a much broader range of tasks, the same fundamental result emerges—a positive manifold. For instance, if the experiment adds in tasks that have a much more visual character, still some people tend to do consistently better and others worse on them all. If the experiment expands to include tasks that involve practical everyday reasoning, the same story.

The critic might also worry that testlike tasks, however diverse, have little to do with performance in realistic situations. But numerous studies have documented substantial relationships between scores on such tests and performance in realistic situations. Formal education is one case in point. Studies consistently show that IQ-like measures predict performance in school, with a correlation coefficient of about .5. The workplace provides another case in point. Studies show that various measures of workplace performance also relate to IQ with a correlation coefficient of about .4 or .5. Also, measures of IQ tend to predict future work performance better than job-specific measures. The next chapter explores such points further.

All this was a remarkable discovery. Why should people who do well on one intellectually demanding task tend to do well on another and also in school and in the workplace? Perhaps there is a something underlying their intellectual performance on tests and in everyday circumstances, a something that *makes* it consistent, some kind of gift, some kind of strength, some kind of insight, something that might be called intelligence.

Inside the Mind's Apple

Newton, so the story goes, went off to make sense out of his experience under the apple tree. Binet strove to make sense of his observations of youngsters in France that displayed profound academic shortfalls. While Newton devised the theory of gravitation, Binet constructed a conception of intelligence as the ability to perform well on a potpourri of intellectually demanding tasks. The mind's apple fell for Binet, and the apple pie he made of it was his eclectic pragmatic conception of intelligence. To sum up the evidence and its import for the mindware questions:

The evidence at hand . . .

- There are more and less intelligent behaviors, apparent in everyday life (visible intelligence).
- Different people display consistently more or less intelligent behavior across diverse test and everyday contexts (the positive manifold).
- One can broadly characterize a person's level of intellectual functioning relative to others (for children, same-age others) with IQ.

MWQ #1. What mechanisms underlie intelligence?

- Binet's answer proposed a potpourri of mental resources, many of which are drawn on by any task.

MWQ #2. Can people learn more intelligence?

- Binet thought so. He said this about slower learners: "What they should learn first is not the subjects ordinarily taught, however important they may be; they should be given lessons of will, of attention, of discipline; before exercises in grammar, they need to be exercised in mental orthopedics; in a word they must learn how to learn." Such experiences would increase their mental age and hence their IQ.

MwQ #3. What aspects of intelligence especially need attention?

- As the above quote signals, Binet thought that will, attention, and mental discipline were key. This view underscores the importance of attitudes, or what I will later call dispositions, in intelligent behavior.

I admire Binet's caution. He recognized from early on that when scientists make up a conception like intelligence, they are only identifying a consistent pattern. This does not say what intelligence *is* under the skin. A positive manifold does not mean that one has to agree with the precepts of Goddard's list, viewing intelligence as a unitary mental process, neural in character, inborn, and unmodifiable by learning. Such judgments make presumptions well beyond the finding of the positive manifold. The coming chapters will reveal whether the further evidence justifies Goddard's list.

When Newton made up the theory of gravitation, it was a theory only in a descriptive sense. He described a pattern of consistency with the equation expressing the law of gravitation. But he did not know what gravity was under the skin, what its underlying mechanism might be. Today, we say in accordance with Einstein that gravity is "really" curvature in space-time induced by the presence of a mass. We have a mechanism for gravity, not just a description.

The question of mechanism is just as central to the nature of intelligence. What accounts for visible intelligence? What lies behind the positive manifold and other phenomena of intelligent behavior? And what are the implications for our conduct as parents, voters, workers, and educators? The mind's apple falls, but exactly how the mind's apple works inside makes all the difference.

3

The Empire of IQ

Numbers are autocrats. They command belief. They impress us with their reality. They compel our respect. When I tell you that the edge of my desk measures precisely .747 of a meter, the edge of my desk takes on a steely presence, as though something so exactly described had to be real.

But let's be cautious of doing too much honor to seemingly precise numbers. In the case of the edge of my desk, I made up the number without even looking.

The numbers we measure the physical world with are even descended from autocrats. On August 22, 1790, Louis XVI of France held an audience with twelve mathematicians and scientists who urged that the monarch approve establishing new more systematic units of measure, including the meter and the gram. The monarch's blessing for this enterprise was one of his last official acts. The very next day he slipped out of town, shortly to be brought back under arrest. But work on the metric system continued, and soon mathematicians and scientists, merchants and engineers around the world were equipped with the new conceptual tools of the metric system.

The power of numbers lies in the precise descriptions they afford and the precise formulations of theoretical relationships they allow, as in the laws of Newton from which one can predict the orbits of the planets and lunar and solar eclipses. The autocracy of numbers lies in the authority they assume; things sometimes sound more real than in fact they are.

This was a risk Alfred Binet recognized when he began his subtle and restrained project to measure the tendency toward intelligent behavior. Around the notion of measuring intelligence has grown up a complex and technical research tradition, a large-scale industry of testing, and a mix of awe, fear, and skepticism regarding what intelligence really means.

Considering the way intelligence testing has dominated both theorizing about and practical applications of the concept of intelligence, it is not too bold to speak of "the empire of IQ." True, a number of developments in the psychology of intelligence profoundly challenge this empire. But there it is, demanding a thoughtful look at its origins and presumptions.

IQ the number is one thing and IQ the empire something else. IQ the number is no more than a measure of the trend of a person toward more or less intelligent behavior across a diversity of circumstances. IQ the empire stands on several further interpretations of what that number means. Goddard's list from Chapter 1 provides a brief preamble to the constitution of this empire, a succinct statement of its basic precepts. In this chapter, I want to draw a clear picture of those precepts, highlighting three from Goddard's list: intelligence as (a) unitary, one kind of thing, (b) based in the physiology of the nervous system, in contrast with learned, and (c) genetically determined. None of these were claims advanced by Binet. Where did they come from? What reasons are there to believe them?

The One and Only Intelligence

Goddard asserted that intelligence was unitary, one kind of thing, whereas Binet had thought of it as a salad of contributing abilities. What happened between Binet's turn-of-the-century pluralism and Goddard's 1920 monism? The key figure on the way to Goddard's viewpoint was the great psychologist-statistician Charles Spearman, contemporary of Binet and formulator of Spearman's *g* for general intelligence.

Spearman introduced his theory in 1904 in a paper entitled with Napoleonic confidence "General Intelligence Objectively Measured and Determined." He had examined data from experiments just like those discussed earlier: People attempted a number of different tasks, getting a score on each. As already mentioned, when experiments like this are done, it's almost always found that the scores relate to one another—people who do well on one task tend to do well on others. In the language of the last chapter, all the correlation coefficients relating scores on one task to scores on others are positive, the finding of a positive manifold. The question was, how to put some kind of a number to this common trend?

Answering this question was Spearman's brilliant technical contribution to measuring intelligence. He developed a mathematical technique that came to be called factor analysis, suitable for attaching a number to the common trend across scores on different tests. The emergent trend toward better or worse performance Spearman dubbed *g* for *general intelligence*.

So how much of performance is general? How much is accounted for by Spearman's general factor, *g*? Statisticians have ways of measuring how much of the variation across people and across different kinds of tests gets captured by a single factor like *g*. Spearman, and others after him, have found that *g* typically accounts for 50 or 60 percent of the variation. This high a percentage is quite respectable. It leaves 40 or 50 percent to be explained by other factors—individual talents, moods of the day, erratic scoring of the tests, and so on. But it represents quite a lot of whatever underlies better or worse performance.

Sometimes *g* is used as a shorthand way of saying general intelligence, as in "Newton must have had a high *g*," meaning high general intelligence or high IQ. However, from a more formal standpoint *g* as a concept is somewhat different from IQ. Psychometricians refer to *g* not as a yardstick for intelligence like IQ but as the name of the single general factor that accounts for better or worse performance across a variety of tests of different character. A high "*g* loading" in a study involving a number of people and tasks means that there is a very strong trend for the people who do well on one task to do well on the others. It's as though all the tasks down deep called on one and the same psychological reservoir, with some people's reservoir fuller than others.

Spearman's Notion of Mental Energy

Although Binet reached no such conclusion, Spearman did. Spearman used all the autocracy of his impressive mathematics to decree a mechanism for intelligence.

Spearman's theory was that there was some kind of mental power or energy in the nervous system. He wrote that the statistically extracted *g* factor

> . . . was taken, pending further information, to consist in something of the nature of an "energy" or "power" which serves in common the whole cortex (or possibly even the whole nervous system).

Spearman saw this energy as a resource delivered to parts of the brain as needed, suggesting that different neural groups

> would thus function as alternative "engines" into which the common supply of "energy" could be alternatively distributed. Successful action would always depend, partly on the potential of energy developed in the whole cortex, and partly on the efficiency of the specific group of neurons involved.

The efficiency of specific groups of neurons allowed for particular talents or abilities in the individual.

The Consequences of a Conception

Clearly Spearman's statistics did not prove his notion of mental energy. They did not show that intelligence in the sense of IQ or *g*—that is, the common trend in more or less intelligent behavior across diverse tasks—had a basis in the neural system. They did not even really show that intelligence had a unitary character. In light of *g* accounting for 50-60 percent of the variability, it was plausible to hypothesize a unitary basis for intelligence, but no more than that.

Nonetheless, Spearman's conception of intelligence as a single essence took hold and, in its long history since, invited invidious comparisons of individuals, races, and ethnic groups. For example, different racial and ethnic groups often show different average scores on intelligence tests. Today the most often aired interpretation is that this phenomenon reflects cultural factors. However, one might maintain—and historically many psychologists did—that fundamental biological factors endow different races with more or less intelligence. This supported systematic efforts to discriminate among different populations because of supposed contrasts in intellectual capacity.

In his engaging and thoughtful *The Mismeasure of Man*, Stephen Jay Gould makes a special point of tracing the history of discrimination founded on such contrasts. For example, a cornerstone in establishing the powerful hereditarian biases were the mental tests devised by Robert M. Yerkes in 1917, together with the leading American hereditarians of the time. Yerkes and his colleagues tested 1.75 million men in World War I to measure pure innate intelligence. The absurdity of these tests lay in the mental ages they supposedly disclosed. The average mental age of white American adults was thirteen, a score just above that of a moron. European immigrants were classified by their country of origin. The average Russian had a mental age of 11.34, the Italian 11.01, the Pole 10.74. And the Negro was the most inferior of all the races since 89 percent scored as morons. But where were the normal adults who presumably established the yardstick for these mental ages?

Rather than questioning the validity of the tests themselves—which revealed that half of the population in America was comprised of morons!—the hereditarians said that ". . . it appears that feeble-mindedness, as at present defined, is of much greater frequency of occurrence than had been originally supposed."

Unfortunately the most devastating effects of these tests extended well beyond the barracks. The results of these army tests were used as propaganda to reinforce and establish social prejudices and unjust social actions. C. C. Brigham, an avid supporter of Yerkes and professor of psychology at Princeton University, praised the army tests as finally providing a "scientific basis" for determining the innate intelligences of various groups and races. Now that intelligence could be measured, America's intellectual heritage could be preserved by testing different immigrant groups and prohibiting those of inferior genetic stock from entering the country. Yerkes wrote in the foreword of Brigham's book, *A Study of American Intelligence,*

> The author presents not theories or opinions but facts. It behooves us to consider their reliability and their meaning, for no one of us as a citizen can afford to ignore the menace of race deterioration or the evident relations of immigration to national progress and welfare.

The tests were also used to propagate segregation and discrimination by limiting access of blacks to institutions of higher education. The trustee of Columbia University and president of the American Museum of Natural History, Henry Fairfield Osborn, wrote in 1923:

> I believe those tests were worth what the war cost, even in human life, if they served to show clearly to our people the lack of intelligence in our

country, and the degrees of intelligence in different races who are coming to us, in a way which no one can say is the result of prejudice . . . We have learned once and for all that the negro is not like us. So in regard to many races and subraces in Europe we learned that some which we believed possessed of an order of intelligence perhaps superior to ours [read Jews] were far inferior.

Spearman himself was far from a fanatic racist. He was not much given to contrasting the intelligence of racial groups. He emphasized that the range of variation within any racial group was far wider than the minor differences in averages from racial group to racial group. That is, although slightly different in their averages, racial groups were much the same in the sprawl of intelligence from the lowest to the highest. He averred that women's lower performance on the tests of the day reflected social factors.

However, others were not so reticent, raising specters such as the dilution of good Anglo-Saxon stock by inferior races and the hopelessness of educating inherently limited minds. Moreover, Spearman was willing enough to pen his approval of the American Immigration Restriction Act of 1924:

> The general conclusion emphasized by nearly every investigator is that, as regards "intelligence," the Germanic stock has on the average a marked advantage over the South European. And this result would seem to have had vitally important practical consequences in shaping the recent very stringent American laws as to the admission of immigrants.

With these egregious ripple effects acknowledged and with Spearman's notion of mental energy very much in question, it is important to honor Binet and Spearman for devising metrics for the mind. IQ and g were enormous leaps forward in the conception of intelligence, distilling mathematically what before was simply the impressionistic observation that some people seemed brighter than others. Moreover, just as with the meter and the gram sanctioned by Louis XVI, IQ and g allowed asking a host of questions that could not be formulated very well without a yardstick for mental agility, questions such as:

- How does intelligence vary over time?
- How does intelligence vary with education?
- How does intelligence depend on knowledge?
- How does intelligence depend on genetic heritage?

- Do some cultures or ethnic groups display greater intelligence than others?
- Can some kinds of instruction or experience make people more intelligent?

Many of these questions are supercharged with sensitive issues about personal, ethnic, and racial identity. But they are provocative and arresting nonetheless.

Finally, it is important to underscore the point that IQ as developed by Binet, and *g* shorn of the theoretical interpretation that Spearman attached to it, cling close to the central phenomenon I emphasized in the previous chapter. They gauge the tendency of individuals to show consistently more, or less, intelligent behavior. The early history of efforts to measure intelligence did not sample behavior in a systematic and rigorous way at all. Rather, the so-called science of phrenology employed measurements of the skull to ascertain which intellectual powers were most developed on the basis of the bumps that supposedly signified more brain power, much as a hump in your lawn signals a gopher beneath. Whatever misgivings there might be about IQ and *g*, they represent something much better than a gopher hunt.

Fast Neurons

My children are enthusiasts of electronic games, well-equipped with Nintendo and other extravaganzas of the video and computer age. Yet here is an electronic game that they would not tolerate for a minute. The player sits in front of a table with a few buttons, holding a forefinger on the closest button (see figure). In a semicircle around this home button are eight others.

The task is strikingly simple. Beside each of the target buttons is a light. One of those lights will come on. When it does, you must lift your hand as quickly as possible from the home button and push the button beside the light that went on.

During one variation of the game, only a single light will come on, always the same one. You simply have to move your finger to the button beside that light as quickly as possible. During another variation, one of two will come on. You do not know which one and have to move your finger to whichever one appears. Another variation features four lights and another all eight.

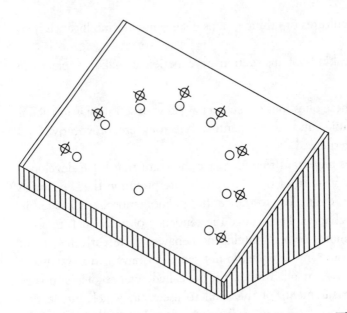

Diagram of Arthur Jensen's choice reaction time apparatus. The empty circles are the buttons, the circles with crosses the lights.

In these days of *The Bard's Tale* and *Ultima*, a few buttons and lights appear dull indeed. And well they might, because, paradoxically, this game is *supposed* to be dull. It is a challenge deliberately constructed to be as mindless as possible, and for the strangest reason: to provide a better probe of intelligence.

Jensen's Logic

The apparatus was developed by intelligence researcher Arthur Jensen. Jensen has been a controversial figure in investigations of intelligence, accused of racism because of his arguments about fundamental differences in intelligence between different racial groups. But the matter of the moment has nothing directly to do with the issue of race and intelligence. It touches not at all on differences among races or any other groups, but rather looks inward toward the fundamental character of intelligence itself.

Jensen's motive was the puzzle of mechanism. Despite Spearman's and others' theories about a neural basis for intelligence, it was quite clear that nothing much had been established about the underlying mechanism of intelligent behavior in any rigorous sense. Spearman could tell stories about mental energy, but how could we come closer to testing whether in fact people of different intelligence functioned differently at the neural level? The dilemma is not unlike that faced by theoretical physicists, who propose on theoretical grounds the existence of neutrinos or quarks. But we still want direct evidence!

Arthur Jensen's apparatus was a kind of mental cyclotron, designed to catch neural efficiency in the act. Its inspiration lay in simple logic: Normally, intelligence is tested with intellectually demanding tasks. However, if what really underlies intelligence in the sense of IQ or *g* is neural in character, a matter of more efficient neural activity in the brain, then one ought to be able to detect this. Seemingly mindless tasks should benefit from neural efficiency too, providing those tasks are the sort that, even though routine, strain the information-processing resources of human beings.

But wait a minute. Exactly what does efficiency at the neural level have to do with the kinds of complex problem solving characteristically demanded by intelligence tests? One possible answer recognizes that speed of processing might translate directly into handling more challenging problems. Thinking is often a little like juggling: The more impressive feats require keeping many balls in the air at the same time. Greater efficiency of information processing might help people to track several ideas at once and discern relationships among them, an ability that should allow better handling of complex problems.

Another answer looks to the cumulative effects of efficiency over the course of years. People who process information somewhat faster than others thereby learn somewhat faster. In the course of time, they accumulate more information, more problem-solving strategies, more complex concepts, and so on. This in turn puts them at an advantage when they face intellectual challenges—on IQ tests or in life.

To probe efficiency of information processing, Jensen devised the "choice reaction time" apparatus illustrated. The name means that the apparatus measures how quickly a person reacts in a choice-making situation among several lights. As the number of active lights increases, so, Jensen reasoned, do the information-processing demands of monitoring the lights and quickly moving the hand to the target light. Thus, the apparatus measures how long it takes for the player to lift a finger from the home button, and when the player's finger strikes the target button. From this data, appropriate calculations can yield a variety of indices of how quickly the player responds and how easily the player takes on the extra cognitive demands of two, then four, then eight lights.

Jensen's Findings

The choice reaction time apparatus yields measures of a number of different aspects of reaction time, for example, the time to lift a finger from the home button when there is only one target button, or two, four, or eight; the rate of increase in reaction time with increasing numbers of target buttons; the variability in reaction time for any given number of buttons, a measure of how consistent a player's reaction time is from one trial to the next.

Studies conducted by Jensen and by others, involving large numbers of subjects, revealed that several of these measures correlate with scores on conventional intelligence tests that pose intellectually challenging problems. As noted earlier, such links are typically gauged by correlation coefficients. The reaction time measures from the Jensen apparatus usually yield correlation coefficients in the neighborhood of .2 with conventional intelligence test scores. Since the maximum correlation is 1.0, this is not impressive, but it is a highly reliable result. A composite of reaction time measures added together does better, yielding correlation coefficients with intelligence approaching .5—still not all that large, but impressive because the Jensen task does not obviously require any intelligence at all.

Inspection Time and Other Measures

Jensen is one among a number of researchers who have looked for relationships between intelligence as revealed by complex, intellectually demanding tasks and measures of simpler performances and even physiological symptoms supposedly closer to the mechanics of the neural system. Of all these, Jensen's approach is perhaps the best known but not necessarily the most compelling.

One measure with an especially strong track record is called inspection time. Like Jensen's choice reaction time, inspection time is a kind of reaction time. In a typical visual version of such studies (auditory and tactile experiments with the same general design and results have also been done), a subject sees two stimuli in a tachistoscope, a device that can display a stimulus for a very brief period of time. The stimuli are very simple, for instance two straight lines a little distance apart, one of which is about half again as long as the other. The subject's task is to discern which line is longer. The apparatus involves an additional twist: After presenting the stimuli for a fraction of a second, it then shows a masking stimulus that washes out the impression of the initial stimuli. The masking stimulus makes the task harder and allows more precise measurements.

Inspection time is defined as the average exposure time of the initial stimuli needed to allow the subject to report correctly with 95 percent accuracy. The idea is that the more rapidly the subject's neural system operates, the briefer inspection time the subject will need. After certain statistical adjustments, inspection time yields a correlation coefficient of about .5 with measures of intelligence derived from intellectually demanding tasks. The .5 is about the same as the correlation from a *composite* of Jensen's measures, an impressive achievement.

Choice reaction time and inspection time are two birds from a flock of diverse reaction time and physiological measures that psychologists have explored in an effort to find out what the neural system does in support of intelligent behavior. Several members of the flock have performed well. As a broad generalization, there are a number of measures that do not obviously involve intelligence in the sense of dealing intelligently with complex intellectual tasks, but that correlate in the medium range and sometimes higher with conventional measures of intelligence.

Neural Efficiency Maybe

What do such findings mean? Jensen maintains that his reaction time measures detect what might be called the basal efficiency of the brain as an information-processing mechanism—how quick and accurate a computer it is. A more precise and rapid nervous system can respond even to a single light quickly and can absorb the increased information load as one goes from one to two to four to eight lights better than a less precise and slower nervous system.

More generally, researchers argue from such findings that intelligence reflects operating characteristics of the human nervous system at the neurological level: neural efficiency of one sort or another. Some people have, so to speak, fast neurons. As mentioned earlier, people whose brains process information efficiently might meet complex intellectual chal-lenges better because they can track more ideas and their interrelationships at the same time, and through a greater accumulation of knowledge and thinking strategies in the course of the years. In neural efficiency, some would certainly venture, lies the very stuff of intelligence.

It is easy to be unhappy with this pattern of results. The idea that our intelligence may be purely a matter of "hardware," like the amount of RAM and the processor speed in a computer, or the horsepower of the engine in a new car, is disconcerting. It seems to limit our potential for growth in uncomfortable ways. However, if our egos are threatened and our pride hurt, we need not panic for at least two reasons: (a) the neural efficiency interpretation is questionable, and (b) in any case, theorists do not claim that intelligent behavior is solely a matter of neural efficiency.

As to (a), the dilemma for researchers is this: It is hard to be sure that more intelligent subjects in reaction time and similar experiments are not treating the tasks as intellectually challenging. Jensen's idea is that when you sit there with your finger on the home button of Jensen's choice reaction time apparatus, there is nothing to do but wait for the light and react. But there are in fact things you can do, if you are a strategic thinker: You can strive to maintain your attention and alertness, try to bring yourself to a hair-trigger edge of readiness, and push away distractions. All such maneuvers have the character of complex thinking that anticipates problems and opportunities. Although the faster reaction-time measures of people with high IQs look like neurological efficiency of some sort, they might in fact reflect the very kind of thinking Jensen's dumbed-down game was designed to eliminate.

Attractive though this interpretation may seem, various tests of the hypothesis have not yielded supportive evidence. In his recent book *Intelligence*, Nathan Brody examines a number of results on both sides of this issue in a thoughtful way and finds no clear resolution. Brody views neurological efficiency explanations of intelligence as "at best, plausible. No more, no less." At present, it simply is not clear which way the causal arrow points: whether some kind of basic neurological efficiency in information processing explains intelligence as measured by complex tasks, or whether whatever helps us to deal with complex tasks also lets us cope better with tasks involving reaction time and inspection time.

Whatever the ultimate resolution of this debate, right now point (b) above is more important to us. No theorist that I know of has attributed intelligent behavior entirely to neurological efficiency. Remember, all the above research focuses on g, which derives from the phenomenon of the positive manifold, the common part of intelligent behavior, the consistency within people of more or less intelligent behavior across very diverse tasks. But a great deal of intelligent behavior clearly has a more focused character. It depends in good part on one or another kind of specialized or semigeneral knowledge. Researchers concerned with the positive manifold use tests and statistical techniques to screen out such influences. But this book examines the roots of intelligent behavior in general, not just the causes of the positive manifold.

Remember also that the correlation coefficients between measurement of reaction time or other nonintellectual tasks and measurement of conventional intelligence range in the neighborhood of .5; this only accounts for 25 percent (the square of .5) of the variation in intelligence as measured by IQ. Although sometimes the correlations are higher, the point remains that a lot remains *un*accounted for. We will return to this theme in the next chapter.

Your Destiny Written in Your Genes

For months, on the wall of a colleague's office at the Harvard Graduate School of Education there appeared in a cartoon by Charles Addams one of the wryest expressions of genetic predestination that I have ever seen. In the picture part of the cartoon was a pair of twins sitting in a patent office looking at one another with a kind of detached puzzlement. Each had in his lap a technical gadget identical in all respects. The caption of the cartoon read, "Separated at birth, the Mallifert twins meet accidentally."

Funny as it is, this cartoon is chilling too. It offers a vision of predestination appalling enough to motivate a dozen erudite philosophical defenses of the concept of free will. We do not like to feel that we are the puppets of our genetic heritage, dancing according to the strings of DNA inherited from our parents. However, we may have to get used to the idea, because a number of astute scholars have argued along such lines.

Inheritance of individual traits is plain reality. Many human traits have been shown to be subject to inheritance. People implicitly acknowledge this when grandparents oooh and ahhh over how Tina or Randy looks just like her mother or his father at their age. Abundant data demonstrate the inheritance of such traits as eye color, skin color, physical frame, tendency to heart disease, and so on. Indeed, one might offer the broad generalization that most everything physical seems substantially influenced by genetics. Therefore, if we believe that intelli-

gence has some kind of organic basis in the brain (although not necessarily a unitary organic basis like general neural efficiency), we should
not be surprised to find that intelligence, to some degree, comes with
the package, a matter of our genetic endowment at birth.

Twins and the Nature-Nurture Question

This amounts to the classic question of "nature versus nurture." Nature
refers to the inborn nature of the human organism, determined by
genetic heritage. Nurture refers to the full sum of a child's environment,
not only formal schooling but the traditions of a culture, the supportive-
ness of parents, the encouragement or discouragement of an elder sibling. Since clearly both nature and nurture are likely to play some role,
the real question is: How much of each?

Without IQ or some other yardstick for intelligence, the "how much
of each" question would be impossible to answer. How can one speak of
how much without a measure? But even with a yardstick in hand, finding an answer has proved challenging to psychologists. Since the question is so fundamental to our understanding of intelligence, it's worth a
few words to understand why the question is hard to answer and how
psychologists have tried to solve that problem.

The basic difficulty is this: The world presents us with a massively
uncontrolled and confounded experiment. Any given person is the
product both of nature and of nurture—a carrier of genes that shape
him or her in a certain way, but also a reservoir of innumerable experiences that cultivate various attitudes, knowledge, and skills. Not only
that, but children are most typically raised by their genetic parents. So
children derive intelligent or not-so-intelligent behavior from their parents both by way of genetics and by way of growing up with those very
parents. Where does nature leave off and nurture begin? The muddling
of factors with one another is a methodologist's worst nightmare.

The most elegant solution looks to identical twins. Every now and
then, circumstances perform a natural experiment that happens to be
just about perfect—the methodologist's dream rather than nightmare.
The ideal experiment follows the recipe of the cartoon mentioned
above. Identical twins are born, and, for one reason or another, separated at birth and raised in differing settings. Such circumstances largely
eliminate the difficulties. First of all, the twins are genetically identical,

rather than just genetically overlapping like ordinary siblings. Second, raised apart and typically by foster parents, they receive their nurture separately from one another.

Other techniques are available to explore the question of apportioning intelligence between nature and nurture, but twins separated at birth studies provide the cleanest cut. What have such studies disclosed? Over a number of investigations, with the application of appropriate statistical techniques, it has been established that around 50 or 60 percent of the variation of intelligence as measured by IQ is determined genetically. Earlier research tended to yield somewhat larger figures than this 50 to 60 percent, but more recent studies have fairly consistently produced degrees of inheritance in this range. The remaining 40 to 50 percent can be attributed to nurturing factors of various kinds.

Opportunity Breeds Predestination

Although this leaves 40 or 50 percent of IQ to be accounted for by nurture, this may not mean as much as one would like it to. University of Virginia psychologist Sandra Scarr has developed the provocative argument that abundant opportunity for nurture, through education for example, may paradoxically *increase* the influence of our genes. Opportunity perversely breeds predestination!

How could this possibly be? The general idea can be summed up in a phrase: In opportunity-rich circumstances, genes select environments. To spell out the idea, let us tell the story of the twin inventors in the cartoon. It might have gone something like this.

Born of an unwed mother, the twins are separated at birth and put up for adoption. One goes to a family in Massachusetts, the other to a family in California. If one had gone to the rural regions of Guatemala, he probably would have become a farmer. But both twins grew up in suburban settings with reasonable educational opportunities of great variety. So, as their interests developed, both could easily gravitate toward science and mathematics.

If either had been raised in poverty, they might not have had access to materials to work with. But in their suburban settings, there was plenty of opportunity to be hands-on, so both were hands-on from the first, doing little experiments, taking radios apart, and so on.

One twin might have entered a liberal arts institution, if it were the only opportunity around. But there were many choices. So, given strong science and engineering interest, the California twin applied to the California Institute of Technology and the Massachusetts twin applied to the Massachusetts Institute of Technology. Both were admitted.

And so on. Sandra Scarr's general idea should be clear. Given a high-opportunity environment, genes have more of a chance to steer people in particular directions. While one might at first think of a high-opportunity environment as a setting that would encourage diverse influences of nurture on intelligence, Sandra Scarr argues just the opposite. In such an environment, exactly because there are so many choices, the tendencies carried in a person's genetic endowment have freest play and wield more influence than they otherwise might in selecting certain patterns of nurture. Thus, opportunity breeds predestination.

Elbow Room

How predetermined should we feel on the basis of these arguments? There may be a matter here of looking at the doughnut rather than looking at the hole. On the one hand, the 50 or 60 percent of intelligence settled by genetic factors is a lot to be locked into. On the other hand, there is an ample portion left unaccounted for—plenty of room for other factors such as parenting, enculturation, and education to make a difference in IQ.

Is the 40 to 50 percent of IQ attributable to nurture enough to feel good about, rather than walled in? Is there some elbow room there? In a broad sense, yes. IQ certainly can change. The next chapter discusses how general education, family background, nutrition, and other factors can influence IQ. However, the elbow room we would really like to see concerns direct efforts to raise IQ through short- to medium-term educational programs. Can we teach intelligence for two periods a week in second grade and make a worthwhile and lasting difference?

Educational efforts to increase intelligence as measured by IQ tests show some, but limited success. Gains are typically modest—six or seven IQ points, less than half a standard deviation, although sometimes larger for more intensive programs. Gains usually last only for a few months to two or three years after special interventions terminate. Students typically show some improvement in school performance after instruction but often not as much as the gain in IQ would suggest: Part of the IQ gain probably reflects the students becoming more test-wise. In *The Bell Curve,* Herrnstein and Murray sum up the circumstances in these discouraging terms:

> Taken together, the story of attempts to raise intelligence is one of high hopes, flamboyant claims, and disappointing results. For the foreseeable future, the problems of low cognitive ability are not going to be solved by outside interventions to make children smarter.

Of course, I disagree entirely with this negative reading of the track record, on three grounds. I will state them briefly here because much of the rest of this book deals with them. First of all, if IQ is our measure, gains approaching half a standard deviation certainly have practical significance, providing they translate into better academic and other performances—and to some extent they do. Second, if such results wash out in two or three years as students return to their usual not very intellectually stimulating settings, this only means that such students may need intermittent booster lessons to sustain their gains. There is nothing odd about this: One might make an analogy with needing to keep in training for a sport.

Third and most important, IQ is the wrong focus for efforts to raise intelligence and the wrong measure of success. IQ is not intelligence but one aspect of the complex phenomenon of intelligence. We need a much broader conception of what intelligence is. A section of the next chapter begins this discussion, and Part II, Learnable Intelligence on Trial, will take a careful look at efforts to improve intelligence, with the focus falling on other meanings of intelligence than IQ. These efforts do often improve IQ a little. But their principal payoffs concern particular kinds of thinking like problem solving or learning for understanding as well as attitudes toward thinking that promote investing mental effort. They enhance certain important kinds of intelligent behavior more than they enhance *g*.

Finally, it is important to recognize what the 50-to-60-percent genetic influence on IQ really means. The figure does not constrain learning opportunities in the way that it seems to. It's tempting to think of the 50 to 60 percent as a fixed quantity like Newton's gravitational constant, leaving a fixed window for change. However, Sandra Scarr as well as Herrnstein and Murray acknowledge that the amount of variation in IQ attributable to genetics shifts according to differences in learning opportunities in the environment.

Imagine, for instance, doing twin studies in a population with enormous differences of educational opportunity—a third-world country with dramatic contrasts from region to region and ethnic group to ethnic group. Now, general education and child rearing both influence IQ considerably, as we will see in the next chapter. So in this setting, twin studies would show a much higher percentage of intelligence attributable to nurture, because the greater differences in nurture would account for more variation in IQ than in our culture.

In contrast, imagine yet another culture with little ethnic diversity, uniform accepted and observed norms of parenting, and a highly standardized educational program administered to virtually all youngsters. Here one would expect to find a greater influence of nature, because nurture does not vary much!

The moral is this: The genetic share of IQ in our culture says hardly anything in itself about how much one might improve IQ, never mind other aspects of intelligence. Perhaps an analogy will help to make this point clearer. Muscle mass is surely heritable too—say 60 percent in our culture. But that figure will depend greatly on the diversity of physical demands and opportunities in the culture. Contrast these three cultures:

- *Schwarzeneggerian (after Arnold Schwarzenegger):* Everyone does hard physical work or pursues vigorous sports in the culture. Since people have equal exposure to exercise, the genetic contribution is high: Differences in muscle mass are largely genetically determined.
- *Oblomovian (after the key character in a Russian novel, Oblomov, who lounged around all the time):* Everyone is a couch potato, letting machines do all the work and having little interest in physical development. Here again, the genetic contribution is high: With minimal exercise universal, genetics still largely determines muscle mass.
- *Allovertheplaceian (this is our culture):* There is great diversity in physical effort, because jobs have different demands and people have varying philosophies about physical development. Here, the genetic contribution is much lower, because environment matters much more.

So where is physical development the greatest? Not where heritability is lowest, the allovertheplaceian culture, but in the Schwarzeneggerian culture, one of the two where heritability is highest, the one that uniformly and strongly supports physical development. This is what we want for intelligence: a culture that through education and in other ways uniformly and strongly supports its development. In such a culture, heritability would be high, but people would be generally more intelligent than they are now.

Is IQ Fair?

The story so far in this chapter itches and irritates. Intelligence as one thing, Spearman's general factor, the correlations between intelligence tests and measures supposedly close to the physiology of the nervous system, the influence of heredity on intelligence as measured by intelligence tests—these are less than uplifting results. We do not like to feel that all our intellectual eggs lie in the one basket of general intelligence, that general intelligence may be as fixed and physical a factor as the height of a basketball player (and if you happen to be short, too bad), or that we are stuck with the genetic legacy of our parents' intelligence. Of course, just because we do not like the sound of something does not change the facts of the matter. But what *are* the facts of the matter? Do such results really hold up or might they profoundly mislead?

One way to press the point probes whether IQ is fair. There are at least two concerns about the fairness of IQ as a measure of general intellectual competence. The first asks whether IQ is culture-fair.

Culture Fair?

Perhaps IQ tests typically make assumptions about a person's cultural background that favor some groups over others. The vocabulary, the tasks, the assumed general knowledge all could easily reflect white middle-class expectations. Such a pattern would help to explain, for instance, why IQ tests consistently show a gap approaching one standard deviation (15 points) between the average score of blacks and that of whites in our culture and about a half a standard deviation between people from lower and higher economic strata.

Of course, researchers developing IQ tests have not been blind to this risk and have tried to design tests that avoid cultural or ethnic bias. The spirit of this quest reaches back to Binet, who trimmed out of his inventories tasks that depended blatantly on school knowledge. Moreover, investigators concerned with the validity of IQ tests have conducted a number of studies about culture fairness. What have they found out?

A careful analysis of this question appears in Arthur Jensen's *Bias in Mental Testing*, and Nathan Brody updates the picture at some length in his recent *Intelligence*. Certainly items on IQ tests can be biased. Brody refers to a classic example from the Wechsler tests, "Who wrote Faust?" While such mishaps can occur, the catch is that diverse and systematic efforts to de-bias tests have not reduced substantially the differences typically found between black and white or other groups. Contemporary statistical techniques allow detecting what items show a bias. For example, in a study conducted by R. A. Gordon, eliminating biased items shrank a black-white difference of .91 of a standard deviation down to .81 of a standard deviation, not much of a reduction.

Someone might object that culture-fair testing is not just a matter of dodging culture-bound pieces of knowledge such as who wrote *Faust*. Different cultures might encourage different attitudes and practices related to thinking and learning. For instance, Jewish people tradition- ally lay great emphasis on learning and scholarship. In many Asian cul- tures, parents urge youngsters to study hard in school and support their school work assiduously. John Hayes discusses this point further in his 1981 book *The Complete Problem Solver*. Factors such as stable homes with both parents present, high income, small family size, and living in urban environments are associated with high IQ. Both groups fall into these categories and both groups indeed do better in school. Sixty-two out of every 100 college age Jews are in college, compared to 27 out of every 100 non-Jews. Jewish college students are proportionately in bet- ter schools than non-Jewish students. Jews have better grade point average than non-Jews. Jews are in Phi Beta Kappa twice their under- graduate proportion. Asians have the lowest school drop-out rate of any group in the country. Dropping out of school "is considered a disgrace in an Asian community." They constitute less than one percent of the American population but are one percent of the undergraduate popula- tion and two percent of the graduate population.

Does this mean that IQ tests show culture bias? If the people of a cul- ture rear their children to invest themselves in thinking and learning, is it unfair that those children tend to score higher on intelligence tests? Not really. Such children exhibit more of what's asked for by the con- ception of intelligent behavior aired in the last chapter—better problem solving, reasoning, logic, vocabulary, information, and so on. They han- dle abstract, complex, intellectually demanding tasks better.

One point of caution: The kind of thinking asked for by IQ tests certainly counts for more in practical terms in some cultures than in others. For instance, members of an agrarian nontechnological culture with little general education would typically score much lower than the norm on IQ tests, even tests without "Faustian" items. But those people would be far better adapted to their circumstances than any Boston-raised Harvard graduate. IQ tests look to be culture fair in that, when well-designed and sensitively administered, they test more or less what they are supposed to. This does not mean that what they test is what everyone in every culture needs.

Prediction Fair?

But is IQ even what people in cultures with complex economic systems and industries need? This concern about the fairness of IQ tests challenges the real-world relevance of what they measure. Do abstract, complex, intellectually demanding tasks have a lot to do with everyday coping in our culture and others like ours? This asks whether the tests are prediction-fair; are they forecasting something about real-world performance or are they just games that psychometricians play?

A considerable body of research underwrites the predictive significance of IQ in industrial cultures. One arena of interest is education. The correlation between IQ and educational performance as measured by course grades and achievement tests ranges in the neighborhood of .5. Another arena of interest is the workplace. Here, a number of studies relating IQ to various measures of job performance show correlation coefficients in the neighborhood of .5 after statistical adjustments for studying groups with a limited range of IQs and for expected inaccuracies of scoring. In other words, IQ matters. It does not matter overwhelmingly—statistically, a correlation coefficient of .5 only accounts for 25 percent of the range of variation in performance, leaving 75 percent to be explained by other factors. But it matters.

In their 1994 book *The Bell Curve*, Richard Herrnstein and Charles Murray document how a number of social ills connect to IQ. People in poverty, unwed mothers, the chronically unemployed, and criminals all show a disproportionate presence of individuals of low IQ. For example, they report that criminal offenders have average IQs of about 92. Able bodied people who are chronically unemployed almost all sit in the bottom 25 percent of the IQ distribution. This does not mean that most people of low IQ are criminals or out of work. On the contrary, Herrnstein and Murray emphasize that the great majority are honest and gainfully employed. The point, rather, is that people of low IQ are over-represented in criminal, unemployed, and similar populations. Low IQ is not destiny but is definitely a risk factor.

Herrnstein and Murray demonstrate that the relationships between low IQ and social ills are *not* masks for educational or economic deprivation. The relationships hold up even after statistically removing the influence of education or socioeconomic background. The relationships also do not depend on race: They hold up when the analysis is limited to non-Latino whites and remain essentially the same with all races and ethnic groups added to the mix.

Herrnstein's and Murray's interpretation of these relationships and what to do about them runs contrary to my position in this book. The authors see intelligence as dominated by genetics, races as carriers of different genetic endowments, and education as of little help. Although I differ on all these counts, the basic connections between IQ and social ills profiled in *The Bell Curve* deserve attention.

In summary, IQ certainly has predictive significance in our culture in a number of ways. I cannot emphasize too much that this predictive significance is limited. For instance, correlation coefficients in the neighborhood of .5, characteristic of much of this work, leave a full 75 percent of variation from person to person unexplained by IQ, ample room for other influences. Nonetheless, IQ points to something of interest and importance.

Fair Implications?

If measures of IQ in themselves prove reasonably culture fair and have some predictive value in industrial cultures, less fair are the implications some people draw from those measures. There mischief often thrives through stereotyping and exaggeration. For example, to say that blacks or people from impoverished backgrounds have lower averages on IQ tests is to tempt some into the belief that blacks or poor people they happen to come in contact with are not very bright. But such a conclusion in fact defiles the meaning of the statistics. The range of IQ is huge in any population. A difference in average scores of the order of half to a whole standard deviation signals a statistical trend with only modest predictive power in an individual case.

What about using IQ as the basis for hiring decisions? Sometimes this may indeed be relevant as one factor among many to consider, but Brody warns about the hazard of overweighing it. Yes, as noted above the correlation coefficient between IQ and job performance often hits about .5. But remember, this figure includes corrections for experimental samples with a restricted range of IQ and for likely modest errors of measurement. Unfortunately, a person making hiring decisions cannot avoid either of those problems. The hirer must choose among applicants whose intelligence probably does not range that widely, because they will have matched themselves to the demands of the job in deciding to apply for it. The hirer also must work with scores of limited reliability, lacking any way of securing more accurate scores. In other words, the statistically corrected .5 yields a more accurate picture-in-principle of the relationship between IQ and job performance, but in practical terms the relationship between the measured IQs of actual job applicants and their performance will be markedly lower and hence much less significant as a basis for choice.

Still more unfair and less warranted is the conclusion that systematic differences in IQ between ethnic or racial groups represent genetic inevitabilities. Brody emphasizes that the causes of group differences in IQ have proved evasive despite considerable investigation. Regarding black-white differences, he sums the matter up this way:

> The reasons for the differences are probably to be found in the distinctive cultural experiences encountered by black individuals in the United States. While it may be difficult to definitively rule out a genetic hypothesis on the basis of the available evidence, I think that it is also fair to say that there is no convincing direct or indirect evidence in favor of a genetic hypothesis of racial differences in IQ.

In keeping with this, intelligence researcher Stephen Ceci in his *On Intelligence . . . More or Less* mentions an informative 1979 review by Sarason and Doris of the literature on immigrants' IQs. They reported that the IQs of first generation Italian-American children were usually within the low average to borderline retarded range (IQs between 76 and 100, with the mid point 87). Italian-American children's IQs were lower than any other ethnic or racial groups except French-Canadians, Blacks, Indians, and Portuguese. Sarason and Doris showed in their review that as the levels of school completion increased among Italian-American children during the first five decades of this century, so did their IQs. Today, Italian-American students' IQs are slightly above aver-

age. Such findings suggest that group differences can easily be a consequence of culture and educational opportunity. For any ethnic or racial
group, cultural assimilation and genuinely equal educational opportunity would wipe out such contrasts.

Although the possible genetic basis of differences in IQ is a complex
technical issue, factors such as the above convince me that Herrnstein
and Murray in *The Bell Curve* overreach the evidence in concluding
that probably the differences are partly genetic.

What can be said in summary about the fairness of IQ? Yes, the significance of IQ differences has often been interpreted unfairly and inju-
diciously. However, from a technical perspective, the measures themselves have survived rather well the assaults of critics concerned about
fairness. With this granted, yet another issue of fairness deserves attention—not about fair measures but about fairly interpreting what lies
beneath the measures, the stuff of intelligence.

Intelligence as Essence

Goddard was not shooting in the dark. Goddard's list gets the support of
considerable evidence from studies of IQ and *g* from the turn of the
century onward. To be sure, a number of cautions were offered and
more are to come in the next chapter. Nonetheless, here is a bird's eye
view of intelligence as seen by the empire of IQ:

The evidence at hand . . .

- More and less intelligent behavior, as observed in everyday life (visible intelligence)
- Different people displaying consistently more or less intelligent
behavior across diverse test and everyday contexts (the positive
manifold)
- Spearman's *g* showing that the consistency accounts for more than
50 percent of the variation in people's handling of novel, intellectually challenging tasks
- IQ as a comparative measure of intelligence relative to others in the
same population
- Correlations between scores on IQ tasks and simple reaction time
and other measures, supposedly closer to the hardware of the brain
- Substantial correlations of IQ between identical twins reared apart

MWQ #1. What mechanisms underlie intelligence?

- One unitary cause of some sort, not the potpourri that Binet envisioned
- In particular, some kind of neurological efficiency
- With genes largely determining neurological speed and precision

MWQ #2. Can people learn more intelligence?

- By and large, no: Intelligence depends mostly on genetically determined physiology.

MWQ #3. What aspects of intelligence especially need attention?

- There is only one kind, *g*, with slim prospects for improving it by learning.

In his *The Mismeasure of Man*, Harvard paleontologist Stephen J. Gould writes with revolutionary spirit about the mischief this hard line on intelligence has done historically. He shows how such a view has provided rationales for limiting immigration, discriminating against blacks and other racial groups, sterilizing the retarded, and much much more. A hard-line view too often has been welcome fodder for the jaws of bigotry, feeding a host of all too human hates and fears.

Gould emphasizes an error of logic called reification. When people reify something, they take a phenomenon and presume that the phenomenon reflects some one essence. The very word "intelligence" nudges in this direction. Compare the adjective intelligent with the noun intelligence. In phrases like intelligent behavior or intelligent person, the adjective intelligent seems simply descriptive. It is not in the business of making theories. However, the noun intelligence suggests one stuff, one kind of thing. Yes, we can keep reminding ourselves that intelligence is simply a name for whatever inner qualities cause intelligent behavior, however diverse—Binet's potpourri of abilities for instance. But we have to be alert, because the word intelligence has a tendency toward reification built into it. So do other similar words like the noun creativity in contrast with the adjective creative. There is always that potentially misleading nudge toward some essence.

It is not so clear that reification is an out-and-out error. One can appreciate the scientific impulse behind reification. It is elegant, powerful, beautiful to assign a plethora of phenomena to a single deep cause. The scientific impulse toward reification is part of the aesthetic of science, a canon of parsimony and theoretical compass that deserves pursuit. The record of successful reification in science is impressive—X-rays, the germ theory of disease, neutrinos, and on and on—all cases where the existence of some *stuff* was posited on the basis of indirect evidence and only later demonstrated in more direct fashion.

But there are a couple of crucial caveats. First, one wants *warranted* reification. To justify speaking of a unitary neurological mechanism for intelligence, one needs evidence that only makes sense in terms of the hypothesis. No one should jump to the conclusion of a single essence because such a conclusion is scientifically neat. In this respect, Spearman with his factor analytic techniques and Jensen and others with their reaction time studies tried to play the right sort of game. They made serious efforts to offer evidence of a single-mechanism concept of intelligence. Although their data do not prove the case, for reasons discussed, they make the case more plausible.

The second caution is that the reified single-mechanism idea of intelligence historically has carried altogether too much baggage along with it. This view of intelligence has been far from a detached laboratory concept, discussed only by white-smocked scientists and professors perched on their podiums. It is a concept that has engendered discriminatory policies on matters from immigration to the sterilization of some criminals. It is a concept that helps to support the questionable practice of tracking in schools, where students deemed to be of different intellectual capacities are assigned courses of instruction that move more slowly or more quickly. Research shows that, for the most part, tracking does not enhance student achievement. Moreover, students deemed less able when tracks are assigned commonly get locked into lower tracks: The slower pace quickly leaves them too far behind to hope to jump up to a higher track. It is a concept that has been abused in hiring policies and practices. Consequently, particular caution should be observed in any move toward a single-mechanism concept of intelligence, in light of the societal ripple effects.

In the end, then, what has the empire of IQ become? It is the vast and thriving testing industry based on IQ that extracts large profits from the educational community, delivers some genuine services on the positive side, and fosters a conception of intelligence as fixed and intractable. It is the long history of IQ imperialism that has provoked and sustained some very questionable actions. But, more than anything else, the empire of IQ is the empire of a magnetic idea, the idea of the one and only pure essence of intelligence. A powerful one in many ways, this idea might be a profound and costly mistake.

4

The Great IQ Roast

Almost everyone is familiar with that charming Hollywood institution, the celebrity roast. In its ideal Platonic form, the celebrity roast must be presided over by Don Rickles, master of kill comedy. The friends and colleagues of a well-known figure, let us say Cher or Michael Keaton, get together with the figure for an evening of fond reminiscences and cutting jokes, a verbal version of the Texas Chainsaw Massacre.

The world of psychology has seen a sustained roast of one of its most notable and notorious celebrities—the idea of IQ. From diverse directions, representing a variety of philosophies and sources of data, psychologists have taken to task the classic conception of IQ. Unlike the Hollywood roast, the Great IQ Roast has often proceeded with little affection for the roastee. Every point on Goddard's list has seen harsh challenges: the notion that intelligence is unitary, that it has its basis in neural functioning, that intelligence is largely inherited, that learning therefore has little impact.

The Great IQ Roast plays a central role in the emerging theory of learnable intelligence that gives this book its focus. The classic theory of intelligence in its extreme form makes little room for learnable intelligence. Rather, intelligence comes built into one's genes like the original equipment of a car or the CPU in a computer. To argue the case for learnable intelligence, one must challenge the classic theory.

Some of those participating in the Great IQ Roast indeed have had the cultivation of intelligence as an agenda. Many others have simply aimed to disclose what they see as flaws in IQ, without any particular brief for education. Whatever the case, the Copernican revolution in our conceptions of intelligence has much to do with those features of IQ that have proved most roastable. If parents, teachers, business people, and policy-makers—indeed, all of us—have any hope of working toward a more intelligent population, a well-done roast of IQ is key. In the pages to come, I will try to survey some major objections to the classic conception of intelligence, take stock of whether and how well the classic conception survives those objections, and appraise the consequent prospects of learnable intelligence.

Multiple Intelligences

Psychometrics is the science of psychological measurement. The classic concepts of IQ and *g* both fall into its camp. Both put numbers to the phenomenon of some people consistently behaving more intelligently than others. Indeed, the prominence of IQ and *g* in theorizing about the mind and in practical matters such as school tracking and employment decisions has fed psychometrics as a discipline. Psychometrics has done well within the empire of IQ.

Nonetheless, much of the criticism comes from within the camp of the emperor—directly from psychometricians concerned with giving the best account possible of the nature of the human intellect. Many of the challenges have dealt with a key claim on Goddard's list and a key characteristic of Spearman's notion of mental energy: the idea that intelligence is unitary, one essence, one kind of ability. Instead, intelligence might be viewed as a composite of different contributing abilities.

Essence or Overlap?

One kind of objection to the classic position acknowledges the statistics and looks to their interpretation. Let it be granted, as Spearman argued, that a single factor, called *g*, accounts for a great deal of the variability from person to person in handling challenging intellectual tasks. This does not imply that the underlying cause of the *g* factor is a single ability. It could still be the kind of potpourri that Binet favored.

As early as 1916, the British psychologist Godfrey Thomson explained

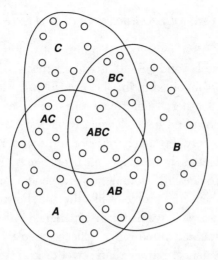

Illustration of Thomson's idea that different tests draw on overlapping sets of the myriad components that contribute to intellectual performance.

how a common trend could occur without intelligence being a single ability. Imagine that there are hundreds, even thousands, of component abilities involved in intelligent functioning. Suppose in principle that they are independent of one another. However, suppose that any given kind of task—logic puzzles, arithmetic problems, vocabulary quizzes—taps many of these components. In this case, performance on any kind of task tends to correlate with performance on any other not because of any single ability underlying intelligence but because of the inevitable overlaps. The above figure illustrates Thomson's argument: The small circles represent the many component abilities that might contribute to intellectually demanding performances, while the large circles represent three different tests that call upon different combinations of those abilities, but with plenty of overlap. On Thomson's interpretation, the *g* factor extracted by statistics represents not a single central intellectual ability but rather the average overlap in the abilities demanded by one task and another—*g* as overlap rather than single essence.

Thomson's argument offers no proof that *g* in fact reflects a grab bag of component abilities, nor any reason to believe that those abilities are partly learned rather than entirely genetically programmed. Nonetheless, Thomson shows clearly that the impressive summative power of the *g* statistic does not imply a unitary underlying phenomenon.

Fluid Intelligence, Crystallized Intelligence, and Beyond

While some like Thomson have looked at alternative interpretations of *g*, others have looked beyond *g* to statistical approaches that suggest a multiplicity of factors involved in intelligence. John L. Horn, professor at the University of Southern California, is one among several who have pressed this case. Horn and his colleague, Raymond Cattell, coined a well-known contrast between *fluid intelligence* and *crystallized intelligence*. Fluid intelligence gauges how adaptable people are to novel tasks, where experience provides little foundation and general reasoning abilities dominate. Number series problems like the one shown in Chapter 2 are examples: Most people have had little experience with them.

In contrast, crystallized intelligence reflects people's accumulated knowledge and experience. Rather than novel tasks, psychometricians use vocabulary tests, general knowledge quizzes, and the like to measure crystallized intelligence. Horn avers that crystallized and fluid intelligence together give a somewhat sharper analysis of intellectual functioning than *g* as a single factor.

Working with an even broader palette, Horn recently has reviewed a number of dimensions of intelligence termed WERCOF factors. WERCOF is an acronym for Well-Replicated Common Factors in intellectual performance. These are some forty-five statistically derived components of intellectual ability falling under several broad categories including abilities of reasoning under novel conditions, visualization and spatial orientation abilities, short-term apprehension and retrieval abilities, and more. For instance, the components contributing to short-term apprehension and retrieval abilities are associative memory (recalling an arbitrary association between one item and another), span memory (recalling a set of elements after one presentation), memory for order (recalling the position of an element within a set), chunking memory (recalling elements by categories), and meaningful memory (recalling items that are meaningfully related). Horn points out that all of these have the votes of many experiments saying that they are parts of intelligence. They help to account for people's performance on a diversity of intellectually challenging tasks.

Flexible Factor Analysis

How is it that Spearman and others can extract a general *g* factor from tests while Horn, Cattell, and yet others come up with a multiplicity of factors? To a degree, this is actually a matter of choice. The technique of factor analysis pioneered by Spearman allows extracting a general *g* from a diversity of tasks given to people. But the technique *also* allows dividing people's performance into a number of subfactors instead. It depends on how the analysis is set up, and that, in turn, depends on whether you want to be a lumper or a splitter, whether you wish to pursue a vision of one highly integrated essence or a vision of multiple intelligences. The lumpers, advocates of classic *g*, could stand accused of making an arbitrary choice. But then, so could the splitters.

However, a closer look at the statistics suggests that perhaps the choice should not be made at all. Rather, the reality of intelligence seems to involve both one overarching factor and a number of only partly distinguishable components. As to components, one reason to believe in them is that appropriate statistical techniques do reveal them. Another is that some of the components behave differently from one another over time and in learning situations. For example, Horn notes that as people grow older, they come to differ more from one another in crystallized intelligence, as measured by vocabulary for instance. In contrast, the range of variation in fluid intelligence remains about the same over the same span of age. The fact that these components behave differently over time rather than remaining in lock step with one another argues that they are truly distinct.

But truly distinct does not mean perfectly distinct. Measures of crystallized and fluid intelligence are highly correlated with one another, and the same can be said for other components of intelligence like short-term apprehension and retrieval. As emphasized in the last chapter, virtually all performances on intellectually challenging tasks correlate: People who do well on one such task tend to do well on others, albeit with individual exceptions. The overlap among the multiple factors amounts to *g*. While *g* may not reflect any single mechanism—remember Thomson's argument that it could simply echo the overlapping of resources required by different complex tasks—*g* is a statistical and practical reality that cannot be dismissed.

Multiple Multiple Intelligences

Different splitters have sliced the pie of intelligence in somewhat different ways. Horn's WERCOF factors have already been mentioned. Another especially well-known example of splitting is J. P. Guilford's *structure of intellect* theory of intelligence. In a series of papers published from 1967 on, Guilford proposed that intelligence involves no less than 150 different components. He arrived at this number through considering five cognitive operations applied to any of five kinds of content to yield any of six kinds of products, for $5 \times 5 \times 6 = 150$ combinations in all. Here is a compact list of Guilford's operations, contents, and products:

> *Operations:* Cognition, Memory, Evaluation, Convergent Production, Divergent Production
> *Contents:* Behavioral, Visual Figural, Auditory Figural, Symbolic, Semantic
> *Products:* Units, Classes, Relations, Systems, Transformations, Implications

We do not have to know just what Guilford means by each of these terms, since we will not go into his theory deeply. However, to catch the spirit of Guilford's approach, consider what happens when you remember your telephone number. You have used a *memory* operation on a *symbolic* representation (*symbolic* refers to numbers and notations) to produce a single *unit*, your phone number. Now a more challenging task: Suppose you figure out the culprit in an especially misleading Sherlock Holmes mystery before you get to the end of the story. This would involve many of Guilford's combinations, but among them would surely be *divergent production*, because you had to use your creativity, applied to *semantic* contents, because you were dealing with words and ideas, to produce an *implication*, who the culprit was.

Guilford proposed that each combination had a distinct statistical presence and a psychological reality. He tried to justify his analysis with statistical techniques, but his approach has been criticized from several perspectives. It seems fair to say that the model as a whole is suspect. However, a number of his components are among those Horn wrote about as WERCOF factors; they seem fairly sound. These include, for instance, all the WERCOF examples listed earlier as examples of short-term apprehension and retrieval abilities: associative memory, span memory, meaningful memory, chunking memory, and memory for order.

A very different and quite recent perspective on multiple intelligences comes from my colleague of many years, Howard Gardner. In his 1983 book entitled *Frames of Mind*, Gardner proposed seven distinct intelligences: linguistic intelligence (dealing with words), musical intelligence, logical-mathematical intelligence, spatial intelligence (as in art, architecture), bodily-kinesthetic intelligence (as in dance, sports), interpersonal intelligence (dealing with others), and intrapersonal intelligence (awareness and handling of self). Chapter 12 discusses his theory further so I will only say a little about it here.

While most of the multiple intelligence theories discussed here come from psychometricians, Gardner represents another camp. Indeed, Gardner's theory of multiple intelligences, or MI Theory as he calls it, is more a reaction to than a variation of psychometric theories. Gardner argues for his seven intelligences not from statistical analyses but rather from studies of brain damage, where certain abilities are commonly lost in company with others; from studies of prodigies and idiot savants, where people display amazing performance in a particular area; and from a general consideration of the kinds of activities that prove central in a complex society. Gardner criticizes the psychometric tradition— even in its more eclectic form—for ignoring facets of the human intellect such as music and kinesthetic abilities.

Nonetheless, Gardner's view shows some kinship to the spawn of psychometry. First of all, Gardner, in company with many psychometricians, believes that the intelligences he proposes reflect in part underlying neurological factors. Second, several of Gardner's intelligences are not so different from those in Guilford's content dimension of intelligence. In particular, Guilford's figural (pictorial and spatial matters) matches Gardner's spatial intelligence; his symbolic (numbers and notations) Gardner's logical-mathematical intelligence; and his semantic facet (words and ideas) Gardner's linguistic intelligence.

What to Make of So Many Intelligences?

Like Guilford's view, Gardner's has drawn considerable criticism. Whatever the resolution in this ongoing debate, it seems confusing that Gardner, Guilford, Horn, and others have proposed different accounts of multiple intelligences. Certainly *g* wins the contest for simplicity and coherence. While the lumpers have one lump on which they agree, the splitters apparently cannot decide how intelligence should be split.

However, this overstates the dilemma. Rival splitters do show considerable overlap. Recall how several of Gardner's intelligences correspond to components on Guilford's list. Also, several of Guilford's components show up among Horn's WERCOF factors. While plainly the splitters face a formidable problem in sorting out components of human intelligence, the phenomena of the mind at least are coherent enough that investigators keep advancing some of the same components.

In the midst of all this, many psychologists still argue for the soundness of the classic g and IQ. Certainly as statistical constructions they remain impressive. They have great predictive power. Comparative analyses have shown that multiple intelligence theories add only a little to this predictive power.

In his recent synthesis of work on intelligence, Nathan Brody of Wesleyan University draws on an analysis by Gustaffson to conclude that the best picture of the situation is a hierarchy. At the top sits g: Without any claims about the underlying causes of g, it remains a fact that a single general factor accounts for a great deal. Moreover, Gustaffson's statistical analyses suggest that g and Horn's and Cattell's fluid intelligence are essentially the same thing, a reflection of greater or lesser ability to handle novel, complex tasks. Besides g there are other factors that refine the picture, factors that represent different kinds of cognitive processing, for example linguistic versus more spatial and pictorial processing. Certainly, the evidence argues that intelligence is more complex than a single essence, even if a single number accounts for a lot.

So how successfully have challenges from the perspective of multiple intelligences been in their roast of the empire of IQ? The insurrection has been limited but important. The g factor retains much of its power and implications for human performance. Nonetheless, a number of other facets of intelligence can be identified with some confidence, facets that the classic Empire left no room for.

Changeable Intelligence

Averring that intelligence was genetically determined, Goddard went on to assert that it was "but little affected by any later influences except such serious accidents as may destroy part of the mechanism." Measured by Goddard's list, the prospects of learnable intelligence look bleak indeed. More broadly, the general impression from the empire of IQ is that intelligence is as fixed as one's fingerprints. You have what you have and that's that.

Here, as happens from time to time with powerful empires, the empire of IQ stands accused of a position it does not take. Although Goddard maintained that intelligence was fixed, this has not been the general stance. Psychometricians interested in intelligence have long recognized that intelligence in the sense of IQ shifts somewhat in response to circumstances.

Intelligence Adrift

Lloyd Humphreys, professor of psychology at University of Illinois, Urbana, and noted intelligence researcher, has underscored repeatedly the changeability of IQ over time. In general, when people take an intelligence test and then retake the same or a similar test shortly thereafter, their two sets of scores show a strong relationship. However, the greater the period from test to retest, the weaker the relationship. In terms of correlation coefficients, scores on a test followed soon by another test correlate in the neighborhood of .95. In contrast, the correlation between a test and another administered a decade later might fall between .63 and .70.

It's tempting to think that shifts in intelligence over time simply reflect inaccuracies in IQ tests. However, if this were the case, people tested just a few days later would show as much drift in their scores as people retested ten years later. Since this is not the case, a much more interesting conclusion ensues: IQ genuinely shifts over time.

Humphreys points out that shifts occur in both directions: Some people get smarter and some not as smart over time, by the measure of IQ. Moreover and rather surprisingly, how smart one is to start with does not influence the direction of drift. A person with a relatively high IQ may experience an increase or a decrease. This is not one of those cases where "the rich get richer and the poor get poorer." Anything can happen.

As to why IQ drifts, there is probably no one answer. Differences in biological maturation might play a role. Nutrition certainly can be a factor. Vitamin and mineral supplements appear to affect IQ slightly, perhaps by impacting the nervous system or perhaps simply by improving general health. In a large California study, some eighth grade students received vitamin and mineral supplements while others received a placebo over a thirteen-week period. There were no resulting differences in verbal IQ, but the group receiving the genuine supplements showed modest superiority in a measure of nonverbal intelligence and also slightly better gains on the California test of basic skills. (Before everyone rushes out to buy vitamins, it must be emphasized that these effects were quite small.)

Child-rearing practices are also implicated. For instance, two studies in France took advantage of circumstances by looking at children born to low socioeconomic circumstances but adopted and raised in high socioeconomic class homes. In both studies, these children showed about a twelve-point edge in IQ, almost a standard deviation and a very substantial gain. In adult life, shifts of social setting and social expectations, or shifts in the level of intellectual challenge in one's professional life, could contribute.

Finally, as we shall see below, formal education is a factor. The basic point is that shifts in IQ over time demonstrate that intelligence is not a fixed quantity.

The Influence of General Education

The IQ of whole populations can change over time. One reason seems to be general education—not education targeted specifically on improving people's thinking but simply more thorough and extended educational experiences in general. For instance, Humphreys highlights a comparison between soldiers subjected to IQ tests during the First and Second World Wars, around 1917 and 1942. Administration of such tests was a standard part of the induction procedures. Over that period, a substantial gain occurred in measures of general intelligence, an increase of about a standard deviation, about fifteen points of IQ. This is a dramatic boost! Humphreys thinks it most likely attributable to the vast expansion of public education between the wars.

Another finding in the same spirit appeared in the last chapter. Sarason and Doris synthesized results about the IQs and education of Italian-Americans during the first five decades of the twentieth century. Decade by decade, as school completion increased, they found a steady advance of IQ. Although it is possible that something else caused an increase in IQ, which helped more Italian-Americans to complete school, the more plausible explanation is that school learning itself boosted IQ.

Brody in his *Intelligence* affirms the influence of education on general intelligence. One study he highlights was reported by Cahan and Cohen in 1989. The study took advantage of the fact that some students because of when their birthdays happen to fall enter school a year before others of nearly the same age. These students end up with nearly a year more schooling than students of almost the same age. They also score systematically higher on tests of general intelligence, much higher than would be explained by the few days' difference in age between them and the students with a year less education. The results of the study establish that schooling increases performance on intelligence tests independent of the differences in age associated with schooling.

One could object that such gains might not mean much. More educated people might score better simply because they were more knowledgeable, not because they were smarter in the sense of general intelligence. Their higher scores might reflect the contamination of intelligence tests with knowledge-based questions.

One answer is to say that a larger knowledge base *is* part of intelligence. But another answer more responsive to the spirit of the objection is to look to the impact of education on fluid intelligence. Recall from earlier in this chapter that fluid intelligence is the side of intelligence that most reflects good thinking on challenging and unfamiliar problems; fluid intelligence seems to be virtually identical with g. Brody points out that increases in the measured intelligence of populations plausibly attributable to more or better education have generally shown at least as much and often more improvement in fluid intelligence as in crystallized intelligence. Tests of fluid intelligence generally pose tasks quite unlike school tasks on the surface and ask for no particular school knowledge. This argues that quantity and quality of schooling impact on intelligence in the sense of g, Spearman's general factor. Therefore results are not an artifact of people just knowing more.

To take stock again of the Great IQ Roast, abundant evidence shows that general intelligence is far from fixed. In all fairness, most advocates of general intelligence as IQ appear not to have claimed that it was, although Goddard did. The changeability of general intelligence signals hope for the possibility of systematically enhancing human intelligence. But it does no more than that. To say that general intelligence is changeable is not to say that we can effectively and efficiently harness whatever factors cause it to change.

Intelligence as Expertise

You can't just think: You have to think about something. Thinking may deal with abstractions but it never occurs in the abstract. Poets think about sonnets, lovers think about kisses, physicists think about quarks, and idlers may think about naps. Thinking always happens in the company of content to be thought about.

Therein lies the seed of one of the most powerful contemporary challenges to the empire of IQ, the notion of expertise. Over several decades, psychologists have become interested in the nature of expertise. What accounts for the agile performance of someone truly steeped in a particular area of accomplishment, be it poetry, love or physics? Perhaps it is general intelligence. Perhaps it is more specific but still broad abilities like visual discrimination, motor control, and deductive logic. But perhaps it is something much less general: simply knowing a lot about what you are doing.

Chess Intelligence

The game of chess looks to be an enterprise of pure logic, a playground for general intelligence. Imagine yourself sitting at the chess board. You see exactly where you and your opponent's pieces sit and every move your opponent makes. You know the rules: which pieces can move how, what constitutes checkmate. You lack for no information, nor is there any element of chance like the rolling of dice or the shuffling of cards. All you have to do is be smarter than your opponent and you will win.

So it seems at least. However, researchers striving to understand just what makes some chess players better than others have built a very different picture of the mechanisms underlying good chess play, a picture in which general intelligence plays a modest role. Indeed, research on chess gave the entire study of expertise its initial impetus. In the 1940s, the Dutch psychologist A. D. de Groot investigated the cognitive abilities of chess players ranked at the master level, as well as of lesser players. While many findings emerged, three point up especially clearly the curious character of expertise and strike a sharp contrast with notions of general intelligence.

One of the most natural predictions about chess play is that the master chess player thinks further ahead. The master reasons in a more panoramic and far-seeing way about what might happen: "Let's see, if I move my rook forward, you'll place your queen there. Then I could bring my knight up there, but you'll surely move yours forward as well. But then I could . . ." and so on. This picture of extensive exploration seems in keeping with our intuition that the chess master has a powerful mind that can keep track of many possibilities.

De Groot set out to check this easy assumption. He investigated the relationship between players' explorations of chains of play before making a move—how deeply and thoroughly they surveyed the possibilities—and the sophistication of their play. The result was a surprise: Amateur players of no great standing explored just about as thoroughly as masters. Yet the masters easily beat the amateurs. Obviously, thinking ahead has importance, yet the scope of one's look-ahead seemed to miss whatever made the difference between the amateurs and the masters. "Chess intelligence" lay somewhere else.

What was the hidden intelligence of the master chess players? If they were not surveying more possibilities with the tool of their powerful general intelligence, what were they doing? De Groot found a clue in the familiar tale that chess masters can memorize the layout of pieces on a chess board at a glance. The tale turned out to be true. De Groot compared the ability of serious amateurs and masters in memorizing a layout, given only a few seconds to look. Masters performed with perfection. Amateurs, in contrast, could only reconstruct the positions of seven or eight pieces.

De Groot made one more comparison, this one strikingly ingenious. He pitted the masters against the novices in the memory task again. However, this time he used arrangements of pieces at random on the chess board, rather than in arrangements that would normally occur in the course of play. The results were startling: The masters became like amateurs, only placing some seven or eight pieces correctly.

What was going on? The contrast between the masters' impressive showing on positions that might occur in the course of play and their mediocre performance on random positions reveals much about the character of chess skill. Apparently, through years of experience, master players learn to see in a quick and intuitive way typical arrangements of pieces. Contemporary psychological theory helps to account for this in terms of a phenomenon called chunking. With experience in a domain, people learn to encode the world in larger chunks that hang together. A chess master, for instance, will not just perceive piece by piece, but will see larger configurations of pieces—a rook on an open file, a fork accomplished by a knight. Able to encode the arrangement of the pieces in the vocabulary of these larger chunks, the master can take in an entire board in the form of a few chunks . . . providing the arrangement is natural to chess.

The results suggested that something very different from general intelligence lay behind the masters' skill with chess. Their chess intelligence depended in good part on quick perceptual insight developed through years of play. Chess masters were not just smart in general; they knew a lot about chess specifically.

Of course, it's no surprise that intelligent behavior in the real world would depend on knowledge. One could not be a good surgeon without knowing a lot about the organization of the human body or a good stock broker without knowing a lot about how the stock market works. What is interesting about the case of chess is that there are not many basics to know: only six kinds of pieces and a few rules. In principle, one might expect a person with very high intelligence to deduce the rest—good positions, good attacks, good sacrifices. In practice, people with high IQs are at the mercy of an experienced player of more modest IQ. Nothing counts like a rich fund of experience.

Horse Racing Intelligence

In the years after de Groot's work, other psychologists repeated and extended his investigations of chess play, most notably Carnegie-Mellon psychologist Herbert Simon (winner of the Nobel prize for his psychological theories about economics) and his colleague William Chase. Still other cognitive scientists began to investigate further areas of expertise in similar spirit—computer programming, physics problem solving, and more. Always the same pattern emerged: Expert performance depends in good part on a large accumulated knowledge base and that allows intuitive perceptual orientation to tasks. Experts can "see" what challenges and opportunities a particular situation affords.

Perhaps the most charming study in this tradition stepped away from traditional intellectual pursuits to investigate handicapping—predicting the winners in horse races. The subjects were people who frequented the horse races year in and year out and claimed to be expert at predicting which horse would finish in what position. Investigators Stephen J. Ceci and Jeffrey Liker located a number of these individuals. They gauged the participants' thinking in several ways. Conventional IQ measures were used. In addition, the investigators examined how well the handicappers scored in predicting finishing positions of horses. Finally, the investigators sat with the participants to see how they reasoned about the horses: the kinds of knowledge they used, how thoroughly they surveyed and balanced the evidence, and so on.

One finding was that some of the handicappers proved much better at the enterprise than others, even though all had had some sixteen years of experience. Second, the handicappers' success was not predicted by IQ: General intelligence seemed to have nothing to do with it. Third, success *did* relate to the complexity of the handicappers' cognition in the context of handicapping. The better handicappers composed judgments that explicitly took into account more interacting factors than did the less successful handicappers.

Here again, as in the study of chess players, knowledge and cognitive processing specific to the activity both counted. Horse racing intelligence was not general intelligence.

Job Intelligence

Chess play and racehorse handicapping come from the world of sports and games. Other areas that have been studied, such as physics, are blatantly academic. What can be said about the workplace? How much does general intelligence count there?

John E. Hunter reports an intriguing attempt to estimate the relative contributions of general intelligence and context-specific knowledge in a very practical context: job performance in a range of jobs including manual jobs. Hunter gathered information on the general intelligence of a number of workers, their knowledge about their jobs, and their on-the-job performance as gauged by supervisors. Hunter employed a statistical technique called path analysis to investigate how these factors related to one another.

The intricacies of path analysis need not worry us here. What counts is the pattern revealed by Hunter's analysis. He found that IQ indeed correlated with job performance, but with knowledge as a mediating variable. This means that the best direct predictor of job performance was knowledge about the job, not IQ. To be sure, IQ did relate to job performance, but not as directly as knowledge. A reasonable interpretation is that higher-IQ workers learn somewhat faster and therefore become more knowledgeable in their jobs sooner. But it's the knowledge that most directly accounts for performance, however long a worker needed to accumulate it.

Richard Wagner and Robert Sternberg conducted an investigation of what they termed the practical intelligence involved in business management. They proposed that how well a person performed as a manager depended a great deal on knowing the ropes. The two developed an instrument called a Tacit Knowledge Inventory for Managers (TKIM) to gauge management practical intelligence. The TKIM posed situations and asked questions about them that seemed to require practical management savvy to answer. The investigators also introduced performance measures to gauge the participants' skills more directly.

They found that people with more experience in management roles showed substantially better TKIM scores. Moreover, TKIM scores correlated with the more direct measures of management performance. IQ scores also correlated with management performance, but not as highly as TKIM scores. Finally, TKIM scores and IQ did not correlate with one another highly, indicating that the practical intelligence captured by the TKIM was an important contributor to management performance not captured by IQ.

Local Intelligence

The moral of these studies and many others like them can be summed up in a sentence: Intelligent behavior depends a great deal on knowledge of a particular activity garnered from long experience—even when the activity seems to be just a matter of logic, as with chess play. That knowledge usually functions rather intuitively and automatically. If you are an experienced chess player, simply sitting down to play chess marshals your chess knowledge. You spontaneously see traps and other patterns that would be invisible to a novice. Options occur to you almost without effort. This does not mean that you make your move quickly. Of course you think for a while. But your extended thinking weaves a tapestry out of those quick intuitions that in turn reflect a large well-practiced knowledge base.

Not only the concept of *g* but many theories of multiple intelligences are calculatedly general. They treat intelligence as cutting across fields and disciplines freely. Some theories of multiple intelligence move toward a more local view. For instance, Gardner makes a case for musical intelligence, logical-mathematical intelligence, and others obviously associated with certain professions. But the strongest proponents of a local view go further yet. It is not music but violin playing, not logical-mathematical intelligence but calculus, around which expertise develops. In a 1994 article, K. Anders Ericsson and Neil Charness put the matter this way:

> Contrary to the common belief that expert preformance reflects innate abilities and capacities, recent research in different domains of expertise has shown that expert performance is predominantly mediated by acquired complex skills and physiological adaptations . . . The effects of extended deliberate practice are more far-reaching than is commonly believed. Performers can acquire skills that circumvent basic limits on working memory capacity and sequential processing.

Intelligence needs to be reconceived not just as multiple rather than monolithic, but as local rather than global in scope, reflecting in-context experience much more than general overarching factors. This looks to be a heavy blow to the empire of IQ.

Strategic Intelligence

While some psychologists questioning the empire of IQ looked for the roots of intelligent behavior in what people know about particular activities, others looked directly to what people know about good thinking. In the late seventies, Stanford University psychologist John Flavell coined a name for a phenomenon that had been recognized in less focal ways before: He wrote of *metacognition,* meaning people's knowledge of and management of their own cognitive functioning.

A harvest of research since has shown that people have a remarkable bundle of beliefs and strategies about thinking and learning. There are, for example, dozens of strategies for memorizing, everything from "read the article over and over" (not a very good strategy, actually) to more elaborate approaches such as making diagrams of the content or linking key points to personal experiences. There are strategies for problem solving: Divide a problem into parts; relate it to problems you already know about. There are general beliefs about learning, ranging from the quitter-oriented "either you get it or you don't" to the more proactive belief that one builds up understandings bit by bit.

This repertoire of beliefs and strategies about thinking and learning begins early. Investigations of young children reveal that, as soon as they can utter complete sentences and answer simple questions, already they have significant metacognitive ideas. Already, they have notions about what makes things hard to remember or when it's difficult to pay attention.

All this leads naturally to a frontal challenge of the empire of IQ. Perhaps general intelligence does not reflect fast neurons so much as strategic knowledge, a repertoire of ways and means for directing attention, memorizing, solving problems, and so on. General intelligence is strategic intelligence.

Strategies Count

Do strategies in fact equip people to behave more intelligently? One way to make the case is to teach people strategies and demonstrate that in fact they function more intelligently. Numerous studies like this have been done, and in a substantial number the cherished result has emerged: The people receiving the instruction came to behave more intelligently in certain ways.

Does this mean that their IQs increased? In some studies this has happened, as for instance with the *Odyssey* program reviewed in Chapter 8. However, an increase in IQ does not always occur and often is not intended or measured. The target is different: Such interventions usually address a specific, important, and intellectually demanding task, for instance mathematical problem solving or reading for understanding and retention. The frequent finding is that the learners indeed become substantially more effective at that task.

As this book unfolds, there will be more and more concern with the role of strategies and related factors in intelligent behavior. Here, I will profile a personal favorite, mathematician-psychologist Allan Schoenfeld's experiments in teaching mathematical problem solving, and then briefly mention a couple of other studies.

The story begins well before Allan Schoenfeld's time, with another mathematician by the name of Gyorgy Polya. Curious about how mathematicians arrived at their solutions to problems, Polya launched an informal investigation of what he came to call the role of *heuristics* in mathematical problem solving. Heuristics is another word for strategies. Heuristics contrast with *algorithms*, such as the procedure for addition, subtraction, or long division. Algorithms guarantee a solution when applied correctly: If you follow the rules for long division, you will reliably arrive at the quotient. In contrast, heuristics are more like rules of thumb. Worth a try, they may or may not help on any particular occasion.

Polya argued that heuristics were the real secret to mathematical problem solving, not formal logic nor, certainly, algorithms. In a two-volume technical work and a more popular book called *How to Solve It*, Polya spelled out a number of heuristics that he felt were key to the problem solving that mathematicians had to do—and perhaps to other kinds of problem solving, too. Among these were such strategies as:

- Breaking a problem into subproblems
- Representing the problem through diagrams
- Relating the problem to problems you have solved in the past
- Generating a simpler problem somewhat like the target problem, trying to solve the simpler problem, and, if successful, applying the same approach to the original problem.

Many mathematics educators took inspiration from Polya's books and tried to put his ideas to work in secondary and college level mathematics education. However, experiments designed to check for better mathematical problem solving generally came up dry. Polya's insights seemed sound, but unknown obstacles stood in the way of the effective use of heuristics.

Allan Schoenfeld carried Polya's torch much further than had his predecessors. Noticing that students after instruction did not necessarily use Polya's heuristics very frequently or aptly, Schoenfeld began to investigate why. One of the most important factors, he decided, was poor mental management: Students did not pay attention to the winding path of their activities in solving a problem. They often did not think to use heuristics they knew and could have applied. They often perseverated in an approach that was not yielding progress rather than trying a new tack. They often gave up without rummaging in their repertoire for another point of entry. Amidst the trees, they lost sight of the forest.

Schoenfeld conducted experiments with his college students in which he took pains to teach a number of heuristics, illustrate them thoroughly in the context of mathematics problems, and introduce a general mental management strategy that would help learners to keep track of their problem-solving process as they worked. The mental management strategy consisted of five phases that aid students in approaching problems systematically:

1. *Analysis.* The student's aim is to get a feel for the problem and gain a deeper understanding by simplifying and reformulating it.
2. *Design.* The aim is to establish an overview of the problem-solving process, develop a plan for how to proceed, and check that detailed calculations are not done prematurely.
3. *Exploration.* The choice the problem-solver makes, instead of implementation, when the problem presents difficulties and no clear solution is evident.
4. *Implementation.* A tentative solution to the problem reflecting a plan that should lead to a solution.
5. *Verification.* The final phase, in which the problem solver checks the solution.

Schoenfeld's investment paid off. The students learning heuristics and the mental management strategy doubled the number of problems solved on a postinstruction test, in comparison with a pre-instruction test. A group of control students received no instruction in heuristics or mental management but went over examples in class like those employed in the strategies group. They also did the same homework. In the control group, problem-solving performance did not increase at all. It was strategies, not just practice, that made the difference.

This study of the impact of the teaching of strategies on mathematical problem solving finds parallels in many other researchers' efforts to examine the impact of instruction in strategies. Let me mention two other examples briefly, to convey some sense of the range of skills addressed. One notable investigation concerned the teaching of reading skills toward better understanding and retention of information. Psychologists Annemarie Palincsar and Ann Brown developed an approach to strategic reading instruction called reciprocal teaching. Middle elementary school students learned to fathom a text's meaning by routinely employing four simple strategies: questioning, clarifying, summarizing, and predicting. The "reciprocal" in reciprocal teaching referred to the system Palincsar and Brown used: The teacher would take turns with the students in leading the conversation and asking the questions, so that students had to accept responsibility for guiding the group much of the time. Palincsar and Brown demonstrated a substantial impact in retention and understanding, often corresponding to two or three years of schooling. The improvements appeared in students' reading for their regular classes and persisted upon retesting a number of months later. In other words, the teaching of reading strategies genuinely empowered the students in a practical way.

Although reciprocal teaching is one of the best known efforts to teach reading skills, such strategies are often taught, and generally with success. In a 1988 synthesis, the researchers Haller, Child, and Walberg surveyed twenty studies and found a substantial positive trend. The approaches improved students' reading on the measures in question by an average of 70 percent of a standard deviation, an impact considered very worthwhile in instructional interventions. Among the most effective strategies were backward and forward searching in the text to clarify obscure points and self-questioning strategies to take the pulse of progress and adjust one's reading.

Let us turn from reading to reasoning. University of Michigan Psychologist Richard Nisbett for a number of years has conducted a program of research investigating whether people can learn certain general patterns of reasoning and transfer them to diverse applications. Recently he summarized this research in a book entitled *Rules for Reasoning*. For example, one study conducted with Geoffrey Fong, Darrin Lehman, and Patricia Cheng examined the impact of graduate study on statistical reasoning, methodology, and if-then reasoning. The investigators found that graduate students in fields that highlighted one or another of these kinds of reasoning showed clear benefits when those kinds of reasoning were tested. For instance, students of psychology displayed superior statistical and methodological reasoning.

This is hardly surprising so far. It seems to be just a case of expertise in a professional discipline. But the research also disclosed that the training had a much broader impact. The students applied these principles to problems that were not at all like professional problems in their fields on the surface. They carried the concepts and strategies across to other settings. For instance, a student who had learned to recognize the need for sizable samples in psychological experiments was also more likely to be cautious about generalizing from one or two cases in problems depicting everyday situations. Looking across his and his colleagues' studies, Nisbett summarized:

- People can make better inferences if they know these rules than if they don't.
- Some people have a better grasp of each of these rules than others.
- Everyone's grasp can be improved by instruction. Different graduate courses, and even different undergraduate majors, emphasize certain of these rule systems, and change students' inferential behavior differentially.
- The instruction can be relatively economical. Perhaps precisely because of the abstract nature of these rules, abstract instruction is effective by itself.
- Notwithstanding their abstract nature, the rules can be made more accessible by teaching examples of their use, and especially by teaching people how to decode the world in ways that make it more accessible to the rule system.
- We can do a much better job of teaching these rule systems than we do.

These examples sample numerous efforts to investigate the impact of teaching strategies or rules to enhance thinking. Such efforts are not always successful—just as with any kind of education—but they have worked often enough to warrant concluding that the teaching of strategies can boost many kinds of intelligent behavior.

Strategies ve'rsus IQ

So strategies count, but how much do they count in comparison with IQ? Perhaps IQ provides most of the furniture of intelligent behavior, with strategies nothing but a polished veneer.

In a 1978 article, University of Pennsylvania psychologist Jonathan Baron examined the relationship between strategies and intelligence. One especially interesting comparison concerned normal and retarded children. Normal children typically use simple strategies to enhance their performance on memory tasks and other familiar intellectual challenges. Quite commonly, retarded children do not use strategies. But do the retarded students really do more poorly because of the strategic shortfall, or because the neural engine in their heads has less power?

This is a question that can be answered by experiment. Several psychologists have investigated how much strategies contribute to simple memory tasks. Such an experiment typically works as follows. First the experimenter compares the performance of mildly retarded children with normal children on a simple task that asks the children to remember several items. Invariably the retarded children perform substantially below the level of the normal children. However, the experimenter notices something interesting: The normal children appear to be using memory strategies such as rehearsing the items subvocally, or reviewing earlier items before the next one comes up. The retarded children tend not to do this.

What really causes the shortfall in the performance of the retarded youngsters? Is it a matter of an organic deficit in the brain or simply the lack of the memory strategies that served the normal youngsters so well? To answer the question, the experimenter directly teaches a memory strategy to some retarded children, a simple strategy such as pausing to review. The experimenter compares the performance of these children with that of normal children. If organic deficits limited the performance of the retarded children, the strategy should make little difference. On the other hand, if strategies were key, then the retarded children should perform much better.

The typical finding is that the retarded children perform much better on the memory task, almost as well as the normal children. Strategies make the difference.

Of course, such studies do not show that retarded children have no real deficits. They assuredly do. Because of organic limits or a deprived environment, they have not learned in the natural course of events strategies that normal youngsters pick up or puzzle out for themselves. Studies like this hardly demonstrate the irrelevance of IQ. However, they do show that sometimes strategic repertoire, more than IQ, is the immediate cause of intelligent behavior.

That points up a theme developed throughout this book: We can help people to behave more intelligently, even retarded people, by expanding their strategic repertoires and nurturing their knowledge and attitudes about thinking and learning. "Is this real intelligence?" you might ask. That depends on what "real intelligence" means, a matter the next chapter examines point blank. In any case, the bottom line in practical terms is acting intelligently in the world—intelligent behavior.

The Importance of Self-Monitoring

Another skeptical question about such studies asks how much the retarded youngsters really learn. Might they not forget the memory trick the next day and perform as poorly as ever? If so, the strategic knowledge provided no more than a temporary fix.

Often when slow students learn strategies, they do forget them or forget to apply them. But not always, and something is known about the conditions for more lasting impact. John Belmont, Earl Butterfield, and Ralph Ferretti reviewed a number of efforts to teach strategies to retarded learners in a 1982 paper. They drew a crucial conclusion. Retarded students will transfer memory strategies to other settings and occasions, *provided* self-monitoring strategies are taught along with the memory strategies. Provided, that is, the students learn to ask themselves questions like, "How might I approach this task? Do I know of any tricks?"

The conclusion of Belmont, Ferretti, and Butterfield is not so different from the insight Allan Schoenfeld came to through his investigations of mathematical problem solving: Strategies alone are not enough, because they often lie fallow. People need to self-monitor to recognize situations where strategies help and seek out strategies to fit the bill.

The larger conclusion for the Great IQ Roast is that the classic idea of general intelligence faces yet another challenge to its authority and autocracy. Strategic knowledge and self-monitoring contribute powerfully to intelligent behavior.

From Clarity to Chaos

Challengers to the empire of IQ have appeared at every gate: psychologists with various models of multiple intelligences, investigators of expertise with their findings about the importance of context-specific knowledge, the champions of thinking strategies and metacognition. All have assaulted the hegemony of IQ and shown up some of its limitations. The result is a new array of evidence and a revised set of answers to the mindware questions:

The evidence at hand . . .

- More and less intelligent behavior, observable in everyday life.
- Different people display consistently more or less intelligent behavior across diverse test and everyday contexts.
- Correlations between scores on IQ tasks and simple reaction time and other measures, supposedly closer to the hardware of the brain.
- Substantial correlations of IQ between identical twins reared apart.
- Some systematic clusterings among subtests of IQ, despite the general trend for everything to correlate with everything.
- IQ changes over time in response to general education, nutrition, and other influences.
- Sometimes performance on intellectually challenging activities does not correlate with IQ.
- General knowledge and skill have a substantial impact on intelligent behavior.
- Specialized knowledge and skill have a substantial impact on intelligent behavior in specialized situations.
- Strategies and metacognition (mental management and self-monitoring) have a substantial impact on intelligent behavior.

MWQ #1. What mechanisms underlie intelligence?

- Neurological speed and precision
- With genes largely determining neurological speed and precision, *or*
- Different neural structures for different kinds of intelligence, *or*
- Extensive common knowledge and skill, *or*
- Specialized knowledge and skill, *or*
- Strategies for memory, problem solving, and so forth, along with metacognition, *or*
- Most likely some messy mix

MWQ #2. Can people learn more intelligence?

- Specialized knowledge and skill, strategies, and metacognitive practices can all be learned in much the same way that anything is learned—through instruction, practice, and experience.

MWQ #3. What aspects of intelligence especially need attention?

- This question is difficult to answer because of rival positions on the most important aspects of learnable intelligence. While some emphasize specialized knowledge and skill, others highlight general strategies and metacognition. Meanwhile, classic *g* theory fights a rear-guard action.

None of the rivals of the empire of IQ has really won over the empire for itself. Yes, sturdy criticisms of IQ have been advanced. They show that intelligent behavior involves a rainbow of causes not considered by the classic theory. However, none of this relegates IQ to the trash heap of the phlogiston theory of heat and other pieces of discredited science. Classic hard-line *g* theorists can still urge that *g* accounts for a large share of intelligent behavior.

And grant this: The classic theory is elegantly simple. It has its austere beauty—one factor, one essence, empowering some people more and some less. As a result of the Great IQ Roast, the pristine clarity of that vision has fallen away into a chaos of contending views about the nature of human intelligence. Although I have presented these diverse perspectives as attacks on the classic view, they also rival one another. The scholars of multiple intelligences, the investigators of expertise, the champions of metacognition and thinking strategies, would all like the empire for themselves. Chaos is not a rare outcome when empires are challenged, and so it is with the empire of IQ. It will take another chapter to rearrange this chaos into a new shape for intelligence.

5

True Intelligence

To *Tell the Truth* it was called. In this television quiz show from the grand old days, the week's broadcast began with three guests introducing themselves in exactly the same words. "I'm J. T. Reynard," one would say, "and I give manicures to pets." "I'm J. T. Reynard," the next would say, "and *I* give manicures to pets." The third followed in kind.

The celebrity panelists asked questions to try to find out who the real J. T. Reynard was, the false Reynards tried to sustain their impersonations, the panelists made their final guesses, and then came the moment of truth. The master of ceremonies intoned, "Will the real J. T. Reynard please stand up." Invariably, the three Reynards glanced at one another expectantly. One would shift a little in his seat. Another would begin to rise and then sit back down. Finally the one, the only, the authentic pet manicurist extraordinaire, rose to greet the audience.

When I wonder about the real nature of intelligence, sometimes I feel like a guesser on *To Tell the Truth*. In response to a simple question about the roots of intelligent behavior, a dozen theories introduce themselves: "My name is such-and-such and I am the one true intelligence." Stories are told: The true intelligence is mental energy, or information-processing capacity in the nervous system, or several specialized computing modules in the brain, or specialized knowledge built through experience, or strategies for remembering and problem solving, or awareness and control of your own thinking.

I want to understand intelligence. I want to know whether and in what ways and with what effort intelligence might be learnable. I want to harness learnable intelligence for the sake of better education, a more alert and insightful political process, more sensitive and fruitful lives in the home and workplace. At the end of all this theorizing, with the innumerable viewpoints set forth, their arguments arrayed, their points and counterpoints analyzed, their favoritisms and anathemas noted, I feel like crying out in heartfelt exasperation, "Will the real intelligence please stand up!"

Three Rival Theories

While there may be a dozen claimants to the title of the one true intelligence, many of them take the same basic approach. By grouping similar ones together, it's possible to identify three basic *kinds* of theories, like the three contestants on *To Tell the Truth*. They are the classic IQ position with some of its variants, the more recent emphasis on expertise as the basis of intelligent behavior, and the viewpoint emphasizing strategies, attitudes, and metacognitive self-monitoring. It is also useful to put a name to each of them:

1. A *neural* theory of intelligence
2. An *experiential* theory of intelligence
3. A *reflective* theory of intelligence

Let us spend a few paragraphs getting each one thoroughly in focus. What is the basic spirit of a neural, an experiential, or a reflective theory of intelligence? Then we can ask, "What hangs on the choice? Is it a matter of truth, priorities, semantics, educational potential? What's at stake?"

If Intelligence Is Neural . . .

Spearman's notion of mental energy, Jensen's notion of efficient response to information load, the research concerning the genetic contribution to intelligence, these and similar theories and findings take a particular perspective on the nature of intelligence. Although such theorists may differ in details, one and all they evoke an image of intelligence as neural in essence.

The spirit of the neural theory is as tough-minded as a Humphrey Bogart role. It emphasizes physical fundamentals. If you want to know the potential of, say, a long-distance racing car, you do not ask how good the driver is. You ask about the engine, its horsepower, how many miles per gallon it gets—you ask about the power source.

Likewise a neural theory of intelligence does not ask about decision-making strategies for life's practical problems or memory strategies for prepping for tests. It does not care how much someone knows about the stock market or calculus. Those are important, to be sure, but they are like the maps in the glove compartment or the driving experience of the driver. They are not the essence of the matter. What really counts is the power of the neural engine under the hood of the skull.

When a person thinks better than another, the neural theory says, most fundamentally it's because this person's neurological system functions better than those of others. It runs faster and with more precision. It operates better because of more finely tuned voltages, more exquisitely adapted chemical catalysts, or a better pattern of connectivity in the labyrinth of neurons. Just as some cars have better engine design than others, some brains are physically superior to others. Although learning assuredly contributes to IQ, neural efficiency more than anything else underlies it.

As measured by the neural theory, the prospects for learnable intelligence are not good. The neural theory says that intelligence is largely a matter of original equipment, genetically determined. To be sure, rich extended learning experiences, especially in the early years of life, may help a little to stimulate neural development. But one cannot expect much.

If Intelligence Is Experiential . . .

De Groot's and Chase and Simon's discoveries about chess mastery, investigations of the acute reasoning of race-track habitués about what horse may win the next race, and dozens of other studies of the role of experience in fine-tuning cognition all point to a conception of intelligent behavior and its causes vastly different from the neural perspective. The experiential view has a one-line message: It's the knowledge of experience that counts.

Nothing counts like it. Your garage mechanic puzzling over the spark plugs, adjusting the carburetor, aligning the wheels, the skilled cook concocting Chicken Kiev or Coquille Saint Jacques, the mathematician making differential equations turn handsprings—all can proceed with judgment and finesse only because of their rich repertoire of experience.

How can something as obvious as the importance of experience be worth mentioning? Because for a long time it was not said loud enough, often enough, or in quite the right manner. The dominant view in psychology used to be that of course experience mattered but not in an interesting way. Good neural equipment allowed a person to acquire knowledge and know-how efficiently in the first place, and apply that knowledge and know-how intelligently after acquiring it. The knowledge merely fed the mental mill of an intelligent reasoner.

But research discussed in the last chapter showed that there was more to it than this. For one thing, the intelligent behavior of deeply experienced people did not always relate closely to IQ; it seems that the intelligent behavior resided in the know-how rather than the neural engine. For another, the know-how involved much more than knowing basic facts and rules. It included a large repertoire of intuitively accessible patterns built up by extensive experience.

As measured by the experiential theory, the prospects of learnable intelligence take a restricted form. The experiential theory avers that intelligence is local, a matter of experience with thinking in particular contexts. Acquiring intelligent behavior becomes a matter of rich experience, reflection, and other factors that support learning to think better in whatever contexts a person needs to function. But what is learned lacks generality.

If Intelligence Is Reflective . . .

The importance of memory strategies to memory, the role of strategies in problem solving, the emergence of metacognition as a significant element of mental development all point to a view of the nature of intelligent behavior and its causes different from both the neural and the experiential theories. With the accent on mindfulness and the artful use of the mind, intelligence seems most essentially and fundamentally reflective.

On the Mississippi river boats that Mark Twain piloted and wrote about with such wit and reverence, the pilot's cabin is perched high in the center, with windows on all four sides. Looking forward, the pilot can see the river unrolling its length to the next turn. Looking to left and right, the pilot can see the banks, the sandbars, the stumps and logs that make the river hazardous and the pilot's work a high art. The pilot has a heightened, distanced point of view, the better to navigate.

So it is with the mind. A theory of intelligence as reflective says that what we find in the physical organization of a river boat or an ocean liner figures centrally in our best use of our own minds as well. Some people are better mental pilots with a more elevated point of view. They more often function metacognitively, monitoring their own thinking and trying to pilot it in effective ways. They cultivate and use more strategies for various intellectually challenging tasks—reading for understanding, personal decision making, problem solving in technical areas like mathematics, conflict management. They benefit from positive "can do" attitudes toward the best use of their own minds, recognizing that thinking often is hard but emphasizing the importance of persistence, systematicity, and imagination.

All this is the mindware mentioned in Chapter 1, defined as whatever kinds of knowledge, understanding, and attitudes make some people better pilots of their own minds than others. Reflective intelligence is made of this mindware. Reflective intelligence helps people score higher on IQ tests as well as handle other intellectual challenges better.

To the competing neural and experiential theories, this reflective account gives some acknowledgment. Certainly the mind must have its physical substrate, its neural engine, and part of people's IQ can reflect that. And certainly to proceed intelligently there must be a storehouse of experience with the activities at hand. It's the same with the savvy Mississippi river pilot, who knows through years of hazardous experience each turn and twist, eddy and race.

But the master river pilot benefits from much more than efficient information processing and knowledge of the landscape. The master pilot stands alert to possible changes, takes a strategic view of time and weather, works through choices about route and schedule with the costs and benefits in mind. And it's the same with people who pilot their minds well—who, to use another common phrase, are good mental managers.

By the measure of the reflective theory, people can learn to think and act much more intelligently. Pilots are made and not born, at least to a considerable extent. Mindware can be acquired.

What's at Stake?

Conflict scars the history of neural, experiential, and reflective theories of intelligence. All three agree on the broad goal: understanding the causes of intelligent behavior. Champions of each have laid claim to the grail of the one true intelligence, the most central underlying cause of intelligent behavior. But what does it matter? What is at stake?

At least three considerations motivate the struggle:

- Constructing a parsimonious theory
- Honoring what one most prizes about human intelligence
- Recognizing human potential in its full spectrum

It's worth taking a close look at each of these in turn. As to the first, science involves a commitment to parsimony in theories. Better to understand a complex phenomenon in terms of one causal factor than two or three. If the case can be made for a neural or an experiential or a reflective theory of intelligence accounting for the larger part of intelligent behavior in a more fundamental way, then this is just plain good science.

To be sure, any such choice risks stripping away some of the richness underlying intelligent behavior. If we adopt a neural theory, we would probably say that a reservoir of experience, while important, accumulates largely because of neural efficiency. We would say that the teaching of strategies may help here and there but fundamentally has little importance to overall intellectual development. We would have to view these contributions to intelligent behavior as somehow less central, more secondary. Similar moves apply if we adopt the experiential theory or the reflective theory wholesale.

But it is not unusual or inappropriate to pay this price. Such moves are commonly made in science to great advantage. Newton's laws, for example, look to fundamental principles at the expense of surface appearances. Recall the principle that an object, once in motion, continues in that direction at that velocity unless diverted by some force. Such smooth continuous motion almost never occurs in everyday experience because friction and gravity interfere. Objects fall to the ground, slow down, and stop. Yet Newton's insight was to view these phenomena as superficial and to look behind them for a deeper order. Choosing one of these three theories of intelligence over the others offers a similar prize if a good case can be made for it.

The second "what's at stake" concerns honoring the signs of intelligence you particularly value. Here individual affinities come into play. A person concerned with programs for the gifted may often find particularly fascinating the polyglot talents of a Bertrand Russell and the special talents of a Mozart. For this person, raw intellectual power occupies center stage. What is more natural than to be drawn to a neural theory, which arguably gives the best account of *g* for general intelligence as well as of special talents. A person concerned with practical getting along in the world may be most impressed with the craft of a seasoned furniture maker, public speaker, judge, or homemaker. To that person, it will seem most important to take an experiential view of intelligence. A person who tracks arguments about public issues may prize the technique, commitment, and alertness of those who manage their thinking well. Such a person will find that a reflective view of intelligence honors this best.

Third and finally, our picture of human intellectual potential hangs in the balance. If we see intelligence principally as neural in character, this discourages efforts to expand people's intelligence through educational programs. Recall from Chapter 3 that the impact on IQ of programs designed to boost cognitive ability generally has been modest. Suppose for the sake of argument we accept the view of Jensen and others that IQ in large part reflects information processing in the neurological system. Then the lackluster educational results suggest that direct instruction has little impact on neural intelligence.

As discussed earlier, historically this posture has stimulated discrimination around issues of immigration, schooling, the handling of prisoners, and more. Even if we can put such practices behind us, the neural view says we should give up on the agenda of producing more generally thoughtful and penetrating graduates and citizens.

If we see intelligence principally as experiential in character, the same conclusion holds for different reasons. From the experiential viewpoint, expertise in circumscribed domains, "local intelligence," is all that one can expect and strive for. However, if we see intelligence principally as reflective, then we can hope to cultivate thinking strategies, thinking attitudes, and metacognition, substantially expanding people's ability to behave intelligently across a range of circumstances.

With so much at stake, it is easy to understand why arguments between the various camps sometimes become acrimonious. A good example has been the firestorm of debate around *The Bell Curve*. While striving to strike a rational tone, authors Richard Herrnstein and Charles Murray at times seem to be either insensitive or deliberately incendiary. Although response to *The Bell Curve* often has been closely reasoned on moral and logical grounds, sometimes it has involved heated responses by writers who clearly have not read the book carefully, because they accuse the authors of ignoring factors specifically taken up in the text of the book. But all the jostling aside, which theory is right? What do the facts and the logic say?

The New Intelligence

In the end, perhaps there is not enough reason for rivalry. To be sure, a choice among the three would have the virtue of parsimony. But nothing about the physical or biological world promises that phenomena of interest always are simple at the core. Not everything allows Newtonian simplification. My colleague Gavriel Salomon, writing about educational psychology generally, recently articulated this as a central principle:

> The complexity of the units, models, and composites educational psychology constructs, manipulates, measures, describes, and explains ought to match the level of complexity of the real-life phenomena under study.

So if neural, experiential, and reflective considerations all contribute abundantly to intelligence behavior, why not acknowledge that?

The contest changes into a collaboration just by a shift of nomenclature. To speak of neural, experiential, and reflective theories of the same phenomenon is to use the language of competition, where the three vie for the prize. Let us use instead the language of dimensions:

> *The neural dimension of intelligence (neural intelligence for short):* The contribution of the efficiency and precision of the neurological system to intelligent behavior. This contribution may involve a single unified factor or some mix of several factors. In any case, it is influenced strongly by genetics and physical maturation.
>
> *The experiential dimension of intelligence (experiential intelligence for short):* The contribution of context-specific knowledge to intelligent behavior. This contribution is learned, the result of extensive experience thinking and acting in particular situations over long periods of time. While the initial ability to learn efficiently in a particular domain may reflect neural intelligence (for example, musical giftedness), the accumulated knowledge and know-how of thinking in that domain constitutes experiential intelligence.
>
> *The reflective dimension of intelligence (reflective intelligence or mindware for short):* The contribution to intelligent behavior of strategies for various intellectually challenging tasks, attitudes conducive to per-

sistence, systematicity, and imagination in the use of one's mind, and habits of self-monitoring and management. Reflective intelligence is in effect a control system for the resources afforded by neural and experiential intelligence, bent on deploying them wisely. Reflective intelligence can be advanced considerably by learning.

Taken together, these three dimensions give us a new conception of intelligence that honors the three aspects of intelligence prominent in contemporary efforts to understand intelligent behavior. In its three-way structure, this conception stands far from Spearman's monolithic mental energy and Goddard's "unitary mental process . . . conditioned by a nervous mechanism which is inborn."

Of course, this collaborative remaking of a competition must be justified by more than just a spirit of reconciliation and harmony. The aim is not to be nice but to be right. The claim is that, nicer or not, a dimensional view is righter. While it is easy to acknowledge that neural, experiential, and reflective considerations all have something to do with intelligent behavior, more than this needs to established. If any one of these makes a minor contribution, it does not deserve the prominence of a dimension. The question comes down to this: Do all three of these kinds of intelligence contribute substantially to intelligent behavior?

Let us test that question. Since I have drawn out of a complex literature the three stark positions—neural, experiential, and reflective—let me also create for each an equally stark skeptic who denies its relevance. We will see whether each dimension survives its skeptic.

The Importance of the Neural Dimension

Imagine a skeptic concerning the contribution of neural intelligence to intelligent behavior. The skeptic might argue for the irrelevance of neural intelligence as follows:

Admittedly, the neurological system contributes to intelligence in some gross sense. When there is neurological damage at birth, as a result of oxygen deprivation, the intelligence of the child is obviously impaired. Likewise, a number of recognized syndromes of retardation involve specifiable types of neural dysfunction.

But those are not the cases of principal interest. We are speaking here about normal individuals with intact neurological systems. Our aim is to account not just for intelligent behavior but for systematic variations in intelligent behavior. Although the human brain obviously supports intelligent behavior, clear causal relationships between variations in neural structure or function and variations in intelligent behavior have not been established. Lacking this, we really have no grounds to attribute differences in intelligent behavior to neurology.

––––––––––

The skeptic makes a telling point: Ideally, an account of neural intelligence would explain exactly what functional or structural features of the neurological system stood behind variations in intelligent behavior. While a few investigators have proposed such functional or structural features, by and large the evidence does not seem compelling enough to sustain any one of them.

However, even in the absence of a fully worked out connection between variations in neurology and intelligence, a number of lines of evidence, some of them mentioned before, suggest some sort of relationship.

- As already noted, there is a substantial genetic influence on general intelligence, which presumably operates through variations in neural function and structure.
- Also as already noted, reaction-time measures such as choice reaction time and inspection time relate considerably to general intelligence. This suggests without proving a physiological component to general intelligence.
- Although people with higher general intelligence might show faster reaction times through strategizing, the evidence is not very supportive of this interpretation: Sometimes teaching strategies for reaction-time tasks impairs performance and sometimes it does not help. In some studies, teaching strategies actually increases the correlation between general intelligence and performance, suggesting that the participants with higher neural intelligence could learn and apply the strategies more effectively.
- Some substances can depress IQ, presumably by influencing neural development and general health. Prenatal alcohol consumption by mothers yields a trend toward slightly lower IQ as measured at age 4. Levels of lead, for instance from ingesting paint, relate to lower IQs. Care was taken in these studies to correct for the influence of other factors, such as parents' economic and educational level.

- Recall from the previous chapter that vitamin and mineral supplements appear to effect IQ slightly, perhaps by impacting the nervous system or perhaps simply by improving general health.
- There is a correlation between general intelligence and brain size of the order of .3, not a high number but a real one. This might be interpreted in other ways than a weak trend toward "bigger brains think better," for instance general health, but it is certainly suggestive.

In summary, it seems sensible to conclude that neurological factors influence intelligent behavior substantially. They appear especially implicated in general intelligence as measured by IQ. However, one should not identify general intelligence exclusively with neural intelligence; recall that education influences general intelligence considerably, a clear argument that some mix of experiential and reflective intelligence contributes to general intelligence. Moreover, people certainly should not think of themselves as imprisoned by their native neurology. This is a matter of making the cases for experiential and reflective intelligence as follows.

The Importance of the Experiential Dimension

Now imagine a skeptic concerning the contribution of experiential intelligence to intelligent behavior. The skeptic might favor a reflective view of intelligence, believing that metacognition and strategies contribute far more than mere possession of knowledge; or, more likely, the skeptic would hold a classic neural position. The skeptic might argue along these lines:

Let me grant that experience and the knowledge and know-how it yields figure in intelligent behavior. You cannot play chess without knowing the rules of the game. You cannot play politics without knowing who to talk to and what to say. But the necessity of knowledge should not be mixed up with a different question: What are the key variables that influence intelligent behavior?

Although knowledge is an essential element, it is not a key variable. Those who are intelligent acquire the critical mass of knowledge they need readily enough, and then use that knowledge with which to think effectively. Intelligence is not *made* of knowledge; rather, intelligence is what equips us for acquiring a mass of knowledge and thinking with it.

Another point concerns generality. By intelligence, we mean what's at least somewhat *general* about a person's capability for intellectually challenging performances. But the knowledge of experience by and large isn't general. It's context specific. So it has no place in a conception of intelligence.

The skeptic mounts an interesting attack on knowledge, granting it a place in the scheme of things but a secondary one. In essence, the skeptic proposes that general intelligence determines what knowledge people gain from experience, so knowledge should not be viewed as a primary causal factor in intelligent behavior.

The trouble with this argument is that it does not jibe with some facts about the nature of intelligent behavior mentioned before, and some further ones as well:

- As related in the last chapter, studies reported by Hunter and by Wagner and Sternberg showed that knowledge, not general intelligence, relates most closely to competence in the work place.
- Also as mentioned, in various studies of expertise, general intelligence may not correlate highly, or at all, with variations in expertise.
- As a generalization, IQ has the most predictive power when people begin to develop competence in an area; its predictive power lessons as learners approach mastery.
- As discussed in the previous chapter, general education has a substantial influence on general intelligence, implicating some mix of experiential and reflective intelligence.
- As mentioned, a substantial component of general intelligence as usually measured is crystallized intelligence, by definition reflecting prior learning.
- The research on expertise discussed earlier shows that perceptual intuition and fluent near-automatic response in areas of expertise clearly are often important for intelligent behavior in those areas, and yet just as clearly do not come effortlessly as a result of a high IQ but with abundant experience.
- Everyday experience shows that people do not generally display professional-level intelligent behavior in more than one or two fields.

In summary, for a number of reasons it's hard to give a good account of intelligent behavior without bringing into play the role of knowledge garnered through experience in areas of specialization. A great deal of intelligent behavior depends crucially on specialized knowledge thoroughly internalized through extended experience. People who lack such knowledge in an area are seriously impaired in many ways, even though they may be very bright in general and may occasionally come to insights less accessible to people steeped in the specialization.

What about the skeptic's contention that by definition intelligence is somewhat general, so specialized knowledge cannot count as contributing to intelligence? There are at least three objections to this. First, as noted above, experience contributes to what psychometricians have in fact called intelligence, in particular crystallized intelligence. Second, it is odd to exclude knowledge from intelligence when *highly* intelligent behavior virtually always depends on a rich knowledge base. Third, the skeptic caricatures experiential intelligence as entirely context bound, a matter of narrow expertise. However, many areas of experiential intelligence are general, relevant over a considerable range of circumstances. For instance, experience in getting along with people, in handling basic arithmetic relationships, or in writing well has all sorts of applications in diverse contexts.

The Importance of the Reflective Dimension

If neural and experiential intelligence virtually demand their places in a theory of intelligent behavior, perhaps reflective intelligence can be dislodged. Let us bring on one more skeptic:

I certainly wouldn't want to speak against self-awareness and the application of strategies where they appear to be useful. However, there is a question of relative importance and primary influence. Intelligent people learn the strategies they need on the side or make them up for themselves. Intelligent people also have the spare cognitive capacity to monitor their thinking and guide it. And, in particular domains, people learn specific relevant knowledge, which provides sufficient basis for them to be as reflective as they need to be. Reflectiveness doesn't cause intelligence but is caused by intelligence.

Like the previous rounds of skepticism, this one simply neglects some basic facts about the way intelligent behavior works as demonstrated by research. In particular:

- As recounted earlier, the teaching of strategies can dramatically improve basic information-processing operations such as memory storage and retrieval, at least in the short term.
- Also, the teaching of strategies can greatly improve performance in plainly intellectually challenging areas such as mathematical problem solving.
- Moreover, teaching metacognitive self-monitoring can help to foster transfer of learning to other circumstances.
- Certain kinds of lapses in thinking are blatant even in very bright people. For instance, in the next chapter I mention some work of my own showing that many people tend to be very one-sided in their thinking, regardless of IQ.
- High general intelligence and relevant knowledge often are not enough for intelligent behavior. Research on expertise shows that sometimes people are bright and knowledgeable in an area of expertise, but very brittle in their problem-solving abilities: They are only good at handling conventional problems in the domain and easily fall apart on more challenging problems. Others who do better draw on more general problem-solving strategies such as the use of analogy, mixed with their domain knowledge. Chapter 9 discusses this point.
- It's not the case that knowledge in an area always leads to better reasoning. Columbia University researcher Deanna Kuhn has conducted a number of studies of reasoning about the causes of released prisoners returning to crime, school failure, and unemployment. In one study, she looked at the reasoning of five parole officers, five experienced teachers, and five philosophers. The philosophers, with no special knowledge of the issues, reasoned much better than the parole officers and the teachers. If anything, Kuhn writes, the parole officers and teachers proved more rigid when reasoning about their areas of expertise than when reasoning about an area where they lacked expertise.
- Similarly, University of Pittsburgh researchers Mary Means and James Voss conducted studies of late elementary and high school students, examining their performance on reasoning tasks in relation to grade, knowledge, and ability as gauged by school-related measures of performance. They found that knowledge of the topics involved in the tasks contributed to students' reasoning of course. But knowledge did not dominate. Ability greatly influenced the quality of students' arguments in terms of kinds of reasons, number

of reasons, qualifications, counterarguments, and so on. Presumably this ability reflects some mix of reflective and neural intelligence.

- It's an everyday observation that often people do not develop robust intelligent behavior in areas where they have a great deal of experience. We do not always and automatically learn from experience, even extended experience. For instance, people play chess or bridge for years without getting much better at it. Reflectiveness about our experiences that leads to restructuring our approach and developing new methods may be one of the missing ingredients.

All in all, the dilemma for a devotee of a particular theory of intelligence—neural, experiential, or reflective—comes down to this: It is much easier to make a case *for* the genuine importance of your favorite kind of intelligence than it is to make a case *against* the significance of the rivals. If we say in *To Tell the Truth* style, "Will the real intelligence please stand up" all three—neural, experiential, and reflective intelligence—should stand up and say in unison, "I am part of the real intelligence." All three would be right.

How the Three Dimensions Work Together

Plainly the neural, experiential, and reflective dimensions of intelligence make up a team: They work together. But how do they combine forces? A simple-minded image of the process might strike a comparison with three men moving a piano up a stairway. All three position themselves and heave, and the piano moves thanks to their pooled powers. But such an image misses something crucial, the very different characters of the three dimensions. They are less like three men than like an ostrich, a salamander, and a sequoia. Yet, diverse as they are, they do function together. I will try to sketch some broad features of how that seems to happen.

Mutual Amplification

The three dimensions seem to amplify the impact of one another, rather than each just adding its share. To honor the familiar saying, the whole is greater than the sum of its parts. Or for a water sports analogy, compare a medley relay race team with a water polo team. The performance of the former is literally the sum of its parts—the sum of the times for each lap by its assigned specialist. However, the performance of the water polo team, as with most teams, depends on the players building off one another, each making the most of what the rest offer.

To get a sense of how this happens with intelligent behavior, imagine a bright young woman I will call Janice who has just begun high school algebra and discovered a fascination with it. Applying herself, she starts to accumulate some experiential intelligence in that domain. Her high neural intelligence helps her to learn algebra faster and with more precision, boosting her experiential intelligence. Also, her high neural intelligence gives her more information-processing power to be reflective with, self-monitoring her learning and steering it in fruitful directions. Moreover, her reflective intelligence leads her to manage her learning systematically and strategically, which boosts her accumulation of experiential intelligence all the more.

As Janice builds experiential intelligence in algebra, concepts and procedures become more automatic, judgments more intuitive. This frees up Janice's neural intelligence for other aspects of algebra, such as complex problem solving. Also, her ripening intuitions allow her to reflect more insightfully and accurately on the course of her problem solving and indeed her learning.

Mutual Compensation

The three dimensions are not easily interchangeable, like three men lugging the piano or three pots of paint of the same color. Nonetheless, in certain respects they compensate for one another.

For example, imagine that Roger, the carpenter down the block, does not have a particularly high neural intelligence and did not do very well years back in the algebra class where Janice now thrives. However, he has been a carpenter for many years, first as an apprentice with rich in-context learning opportunities. Gradually he has mastered the craft. His accumulated experiential intelligence makes him a good carpenter, and not just in a routine sense. He has been around enough and seen such a variety of problems that he is a pretty good problem solver as a carpenter too.

Along the way, he has learned to be somewhat reflective about his work: to stand back, ponder, plan, anticipate pitfalls. In fact, he carries these practices over into other parts of his life besides carpentry. "Take your time, follow the steps" he tells himself, not just over building a staircase but filling out his tax returns. "Think about what could go wrong—like those costs going up," he tells himself, not just about the lumber for a job but also about his children's education after high school. Although not intellectually gifted like Janice, he has developed considerable experiential and reflective intelligence that stand him in good stead. In fact, at this point in his development, his neural intelligence may not matter very much to the intelligent behavior that shines through in his carpentry—remember again the experienced race track devotees, whose readings of the horses had little to do with IQ.

Just as reflectiveness and experience can help to compensate for ordinary or indeed less-than ordinary neural intelligence, high neural intelligence can make up in part for experiential and reflective shortfalls. Reuben, the class math genius, starts with raw intelligence. Although the same age as Janice, he finished algebra two years ago. He may not be a very strategic learner, but, as the saying goes, he soaks up knowledge like a sponge. He does not need to know a lot beforehand because he learns it so fast, and he does not need to be so reflective because he gets his head around things so easily.

Notice that these are only partial compensations. When Reuben finally hits a topic that is genuinely difficult for him, he may suffer for the lack of reflective learning strategies. But, with such qualifications granted, high neural intelligence helps make up for shortfalls in the other two.

Distinctive Contributions

With all this said about how the dimensions work together, each tends to come to the fore in certain circumstances, carrying the greater burden. *Neural intelligence particularly supports initial learning and special talents.* Recall that general intelligence, which presumably reflects the neural dimension to a considerable degree, predicts rate of learning in unfamiliar activities particularly well. If you are getting started with Shakespearean sonnets, nuclear physics, or reggae music, your early learning will be aided considerably by the neural intelligence you have to work with. You will face less of a front-end hump. Next most helpful will be reflective intelligence, if you have accumulated a good repertoire of learning strategies.

A good case can be made for a genetic and neurological basis for striking talents in music, sports, mathematics, and other fields. Such talents often begin to show themselves when children are quite young. A child can be talented in one area much more so than in others, or a polyglot talent, good at many things. With this said, a caution is in order. People should not write off areas of enthusiasm simply for lack of a dramatic talent. On the contrary, extensive deliberate practice often eventually yields ample mastery through experiential and reflective intelligence, even at the professional level.

Neural intelligence also particularly supports general human talents. The theme of talents applies at the level of the human species as well as that of the individual. Human beings have special talents provided by the neural engines in our heads. For instance, considerable evidence argues that the human brain is well-equipped for language learning. We have a sense of self and can reflect on ourselves, whereas most other animals show no signs of such a capacity. Plausibly, this capacity underlies our power to reflect on our own thinking, the precondition for developing reflective intelligence.

Experiential intelligence particularly supports day-to-day expert thinking in a domain. As discussed in the last chapter, expertise has become one of the most widely studied phenomena in psychology over the past three decades. A number of investigations argue that expertise in a domain depends on an extensive base of knowledge about different situations and how to deal with them, a base acquired through years of experience. Intelligent behavior depends on this knowledge base in ways not readily made up for by high neural or reflective intelligence, although they may help.

Experiential intelligence also particularly supports coping with recurrent everyday situations. People acquire experiential intelligence not only in specialized domains like chess, physics, or sailing, but also in such common contexts as sustaining a dinner conversation, developing a friendship, shopping in a supermarket, organizing a party, or mowing the lawn. Such activities are not what we ordinarily think of as domains of expertise because almost everyone achieves considerable competence in them. Nonetheless, the same psychological mechanisms appear to be at work, empowering people to function smoothly and effectively.

Reflective intelligence particularly supports coping with novelty. Novel situations by definition are not well-served by experiential intelligence. In unfamiliar circumstances, experiential intelligence has little to offer. If you take up playing bridge having never played any card game seriously before, or through a promotion for the first time have management responsibilities, you can benefit from reflective intelligence by thinking about the challenges and consciously and strategically striving to cope with them. In familiar circumstances with an unexpected twist, experiential intelligence can be downright misleading, prompting an automatic response that does not suit the occasion. If you are a U.S. citizen on holiday in England and rent a car, you may have to sustain a reflective alertness to keep yourself driving according to England's left-side convention.

Of course, neural intelligence also helps in coping with novelty, since novelty always throws one into the initial phases of learning. Neural and reflective intelligence aid each other in such circumstances, neural intelligence providing the raw information-processing power managed by reflective intelligence. The most distinctive contribution of reflective intelligence comes in the following category.

Finally, reflective intelligence also particularly supports thinking contrary to certain natural trends. An especially important role for reflective intelligence occurs in situations that require breaking set ways, unseating old assumptions, and exploring new ones.

Consider for instance an advertising executive reaching for a startling new advertising campaign for a product, or a physicist questioning prevailing theories of subatomic structure. The advertising executive and the physicist particularly need flexibility. Unfortunately, most people tend to think along narrow paths. Neither high neural intelligence nor the familiarity built by experiential intelligence banishes this tendency. For example, a person with high neural intelligence and great knowledge in an area can easily prove very narrow minded, seeing only one side of a situation. For another example, most people incline toward what is sometimes called solution mindedness, trying to address the task at hand directly without much reflection on what the problem is, different ways in which it might be described, or indeed whether it is worth solving at all. As a control system for neural and experiential intelligence, reflective intelligence has the responsibility of bucking the trend, harnessing the mind's resources in more powerful patterns that break out of the typical ruts of thinking.

The Prospects of Learnable Intelligence

The last three chapters told rather different stories about the underpinnings of intelligent behavior. Binet's potpourri conception gave way to the more technically sophisticated view of Spearman, with his statistical theory of *g*, and this in turn partly dissolved in a soup of rival perspectives at the end of the last chapter. In this chapter, with the organization brought by the idea of neural, experiential, and reflective dimensions of intelligence, something like a coherent theory of learnable intelligence at last appears. A list of the contributing evidence along with answers to the three mindware questions summarize the theory so far.

The evidence at hand . . .

- More and less intelligent behavior, observable in everyday life.
- Different people display consistently more or less intelligent behavior across diverse tests and everyday contexts.
- Correlations between scores on IQ tasks and simple reaction time and other measures, supposedly closer to the hardware of the brain.
- Substantial correlations of IQ between identical twins reared apart.
- Some systematic clusterings among subtests of IQ, despite general trend for everything to correlate with everything.
- IQ changes somewhat in response to general education and other influences.
- Sometimes performance on intellectually challenging activities does not correlate with IQ.
- General knowledge and skill have a substantial impact on intelligent behavior.
- Specialized knowledge and skill have a substantial impact on intelligent behavior in specialized situations.
- Strategies and metacognition (mental self-monitoring and management) have a substantial impact on intelligent behavior.

MWQ #1. What mechanisms underlie intelligence?

Neural Intelligence (in large part genetically determined)

- Neurological speed and precision.
- With genes a major influence.
- Different neural structures for different kinds of intelligence, including individual talents.

Experiential Intelligence (learned)

- Extensive common knowledge and skill.
- Specialized knowledge and skill.

Reflective Intelligence (learned)

- Strategies for memory, problem solving, and so forth.
- Mental management (mental self-monitoring and management, sometimes called metacognition).
- Positive attitudes toward investing mental effort, systematicity, imagination.

MWQ #2. Can people learn more intelligence?

- Yes, experiential intelligence can be expanded through extensive experience. Reflective intelligence can be expanded through instruction or self-instruction and experience that cultivates metacognition, strategies, and attitudes conducive to good thinking.

MWQ #3. What aspects of intelligence especially need attention?

- This analysis of learnable intelligence suggests that efforts to cultivate intelligence should focus on reflective intelligence, the control system for neural and experiential intelligence.
- One emphasis should be devising and using strategies relevant to broad thinking challenges like remembering, problem solving, and decision making.
- Mental self-monitoring and management should be another emphasis.
- The cultivation of positive attitudes should be a third.

Without question two of the three dimensions of intelligence can be advanced by learning—experiential intelligence through in-depth experiences and reflective intelligence through the cultivation of strategies, attitudes, and metacognition.

Learnable IQ?

How does IQ figure in the prospects of learnable intelligence? Specifically, will teaching reflective intelligence increase IQ? How much? And how much does it matter?

Yes, extensive cultivation of reflective intelligence can increase IQ, as already discussed in Chapter 3. Strategies and attitudes of decision making, problem solving, and so on abet performance on IQ tests as well as on other intellectually challenging tasks. This may seem surprising in light of some psychologists' interpretation of IQ as reflecting neural intelligence. But remember, it's well established that nurture as well as nature affects IQ. In thinking of IQ as neural at the root, psychologists like Arthur Jensen are advancing what they see as most theoretically important about IQ, not saying that IQ as ordinarily measured involves nothing else.

However, the impact on IQ will be modest. Learners will gain much more ability in the particular kinds of thinking focused upon—say making everyday life decisions or solving math problems—than in their general IQ. Interventions of modest scope may often empower learners in particular areas of thinking with no impact on IQ.

Why? Not because IQ is entirely or even largely neural but because of the way IQ is constructed statistically. Remember, IQ reflects the positive manifold of correlations among virtually all intellectually challenging tasks. By design, IQ is the most general possible gauge of cognitive ability. Therefore, it shows the most inertia. A comparison with athletics helps to make this point clear. Suppose you wanted to improve someone's—call her Paula—general athletic ability—call it her athletic quotient or AQ. By coaching tennis, you could improve Paula's tennis game greatly, by coaching running her running, by coaching soccer her soccer, by coaching calisthenics her muscular strength and flexibility. Paula might never become a champion, but any good coach can do a lot in a particular sport and for physical conditioning.

However, how much would this effect Paula's overall AQ? Some, to be sure, because the competencies, flexibility, and strength developed by the regimen would spill over to enhance performance in many athletic activities not specifically trained. Still, Paula would advance less in her overall AQ than in the target activities.

It's the same with IQ. One cannot expect IQ to respond to instruction as much as areas of intelligent behavior specifically targeted for instruction. This is why IQ is the wrong measure for learnable intelligence. It is the toughest possible standard and often not the one that counts. For instance, if we are teaching youngsters to read for understanding or to solve math problems better, we want them to get much better at that—and research shows that they can. If their IQs go up a little too, this is welcome but unnecessary frosting on the cognitive cake. To dismiss the program because it fails to impact on IQ would be wrongheaded entirely.

The Intelligence Gap

Intelligence can be learned, so I've argued and will argue more fully in the chapters to come. If this does not happen as much as we would like it to, why not? How do common conditions of learning in home and in schools, in the workplace and the marketplace, leave us with an intelligence gap?

Here are the basics of an answer pursued in later chapters. Although experiential intelligence reflects knowledge in a domain, it is much more than a heap of facts and algorithms, just as a building is much more than a heap of bricks. Conventional instruction in the subject matters comes close to providing a heap of facts and skills, not so different from a heap of bricks, with the main hope that the learner will magically transform the heap into a building.

Some students do just this—mostly the better ones, fueled by high neural and reflective intelligence. But many do not, because the typical educational setting does little to spark the development of rich and well-integrated experiential intelligence in a domain. In contrast, apprenticeship settings, other sorts of on-the-job learning, and certain richer kinds of school experience have much more of a chance of enhancing experiential intelligence.

Reflective intelligence, as the control system for experiential and neural intelligence, offers the greatest hope for an all-round improvement in people's intelligent behavior. Typical schools do no better with reflective intelligence than with experiential intelligence. The next chapter mentions research showing that conventional high school and college education has hardly any impact on general reasoning abilities. The cause of the shortfall is no further away than the nearest lecture or textbook: Hardly anything in conventional educational practice promotes, in a direct and straightforward way, thoughtfulness and the use of strategies to guide thinking. Those students who acquire reflective intelligence build it on their own, by working out personal repertoires of strategies. Or they pick it up from the home environment, where some parents more than others model good reasoning in dinner table conversation, press their children to think out decisions, emphasize the importance of a systematic approach to school work, and so on.

Whereas some workplaces offer much more experiential learning than typical school settings, the same cannot be said for reflective intelligence. In general, neither the ordinary school nor the ordinary work-place models or promotes the stand-back strategizing that is the hall-mark of reflective intelligence.

To put it all into a few words, the emerging science of learnable intel-ligence leaves an enormous gap between theory and practice. To be sure, there are many more puzzles to be worked out in the theory of intelligent behavior. However, enough is known to conduct education in ways much friendlier to the development of experiential and reflec-tive intelligence. Only in a few sites do such things happen. The promise is there, but the path to success is plagued by a hundred mal-adies from sheer unawareness of the prospects to stark fear of the conse-quences of a genuinely more thoughtful population.

Part II

Learnable Intelligence on Trial

6

What's Wrong with
My Neighbors' Thinking?

On July 3, 1988, at approximately 10:45 AM, an Airbus carrying 290 passengers and crew took off from the Bandar Abbas airport in Iran on route to Dubai. This routine beginning of Iran Air Flight 655 was the prelude to a tragedy and an international incident that profoundly embarrassed the armed services of the United States of America.

The situation between Iran and the United States was tense at the time. U.S. cruisers were stationed in the Persian Gulf offshore from Iran. Little more than half an hour earlier, three small boats had fired on a helicopter from the U.S. cruiser *Vincennes*, and later a skirmish had followed between the *Vincennes* and the U.S.S. *Elmer Montgomery* and a flotilla of Iranian launches, in which two were sunk. Nerves were on edge. Was an attack with more force in the offing?

Within seven minutes of the departure of Flight 655, the potential for disaster coalesced into reality. The technical crew aboard the *Vincennes*, detecting a plane on radar, interpreted it as potentially an F14 on an attack course. *Vincennes* Captain Will Rogers recognized the possibility of a mistake and, in the brief minutes between initial detection and the final moment of decision, sought to confirm or deny whether the oncoming aircraft posed a threat. Radio messages warning off the seemingly aggressive aircraft received no acknowledgement. At 10:54, as the aircraft advanced to put the *Vincennes* within range of its weaponry, Rogers ordered the launching of two Standard-2 surface-to-air missiles. The Iranian Airbus was blown out of the air, killing all passengers and crew aboard.

The next day, the newspapers were aflood with speculation and the international airwaves full of recrimination for this aggressive act on the part of the U.S. Navy. How could such a tragic decision have been made? The first words from the armed services gave a supportive interpretation of the U.S. action. On the very day of the disaster, Admiral William J. Crowe, chairman of the Joint Chiefs of Staff, reported a number of anomalous circumstances that made the Iranian plane's threat seem all too real. The plane supposedly was not advancing along the established departure corridor. It was descending rapidly from 9,000 feet toward the *Vincennes*. It's identification beacon was emitting a signal characteristic of an F14's. The plane had not responded to direct efforts to warn it off.

However, from the first, there were doubts about this account. Gradually, a picture emerged rather different from the initial reports. It was established that the departure of the Airbus had been routine and orderly in all respects. The plane proceeded in proper fashion within the invisible boundaries of its allotted air corridor. True, the pilot of the Airbus had not responded to—but probably had never picked up—the warnings from the *Vincennes*. Up to the moment when the Standard-2 missiles bored into its fuselage, the plane was ascending, not descending.

Subsequent investigation argued that the technical equipment on board the *Vincennes* delivered confusing information and that subordinates who recognized the possible confusion did not alert Captain Rogers to it. Such mishaps of information handling regrettably are not rare. It is the nature of the human organism to hang back from redirecting authority, to project fears and anxieties, to see what is not there, and to miss what is there. Yet that is not the whole of the story. If the events that unfolded on the *Vincennes* constituted one grievous lapse of thinking under time pressure, there was another with no time pressure and few immediate consequences that struck me even more. This second lapse of thinking was the reaction of the people of the United States to the incident.

I was away from home attending a conference in the midwest when the debacle exploded on network news and into the headlines. With concern, I followed the unfolding story daily in the *USA Today* provided by my hotel. On July 6, the third day after the incident, the editors of

USA Today printed on the front page the results of a poll taking the pulse of the American public about the incident. Their first question asked directly, "Was the captain right to shoot?"

"Yes," the statistics said, 75 percent feeling the U.S. action to be fully in accord with the data available to the captain and crew at the time. Only 10 percent judged the action inappropriate. And, the clincher, only 5 percent of those polled felt any need for additional information.

It is natural and appropriate that people would favor their own nation. So did I—hoping and indeed inclining to believe that circumstance, not misperception and misjudgment, had triggered the decision that triggered the missiles that downed the Airbus. However, what worried me about the statistics was the mere 5 percent who felt any need for more information. The newspapers were full of claims and the counterclaims, the Naval reports and the doubts, the launching of inquiries, the spiraling of confusion, the beginning swell of hard information about what had transpired. Yet, in this sea of flux and ambiguity, only 5 percent! How could people feel such unreasonable confidence in their judgment?

This worries me. We have a population most of whom demonstrated not one whit of appreciation for ambiguity, crosscurrents, confusion, and the potential role of evidence in bringing into focus an accurate picture of events. These are my neighbors, the same people who vote for presidents, serve on school boards, and raise the next generation at least somewhat in their own image. What's wrong with my neighbors' thinking? Or—yes, let's admit it—is there something wrong with my thinking in thinking there's something wrong?

If It Ain't Broke, Don't Fix It!

I tell this story because many people doubt the need for better reflective intelligence. At least for normal adults, is there any real shortfall that invites attention? Most folks, the story goes, are intelligent enough already for most of what they need to do. The third mindware question, which asks what kinds of intelligence need the attention of learners, gets a simple answer: None, really. "If it ain't broke, don't fix it!"

To be sure, all the world recognizes that mistakes from time to time get made, options overlooked, evidence neglected, consequences ignored, and so on. But what creates trouble from time to time may not pose a serious threat to human well-being. On the whole, day by day, week by week, do people not function pretty well? Step by step, measure by measure, does the body politic not press along quite adequately if not entirely perfectly? Is it not so that, advertising campaign by campaign, product by product, the economic world progresses, despite occasional setbacks? "If it ain't broke, don't fix it!"

As to the plane disaster, a tragedy certainly. But as to the overconfident reaction of the U.S. public, someone might object that whether people reason poorly about a news event is no measure of how well they reason about their own more immediate concerns. Perhaps people think well enough in situations closer to their lives—in deciding whom to marry, what school to attend, what stereo to buy, where to live, what career to adopt, what job to attempt, what candidate to support, and so on. "If it ain't broke, don't fix it!"

Without a doubt, such a posture brings with it all the comfort of a down-stuffed quilt on a chilly Maine morning. It's much easier to believe that there is not much of a problem with ordinary everyday thinking. However, the "it ain't broke" attitude deserves a hard look. Is it really true that the third mindware question should be answered by saying that intelligence does not need educational attention? Is it a fact that there is nothing much wrong? Is it really so that your neighbors' thinking is on the whole quite good? The story of the *Vincennes* is an anecdote, but what does systematic evidence say?

A number of investigators in psychology, philosophy, history, education, and other disciplines have addressed this issue. To preview the rest of the chapter, here is what the findings point to. The Iran plane disaster and the shaky thinking it revealed are not anomalous, rare events. Thinking equally questionable occurs all the time, although without the conspicuous publicity or the starkly tragic consequences. The "it ain't broke" posture toward everyday thinking is naive. Just the contrary, considerable evidence from many quarters documents human failings in quite straightforward aspects of sound judgment, due attention to evidence, and creative exploration of options.

The psychological literature on thinking and difficulties with thinking is huge. Often, investigations have focused on somewhat technical aspects of thinking, for instance how well people reason with syllogisms, how well people take into account the laws of probability, or how well people recognize the need for a sizable sample to warrant a sound generalization. But I will not do that here.

To explain why, let me start with an example of a technical kind of reasoning, a problem of deductive logic:

Given that some oranges are green,
And all apples are red.
Which of these statements follow logically:
    (1) Therefore, some apples are not oranges.
    (2) Therefore, some oranges are not apples.
    (3) Nothing can be concluded.

Various factors make reasoning about such problems challenging. One is that we already know the true situation about apples and oranges. It's simply not the case that all apples are red, but the problem gives that as a premise so we have to work with it. Moreover, we already know that (1) and (2) are both true—in fact, not only are *some* apples not oranges, but *all* apples are not oranges, and vice versa. It's hard to set aside what we already know and look only to the logic of the statements. Another factor is this. Never mind what we already know, complex crisscrossing relationships are involved. For instance, even if we use X's and Y's instead of apples and oranges—some X's are green, all Y's are red—it's still hard to think about. You may want to draw a diagram.

So what is the correct response? Well, answer 1 does *not* follow logically from the premises, even though it is in fact true. However, 2 does follow logically: If some oranges are green, consider the green ones. Those oranges certainly cannot be apples, since the second premise says that all apples are red. So therefore those oranges are not apples.

People generally perform quite poorly on such logic problems. Focused programs of research have taught psychologists a lot about the mental processes people use in trying to cope with logic problems and the pitfalls people commonly fall into. I could bring in studies of logic problems and other somewhat technical kinds of reasoning and discuss them at length; most explorations of shortfalls in thinking do so.

However, would that seriously challenge the "it ain't broke" position? To be sure, how well people handle such conundrums *may* say a lot about how well they reason about more everyday kinds of problems. But maybe not. Maybe everyday reasoning makes somewhat different kinds of demands. I would rather question the "it ain't broke" position with thinking situations that have a more commonplace character in the first place.

So I have chosen some studies that treat very ordinary nontechnical kinds of thinking that occur frequently in everyday life, principally making decisions and justifying conclusions in situations that do not invite either formal deductive logic or quantitative probabilistic reasoning.

The March of Folly

The March of Folly is the title of a 1984 book by the prolific and provocative Pulitzer prize–winning historian, Barbara Tuchman. Her data is that of history, not the psychologist's laboratory, and so in some ways more real and telling: If shortfalls in thinking commonly occur on the scale of empires and grand events, affecting thousands and millions of people, there can be little question of dismissing aberrations in human thinking as minor, rare, and hardly worth a worry.

Tuchman argues that, as the yarn of world history unwinds, again and again it is stained by what she calls *folly*—by events transpiring in sorry, hurtful, and sometimes disastrous ways on a momentous scale, for lack of good thinking. Her notion of folly is specific and carefully crafted. Folly in government concerns not any moral turpitude but something utterly pragmatic: "Pursuit by governments of policies contrary to their own interests." Moreover, three conditions have to be met to signal the profound lack of good thinking that counts as "ideal" folly:

1. The policy "must have been perceived as counter-productive in its own time, not merely by hindsight. . . . To avoid judging by present-day values, we must take the opinion of the time and investigate only those episodes whose injury to self-interest was recognized by contemporaries."
2. "A feasible alternative course of action must have been available." Otherwise, the matter could not be helped.
3. "The policy in question should be that of a group, not an individual ruler, and should persist beyond any one political lifetime. Misgovernment by a single sovereign or tyrant is too frequent and too individual to be worth a generalized inquiry."

Not surprisingly, one of Tuchman's prime examples of folly, the closing case of her book, was the U.S. involvement in Vietnam. Since that story as been so much told, let me offer another—King George's handling of colonial politics during the time of the American revolution. Politics, it is said, is the art of the possible. More than anything else, according to Tuchman, the folly of King George and his regime lay in persisting in a stubbornly impractical view of the thriving American colonies and their spiraling restlessness. The American colonies, after all, were a long way off—not an easy arena for a military action or a prolonged occupation. Moreover, in dealing with Americans, Britain would be trying to thwart people of their own stock, as familiar as they were with weaponry and the art of war, and, as it turned out, quite willing to wage battle in unexpected and scurrilous ways.

So it was that, when complaints were lodged, when the British applied sanctions, when this fulminated yet more protest, when the talk of some moved toward arms and independence, one would have thought that George and company would exercise some prudence and strike a deal or, if that would be too much of a concession, find graceful ways to ease off. In politics, there are almost always graceful ways.

But no. King and company were fixated on matters of policy—these were *our* colonies, our sons and daughters, from which we would brook no disobedience. Greed was also a factor. The colonies represented a major market for tea and other goods, with tea a legal monopoly for Britain, although in fact Holland sustained a brisk trade with North America in smuggled tea. Profit from colonial trade was worth far more than any likely yield from taxation. However, England insisted on taxation as a point of principle. Benjamin Franklin's advice, "Everything one has a right to do is not best to be done," fell on deaf ears.

One old saying deserves another: From "politics is the art of the possible," let us move to "half a loaf is better than none." Within British government there were certainly voices that recognized the risk of no loaf at all, and spoke out for different handling of the circumstances. But George and company were committed to their folly. Events rolled on toward war, with hardly a thought to the juggernaut reality of an independent America.

Lest it be thought that violent revolution is the inexorable consequence of colonialism, Barbara Tuchman took care to sketch in the contrast case of Canada. Britain and the monarchy, she notes, had learned from their sorry experiences with what became the United States. In the 1830s, tensions began to develop between English-speaking Canada and the crown. But this time a more cautious course was taken, leading to a pattern of amiable and fruitful relationships that survives down to the present day without the stark break that characterized American and British relations.

These are not Barbara Tuchman's only examples of folly. Her book is a virtual parade of these sad clowns of history. She notes the fall of Montezuma, for example, an entire nation handed over to a few dozen Spaniards. For her very first example, she chooses one probably apocryphal but nonetheless illustrative, the siege of Troy and the tale of the Trojan Horse. As the *Odyssey* tells the tale, the deception of the Trojan Horse was actually suspected. Some of the Trojans recognized that soldiers might hide inside such a construction. During the wild revels in celebration of the seeming withdrawal of the Greeks, some actually heard odd sounds within the belly of the horse. Yet the party animals of Troy dismissed it all as mere imaginings. Blind in the face of threat, folly rode confidently to disaster.

John Wayne Reasoning

The three Apaches are nowhere in sight. "But they're up there," drawls John Wayne, "behind them rocks. And they've got Mary O'Doole with 'em."

As if to confirm his words, a cry, suddenly interrupted, sounds from the helter-skelter of boulders above. One of the posse speaks up: "Look, there's nine of us and only three of them. We just move in kinda slow like. Pretty soon we'll be on top of 'em."

"Nah," says John Wayne. "They'll finish her off for sure. Look, I'm heading around back of this pile of rocks. The rest of you stay here, move in slow. And I'll come up behind."

"Well, I dunno," one says skeptically.

"For the sake o' Mary O'Doole, that the way it's gotta be," says John Wayne. "Let's move."

That's leadership, and we love it. We love the firm hand in a crisis, the sense of vision and purpose that sweeps others along toward a bold action. In our political leaders and our movie heroes, in our generals and our CEOs, we hunger for the confident individual who sees plainly the one true course and seizes the helm.

In many situations, decisiveness is certainly a virtue. Moments of crisis often demand decisiveness: Even an arbitrary choice that leads to action may prove a better bet than prolonged hesitation. Rich experience in an area often prepares us to be both decisive and correct in our quick decisions—a consequence of experiential intelligence. However, with such qualifications acknowledged, we always have to remember that decisiveness for the sake of decisiveness is, well, bad thinking.

How real is this seeming trend toward overadmiration for the firm stance? Some evidence for its reality comes from a study conducted by Jonathan Baron, professor of psychology at the University of Pennsylvania, a champion of thoughtful reasoning and an investigator of how people reason about everyday matters. Baron suspected that many people viewed having a firm clear position as a virtue in itself, more of a virtue than considering all the factors in a situation. He set out to test his hypothesis.

Baron collaborated with John Sabini and Andrea Bloomgarten in several studies with somewhat similar designs. A number of college students (who have had plenty of opportunity to develop skills of thoughtful reasoning) responded to several arguments on an everyday issue, each generated by a different person, so the students were told, although in fact all were written by the investigators. Some of the arguments took strong stances pro or con on the issue, not considering the other side of the case. Others concluded for one or the other side of the issue, but explored arguments on both sides. The subjects were asked to grade the quality of the thinking in the arguments.

Some students thought that the one-sided arguments represented better thinking. Moreover, asking the students to write out their own thinking on another issue, the investigators found that they practiced what they preached: The students who valued one-sided arguments over two-sided arguments also showed a tendency to think about the other issue in a one-sided way. Baron speculates that they may have been applying tacitly a standard rather different from good thinking: the standard of expertise. They may have sought the clear confident answers that come with expertise, rather than the play of point and counterpoint characteristic of sound reasoning.

In sum, Baron identified in some students an attitude toward everyday reasoning that in its strongest form one could call John Wayne reasoning. If you are a John Wayne reasoner, you honor and pursue a tough-minded clear-cut black-and-white vision of the question at hand over a thoughtful exploration of the pros and cons. If you have the expertise, the experiential intelligence, to back it up, you may be right—but if you do not, or if the situation outstrips your expertise, you may very well be wrong. Another more technical name for John Wayne reasoning is my-side bias, and sometimes confirmation bias is used in much the same sense. In a number of studies of reasoning besides Baron's, people display a strong my-side bias, accumulating evidence on the side of the case they lean toward and not searching for or discounting evidence representing other perspectives.

Mindlessness

Sally Merrimak, Professor Fulsome's secretary in the Department of Psychology at William James Hall of Harvard University, had a pile of photocopying to do, handouts for Professor Fulsome for his upcoming talk at the annual meeting of the American Psychological Association. She had just settled in for a long session of photocopying when a youngish woman made an appearance at the door of the copy room. "Hi. Sorry," the woman said, "But can I cut ahead of you? Because I have some copying to do."

A good-hearted person, Sally gave way as you or I well might. Sally had not noticed a peculiarity of the woman's request: She gave a reason for her need, but an *empty* reason: "Because I have some copying to do." Of course she had some copying to do, why else would she be asking to cut ahead?

Are empty reasons that powerful? It seems that they are when Sally or others are not very attentive to what they are doing. The youngish women made a number of appearances at that same photocopy machine over several days, asking to cut ahead of people. Sometimes she would give a genuinely reasonable, if brief, reason: "I have to get these done within half an hour." Sometimes she would give no reason at all, asking simply whether she could cut in. The curious finding was this: When she simply asked to cut in, she was often refused. When she gave a reason, her request was often granted—and just as often no matter whether the reason was substantive or empty. In other words, Sally and others were not really listening to what the woman said, but only its form—the woman said "because" and gave a need.

Sally Merrimak, along with many other people who unwittingly participated in this experiment, got suckered. She displayed what Professor Ellen Langer of the Harvard Department of Psychology terms "mindlessness." Sally and Professor Fulsome are not real people, but the study outlined here was actually conducted in William James Hall by Langer. Through this and a number of other cleverly conceived investigations, Langer has demonstrated the phenomenon of mindlessness over and over again. She has been able to show how commonly people do not really think about what they are doing.

Mindlessness is not just a laboratory phenomenon, Langer stresses. She relates this personal anecdote, for example. A store clerk noted that she had not yet signed a new credit card. So she signed it on the spot. The clerk dutifully proceeded to compare her signature on the credit card with her signature on the credit slip for security purposes, never thinking that of course they would match: She had just signed both.

What causes mindlessness? Langer points to the role of automatization in human behavior, the formation of habits of information processing that let us get on with the routine business of the day without fretting and fussing over each little detail. Up to a point, such a transformation from the mindful to the routine is very useful, indeed essential, to human behavior. We would all go crazy over the details of getting from one side of the room to the other, if we could not delegate much of the routine to automatic processes.

However, a price is exacted. We end up responding in many ways on many occasions to the sketchy forms of things rather than their subtle contents. The next chapter develops this and related themes at more length.

A Study of Everyday Thinking

What do we really know about our neighbors' thinking? And which neighbors? A number of years ago, I became interested in understanding more about how people in different walks of life reason and whether formal education helps them to reason any better. Around 1974 I began a series of investigations taking a systematic look at the reasoning of a cross-section of people representing several different ages, professional interests, and degrees of education.

The focus fell on everyday reasoning about public issues—how people thought about the concerns that they had to manage as voters and citizens. For example, these were the days of high paranoia about the cold war turning hot, and of hope that perhaps something could ease the tension. With that in mind, one of the questions we used in the research asked, "Would a freeze on the development of nuclear weapons reduce the chances of a nuclear war?" For another example on a much less global level, around that time many people in Massachusetts were campaigning for a "bottle bill," requiring a deposit on all beverage bottles. The aim was to reduce the clutter of discarded bottles spoiling the parks and roadsides. The merits of this candidate law were fiercely debated at the time. Therefore, we made one of our questions, "Would a five-cent deposit on bottles and cans significantly reduce litter?"

To see how people might answer such questions, ponder for a moment the Cold War issue. A simple response on one side of the case might be, "Sure, a nuclear freeze agreement would reduce the chances of nuclear war. After a while, there would just plain be fewer weapons to fight with." A simple answer on the other side might say, "No, not really. You can't trust the Russians to honor the spirit of such an agreement anyway."

A more complex argument would recognize several points on both sides. Favoring reduced chances of war would be the existence of fewer weapons, the symbolic significance of the freeze agreement, possible follow-up negotiations for related agreements, and the lesser likelihood of nuclear proliferation in other nations given the freeze agreement. Arguing against reduced chances of war would be questions of trustworthiness of both parties; the fact that, even with a freeze, plenty of weapons exist to vaporize civilization; the possibility that complacency nurtured by the freeze would actually make us more careless; the notion that wars get triggered by spiraling events that have little to do with available weaponry anyway. Of course, a great deal more could be said on either side of the case.

We probed people's thinking about such issues through one-on-one personal interviews. We cast a wide net, including 320 people in all, with students ranging from high school freshmen to doctoral candidates and nonstudents including many who had no college degree as well as a number who had a degree. We gave people time to think before answering. The instructions were carefully framed to avoid words like "argument"—we did not want to put people into a contentious frame of mind, where they felt that they had to take a strong position and defend it. We probed for any ideas that the participants had on either side of the case.

I will briefly outline several results from this study of your neighbors' thinking.

1. How well do people reason? As a trend, not too well. The arguments that people gave about the bottle deposit issue, the Cold War issue, or others were generally sparse and showed a strong my-side bias. The typical participant would adopt a position and offer two or three reasons for it, none or one against it.

2. *What kinds of logical errors did their reasoning show?* A number of logical errors or *fallacies* have been identified in the literature on reasoning. One of the best known is *affirming the consequent*; it takes the fallacious form A implies B; B, therefore A. For example, if you were told that if it's a zebra it has black and white stripes, saw a creature with black and white stripes, and concluded confidently that it was a zebra, you would be affirming the consequent. Laboratory research shows that people are quite prone to such logical lapses when they face verbal problems that call for strict deductive reasoning.

However, this was not the case for the everyday issues on which we gathered data. As a generalization, there were few technical errors of logic like affirming the consequent. Rather, for the most part, people's arguments were weak because they left important considerations out of the picture altogether. By way of illustration, recall one typical response mentioned above to the question whether a nuclear freeze agreement would reduce the chances of nuclear war: Yes, because fewer weapons to fight with means less chance of nuclear war. In trend, participants largely ignored the side of the case opposite their own; for instance a person who offered the "fewer weapons" argument might mention no factors that could provoke escalation into a nuclear war anyway. Participants did not explore possible objections to lines of the argument in support of their own side of the case, for instance, never asking "Aren't even a small number of nuclear weapons quite sufficient to start a nuclear war?" Participants often did not even muster very many lines of argument in support of their own side of the case, sometimes even mentioning no more than the single "fewer weapons" argument. In summary, their sins of reason were sins of omission rather than commission.

3. *Do people reason as well as they could?* One might think that people would explore the issues as thoroughly as their knowledge and ability allowed. Certainly we encouraged them to, asking them more than once to think more if they thought it would advance their understanding of the issue. They seemed to comply in good spirit. Apparently, they believed they had thought the matter through as much as they could.

But this was not the case. In a later round of research, we explicitly checked whether people could think of factors on the side of the case opposite their own, whether they could make up objections to their own lines of argument, and whether they could generate more lines of argument in support of their own position. We found that they could easily do all three if directly asked. In terms of the above example, a person who initially only answered with the "fewer weapons" argument, could easily give arguments on the other side, objections to their own main argument, and additional arguments on their side. Most dramatically, people produced an average of 700 percent more arguments on the side of the case opposite their own, a sevenfold improvement. In other words, people tended to think they had reasoned about the issues as much as they could, but, when asked, proved cognitively capable of a considerably richer exploration.

4. *Does typical education improve people's reasoning?* Not to any great degree on the measures we employed! We compared high school freshmen with high school seniors, college freshmen with college seniors, and first year with fourth year doctoral students. We found only very slight increases in elaboration of arguments and attention to different sides of the case across three years of education, from the first year to the fourth year in high school, in college, and in graduate school. While the students presumably advanced in subject-matter mastery, they did not seem to learn to explore general issues much more thoroughly or in a fairer way.

This should be distinguished from a rather different question: Did people in college undergraduate programs reason better than those in high school, and people in graduate school better than those in undergraduate programs? The answer there was yes, but not because of anything schooling taught them. Remember that the first year to fourth year differences were minor. Rather, admissions requirements to college and to graduate school apparently select for people who are more able or inclined to develop lines of argument more fully.

5. *Do people learn to reason better in the "school of life?"* Perhaps people out of school for some time, learning the lessons of practical everyday living, would develop richer and fairer ways of thinking. Not according to our data. The groups ten years or more out of school performed in about the same way as the school groups. Age was uncorrelated with reasoning performance in our out-of-school population.

6. *Does high general intelligence lead to better reasoning?* Yes and no. The answer depends on what aspect of reasoning you consider. At the end of our interviews with participants, we asked them to take a short-form IQ test. We found that participants with a higher IQ tended to produce considerably more elaborate arguments on their own side of the case, but not on the other side of the case. High general intelligence did not lesson

my-side bias. I have always felt that this was an especially important finding, because we tend to identify good thinking with high general intelligence. Yet here it emerges that high general intelligence does not allay my-side bias, one of the fundamental challenges to good thinking.

An especially telling version of this result came from a subsample of students of law. The students were quite bright in the sense of IQ. Moreover, in their education, they are of course taught to anticipate and pay heed to the other side of a legal dispute, if only to argue their own side better. Presumably in professional contexts they learn to do so. Nonetheless, in the context of these everyday reasoning tasks, arguing only with themselves and trying to get at the truth of an issue, the student lawyers proved to be very prone to my-side bias. This does not mean that all the student lawyers reasoned in a one-sided way. There were exceptions in this population just as in the other populations studied. But the trend toward my-side bias was dramatic.

In summary, from this study and several follow-up investigations, a troubling picture of your neighbors' thinking emerged. Although some people showed very good reasoning, by and large it appears that people do not reason nearly as well as they can. People seem to lack a sense of how much they can and should explore an issue to reach confident conclusions. They are particularly prone to my-side bias, building up their own position with hardly a thought to evidence on the other side. Conventional schooling—even advanced schooling—helps little. Finally, high general intelligence helps largely on your own side of the case, leaving my-side bias insidiously intact.

Let us stand back for a moment. Section by section, paragraph by paragraph, examples about folly in history, one-sided "John Wayne" reasoning, and one-sided and underelaborated reasoning have challenged the comfortable "it ain't broke" position. Yet by now, just as we often feel that something is too good to be true, we might feel that all this is too bad to be true. Human thinking cannot be that bad! How could we survive? How could we function? Granted that the world is not a utopia, still how could we have come this far?

The answer of course is that we could not have. Most of the time human thinking must work fairly well. I do not want to argue that we human beings think badly in general. I do not even want to argue that hasty, narrow, and biased thinking are always bad. In fact, in emergencies or in socially repressive situations where fair-mindedness puts you at risk they can be adaptive. But I do want to argue that hasty, narrow, and biased thinking commonly do work against our best interests and that we think badly often enough to worry about and do something about it.

The real question is not whether we *usually* think badly—clearly not—but why we think badly now and again when it looks as though we could do better. In Chapter 1, I hinted at an answer. I suggested that we find ourselves caught in an evolutionary double bind, with a mental organization that functions very well in most circumstances but has some traps built into the way it operates. Basically, the situations reviewed in the last several sections spring these traps—as, unfortunately, do situations in our everyday lives from time to time.

In the next chapter, I will examine head-on what this evolutionary double bind is and how it works. For now, let me continue to pile up evidence that challenges the comfortable "it ain't broke" position, not because human thinking is very broke, but because it has a few serious cracks.

A Sampler of Other Evidence

I have no ambition to become the Edgar Allen Poe of cognition. Perhaps it is enough to say that there are many other dark tales to be told, and to offer a brief sketch of some of them.

History and High-Stakes Thinking

History is a natural place to look, because episodes of history provide us with high-stakes cases of thinking in action. Besides Barbara Tuchman's book, there is, for instance, Gordon W. Prange's well-known *At Dawn We Slept*, the story of the events leading up to the attack of the Japanese on Pearl Harbor. As Prange documents, many indications of a potential attack came to light before the event itself; yet no one took the evidence seriously enough to mount countermeasures.

Recent history gets a look in a fascinating book by Harvard University scholars Richard Neustadt and Ernest May called *Thinking in Time*. The authors examine the political reasoning during such high-tension episodes as the Cuban missile crisis and the Bay of Pigs debacle, arguing that sometimes the thinking of statespersons and politicians has proven astute, on other occasions remarkably obtuse. One key factor in astute thinking, they urge, is a systematic effort to see the situation from the perspective of the other side—the Russians or Cubans, for example.

Legal Reasoning

Thinking in legal contexts, another arena of argument where we want nothing but the best, has also come under scrutiny from a number of directions. For example, Elizabeth Loftus in her *Eyewitness Testimony* documents the profound unreliability of witnesses in many circumstances and the general misunderstanding of problems of witness reliability among jurors, judges, and the legal system in general. The law vests enormous weight in the eyewitness, crediting that person with high authority in reporting accurately what transpired. Unfortunately, extensive research shows that eyewitnesses are often mistaken in crucial ways, even when there is no question of bad illumination or observation at a distance. Poor thinking enters in by two doors: in witness's uncritical accounts of what they saw—often more a reconstruction from fragments of memory than a replay of some mental tape recorder—and in jurors' and judges' easy acceptance of such reports.

One horror story reported by Loftus concerns the case of Charles Clark, who was sentenced to life imprisonment after being charged with shooting and killing the owner of a clothing store at the scene of a robbery. The daughter of the owner identified Clark in a police lineup as the perpetrator. Even though Clark's landlady testified that he was home the entire day the murder occurred and one of the other defendants said that Clark had no part in the murder, the single eyewitness testimony of the daughter outweighed all other evidence.

Clark repeatedly petitioned for a new trial, but only after thirty years of imprisonment was Clark vindicated. The early transcripts revealed that the victim's daughter said that she could not identify Clark as one of the robbers. The girl admitted that she identified Clark as the man who shot her father only after the authorities pointed Clark out to her before the lineup as being guilty.

In many other ways, jury trials raise concerns about the quality of human reasoning. A number of studies have scrutinized the reasoning of jurors, disclosing an array of problems also found in other settings, such as my-side bias. University of Melbourne psychologist Jeanette Lawrence, writing about the thinking of judges, shows how, in passing sentence, different judges can project onto the same case very different interpretations of motive and context—all of them unwarranted by the available information—and thus render very different sentences.

For instance, trial judges define for juries the criteria for determining reasonable doubt in different ways, with definitions ranging from a doubt "for which any reason can be given" to a doubt that is "not trivial or imaginary." One study that examined the deliberations of six mock juries in an actual rape trial revealed that guilty verdicts occurred more often with lax definitions of reasonable doubt.

How a judge decides on a tough or lenient sentence depends on how the judge interprets and classifies the information presented by the defendant. The following shoplifting case illustrates how judges do not view information presented in a case in a uniform way:

> Maria, an unemployed domestic worker whose husband was also unemployed through illness, stole goods worth $47.50 from different parts of a city store while accompanied by her two children. The security staff stopped her and recovered the stolen items. She had no previous convictions.

Different judges use the same information to make their own inferences. For example, regarding Maria's economic problem, one tough judge used that information to decide that she could not pay a fine that he thought appropriate, whereas a lenient judge used that same information to infer that her financial troubles most likely were the cause of the offense. One focused on the event in the store, the other on the life circumstances of the defendant.

Reasoning in School

Within the world of education, research conducted by the National Assessment of Educational Progress has persistently documented short-falls in school children's reasoning. While one might not be entirely happy with the levels of literacy and numeracy achieved, the American educational system equips most students with a routine competency. However, the findings for more demanding intellectual performances are cautionary. Well-organized and compelling writing is a stumbling block for a high percentage of youngsters. Much more than computation, story problems in mathematics cause students difficulty. Students may remember what they read adequately but tend to have difficulty drawing inferences.

For example, the Monday newspaper has an article discussing how Senator Berenson stood against gun control legislation but favored deregulation of airline fares. Suppose you ask these students how Senator Berenson probably would vote on a proposal to establish nationwide automobile emission standards as an antipollution measure? You would like the students to recognize a trend against government control in Senator Berenson's positions and conclude that the Senator would vote against emission standards. But this is just the kind of pattern that students commonly do not detect.

Relatedly, students even at the college level commonly display fundamental misunderstandings of concepts that they have studied. For example, students who can readily solve numerically-based problems involving Newtonian dynamics mishandle problems that require a qualitative account of what forces are acting on objects and how they would move. Here is a case in point: Through a freak mishap, a bowling ball falls out of the cargo hold of an airplane, as the airplane proceeds along its way. Disregarding any effects of air friction, when the bowling ball hits the ground, will it be (a) behind the plane, (b) directly under the plane, or (c) ahead of the plane? And why?

The right answer is (b), directly under the plane, because the bowling ball shares the forward motion of the plane as it falls out of the cargo hold and preserves that forward motion despite its downward fall. This follows directly from Newtonian principles students have studied and often learned to handle fairly well in their mathematical form. However, many students do not see through the formalism of the mathematics to the underlying phenomena, and tend to assimilate Newtonian conceptions to common-sense but mistaken intuitions. In general, performance on activities that demand thought and understanding falls much further below ideal expectations than performance on routine activities. Certainly this is expectable, but it is regrettable nonetheless and sets a clear agenda for educational improvement. In this spirit, readers may want to consult my recent book *Smart Schools*.

When Mixed Evidence Strengthens Belief

Innumerable laboratory studies that mimic natural situations also speak to the fallibility of human thinking. One of the most disturbing experiments I know of, reported by C. G. Lord, L. Ross, and M. Lepper in 1979, explored people's postures on use of the death penalty. Before exposing them to a mix of evidence on both sides of the case, the experimenters recorded the participants' initial leanings: What position did they favor and how confident were they of their views? Then the experimenters had the subjects read through the deliberately mixed body of evidence that pointed in no clear direction.

If people were more reflective about their reasoning—a matter of reflective intelligence—the mixed evidence would have reduced confidence. However, as a strong trend, people on both sides of the issue stuck to their positions and even became more confident. How could this be? The experimenters found out by examining in more detail the subjects' attitudes toward the evidence that had been offered. They discovered that the "pro" subjects unreflectively took the "pro" evidence as reinforcing their position but tended to dismiss the "con" evidence as biased or misleading. So they become more confident in their position. The "con" subjects behaved in mirror image way, taking encouragement from the "con" evidence and dismissing the "pro" evidence. Thus the same mixed evidence can reinforce people in their polarized positions, a unsettling pattern in human reasoning. Why this pattern? It has to do with the evolutionary double bind mentioned earlier and explored in the next chapter.

Causal Reasoning

In her 1991 book *The Skills of Argument*, Columbia University Professor Deanna Kuhn reports the results of a major experiment probing people's causal reasoning. Kuhn worked with three issues on which many people have views:

• What causes prisoners to return to crime after they're released?
• What causes children to fail in school?
• What causes unemployment?

She and her colleagues asked for participants' reasoning on these issues and drew out their reasoning further through interviews. The participants in the main sample included people ranging in age from fourteen to into their sixties and representing various levels of education.

The reasoning Kuhn and her colleagues found ranged along a spectrum between two poles. At one pole, people seemed to reason

> . . . never having considered that things could be otherwise. At the other pole, knowing is an ongoing, effortful process of evaluating possibilities,

one that the ever-present possibility of new evidence and new arguments leaves never completed.

Kuhn found a pattern of performance closer to the first pole than the second.

Some subjects appeared to feel that all knowing is factual and certain. In fact, they seemed content to leave the reasoning to the experts. When asked "do experts know for sure what causes school failure?" one subject's response was, "If they're experts, they know." Another subject reached a general conclusion about expert certainty from a specific personal incident: "I would have to say yes, because they have proven to me. In my old school we had guidance counselors and they knew what was wrong with me."

More weak reasoning occurred when subjects were asked to provide evidence to support their views. Some people thought that evidence was irrelevant and unnecessary and subscribed to "argument by telling." One respondent put it this way: "I wouldn't really give them evidence. I would just try to convince them that that was the reason why. (Experimenter: How would you do that?) I'd keep at it, you know, keep telling them that, yes, this is the reason, this is the reason . . ." Another discarded evidence in favor of intuition: "I would not try to give any evidence. I only . . . when it comes to kids, I work by my good instinct."

Some subjects who did manage to provide examples to support their view treated examples not just as evidence but outright proof. When asked to give evidence to convince someone about the causes of children failing in school, one person responded:

> . . . I could give examples . . . Because if I could give examples, they couldn't disprove my examples since they really happened. (Experimenter: Is their anything further you could say to help show that what you've said is correct?) I could ask them if it ever happened to themselves. (E: What would that show?) Well, then, if it did, it would prove it very well.

In this case the person's examples aren't used as supporting evidence; they settle the question.

To mention a few generalizations, at least half of the participants were very certain of their explanations, despite the genuinely vexed character of the issues used. Only about a third could even generate alternatives and only about a third could articulate what sort of empirical evidence would challenge their theory. Level of education completed made a substantial difference in the participants' performance (I would interpret this as a consequence of selective admission policies for higher levels of education, as discussed in the previous section). Age and sex had no impact.

Decision Making

A study conducted by Jonathan Baron and colleagues Laura Granato, Mark Spranca, and Eva Teubal focused on the decision making of children and early adolescents. The participants, ranging in age from about seven to fifteen, thought about a series of common-sense decision-making situations and responded to queries from the researchers. For instance, one situation ran as follows:

> *Problem.* The coach of a basketball team says that everyone has to go to practices if they want to play in the games. Bill is the best player on the team. He missed three practices in a row, just because he felt like watching TV. Of course, Bill was so good that he would still help the team even though he had missed the practices. If you were the coach, how would you think about whether to let Bill play in the next game?

Baron and his colleagues looked for—and found in abundance—several kinds of bias and blindness that impair good decision making. One impediment related to the above problem concerned *precedent.* Participants failed to take into account the fact that making a decision in a certain way on one occasion tends to set a precedent for later occasions that may create problems. For instance, one problem with the coach letting Bill off in the above story is that it would set a precedent for others to expect similar tolerance. In fact, fewer than 15 percent of the participants spontaneously recognized anything like precedent setting as a concern.

Here is another sample:

> *Problem.* You saw an accident. A friend of yours ran into someone else's car. You hoped that the accident would not be blamed on your friend. You decided to lie to the police about whose fault the accident was, if they asked you. The police came. You expected that they would blame it on the other person, even though it was your friend's fault. They didn't ask you. You did not speak up to tell the truth. Is this just as bad as if you had lied?

People often responded to this problem with *omission bias*. This means treating inaction as though it were not an act for which one was responsible. For instance, you might feel that keeping silent in the above situation is better than lying if directly asked. The authors argue that this is an error of reasoning, one which about three-quarters of the subjects displayed.

Before the following problem, participants responded to another that invited them to reason about the pros and cons of wearing seat belts. They did reasonably well, generating the usual kinds of factors. For instance, seat belts prevent you from being thrown through a windshield. Then the subjects faced this situation:

Problem. Jennifer says that she heard of an accident where a car fell into a lake and a woman was kept from getting out in time because of wearing her seat belt, and another accident where a seat belt kept someone from getting out of the car in time when there was a fire. What do you think about this?

People reacted to this task with an error of *probability*. They failed to take into account the relative probability of different scenarios. Getting trapped by your seat belt in a fire or under water seems much less probable than being thrown through a window for lack of a seat belt. Even if people should disagree about this, at least probability is an issue. However, most subjects never raised it at all, treating the fire and lake scenarios as though they were as likely as anything else that might happen. Finally:

Problem. The principal of a private school, for kindergarten through sixth grade, is wondering whether she should have a rule requiring students to wear uniforms to school or not. What do you think?

With this and similar items, the subjects showed considerable *my-side bias*. As discussed before, this means little exploration of reasons contrary to one's position and a preference for interpreting evidence as suiting one's own position.

My Thinking

This parade of problems in human thinking is discomfiting. It provokes a natural defensive question: "Who's in a position to judge when someone's thinking is not so good?" Who am I to judge, or you, or this philosopher or that psychologist? The question is legitimate because when person A looks at person B's thinking and finds it wanting, person A may simply not understand the context or intentions of person B. Person B's thinking, rightly understood, could be just fine. Perhaps in fact there is not much bad thinking around after all.

I have two answers to this puzzle of who's in a position to judge, a logical one and a pragmatic one. The logical one goes like this: If A concludes that B's thinking is wanting, indeed A may be mistaken. But there is certainly inadequate thinking somewhere in the picture. Either A is right and B's thinking is wanting, or A is wrong and it's A's thinking itself that is inadequate. To generalize, the very fact that people often feel that others' thinking is wanting is proof that there is considerable faulty thinking around, although sometimes it's the faulty thinking of the critics rather than that of those criticized.

My pragmatic answer to the puzzle of who's in a position to judge goes like this. Over the last pages, I have tried to deal with the question of "who's to judge" in a practical way. I have sought examples where I think most people would agree that there is something important awry with the thinking in purely common-sense terms, without needing to resort to any arcane psychological or philosophical criteria. While it is certainly true that one can debate into oblivion some of the concerns raised by psychologists' and philosophers' technical scrutiny of people's thinking, I argue that it is hard to dismiss anywhere near all the problems that seem to appear. It is hard to make the "it ain't broke" argument, even if it ain't as broke quite as often as those who take the most jaundiced view might think. In fact, I would suggest that most people commonly find genuine shortfalls not only in others' thinking but even their own. The very ordinariness of such mental mishaps makes a case for their reality. Let me illustrate with a personal story.

I had known Carolee for years. She was a good friend and colleague, one who lived in the Boston area. But I rarely saw Carolee, because the pattern of our lives left us in different places at different times. So, when we both were going to attend a conference near Washington D.C. awhile ago, I looked forward to catching up.

However, there was so much also going on at the conference that we did not have time to talk. So we cross-checked plane flights. She was returning to Boston on Delta, about twenty minutes after my return flight on Northwest.

"Look," I said. "If we have enough lead time when we get to the airport, I'll go to Delta with you and see if I can get a seat. Then we can have our conversation."

Unfortunately, the hotel van taking us and others to the airport did not get there as early as we would have liked. As it pulled up in front of the Northwest terminal, with the Delta terminal some distance away, I did a time check. "Let's see," I said. "If I go with you, I'll have to see if I can switch airlines. Maybe there'll be a seat on Delta and maybe not. If there isn't, I won't have time to get back to Northwest for the flight I have. I don't want to get stranded." So we agreed to forget about flying together and meet for lunch sometime soon in Boston.

No more than thirty seconds later, as I was walking into the Northwest terminal, I realized my mistake. I had been thinking only in terms of me going to the Delta terminal with Carolee to try to change to her flight. But why shouldn't she change to my flight? It was obvious—the same plan in reverse. Moreover, it was actually a better plan, because my flight left well before hers. It would have worked too: When I boarded the plane I found there was plenty of room.

Carolee and I had lunch a few weeks later. I told her about how I had missed the obvious solution. "Yes," Carolee said. "You know, it's funny, I realized the same thing myself a few minutes later. Also, the Delta flight turned out to be pretty crowded, so that's the only way it would have worked."

This was a small not very important mishap of thinking. Life is full of them, along with occasional ones important enough to matter a lot. I tell this story to confess that, although I try to be mindful and strategic, the kinds of lapses surveyed in this chapter plague me too—and all of us. The chapter title "What's wrong with my neighbors' thinking?" contains a calculated irony. When we complain about thinking going astray, it is generally not our own thinking but someone else's—a neighbor, or the town manager, or the school principal, or the president, or the manufacturer that produced the lemon of a car that we, with reasonably careful shopping, purchased.

However, what is wrong with our neighbors' thinking is quite typically wrong with our own thinking. My neighbor, and I, often cruise through life mindlessly. We slip into a bullheaded John Wayne attitude toward the world, valuing the robust one-sided position over the reflective two-sided one. We settle for the simple story line that makes superficial sense of a situation rather than the complicated bundle of stories that can usually be told in any pro/con examination of an issue. We miss the creative opportunity because we have not challenged our tacit assumptions, not seen the boundaries that constrain our thinking.

While Part I dealt largely with the mechanisms of intelligence, in this chapter I have focused on the third mindware question, which asks what kinds of intelligence need learners' attention. Some would hold that none do in most cases—people get along quite well. If it ain't broke, don't fix it. My argument in this chapter is that such a stance is simply mistaken. To sum up:

MWQ #3. What aspects of intelligence especially need attention? At least these:

- Avoiding hasty judgment, recognizing the need for evidence (concern raised by public reaction to the *Vincennes* incident).
- Seeing past one's policies and positions creatively and insightfully to serve one's interests better (concern raised by Barbara Tuchman's analysis of folly).
- Open-mindedness, avoiding my-side bias (concern raised by Jonathan Baron's research, the Lord, Ross, and Lepper study of beliefs concerning capital punishment, Deanna Kuhn's research on causal reasoning, my own research, and many other findings).
- Relatedly, well-elaborated open-minded reasoning on both sides of an issue, with objections considered (concern raised by studies conducted by my colleagues and me).
- Generating multiple interpretations or perspectives (concern raised by Neustadt and May in their *Thinking in Time* and by Deanna Kuhn's research on causal reasoning among others).
- Maintaining mindfulness (concern raised by Ellen Langer's experiments on mindlessness).
- Caution about the idea that seeing is believing (concern raised by Elizabeth Loftus's work on eyewitness testimony).
- Caution about projecting interpretations unwarranted by the evidence (concern raised by Jeanette Lawrence's studies of judges).
- Attention to factors in decision making such as the probability of scenarios considered, precedent setting, and the notion that inaction is itself an action (Jonathan Baron's decision-making study).
- Drawing inferences from reading (concern shown by the National Assessment of Educational Progress among others).

- Writing in a well-organized persuasive way (same source).
- Understanding key concepts in science and mathematics (same source).

Shortfalls in our thinking are all too real and all too frequent. They muddy the slow Amazon of history, make more turbulent the maelstrom of politics, clog the flow of economies, and cloud the brooks and streams of everyday life. In the name and with the hope of learnable intelligence, it's imperative to understand why, from time to time, thinking goes awry.

7

The Intelligence Paradox

"Homer himself hath been observ'd to nod," wrote the Roman poet Horace. In Homer's *Odyssey* and *Iliad*, not all fits together as neatly and perfectly as it might. In the *Iliad*, for example, Helen tells Priam things that he should already know. A duel, an affair of honor, occurs a few hours after a similar duel has ended in a fiasco, followed by the breaking of a solemn truce. Phoenix plays an important part in an conciliatory embassy to Achilles, but makes no appearance as the group sets out or upon their arrival.

Scholars and enthusiasts of Homer gently acknowledge the bard's failings with the phrase "Homer nods." They might as well be speaking of all of us. If our first recorded genius of epic poetry nods, what about the rest of us? The previous chapter argued that most of us nod a good deal in our thinking. We reach conclusions in one-sided ways, adopt overfirm stances, miss opportunities that in retrospect seem plain, fail to sustain an alert state of mind, and so on. While the nods of Homer are benign— the *Odyssey* and the *Iliad* are tall tales we can marvel over with little concern about whether they completely hang together—many of our nods in real family, business, and political life have grave consequences.

Yet there is a puzzle to all this. Taking the last chapter as a measure, one could get the impression that there are more nods than anything else. One might think that most people's thinking is less at the Homer-the-poet end of the spectrum and more at the Homer Simpson end of the spectrum. How can it be then that on the whole, day in and day out, people get along? How can it be that so many people live their lives reasonably comfortably and competently? As the popular phrase puts it, how can we be so smart and yet so dumb? Or, as psychologists Richard Nisbett and Lee Ross quipped, "If we're so dumb, how come we made it to the moon?"

I call this puzzle the *intelligence paradox*. It is indeed striking that most of the time most human beings function cognitively in a very sophisticated way. For example, with the help of their neural intelligence and plenty of experience, almost all children learn to navigate about their environments, handle objects in complex ways, communicate fluently in their native language, and more or less get along with other people. Given reasonable educational opportunities, most children learn to read and write after a fashion and to do basic arithmetic. By the time of adolescence, most people have accumulated an immense amount of knowledge, not necessarily book knowledge but knowledge about the world of the streets, videogames, movies, baseball, and whatnot. Many of these cognitive achievements have proved difficult to explain in detail or model on computers. They are remarkable accomplishments of the human organism. Nonetheless, despite what one has to call the virtuosity of human cognition, people commonly hit sour notes when it comes to thinking well. How can this be?

A resolution of the intelligence paradox is fundamental to formulating a theory of learnable intelligence. Without such an understanding, the roots of human difficulties with complex thinking remain unclear, as do ways to help. That sets the mission for this chapter: to understand the intelligence paradox—why Homer and all of us nod, or how we can be so smart and yet so dumb.

Is the Paradox Real?

The easiest way to dissolve a paradox is to declare one or another side of the paradox false. However, instead of dissolving the paradox, I want to defend it. I believe that the paradox is real: Human beings actually do function quite well most of the time, yet display shortfalls of thinking far too often for their own good.

The usual approach to dissolving the intelligence paradox is to argue against the idea of human unreasonableness, holding that by and large seemingly unreasonable thinking is not in fact unreasonable. In his recent book, *The Fragmentation of Reason*, philosopher Stephen Stich reviews skeptically a number of such perspectives. For example, one protest to the notion of human unreasonableness is Darwinian. Roughly, the idea is that human beings, as biological organisms that have survived for hundreds of thousands of years, could not possibly function in fundamentally irrational ways, or humans would have been dead long since. Plausible as this argument sounds on the surface, it is subject to a number of objections. One of the simplest is that adaptations have a competitive rather than an absolute character: An organism does not have to be perfect to thrive, just more effective than the competition. As Darwin himself pointed out emphatically in *The Origin of the Species*, many organisms are far from ideally adapted. In fact, he took this as a key piece of evidence for the reality of evolution and natural selection.

Another kind of protest to the idea of human unreasonableness says that people only look unreasonable because certain standards of reasoning are impossible ideals. Stich agrees that this is sometimes so. For instance, people commonly are inconsistent, a kind of lapse in reasoning. However, the mathematics of the computational processes necessary to maintain full consistency checking in a collection of beliefs shows that it is computationally impractical. Although obviously people can strive to avoid gross inconsistencies, a fully consistent set of beliefs is an impossible ideal. As Stich expresses at another point, ". . . it seems simply perverse to judge that subjects are doing a bad job of reasoning because they are not using a strategy that requires a brain the size of a blimp."

While this problem of an impossible ideal holds for some kinds of supposed unreasonableness, Stich points out that there are many others where it does not. In the previous chapter, I tried to highlight kinds of unreasonableness where the thinkers in question might well have done better. In my own studies on informal reasoning, my colleagues and I actually checked whether the participants were cognitively capable of doing better by asking them to try to think in patterns they had not spontaneously exhibited. As a broad generalization, we found that they were capable of doing so.

Yet another line of objection to human unreasonableness is the idea that supposedly good thinking is not always adaptive, and therefore not really good. For example, in the last chapter I emphasized the problem of my-side bias—looking only or mostly at your own side of the case. In a repressive social setting with strong community beliefs, my-side bias about the norms of the society is a positive asset so long as my side is everyone else's side too. Broad-mindedness can be downright dangerous.

Stich sees this kind of argument as a real concern and emphasizes that pragmatic criteria for good thinking are needed: Genuinely good thinking should help people attain their goals. If it does not, but merely matches some academic ideal, it is suspect. In somewhat the same spirit, cognitive psychologist Jonathan Baron has argued for a goal-oriented conception of good thinking. Patterns of thinking can be called good insofar as they help thinkers to attain their goals. To return once more to the case of my-side bias, biased thinking may sometimes be good thinking, in the sense that it helps one to attain goals such as social solidarity, aiding one's survival and well-being. This does not mean that in general people would be better off thinking narrowly but only that in certain contexts on certain kinds of issues they would.

This pragmatic criterion for defining good thinking seems sensible to me, although certainly it is subject to debate. In any case, I chose the arguments in the last chapter with pragmatic factors in mind. The kinds of lapses in thinking reviewed were, I suggest, kinds of lapses that at least very often would not be in the best interests of people. Indeed, it's worth recalling that this was actually one of the criteria for *folly* as defined by Barbara Tuchman: behavior that ran against the very interests of the perpetrators.

The bottom line is that it is not so easy to argue away the intelligence paradox on Darwinian, impossible ideal, or other grounds. Much more often than would be desirable, people show shortfalls in thinking contrary to their own best interests. The puzzle of the intelligence paradox still remains: How can we be so smart and yet so dumb?

Intelligence Traps

It will help in probing the intelligence paradox to make a broad generalization about the kinds of things that tend to go wrong with human thinking. By and large, the literature on thinking deals with fairly particular kinds of shortfalls. As noted in the last chapter, considerable laboratory research concerns difficulties in syllogistic reasoning, as with *affirming the consequent*, or in reasoning with probabilities. Others examining how people reach conclusions from evidence speak of *confirmation bias*, or *my-side bias*, the tendency to seek out evidence confirming your prior belief and to ignore or dismiss contrary evidence. Psychologists concerned with people who seem to manage themselves poorly look in part to a cognitive style trait called *impulsivity*, the tendency not to take thought before acting. Others focus on *cognitive dissonance*, the inclination to rationalize our own behavior to ourselves, interpreting our own motives after the fact as more coherent than perhaps they actually were. Investigators concerned with creative thinking point to *functional fixedness*, the way people's perceptions get locked into the normal functions and roles of things. For example, because of functional fixedness, people tend not to see a paper clip as a potential tool for fishing a lost ring out of a drain.

From *affirming the consequent* to *functional fixedness*, these are one sprinkle from a huge pepper shaker of ways scholars have labeled the mishaps of thinking. Searching for an overarching generalization, several colleagues and I evolved the following scheme, which captures many problems of everyday thinking. We identified four "defaults" of human thinking: People tend to think by default in ways that are *hasty, narrow, fuzzy,* and *sprawling*.

To say a little more about each:

- *Hasty thinking.* This includes impulsiveness and mindlessness, Ellen Langer's notion from the previous chapter of how people react without thinking about what they are doing.
- *Narrow thinking.*This includes my-side bias, functional fixedness, and other respects in which people tend to think in narrow patterns.
- *Fuzzy thinking.* This refers to problems of clarity, precision, and distinction-making in human cognition. For instance, many youngsters have difficulty sustaining high precision in supposedly routine tasks such as arithmetic problems, and fail to differentiate fundamentally different concepts such as weight and density. For an adult example, we may hear a politician appeal to democracy, but not know or ask what the politician's version of democracy is.
- *Sprawling thinking.* Very often, human thinking about a vexed matter wanders endlessly around the intricacies in a disorganized way without ever converging. For instance, when thinking over an office dispute, you may find your mind bouncing from the personalities involved to the causes to possible fixes to who said what to what they should have said, around and around without ever settling on an overview of the situation.

These intelligence traps are called not just faults but defaults of human thinking for a reason. What happens by default happens automatically when no special action is taken. For example, if you do not keep up your insurance payments, your policy gets canceled by default. When a person dies intestate, the person's property goes to relatives as specified by the laws of the state, by default. The same appears to be so with hasty, narrow, fuzzy, and sprawling thinking. It seems that without special attention, the mind tends to fall into these intelligence traps. Only when we do something to keep our thinking in order do we escape the potholes of cognition.

The Pattern Machine

It is time to tackle the intelligent paradox head on: Why indeed are we so smart and yet so dumb? In scientific inquiry, paradoxes often signal missing parts of a puzzle. If the default tendency toward hasty, narrow, fuzzy, and sprawling thinking makes us dumb at certain junctures, perhaps much of the time thinking something like that actually makes us smart! More precisely, I want to argue that rapid, focused, routine responding, which sometimes might be hasty, narrow, fuzzy, and sprawling, serves very well most of the time.

Gradually over the last half century cognitive scientists investigating the workings of the mind have built a picture of the mind's approach to most of cognition, how the bulk of mental work gets done. They have discovered something fundamental. More than anything else, the mind is a *pattern machine*. Through experience, our brains become attuned to familiar and useful patterns in the world and replay them efficiently and reflexively.

Chapter 4 already touched upon this particular revolution in the conception of mind, reviewing how chess masters play the game so well. The key was rapid perception of the dangers and opportunities of the chess board—a kind of pattern recognition built up through years of play. One simple symptom of this rapid perceptual sizing up is the reaction time of master-level players. Shown a chess position, they will arrive at a tentative move within seconds. To be sure, they will then think carefully and sometimes choose a different path—a "sometimes" crucial in competitive play. Nonetheless, most of the time they stick with their first choice. Studies in the same general spirit have been conducted for a number of disciplines. In physics, for example, research pursued by Carnegie-Mellon psychologist Jill Larkin and others has shown that expert physicists orient quite rapidly to the core challenges of problems posed to them, much as chess masters see quickly and clearly the hazards and opportunities of chess positions.

Knowledge Compilation and Production Systems

All this has evolved into a picture of what happens when people address, struggle with, and gradually master a domain of activity—chess play, physics problems, language learning, or for that matter a professional craft. Initially, a learner struggles with the situation, exploring possibilities, encountering problems, trying out solutions, and so on. Gradually, through personal discovery and instruction, the learner discovers various ways to handle the various situations that arise, building up what I have called experiential intelligence.

A process occurs that cognitive psychologists call knowledge compilation. When a person discovers, perhaps through elaborate exploratory thinking, a regularity like "In Situation A, do Action B," a pattern recognition mechanism often gets set up in the brain to monitor for Situation A in the future. The next time that Situation A occurs, the person does not have to reason his or her way to Action B. Rather, Action B gets triggered automatically.

One way of representing these A-B links is through a formalism called production systems. Each A-B link is called a production. Competence in any activity from solving physics to playing on jungle gyms supposedly resides in a large special-purpose production system that encapsulates the many A-B links needed to handle the activity efficiently based on past experience.

Of course, experiential intelligence consists of more than just vast libraries of reflexes. For instance, master chess players, besides reflexes, have considerable explicit knowledge about chess that they can discuss, teach, write about, and ponder. Nonetheless, a large part of the chess master's, and others', experiential intelligence lies in the repertoire of productions in various special-purpose production systems.

Knowledge Compilation and Intuition

Knowledge compilation makes the thinking of experienced chess players, expert physicists, and other experts in other domains very intuitive. By definition, an intuition is an idea that comes to one with little conscious cogitation or rationale. Exactly this occurs when a master chess player looks at an opponent's position and quickly sees a likely response, or an experienced physicist looks at a physics problem and quickly sees that it can be approached by an energy balance equation. The compiled knowledge of the expert allows the expert to think in bigger leaps with an intuitive feel to them, rather than plodding along step by step. In other words, experiential intelligence in an area makes us capable of good intuitions.

Notice that this view of intuition carries a warning: Intuitions can be unreliable. Good intuitions depend on our having built up the experience. A novice in an area may very well feel strong intuitions, but they will tend to miss the mark.

Even for the expert, intuitions have a double edge. There is no guarantee that the expert's intuitions are always right. They reflect the compiled knowledge base, and the compiled knowledge base may be narrow or misleading in the face of a novel problem. When an expert's intuition happens to be wrong, it nonetheless feels just as compelling as a right intuition, a hard trap to escape.

Connectionism and Neural Networks

In recent years, another paradigm has arisen within cognitive psychology to challenge some of the precepts above. The notion of production systems pictures what I call experiential intelligence as in good part a bank of A-B rules, productions. In contrast, advocates of a new school of thought called connectionism urge that the brain does not work in such a computerlike way. A rule like Situation A, Action B is not stored as such in a particular place in the brain. Rather, the brain builds an association between A and B distributed throughout the neural network of the brain, somewhat as each region in a hologram contains a complete low-resolution image of the same object. Other associations besides the A-B association in question occupy the same space.

The details of how A-B associations could be distributed throughout a system rather than stored in one place as a rule would take us far afield of our immediate concern with the intelligence paradox with little profit—the debate between the classic cognitive psychology position with its underlying brain-as-computer metaphor and the connectionist position with its underlying idea of a neural network continues vigorously today, and many intermediate positions have evolved. The point I want to emphasize is that, despite the debate on how the brain works, classic cognitive psychology and the new connectionist perspective agree on some fundamental operating characteristics of the brain. In particular, the brain functions as a pattern-recognition device that yields rapid response to patterns in areas of great experience.

The Intelligence Partnership

This general picture helps me to articulate what I think is the partnership relationship between reflective and experiential intelligence in learning. Reflective intelligence—positive attitudes about investing effort in thinking, self-monitoring and regulation, use of decision-making strategies, and other kinds of mindware—figures more when productions in a production system are getting built up. Then the learner is searching for opportunities the hard way, exploring, trying out conjectures, and so on. This requires mindful consideration of options, following trains of inference, challenging assumptions to discover new possibilities—all aspects of reflective intelligence, the higher-order organization of thought. On a connectionist viewpoint, the brain does a certain amount of extracting patterns from experience automatically. Nonetheless, considerable exploration and trial-and-error are needed to provide a rich base of experience, exploration and trial-and-error that benefit from the direction of reflective intelligence.

One might say that reflective intelligence functions as the leading edge of experiential intelligence. What reflective intelligence discovers gets sifted, compiled, and stored up as part of experiential intelligence. At any given point in time, behavior in a familiar area (chess, playgrounds, physics, or whatever *you* happen to be familiar with) gets guided largely by experiential intelligence, as productions in the production system trigger or neural networks fire and the person relies in other ways on detailed stored knowledge. However, the leading edge of the person's behavior—the unusual, the novel, the problematic, the non-routine—prompts people to combine their reflective intelligence with their experiential intelligence to try to cope and indeed thrive.

Finally, neural intelligence fits into the picture as the underlying hardware that supports these processes.

The partnership between reflective intelligence and experiential intelligence can be viewed as a consequence of biological evolution, an adaptation of great subtlety and complexity for coping effectively with a risky world. Without reflective intelligence, we would not accumulate experiential intelligence nearly as well. And without experiential intelligence, we would be too reflective for our own good. Alan Newell, one of the founding fathers of the information processing perspective on cognition, argues in his 1990 synthesis *Theories of Cognition*, that the accumulation of experience about particular situations in reflexive form is a fundamental information-processing strategy. Evolution would push any complex organism in this direction. Creatures that tried to deal with the world mostly by reasoning things out reflectively, with little knowledge compilation, would simply perish in the rough and tumble. For lack of quick recognition, they would less often seize fleeting opportunities and dodge sudden dangers.

Why Homer Thrives

Recall that Homer nodded only occasionally in the *Iliad* and the *Odyssey*. Most of the time, he thrived. The pattern-machine perspective helps to explain why, despite the many shortfalls of human thinking, Homer and the rest of us function fairly well most of the time. Most of the time, experiential intelligence supports behavior. People rely on a vast store of experiences built up over years and held in a stockpile of productions.

In this connection, it's worth identifying the exact poetic tradition that Homer represented. Homer was what Albert Lord calls a singer of tales, a bard in an oral epic tradition. Oral epics were sung by wandering singers in a number of world cultures. Lord himself investigated oral epic practices still surviving in Yugoslavia in the 1930s. Homer is our name for the singer of the *Iliad* and the *Odyssey*, epics transcribed by unknown persons around the sixth or seventh century B.C.

It's natural to ask how Homer or any bard could sing a tale many thousands of lines long. Did this represent a prodigious feat of memory? On the contrary, Lord showed that singers composed their songs on the spot—but not out of nothing. They relied on plots they had already heard, on set scenes that might occur with minor variations from tale to tale, and on phrases and lines with the versatility to be plugged into different poetic settings with little or no modification. Thus, for instance, one description of a hero might sound pretty much like another except for the name and a few details.

The moral of all this is that Homer, as transcribed, was functioning very much in the pattern-machine manner of experiential intelligence, relying on a large repertoire of patterns that with flexible modification allowed him to compose on the spot a new rendering of the epic. Homer nodded only occasionally because what Homer or any singer of tales does on any one occasion is not typically a radically new performance, but a performance strongly supported by a repertoire of patterns garnered through experience and assembled fluently and intuitively to serve the moment.

Thus did Homer nod only occasionally. Thus do we all, in familiar circumstances, relying on our stockpile of patterns stored up as part of our experiential intelligence. One might call experiential intelligence the 90 percent solution. For 90 percent of the time it serves us well (of course, 90 percent is a somewhat arbitrary figure here, to convey the spirit of the point).

To be sure, our stockpile of patterns may have a few errors in it. However, by and large, it is a stockpile filtered through the test of practice. It efficiently and effectively informs our actions. It equips us to function reflexively when time is tight or the matter is not important enough for deliberation. It also feeds us information for more extended reasoning with reflective intelligence. Just as chess masters use their experiential intelligence as the raw material for reflective thinking that sometimes changes the move that seems most promising at first, so do we all think reflectively, summoning knowledge, imagery, and intuition from experiential intelligence.

This picture also clarifies how we can in the long run evade the worst effects of our fragile reflective intelligence, plagued by the default tendencies as it is. In most areas—family life, business, and so on—we have years to accumulate experience. If we do not reflect so well on one occasion, we have another chance and another. Whether things work out well or badly, the results tend to get captured by the pattern machine so next time we know better. Not through impeccable thinking on any one occasion, but through somewhat hit-or-miss thinking over many occasions, we gradually sort things out. We incrementally come to function quite well in familiar activities.

Why Homer Nods

All of this also helps to make clear why Homer nods, in fact why all of us nod, not always thinking and acting at our best. If experiential intelligence is the 90 percent solution, there remains a 10 percent problem.

For one thing, even in the midst of familiar activities, from time to time we simply slip. More importantly, not all activities are familiar. Inherently, experiential intelligence prepares us less well for novel circumstances than for familiar circumstances. Less supported, we are more likely to lapse.

However, these two points do not really resolve the intelligence paradox. The heart of the paradox lies in the observation that people seem to fall into the intelligence traps unreasonably often, thinking in a hasty, narrow, fuzzy, or sprawling way when there is no need to and indeed a need not to. Again, the word default has relevance. It signals the trend of human cognition. But why this trend?

I think the answer is this: The pattern-driven character of experiential intelligence actually gets in the way of reflective intelligence. Experiential intelligence nudges us toward patterns of thinking that work well when all goes pretty much as expected but that can easily become hasty, narrow, fuzzy, or sprawling in less supportive circumstances. Even though experiential and reflective intelligence form a kind of partnership for learning, as discussed before, there is also a deep inherent conflict between them.

This is the evolutionary double bind mentioned briefly in chapter 1. Even as evolution has equipped us with a neural system capable of supporting experiential intelligence, reflective intelligence, and their partnership, it has saddled us with a conflict between the two that sometimes prevents reflective intelligence from doing its best work. We would not do very well without them, but with them we have certain problems too, a double bind.

To see how the partnership of reflective and experiential intelligence limits itself, let us take a tour through the four defaults identified earlier.

Hasty Thinking

Recall that experiential intelligence functions in large part through the reflexive pattern machine of the human mind. The pattern machine tends to suggest a response right away if a familiar pattern appears in the situation. In other words, it acts on impulse. The impulse usually suits familiar situations nicely. However, it may not serve unusual situations or familiar situations with an unexpected twist. Moreover, when a basically familiar situation involves more complexity than usual, experiential intelligence can easily respond to some features of the situation while missing others with important implications.

For instance, a job applicant makes a terrific showing. He proves personable and articulate. He reminds you strongly of the best person who ever filled the post. Within a week you discover that the new employee writes slowly and awkwardly. Although you knew this was a key skill and should have been more cautious and reflective, you got carried away by your overall impression.

Narrow Thinking

Recall that the pattern machine builds up a repertoire of patterns from the past. Naturally, those patterns tend to dominate cognition: They are the very bricks and mortar of cognitive functioning. Most of the time, people gain enormous efficiency by relying on them. The Catch 22 is that their reflexive emergence inhibits exploration of other patterns. In novel situations or familiar but unusually complex situations, just this is likely to happen.

Previously I have placed my-side bias in the foreground as an example of narrow thinking, so here is a different kind of example. You enter a rather crowded lounge. You spy a comfortable chair and go over but see that someone has spilled a drink on the cushion. You look around but find nothing to wipe up the mess with, and anyway the cushion would still be damp. So you resign yourself to sitting on a nearby coffee table. Two minutes later someone comes along, takes a look at the same cushion, turns it over, and sits down.

Why didn't you think of that? Perhaps because your experiential intelligence immediately led you to a narrow definition of the problem: Clean up the mess. When you realized that would not work, you abandoned the problem as unsolvable. Such cul-de-sacs of thinking occur all the time. Led to look at something in one way, we never get around to looking at it in another.

Fuzzy Thinking

Here it is important to note a characteristic of the human pattern-recognition system, how readily we recognize camels in clouds, faces in leaves, and so on. In other words, the human pattern-recognition system readily overgeneralizes. Sometimes we realize we are overgeneralizing: Although we see a camel in a cloud, we hardly mistake it for a camel. However, often we just plain make mistakes. Someone calls someone else's name and you think you hear your name. A paper bag blowing across the road momentarily looks like a dog, so you swerve your car.

The basic problem is this: Patterns fundamentally different underneath are often enough alike on the surface so that they lead to confusion and trigger mistakes. For example, youngsters studying science find it difficult to hold onto subtly distinct concepts. Mass and weight are sort of the same: The more mass the object has, the heavier it is on Earth—but only sort of the same: Way out in space a massive object has no weight at all. Density and mass are sort of the same: A dense object has a lot more heft than a less dense object of similar size—but only sort of the same: Density refers to mass per unit volume, so a little chip of that object will have the same density as the whole thing. It's easy to get muddled about the differences between mass and weight, density and mass, or law and justice, privilege and right, or need and desire. Yet effective thinking often depends on making such conceptual distinctions clearly.

Sprawling Thinking

Finally, thinking tends to sprawl simply because, in unusually complex or novel situations, our pattern-driven minds keep recognizing new possible connections and pushing us for a few seconds in the direction of the latest connection. Then another connection from another direction emerges, and we go off in that direction.

Suppose, for example, that you set out to buy the first home you have ever owned. You ponder what features you want: A large yard, you think. But that means more cost: How will you finance it? Yes, financing, that means you have to have a sense of costs. Where can you find out about costs? The newspaper, right here beside you. But wait, do you want to live in close to town or further out? Thus one thought leads to another and yet to another in crazy quilt manner. To generalize, sprawl is an accidental side effect of pattern-driven experiential intelligence in circumstances where experiential intelligence does not have a clean path to follow.

More Evidence: Cognitive Shortcuts

A close-up view of two particular paths of pattern-driven reasoning shows how our pattern machine sometimes gets us into trouble. In the 1970s, psychologists Daniel Kahneman and Amos Tversky identified and investigated a pair of cognitive shortcuts that account for a good deal of faulty reasoning. They called them the *availability heuristic* and the *representativeness heuristic*. For the first, when people make judgments of frequency or likelihood of something, they often do so based on how easy it is to retrieve from memory or imagine something—its availability to their minds—instead of surveying the possibilities more carefully. On the representativeness heuristic, when people categorize something, they often do so based on how well the something fits ideal or stereotypical attributes, neglecting other relevant information.

In their 1980 synthesis, *Human Inference*, Richard Nisbett and Lee Ross profile these and other ways that judgment sometimes falters. They illustrate risks of the availability heuristic as follows:

> An Indiana businessman confides to a friend, "Did you ever notice how many Hoosiers become famous or important? Look anywhere—politics, sports, Hollywood, big business, even notorious bank robbers—I couldn't guess the exact figures, but I bet we Hoosiers have far more than our fair share on just about any list in *Who's Who*."

Sure, the businessman is proud of his home state. But he need not be exaggerating deliberately. He can think of many more famous people who are Hoosiers because he reads the local newspaper, notes in national periodicals when Hoosiers do well, and so on. Hoosiers are more accessible in his memory, creating a cognitive illusion of high frequency. In their book, Nisbett and Ross assemble a mountain of evidence for the distorting effects of the availability and the representativeness heuristics on human judgment, including causal reasoning, the making of predictions, the beliefs and theories that people hold, and more.

How do these cognitive shortcuts shape and sometimes misshape perceptions that matter to us? Recently I came across a case in point that deals with something very central—how we feel about the general state of life. A November 1994 survey from the Massachusetts Mutual Life Insurance Company has many parallels with Nisbett's and Ross's illustration. Reported under a headline entitled "For Most in US, Problems Lie Elsewhere," the survey found that many Americans are profoundly concerned about the state of the nation. They see a systematic collapse in Congress, schools, and neighborhoods—but not their own! They announce their general satisfaction with their own legislator, their children's school, and the safety of the neighborhood where they live.

Why should people be optimists up close but pessimists at a distance? Yes, it may help them to feel better. But there is a plausible interpretation in terms of the availability heuristic. People learn about their immediate circumstances through direct experience and get a certain mix of positive and negative signs. However, they learn about other circumstances through the media, which often filter events for sensational interest. Newspaper articles about serene neighborhoods and solid committed legislators do not compete well for space with those about gang wars and sell-outs. The jaundiced filter of the media may create the very reverse of the maxim that the grass is always greener on the other side of the fence, a world where the grass is always yellower. The double risk is that we end up overcritical of problems far away and overtolerant of problems close to home that we are more likely to be able to do something about.

The availability and representativeness heuristics are part and parcel of the pattern-driven character of perception. When we rely on what we can easily bring to mind (availability) or key attributes (representativeness) to make a quick judgment, we are directly tapping our accumulated library of experiential intelligence, assuming that it reflects accurately the world we navigate through. Usually it does, and we would be foolish not to use such cognitive shortcuts most of the time. But sometimes it does not.

The Intelligence Paradox Affirmed

Instead of resolving the intelligence paradox, all this affirms it. To summarize, we human beings have an elegant system for long-term moderate success: We puzzle things out in novel and complex situations with the help of reflective intelligence and, as we succeed, the results get captured by our mind's pattern machine, becoming part of our experiential intelligence. Our behavior in similar situations in the future becomes better tuned, more fluent, more adaptive—more intelligent in those contexts, in other words.

However, the very success of this system sometimes has a backlash effect on the functioning of reflective intelligence. Reflective intelligence tends to misfire more often than it might exactly because the pattern-recognition system it has fed in the past continues to function exactly as it is supposed to, constantly throwing up patterns that may prompt hasty action, fixate the mind on a narrow pattern, gloss over important differences, or send thinking sprawling through a maze of haphazard connection-making.

Overall, the system works fairly well and overall people function fairly well. However, in the details of its architecture, experiential intelligence coupled with reflective intelligence is somewhat self-limiting. The very effectiveness of the experiential system somewhat undermines the effectiveness of the reflective system.

More Causes of Defaults in Thinking

While the pattern machine of the human mind seems to contribute considerably to default tendencies in thinking, it is certainly not the whole story. Other factors appear to aggravate the slippage toward hasty, narrow, fuzzy, and sprawling thinking. Here are several that deserve consideration.

Ego Defense and Other Passions

My discussion so far has been rather dispassionate, but we are passionate creatures. We invest ourselves in the positions we take, the directions we pursue, the thoughts that we think. These intimate commitments shape and sometimes distort our thinking.

Much of the impact of feelings on thinking falls under the general umbrella of ego defense. Most of us surely seek to defend and overdefend viewpoints about the world that lie close to our conceptions of ourselves and our roles in relation to others. I may well be able to think better about my neighbor's position on an issue that I care little about than I can about my own position on an issue that I care very much about. When my position is at stake, I am more likely to be hasty—after all, I already know what I think, so why think more? I am more likely to be narrow—I do not even *want* to ponder the other side of the case. I am more likely to be fuzzy—my own view seems to fit together nicely, so why should I probe it for confusions and incoherences? But perhaps I am not more likely to be sprawling, because my thinking about the matter is largely a review and elaboration of my invested position, which keeps me from wondering and wandering.

Many particular passions amount to variants of ego investment. Anger, for instance, casts the self as antagonist of some other party perceived as threatening, and sexual love casts the self as partner in an intimate relationship. Thoughtful distance is not likely amidst such storms of feelings.

Nor is this so strange. Anger, love, and other powerful passions are adaptations for survival. They energize us for defense and procreation. Were people dispassionate, especially in rough-and-tumble earlier times, the human race probably would not have made it. Remember, sophisticated thinking is only one survival adaptation, and indeed a latecomer in the pageant of evolution. Other survival systems are at work at the same time, sometimes dominate, and sometimes *should* dominate. When we fight or flee, our anger and fear are feelings part and parcel with the quick boost of adrenalin surging through our bodies. Although many people's lives are less risky today than hundreds of years ago, from time to time we still need that shot of energy more than a quiet period of reflection. As is said of a well-known credit card, so also with our capacity for fear or anger: Don't leave home without it!

All this notwithstanding, passions in general should not be viewed as antagonists of good thinking—it all depends on the passion and indeed the circumstances. Harvard philosopher Israel Scheffler has written eloquently of what he calls the cognitive emotions, feelings that support thinking rather than bumping it off course. He points up such feelings as love of truth, curiosity, and surprise. Because you want to get at the truth, you seek evidence. Because you are curious, you investigate. Because something surprises you, you ask yourself why you expected anything different. Such feelings as these nudge us and sometimes drive us to make better sense of the world and ourselves.

Scheffler's insight is fundamental. Thinking at its best is a passionate, not a dispassionate, enterprise. Thinking involves commitment, intellectual adventuring, sturdy perseverance in the face of obstacles, and so on. It is worth adding that the intensity of feelings figures in the picture as well. Love or anger are not specifically cognitive emotions in Scheffler's sense, because, in contrast with curiosity or love of truth, they do not deal specifically with the challenge of coming to know and understand. However, mild anger or moderate love may often sharpen thinking by keeping us alert and attentive.

The particular effects of particular passions aside, Antonio Damasio in his 1994 *Descartes' Error* makes a systematic case for the role of affect in intelligent behavior. He documents studies of brain damage that show a surprising association between loss of strong affective responses and loss of the ability to make sound decisions. One striking case concerns a man called Elliot who suffered highly localized frontal lobe damage from a brain tumor and the operation that successfully removed it. Remarkably, Elliot emerged from this trauma entirely functional to all immediate appearances—articulate, intelligent, witty, mild-mannered. Nonetheless, two other features of Elliot's condition stood in testimony to his deeply injured state. He had no strong emotional reactions to situations. And he could not keep his life in order. At work, he would spend all day on a minor detail, losing track of the whole, or go off on a tangent altogether. He invested unwisely. He used his time poorly. In innumerable ways, he made poor life decisions.

Investigating Elliot's dilemma, Damasio conducted an elaborate program of cognitive testing. Elliot's mental capacities seemed intact. He scored high on IQ tests and dealt successfully with a whole range of other challenging cognitive tasks. Moreover, he showed no abnormalities on an elaborate test of personality. Yet something was profoundly amiss. Damasio puts it this way:

> I began to think that the cold-bloodedness of Elliot's reasoning prevented him from assigning different values to different options, and made his decision-making landscape hopelessly flat.

Damasio argues from this and several other lines of evidence that synthesizing the factors in play when we make complex decisions crucially involves our affective responses.

In summary, feelings related to ego defense frequently aggravate the default tendencies of human thinking. This granted, we also need to recognize that good thinking is a passionate rather than a bloodless enterprise.

The Cognitive Load Bottleneck

In 1956, the psychologist George Miller published a renowned article entitled "The Magical Number Seven, Plus or Minus Two: Some Limits in Our Capacity for Processing Information." In this article, Miller drew upon a number of results from various investigators to argue for a fundamental limitation in human cognition. When we think, Miller urged, we have to keep track of what we are thinking about in what is usually called short term memory—the kind of memory you use when you look up a number in the phone book and keep it in mind until you finish dialing. Miller noted that short term memory appears to have quite a limited capacity. Adults typically can hold from five to nine pieces of information in mind at a time. For example, it is not difficult to recall a seven-digit number from the phone book as you reach for the telephone, but a ten-digit long-distance number can cause you trouble.

We can ask questions about Miller's thesis: What is a piece of information? Do pieces of information come in different sizes? Is there really a distinction between short-term and long-term memory? The professional journals have thrived, as psychologists have analyzed and experimented. But all agree that Miller identified a fundamental operating characteristic of cognition. Whatever the technicalities of counting and measuring pieces of information, the rough truth holds up that people cannot keep track of very much unfamiliar information at any one time. The number of things that need attention simultaneously is called *cognitive load*. When the cognitive load gets high, pieces of information simply drop out of short-term memory.

The cognitive load bottleneck contributes to some of the defaults of thinking. Narrow thinking is lower in cognitive load: There is less to keep track of. Fuzzy thinking avoids differentiations that otherwise require cognitive capacity. Sprawling thinking occurs in part because, in thinking about complex matters, people simply lose track of where they are through cognitive overload.

Literate cultures incorporate an important partial solution to the cognitive load problem: thinking on paper—or blackboard, computer, anything that can function as a scratchpad. Writing and drawing are usually considered tools of communication, but they are also very much devices for thinking at the moment. By thinking on paper, people can manage far more pieces of information than Miller's seven plus or minus two quite handily.

Unfortunately, although few would attempt intricate arithmetic or algebra without paper and pencil, people surprisingly often try to reason out complicated matters of personal destiny, political choice, family commitment, and so on, in conversations with themselves and others, without ever touching a pencil. They seem not to realize that in juggling a huge array of factors they are dropping several along the way. This inevitably tips thinking toward the defaults. About anything complicated and serious, it's wise to think on paper at least some of the time.

Misguided Beliefs and Strategies

Besides the influences of pattern-driven cognition, ego defense, and the cognitive load bottleneck, something else gives the defaults an unwelcome boost: certain beliefs about and attitudes toward thinking.

For one example, recall the research of Jonathan Baron on argument discussed in the last chapter. Baron discovered that many people view one-sided arguments as better than two-sided arguments. They find in one-sided arguments virtues such as firmness and decisiveness, buying into what I called John Wayne thinking. Such people hold a misconception about the nature and power of reasoning, a belief that promotes narrow thinking.

For a second example, many people believe that sheer repetition is a good way to memorize something. In fact, it is a mediocre method. Much more rapid memorizing comes from any approach that emphasizes finding familiar chunks, identifying patterns, and building associations in what you are memorizing. Why do some people invest in sheer repetition? Probably because it does help some, they have heard correctly and experienced for themselves that it helps, and they have not had a chance to learn about more sophisticated ways of memorizing.

For a third example, many people strongly value quick intuitive thinking over more extended reflective thinking. Popular culture even testifies to the point: I remember a beer commercial from several years back with the slogan, "When it's right, you know it." What was right in this case was supposed to be the taste of the beer, but the general message seemed to be that you know intuitively and automatically when something is right for you. This belief may stem in part from the romantic era in European history that, among other things, romanticized the workings of the mind (see my 1981 book on the nature of creativity, *The Mind's Best Work*). Or it may be connected to people's reluctance to admit that they have to work hard on problems from time to time. Research shows that people sometimes conceal or avoid hard thinking because they think it will be perceived as a sign of lower intelligence. In any case, whatever the causes, the trend to value intuitive over reflective thinking is clear.

Clear, but not so wise. To be sure, intuition certainly has great importance in human cognition. Recall that intuition fundamentally is a consequence of experiential intelligence. After extended experience with a situation, we often internalize its characteristics and develop generally sound sensitivities about what to expect and what to do. Unfortunately, in new areas of experience, we often feel compelling intuitions that are baseless and simply wrong. Also, intuitions grounded in experience can sometimes be wrong because they are too narrow, not respecting changed circumstances.

In summary, intuition is a real and important mode of cognition, but nothing about it protects it from error. Whether one is better off dealing with something intuitively (through the quick mechanisms of experiential intelligence) or reflectively (through deliberation and strategies that also of course call upon experiential intelligence for judgments) is a subtle matter of the right move for the right moment, not subject to a sweeping generalization like "When it's right, you know it."

To these three, it's worth reminding ourselves of one more example: the belief in the neural and genetically fixed character of intelligence. This belief stands in the way of efforts to cultivate reflective intelligence, making of it a Mission Impossible. The first chapters of this book explored that issue at length.

These four examples illustrate a general lesson worth taking to heart: Our thinking occurs against a backdrop of our beliefs about and attitudes toward thinking. Those beliefs and attitudes may support good thinking practices, but often undermine them.

Technical Knowledge Gaps

Suppose I offer to play several rounds of a coin-flipping game with you. You can choose either game A or B. In game A, you get $2.00 no matter whether the coin comes up heads or tails. In game B, you get $10.00 if the coin comes up heads, but you lose $5.00 if the coin comes up tails. Which game would maximize your profits, A or B? In his *The Complete Problem Solver*, Carnegie-Mellon University psychologist John Hayes offers this example as a simple illustration of decision making under conditions of risk.

The question is not easily answered without knowing something about probabilities and how to handle them. The right concept to apply in this case is called expectation value. If an event occurs with a probability p, and the event carries value V, then your average return over many occurrences of that event will be pV, the product of p and V.

Expectations allow figuring out whether to choose game A or B. For game A, your expectation is always $2.00, which you get no matter how the coin falls. For game B, the probability of a head is .5 and the payoff for a head $10.00, so your expectation is $.5 \times \$10.00 = \$5.00$. But what if it comes up tails? The probability of tails is also .5, and the payoff is –$5.00, so your expectation is .5 × –$5.00 = –$2.50. Summing the expectations, $5.00–$2.50 = $2.50, your average gain per round. So you will do better to choose game B by an average of fifty cents per game.

While the two-games scenario is artificial, just such decisions arise from time to time in real-life circumstances. Expectation values have relevance to gambling of any sort. They also figure in insurance rates, personal decisions as to whether to buy certain kinds of insurance, decisions about medical treatments involving various costs and risks, and in other matters.

Expectation values are one example of yet another category of causes for the four defaults—a category that might be called technical knowledge gaps. The point here is simply that some occasions of thinking, even when not located within the technical demands of a particular profession, call for a modicum of technical sophistication about probability, statistics, logic, or related matters. Lack of such knowledge seems to hit the default of fuzzy thinking hardest. For instance, if you do not happen to know about expectation values, you are likely to choose game A versus game B in a fuzzy manner, not well-grounded in the mathematics of probabilities.

Over the past thirty years, a number of psychologists have examined closely the difficulties people experience reasoning with probabilities and statistics. Those difficulties have proved both varied and persistent. Even people who have had instruction in probability and statistics commonly make mistakes. The challenge goes beyond simply not knowing the appropriate computations; people often suffer from persistent but mistaken beliefs about the way probabilities work.

One of the best known of these beliefs is the so-called gambler's fallacy, the idea that the law of averages makes events even out over time. John Hayes offers an apt example of this as well. He notes that a sports commentator emphasized how the Oakland Raiders (as they were called then) had a good chance of winning the Super Bowl game. Why? They had lost several Super Bowl games over the past years. So they were "due." Unfortunately, the law of averages does not work this way. If, for instance, you flip a fair coin and it comes up heads three times in a row, the probability of it coming up heads or tails on the next throw is still 50-50. The law of averages does not imply otherwise for coins, nor does it for the Oakland Raiders either.

Another important area of confusion and misunderstanding concerns sampling—how much of a sample do we need to be confident of a generalization? How much more reliable are larger samples than smaller samples? People often have a poor sense of this and either settle for samples that are far too small or seek a much larger sample than needed. A well-known demonstration of people's fuzzy sense of sample size and its implications comes from one of many studies on such matters by psychologists Amos Tversky and Daniel Kahneman. Boys and girls in general are born with equal frequency. Now suppose that on a particular day 60 percent of the babies born in a hospital were boys. Would this be more likely in a small hospital (fifteen babies born per day) or a large hospital (fifty babies per day)? Subjects in their experiment revealed no preference. In fact, the 60 percent is far more likely in the smaller hospital; chance deviations of a given percentage from the expected average occur much more often in small samples than in large samples.

The perils and pitfalls of reasoning with probabilities go on and on, but there is no reason here to go on and on about them. These few examples suffice to make the general point: There are areas of reasoning we cannot expect to handle well just by living our lives in a thoughtful way. They involve a modicum of technical knowledge. Moreover, for the uninitiated—and even for the initiated but unalert—these areas of reasoning are fraught with misperceptions and misconceptions that can lead to bad judgments.

Hope for a Better Homer

The chapter to this point bears summing up in terms of mindware questions 1 and 3. To take them in reverse order:

MWQ #3. What aspects of intelligence especially need attention? Generalizing over a number of shortfalls in human thinking, there are broad default tendencies toward:

- Hasty thinking
- Narrow thinking
- Fuzzy thinking
- Sprawling thinking

These default tendencies trace back to the mechanisms of intelligent behavior:

MWQ #1. What mechanisms underlie intelligence?

Reflective intelligence, the control system for experiential and neural intelligence, faces several obstacles inherent in experiential intelligence and other aspects of human psychology, namely:

- Most fundamentally, the pattern-driven character of experiential intelligence, which generally serves us well but sometimes makes cognition hasty, narrow, fuzzy, or sprawling. Also . . .
- Ego defense
- The cognitive load bottleneck
- Misguided beliefs and strategies
- Technical knowledge gaps

It becomes clear that the question is not so much *whether* human intelligence works well as *when*. As Jeremy Campbell in his *The Improbable Machine* put it, "A paradox of the worldly brain is that it needs to be as bad as it sometimes is in order to be as good as it usually is."

Most people's minds yield the best results when there is plenty of time, little novelty or need for novelty, no more than normal complexity, and low risk. This is the 90 percent solution of experiential intelligence. Suppose, for example, you learn to play the card game bridge. There is plenty of time and low risk in supportive social settings. At first there is great novelty and complexity, but the game is bounded by its own rules, so you learn to deal with many of the factors that make the game complex, and surprises become rarer. Moreover, even if you do not become a really good player, at least you become a comfortable player, and the risks are still low.

For middle-class human beings, much of life is a cozy game of bridge. Most of us have plenty of time to learn to read, to make friends and get better at making and keeping friends, to get used to most new jobs, and so on. In such situations, reflective intelligence does not have to function marvelously. We fall into the intelligence traps and work our way out of them and life goes on. To be sure, insofar as our reflective intelligence functions better, it helps us to get off to a faster start and keep open to new opportunities. But, insofar as it does not, we become fairly functional over time.

Even if we do not progress as far as we might, the low risk factor saves us from harm. The social dimension is important here. Very often, individuals get protection from making an error because someone else in the situation sees more clearly, or protection from the consequences of an error because someone proves forgiving or repairs the damage. People with greater experiential intelligence—parents, coaches, teachers— deploy it in behalf of their charges, who at one and the same time gain short-term protection and an opportunity to learn. Many of the most notable achievements of human intelligence (although by no means all) enjoy a clearly collective character and muster rigor through formal methods. Earlier in the chapter, I quoted the quip from Nisbett's and Ross's *Human Inference*, "If we're so dumb, how come we made it to the moon?" Here it's apt to quote part of their answer as well:

> Humans did not "make it to the moon" (or unravel the mysteries of the double helix or deduce the existence of quarks) by trusting the availability and representativeness heuristics or by relying on the vagaries of informal data collection and interpretation. On the contrary, these triumphs were achieved by the use of formal research methodology and normative principles of scientific inference. . . . no single person could have solved all the problems involved in such necessarily collective efforts as space exploration. Getting to the moon was a joint project, if not of *idiots savants*, at least of savants whose individual areas of expertise were extremely limited.

All of this is fine as far as it goes. The catch is that often neither we nor the person beside us is an expert. Also, many situations leave us short on time, or continuously pose novelty, or ask us to break out of a rut we are in if only we could see that we are in it, or pose complexities that we would need to stretch to deal with. Sometimes these situations also involve high risk. Recalling again Barbara Tuchman's reflections on history, political crises often present urgent, novel, complicated, and high-risk circumstances. To turn back to the personal level, there are personal trials: facing a tax inspector, breaking up with a spouse or lover, getting fired, seeking a new job, moving to a new town. In such circumstances, not just the so-so but the best functioning of reflective intelligence becomes important. Moreover, such situations are not rare. They are the 10 percent problem left over by the 90 percent solution of experiential intelligence. Some people in this world live in time-pressured, changing, complicated, and risky circumstances much of their lives. All of us face them occasionally.

Besides crises, there are innumerable activities that we need to handle periodically but not often enough to develop expertise. For example, filling out your income tax may be a new problem every time around. The laws change and you also forget from one year to the next. Then there are situations that by design provide constant novelty and increasing complexity. Schooling, for instance, continuously exposes learners to new more advanced information and skills, so reflective intelligence helps students to cope better with the demands of schooling.

In summary, there is little reason to be cavalier about the shortfalls of reflective intelligence as it usually functions. Although the experiential-reflective partnership of human intelligence as a whole works rather well in conducive circumstances, things diverge from this cozy cognitive Eden often enough to warrant concern. Urgent, novel, complex, or risky situations come up and sometimes catch us in that evolutionary double bind—making not-quite-right experiential responses that pre-empt more reflective responses. Into the intelligence traps of hasty, narrow, fuzzy, and sprawling thinking we fall.

For the 10-percent problem left over by the good work of experiential intelligence, people need a 10-percent solution—the solution provided not just by so-so but by really good reflective intelligence that helps us to avoid the four intelligence traps and other hazards of thinking. If better reflective intelligence is a general goal, what about a direct approach? Not to mince words, can one teach mindware? What actually happens when it's tried? To these questions, the next chapter turns.

8

Intelligence Can Be Taught

Bumblebees can't fly. Most of us have heard that classical aerodynamics makes this prediction. The story serves nicely as a warning
about the intellectual autocracy of theory. Since bumblebees do fly,
there is clearly something wrong with the theory.

Now I have no idea whether it's true that classical aerodynamics
implies land-bound bumblebees, but certainly the classic view of intelligence as expounded by Goddard and others says that intelligence can't
be taught. One can argue theory forever around such issues, but it's better simply to look for bumblebees. In fact, here and there in the previous chapters, I reviewed teaching experiments where students had
learned to think better in one or another respect. This chapter is committed not to the occasional bumblebee but a swarm of them.

In 1975, Arthur Whimbey, a psychologist with a background in psychometrics, published a book entitled *Intelligence Can Be Taught*. Whimbey urged the need to rethink in fundamental ways our conceptions of
intelligence, to question assumptions about its genetic determination
and intractable character. Whimbey argued that intelligence could be
taught, not only on principled grounds but on empirical grounds. He
invoked the rule of logic that what is actual is possible. Whimbey maintained that intelligence had been taught, so certainly it could be. The
pages of Whimbey's book are filled with cases in point—interventions

that enhanced the cognitive functioning of preschool children, studies that helped poorly-performing college students to take a more organized and effective approach to their academic work, courses that focused on enhancing performance on IQ tests and succeeded in doing so.

Whimbey emphasized some of the problems of thinking highlighted in the last chapter. In comparing low- and high-aptitude college students, Whimbey noted that the low aptitude students displayed a number of limitations. They showed more interest in right answers than in how one got to an answer. They tended to tackle problematic situations in quick and superficial ways. Reluctant to invest effort and proceed carefully, they often fell prey to trivial errors. In other words, they tended to fall into two of our intelligence traps, the defaults of hasty and fuzzy thinking.

Pursuing the hasty-fuzzy problem, Arthur Whimbey and his colleague, science educator Jack Lochhead, produced a book, *Problem Solving and Comprehension*. Designed for high school and college students, the book focused especially on remedying hasty and fuzzy thinking and encouraged students to develop good mental habits of careful analysis and application of information in reading and problem-solving situations.

In many ways, Whimbey's *Intelligence Can Be Taught* was ahead of its time. In 1975, the interests of cognitive scientists were just beginning to turn toward the cultivation of thinking abilities. Far more researchers take this area seriously today than was the case then. At that time, some of the major programs designed to teach thinking did not even exist, and others were in their early stages with not much in the way of a track record to ponder and interpret.

Whimbey was right: Intelligence can be taught. In particular, what I call reflective intelligence can be cultivated in a variety of ways that mute the destructive effects of the four intelligence traps. In Chapter 4, I began to build this case. I discussed mathematician-educator Alan Schoenfeld's success in teaching mathematical problem solving. I mentioned good results on teaching reading strategies that boost students' understanding. I noted research on college students' learning of if-then, statistical, and methodological reasoning, that showed a double success. Students both advance in the skills most important to their areas of study and carry those skills over to other contexts.

The goal of this chapter is to illustrate the enterprise and give further evidence that it works. I focus on four well-known programs that have existed for a number of years. Each involves a bundle of materials. Each aims at classroom settings, not the only place where one might hope to boost reflective intelligence but an important one. Each has a somewhat different style. Each has undergone formal evaluation and has proven at least somewhat successful in improving learners' thinking.

While these four examples all take the form of separate courses, there is another approach entirely: integrating the teaching of thinking with subject-matter instruction. Often called *infusion* because attention to thinking gets infused into subject-matter instruction, this approach developed much later than the use of separate courses and hence lacks the track record of research. It promises much, however, not only for the teaching of thinking but for enhanced subject-matter learning. Accordingly, a section toward the end of the chapter illustrates some infusion programs.

There are many other approaches than those highlighted here, including some at least as ingenious. For a more thorough review of school-based programs, readers are encouraged to look to *The Teaching of Thinking* by Raymond Nickerson, David Perkins, and Edward Smith, or several other sources listed in the bibliography. Moreover, efforts to cultivate reflective intelligence by no means sit solely inside the walls of schools. A number of books and programs speak to the worlds of business, professional, and everyday life, aiming to foster people's creativity, understanding, decision making, group collaboration, and other kinds of thinking. Examples are as diverse as Peter Senge's well-known *The Fifth Discipline*, which focuses on systems thinking as a tool of management, and Edward de Bono's *Six Thinking Hats*, which highlights six viewpoints that, used in turn, expand creative and critical thinking around an issue. Books and programs appear from time to time for specialized areas like creative writing, medical diagnosis, industrial design, and more.

With such a smorgasbord of possibilities, why do I focus in this chapter on primary and secondary education? Because the aim here is to bring forth evidence, to build a case. Almost all the research about the effectiveness of interventions has occurred in elementary and high school settings. Where the evidence lies, there we will go.

Project Intelligence

The Style

Unabashedly, I begin with one of the programs I have worked on, although only as one among several authors. If you were participating in the Project Intelligence course, at one point you would find yourself sitting in a classroom with your fellow students pondering something very odd in its very ordinariness: a pencil.

"What is there to think about?" you might ask yourself. After all, you have been using pencils all your life.

However, some probing questions would lead you on. For instance, what are the purposes of a pencil? What can you use them for? "Writing," you might answer. "Drawing, shopping lists," and so on. But what about less conventional purposes? This is a little harder, but in a few moments you'd have some answers here as well: "Propping a window open, scratching your back, putting holes in a piece of paper for a three-ring binder when I don't have a paper punch."

Now, what *features* does a pencil have? And *why* those rather than others for the pencil to do its job well? Some answers come easily here too: "The lead makes the mark. The eraser lets the pencil erase." But how about the round shape? "Well, maybe that makes for a more comfortable grip." But some pencils are hexagonal rather than round. Why? "Well, let's see . . . they won't roll on desks so much. They maybe allow a better grip. The flat sides provide better space for advertising."

Through such questions as these, you and your classmates delve deeper and deeper into an analysis of a perfectly ordinary object you would pay no attention to otherwise. You find yourself with a new appreciation of the logic and the ingenuity of an ordinary household pencil *and* of human inventiveness.

Notice that all these questions focus on the pencil as a *design*, something invented to suit purposes (writing, drawing, etc.) and fine-tuned to do so. Not only pencils, or chairs, or automobile tires, but much more abstract things can also be viewed as designs and understood better using the same kinds of questions. In fact, the aim of looking at pencils and other concrete examples is to sensitize you to designs generally. Here is a brief sample of things much less concrete than a pencil. Questions about purpose, features, rationale, and so on, make just as much sense with these as for the pencil.

- Lines at supermarkets and banks, for example, are inventions to deliver orderly service to customers.
- Songs are inventions that give us pleasure, often foster solidarity when we sing them together, honor organizations as with national anthems, and so on.

- Scientific theories are inventions to deliver explanations about puzzling phenomena.
- A library is an invention for sharing access to a large reservoir of books.
- A librarian is a role invented to help with the orderly running of libraries.
- Forms of government are inventions that take different approaches to organizing society, protecting people's welfare, and indeed sometimes taking advantage of people on a large scale.

Analyzing designs with key questions is only part of the story. Later on, you find yourself not just analyzing but designing things yourself. For instance, you are asked to retrieve a ring lost down a drain. What kind of gadget could you design to help? Following a strategy, you generate several different approaches to the problem, then selecting the approach that seems most promising. Then you elaborate its details. What would you make the gadget out of? How much material would you need? What weak points might it have and how could you fix them?

All this is about inventive thinking, the component of Project Intelligence I worked on. Lessons from different units of Project Intelligence would bring you problems of quite a different sort. For example, you might find yourself puzzling over cartoon aliens from another world. Certain aliens are Bebenians and others are Tisars. But they look rather alike. By inspecting the aliens carefully, can you determine what the key features of Bebenians versus Tisars are? Still another unit asks you to reason about problems demanding deduction. Still another introduces a systematic strategy for making decisions, considering the factors that apply and evaluating each option in terms of each factor.

The Philosophy

Project Intelligence emerged from a remarkable national commitment made by the government of Venezuela for six years commencing in 1978. Luis Alberto Machado, a thoughtful politician with a long-time commitment to educational and intellectual development, was appointed Minister of State for the Development of Intelligence. Minister Machado searched around the world for programs that might be implemented on a smaller or larger scale in Venezuela, to enhance the cognitive development of people from birth through adulthood.

Two of the other programs reviewed in this chapter were brought to Venezuela, although they were developed elsewhere: Edward de Bono's CoRT program and Reuven Feuerstein's Instrumental Enrichment. Indeed, CoRT was implemented in some version throughout most of Venezuelan primary education. However, seeing the need for an absolutely up-to-date program, the government of Venezuela commissioned a team of researcher-developers from Harvard University and the Cambridge, Massachusetts, consulting firm of Bolt, Beranek, and Newman to develop a course to teach thinking.

The resulting "Project Intelligence" produced the Project Intelligence course, called, in its English version, *Odyssey*. I was one of several authors of Project Intelligence, responsible with my colleague Catalina Laserna for the unit on creative thinking. The opening example, about the pencil, comes from that unit. Development of the course was directed by Raymond Nickerson of Bolt, Beranek, and Newman, and Richard Herrnstein of Harvard University.

The philosophy behind Project Intelligence was eclectic. We recognized that thinking involved many facets. A course to teach thinking should develop students' abilities in a variety of areas. Strategies were important—for example, strategies for problem solving, decision making, or creative thinking. But spirit was important too. Learners needed a zest for thinking, an analytical but an adventurous spirit.

As a matter of design, the developers sought not to put all their eggs in one basket. Each lesson would be of value in itself. If some lessons failed, others independent of them would succeed and students would still gain.

The development team also viewed certain skills of categorization and classification as fundamental (although there was some controversy on this point). They would be introduced first, with other skills focusing on more "practical" activities such as decision making, problem solving, and creativity to follow.

The Design

The Project Intelligence course, or *Odyssey*, consists of six units of instruction comprising about one hundred lessons in all. Although the lessons were originally written for seventh grade students in Venezuela, they can be used with minimal adaptation with somewhat younger and older students quite readily. Here are the topics of the units:

1. *Foundations of Reasoning,* including observation, classification, ordering, analogies, and spatial reasoning.
2. *Understanding Language,* including attention to word relations, the structure of language, and reading for meaning.
3. *Verbal Reasoning,* addressing assertions and arguments. (It must be noted that this unit was never carried into its final form, for a variety of reasons.)
4. *Problem Solving,* emphasizing various kinds of representations, mental simulation, trial and error, and inference as ways of solving problems.
5. *Decision Making,* introducing a systematic approach to gathering and evaluating information in order to make a careful decision.
6. *Inventive Thinking,* highlighting the concept of design as a way of developing students' awareness of the inventions all around them and introducing strategies for creative design.

The Project Intelligence lessons themselves are rather carefully scripted. Dialogues between teacher and student are illustrated in detail, not to put words in teachers' mouths but to offer a model of what teacher-student interactions might sound like. Generally, the lessons introduce or provide further elaboration and practice on a strategy for dealing with the type of problem of concern—hierarchical classification, decision making, inventive design, and others. The lessons make room for abundant practice, including exercises at the end for the students to undertake individually or in small groups, along with suggested responses to help the teacher to support and evaluate the students' work.

The materials themselves include a teachers' guide with the scripted lessons as discussed above; and workbooks for each student. The workbooks support the presentation of Project Intelligence ideas by the teacher and provide the exercises. Across its units and lessons, Project Intelligence deals with all the thinking defaults. The emphasis is always on thoughtful extended analysis and exploration, contrary to the human leaning toward hasty thinking. The units on inventive thinking and decision making particularly honor looking beyond the obvious to seek the unusual approach, a matter of broadening beyond narrow thinking. The Foundations of Reasoning unit as well as lessons from various points in Project Intelligence focus on careful systematic thinking and the marshalling of evidence to verify tentative solutions. Finally, Project Intelligence offers several overarching strategies, for instance for decision making and for inventive thinking, that help to organize thinking and avoid sprawl.

The Success

Project Intelligence was evaluated during the academic year 1982/83 in a large-scale experiment in the Venezuelan city Barquisimeto. The implementation taught about one-half of the Project Intelligence lessons, including some from each unit. The Venezuelan school year and the time available for the lessons did not permit a more thorough implementation. It was suggested that Project Intelligence in its full form might be used over two years. The course was taught in three Barquisimeto schools, involving twelve classes and more than 450 students. Control groups of students were identified in other seventh-grade classes in other Barquisimeto schools.

The assessment was one of the most elaborate ever conducted in the teaching of thinking. Before and after instruction, the treatment and control students received several tests of general academic aptitude. In addition, "target abilities tests" probed whether the students learned the specific thinking processes fostered by the six units. On top of that, the students were asked to undertake a brief open-ended design task, to gauge whether the Inventive Thinking unit had enhanced their inventive design abilities (the target abilities test for the Inventive Thinking unit was more knowledge oriented than performance oriented); and to write their reasoning about a simple issue, to test for transfer to everyday reasoning.

On most measures, the Project Intelligence group outperformed the control group. While some gains would be expected as a result of maturation and a year of schooling, the Project Intelligence students displayed markedly greater gains than their control-group peers. The edge for the Project Intelligence group was real but modest on the general academic aptitude tests. In terms of IQ, it corresponded to from 2 to 7 points. The Project Intelligence students showed a substantially greater advantage on the target abilities tests: They learned the thinking processes that the course taught.

Of special interest to me were the open-ended design task, because it tested inventive thinking in a more meaningful way than the target abilities test; and the everyday reasoning task, because everyday reasoning had not been directly addressed by the Project Intelligence materials. On the open-ended design task, the Project Intelligence students performed far better than the control group students. The students were asked to design a table for a very small room. The Project Intelligence students included twice as many features in their tables to cope with the small size of the room; they specified far more detail in elaborating their designs; and in several other ways showed superior performance.

On the everyday reasoning task, the Project Intelligence students offered about 25 percent more reasons for their positions on the given issue than did the control group students. Although the more elaborate reasoning was gratifying, it is also important to say that neither control nor Project Intelligence students offered very sophisticated arguments on the issue.

Regrettably, a change of the political party in power in Venezuela led to less active government interest in the development and testing of such programs. They remain available in Venezuela on an elective basis and are used here and there. However, no follow-up information is available concerning the students who participated in the Project Intelligence course or in other interventions from that era. Besides follow-up information, the Project Intelligence analysis lacks any examination of transfer to school performance. We do not know whether the intervention enhanced the academic performance of the participants during the test year or after. Despite these gaps in the picture, over a wide range of intellectual performances, the Project Intelligence students showed an edge. Intelligence can be taught by Project Intelligence.

Reuven Feuerstein's Instrumental Enrichment

The Style

If you were studying the first "instrument" of Reuven Feuerstein's Instrumental Enrichment program, you might encounter a problem something like that shown in the following figure. Someone sitting beside you to help would ask a strange question: "What do you think that you are supposed to do?"

You do not have great difficulty getting ideas. "Probably," you might say, "I'm supposed to look for where the shapes on the left occur in the patterns of dots on the right." And you give it a try.

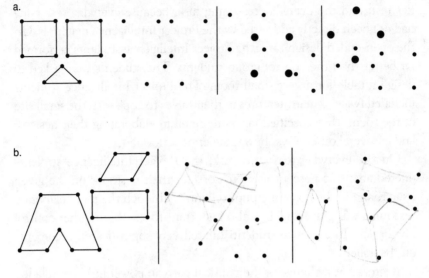

Illustrative tasks from Instrumental Enrichment.

Yes, it turns out that the shapes *can* be found among the dots. Example (a) even offers clues about where to look in the form of the larger dots. These probably helped you to figure out what the task demanded in the first place. With the help of the person sitting beside you asking questions, you gradually sort out more rules of the game. You should look for the figures among the dots. Figures must be the same size, although they may occur in rotations. You cannot use the same dot for two different figures.

"Easy enough," you think. But is it? As you progress through a number of these, the puzzles become more difficult. Example (b), for instance, does without the enlarged dots and includes the complex shape on the lower left, one not so easily sought among the scattered dots.

Along the way through this series of puzzles, you find yourself in the midst of some unusual interactions with the person sitting beside you. He or she might prompt you to explain your strategies: "What is your plan now? How well did it work out?" The person might support your concentration: "Let's keep at it. We're almost ready to go on to the next problem." The person might even explain a concept like strategy, to help you understand what you are doing: "A strategy is your *plan* for how to find the dots—or how to do anything else."

The Philosophy

Reuven Feuerstein is an Israeli psychologist-educator drawn into the problems of teaching intelligence by circumstances surrounding the founding of the state of Israel. After World War II, Israel saw massive immigration, including large numbers of adolescents from impoverished and socially sparse surroundings. Many of these children seemed to be retarded: Certainly they scored three to six years beneath their age norms on standardized tests of intelligence. But Feuerstein was skeptical—how could so large a population exhibit retardation? Experimenting with some of these youngsters, Feuerstein became convinced that their shortfalls reflected lack of cognitive skill rather than genuine retardation. He came to call such people retarded *performers*, people who performed in a retarded manner but often had ample potential for learning and thinking.

For such individuals—and indeed for a wider range of people including ones genuinely organically retarded—Feuerstein developed a program called Instrumental Enrichment. Several points sum up the philosophy of this program.

First of all, Feuerstein emphasized that learning should be thought of as a *mediated* process. People characteristically do not learn alone, but with the help of someone standing by and supporting the struggle with the task at hand, perhaps a parent, a teacher, an older sibling. Beyond providing moral support, good mediators offer crucial cognitive guidance, directing the learner's attention to important features, posing questions, suggesting what to attend to next, and so on. Such actions often make a dramatic difference in the complexity of the task a learner can attempt and the learner's success with it. Feuerstein urged that the role of a mediator is crucial in learning, especially in learning complex cognitive skills. Indeed, the retarded adolescents that originally stimulated his quest were deprived by circumstances of the kinds of mediated learning experiences that would have helped them to develop normally.

Second, Feuerstein analyzed the kinds of deficits he saw into a number of cognitive processes, falling under three broad categories: information input, elaboration, and output. For instance, under input he noted problems of blurred and sweeping perception and impulsive behavior; under elaboration, difficulty in sifting relevant from irrelevant information and lack of systematic strategies for hypothesis testing; under output, *egocentric* communications (a technical term for not taking into account others' prior knowledge) and trial-and-error behavior. Feuerstein sought an approach that could build up learners' strengths in these fundamental areas.

Third, Feuerstein viewed with skepticism efforts to enhance retarded performers' cognitive abilities through regular subject-matter instruction. After all, these were youngsters who often did not think well of themselves as learners and who had developed negative attitudes about school subject matters. Also, they typically had scant general knowledge and skills; school instruction often assumes a considerable background. Better, Feuerstein reasoned, to develop learning experiences that have a very general abstract character and demand very little in the way of prior knowledge.

Fourth, Feuerstein conceived students' difficulties as attitudinal as much as cognitive. He wished not only to equip students with better cognitive skills but to instill in them positive, proactive attitudes toward thinking and learning and self-reliance as thinkers and learners.

The Design

Over the years, Reuven Feuerstein developed his inquiries into a program to advance learners' cognitive functioning. The program itself consists of fifteen units, or instruments as Feuerstein calls them, each including several paper and pencil exercises addressing one or more deficient cognitive functions. The dots examples were drawn from one of these units, called, appropriately, Organization of Dots. While this instrument has a particularly abstract visual character, some of the instruments connect more to everyday knowledge and situations, for example, thinking about time, speed, and distance relationships, or compass directions. Even so, Feuerstein took care to keep dependence on extensive prior knowledge low.

Key to the instruction is the mediator. In a typical Feuerstein setting, the mediator works with one learner or with groups small enough to allow careful discussion and some individual attention. In the case of a single learner, the mediator sits with the learner and directs the learner's attention to the next problem. The mediator asks what the learner thinks he or she should do, prompts the learner to ponder what strategy to use, asks how the learner knows a possible answer is right or wrong, draws the learner's attention to inconsistencies, encourages the learner to check.

In other words, the mediator provides the mediated learning experience so important to Feuerstein's theory. Not just mental calisthenics, the exercises basically are occasions for the learner to face complex, cognitively demanding tasks with the help of mediation. The learner learns not just by working the tasks but from the mediator's questions and prompts. Over time, the learner internalizes those questions and prompts—that is, forms a mental habit of attending to them—and becomes more self-mediating.

Another responsibility of the mediator is *bridging*, helping the student to carry over ideas from the exercises to more applied contexts, for example school studies. The mediator aids the student in making such connections and encourages the student to follow through on them. A mediator might for instance ask students what difficulties they had with arithmetic problems, ask how those difficulties are like and unlike those that students experience with the Feuerstein puzzles, ask whether any of the same strategies apply—which of course they do—encourage students to work arithmetic problems deliberately and strategically, just as they have with the Feuerstein tasks, and so on.

Mediating a learner's approach to a typical task from Instrumental Enrichment benefits from specific knowledge of the program. However, it's worth emphasizing that the general idea of mediation and its basic style can apply to almost any learning situation. When you sit with a son or daughter over a puzzling algebra problem, ask what the problem is, notice that the answer you get leaves out something, point to that something in the problem statement and ask how it fits in, get an answer that doesn't quite make sense, ask about the particular point that doesn't quite make sense, and so on, you are mediating. If in contrast you simply tell your son or daughter how to work the problem, you are not. The art of mediation consists in good part of providing just enough help, usually in the form of questions, to keep the learner moving on the problem without solving the problem for the learner.

Recalling the thinking defaults of hasty, narrow, fuzzy, and sprawling thinking, it is easy to see that Instrumental Enrichment addresses them all to some extent. A specific responsibility of the mediator is to press students to stop and think: no hasty responding allowed here! Over time, students take this to heart and form habits of proceeding deliberately by themselves. Also, the mediator puts great emphasis on eliminating sprawl, sticking to the task, and approaching it in systematic ways. Again, in time students begin to internalize these habits of mind.

The mediator presses for clarity and precision: *Why* do you think that answer is correct? What's the difference between this answer and that possible answer? Pursued persistently as a matter of habit by students, such queries work against fuzzy thinking. Finally, the mediator may sometimes encourage different views of the matter: What other approaches might you take? By and large, however, Instrumental Enrichment places great stress on systematic and convergent thinking and not so much on imagination and divergent thinking.

The Success

Instrumental Enrichment has been available for some time. It has been used with a diversity of populations including individuals deprived by circumstance of mediated learning experiences (as with the Israeli immigrants) but otherwise normal; the educable retarded, such as Down's syndrome children; and normal and gifted students. Although the program may well benefit normal and gifted students, it was not particularly designed for them, nor does Feuerstein himself advance claims about the program's appropriateness for such populations. So here the focus falls on the program's track record with slow learners.

One study conducted in Israel compared treatment groups of slow learners receiving two years of Instrumental Enrichment with others receiving a general enrichment program. Students benefitted more from Instrumental Enrichment. A variety of measures assessed the impact of the two approaches, including tests of general intellectual aptitude and of interpersonal conduct, self-sufficiency, and adaptation to work demands. Not always, but on several tests, the Instrumental Enrichment students showed an advantage. Also, two years later a number of the students from both approaches entered into the Israeli army, automatically receiving at that time the Army intelligence test. The Instrumental Enrichment students scored approximately normal and several points higher than the students who had received the other treatment. This demonstrates persistence of impact after two years.

Feuerstein and his colleagues also proposed a hypothesis of divergent effects. By this they meant that Instrumental Enrichment would help students to learn to learn. As better learners, students of the Instrumental Enrichment program would continue to widen the gap between themselves and others as time went on. Some evidence for this hypothesis was found in the above study.

A variety of other studies have shown that Instrumental Enrichment often yields a significant, although not large, impact on conventional intelligence-measuring instruments, especially on visually oriented sub-tests. Sometimes an impact has not been found on school performance, but sometimes it has. As mentioned earlier, Instrumental Enrichment often has been used with ordinary students rather than slow learners. A case in point is a 1991 study of an implementation in a school setting conducted by Nigel Blagg. Improvements in classroom behavior resulted but not in academic performance or on standardized tests; it's noted however that the time with Instrumental Enrichment was only about half what Feuerstein might have hoped for.

Certainly much depends on the thoroughness of the treatment, the quality of the mediation (which is quite an art and requires special training), and attention to bridging from the instruments to other applications (an aspect of the program often neglected). The evidence for effectiveness appears best for slow learners, the original target population. It is reasonable to conclude that Instrumental Enrichment in full and careful implementations can have a significant and worthwhile impact on the cognitive functioning of slow learners. Intelligence can be taught by Instrumental Enrichment.

Edward de Bono's CoRT

The Style

Imagine you were taking a course of instruction in thinking developed by the British thinking skills expert Edward de Bono. Called CoRT, an acronym for an organization named the Cognitive Research Trust founded by de Bono, the course might present you with this deliberately bizarre proposition:

All cars should be painted bright yellow.

That's not just taxicabs, but literally all cars. What do you think of this idea? Chances are you would have a gut reaction: "What a stupid idea!" And maybe you would be right. However, the CoRT program encourages you not to be so hasty. At least, CoRT says, let us ponder crazy ideas, push them around for a while, and discover what might be made of them.

CoRT recommends that you apply thinking operations to this idea. A likely candidate might be one of the best-known CoRT operations, a PMI. Like the name of CoRT itself, and like most of the other CoRT operations, PMI is an acronym. It stands for "Plus, Minus, and Interesting" points about the proposition at hand. Doing a PMI means trying to list out such points.

In the case of painting all cars bright yellow, negative points probably come to mind most readily. It's easy to recognize, for instance, that yellow cars might get boring; you would have a hard time finding your car in a parking lot; people who did not like the color yellow would be disappointed; dirt would show more; people might miss the individuality of their cars.

However, one of the points of a PMI is to push the reasoner beyond first reactions, whether positive or negative. Turning to the Plus side of a PMI, you might surprise yourself by discovering a number of advantages to the "all cars yellow" scheme. For example: The price of yellow paint would go down; cars might be easier to see at night; you would have less to decide about in choosing a car; cities might look neater, with those rows of trim yellow vehicles; car washes would benefit, as drivers sought to keep their yellow cars clean.

While any notion has its positive and negative sides, there are also just plain *interesting* features that invite further inquiry. Under *Interesting,* one might list this for the yellow cars: Would manufacturers develop different shades of yellow to satisfy customers' hunger for individuality? What strategies would people figure out to find their cars in parking lots—perhaps personal flags hung on the antennae? Would body styles become more distinct and baroque to make up for the uniformity of color? Would the experiment with cars inspire other similar experiments; for instance, what if all left shoes were colored red, all right shoes green?

Especially if you applied your PMI to the idea of yellow cars in a group, you would be startled by the number of positive, negative, and interesting ideas harvested from the participants. At the end of it all, you might still feel that painting all cars yellow was not a very good idea. But you would also realize that it was not as bad an idea as it first seemed. You would recognize that ideas have a hidden complexity: multiple positive, negative, and interesting features that demand exploration for a good understanding and a good assessment.

The Philosophy

Edward de Bono came to the teaching of thinking not from a psychological background (in fact, he holds a medical degree) but out of interest in thinking in the worlds of business and education. De Bono argues that natural thinking typically falls into ruts. To bump our minds out of these ruts, we need thinking tools to redirect our thinking into more fruitful paths. While spending much of his time consulting for the business world, de Bono has committed a significant portion of his career to the development and dissemination of CoRT and other programs.

Part of the aim of CoRT, de Bono explains, is to equip people with appropriate tools. But another side of CoRT is to encourage people to think of themselves as thinkers—as people ready and able to think more imaginatively and analytically about any situation. In CoRT and in his other work, de Bono seeks not just to build strategic repertoire but to cultivate a change in mindset.

In designing for the practical teaching of thinking, Edward de Bono repeatedly emphasizes the importance of robust materials that can be put into place easily. This certainly is one of the features of the CoRT program. Its mnemonics such as PMI and its well-articulated lessons support a relatively straightforward implementation.

De Bono also declares that his primary concern is improving thinking not in academic contexts but in practical everyday life. CoRT may or may not affect academic performance, he says. However, it should improve everyday decision making, opportunity finding, problem solving, and so on.

The Design

The CoRT program includes six units, each comprising about 10 lessons. The units have different foci. Unit I, called *Breadth*, emphasizes stretching the mind to find aspects of a situation likely to be neglected. For example, Unit I includes PMI, which urges evenhanded attention to positive, negative, and interesting features of a situation. It also includes CAF (Consider All Factors), which encourages casting a wide net for the many sorts of factors that might figure in a situation; and OPV (Other Points of View), which asks thinkers to consider points of view on the matter other than their own.

To mention some other units, CoRT II is called *Organization*. In some contrast to CoRT I, its aim is to help the thinker direct attention in a systematic and focused way to the topic at hand. CoRT III, *Interaction*, deals largely with evidence and argument. CoRT IV, *Creativity*, emphasizes generating and sifting ideas.

The CoRT lessons require about half an hour to teach. Many of the lessons introduce operations, such as PMI. Others consolidate them and knit them together. Unit I should be taught first, de Bono avers, but the others can be taught in any order. In practice, many applications of CoRT *only* use CoRT I and sometimes a little more. It is very rare that CoRT is taught through from beginning to end.

As even this brief description shows, CoRT fairly transparently addresses the thinking defaults identified in the previous chapter: hasty, narrow, fuzzy, and sprawling thinking. By providing and encouraging the use of operations, CoRT works against hasty thinking. Because many of the operations broaden thinking, CoRT helps with the problem of narrow thinking. Indeed, this is probably its forte. Because some operations deal with ordering and prioritizing, CoRT helps to some extent with fuzzy thinking. Because some operations and other features help students to organize their thinking better, CoRT addresses sprawling thinking.

Of course, this does not mean that CoRT is a comprehensive program, any more than any other single program is likely to be. The four intelligence traps are vast; they make room for all kinds of mishaps and a diversity of sorts of thinking. Nonetheless, CoRT plainly touches on all four.

The Success

There is considerable evidence of the success of CoRT, although some of it not as deep as one would like. De Bono himself reports several informal experiments that show that certain of the CoRT operations have an immediate positive impact. For example, they do broaden thinking, leading people to consider many more pros and cons and other facets of situations. As a result, the CoRT operations lead people to see situations in more balanced, less shoot-from-the-hip ways.

In the years 1979–1983, a version of CoRT was implemented in a large number of school systems in Venezuela for ten, eleven, and twelve year olds. As part of this work, a sizable number of children took pretests and posttests designed to gauge the impact of the program. The tests involved characteristically de Bono-like tasks, such as the yellow cars situation. Analysis of results revealed that the youngsters performed much better than control students who had not received the program. They generated far more ideas and expressed those ideas in more complex and abstract ways. However, this study did not probe whether CoRT improved students' academic performance nor whether students took the CoRT tools to heart and put them to use in their personal lives. Many anecdotes testify to the latter, arguing that the personal-life connection worked for some students. However, whether it did for most is hard to say.

The deepest and most thorough investigations of CoRT have been conducted by the Australian psychologist John Edwards and his colleague Richard Baldauf. Edwards and Baldauf examined the impact of the first unit of CoRT (ten lessons) on students' general intellectual performance and on school performance specifically. They found that CoRT can have a modest impact on scores on IQ tests. It can also have some impact on performance in school subject matters. One study revealed gains in science performance but not in social studies, whereas the CoRT operations and general spirit appear to suit social studies more straightforwardly than science. A later study confirmed an impact on IQ, fluency, and originality on the Torrance Tests of Creative Thinking, and this time on achievement in language arts and social science but not science and mathematics.

In summary, it is reasonable to conclude that CoRT has considerable impact on thinking about the kinds of imaginative *or* common-sense situations highlighted in the CoRT materials, at least when children think to deploy the CoRT tools. Also, there can be some impact on general measures of intelligence and on school performance. As is often the case with educational evaluations, little information is available on whether CoRT effects persist or are soon forgotten by learners and on the extent to which learners carry CoRT into their personal lives, anecdotes aside. Nonetheless, CoRT is straightforward, ingenious, and quite easy to apply. Intelligence can be taught by CoRT.

Matthew Lipman's Philosophy for Children

The Style

You are a sixth grader encountering for the first time a program called Philosophy for Children. Not so clear about what philosophy is anyhow, you find yourself of all things reading a novel. *Harry Stottlemeier's Discovery*, it's called. "Discovery?" you ask yourself. "What could the discovery be? . . . aliens from Mars, a cure for cancer, a drug cache?"

Harry Stottlemeier's discovery turns out to be something of an entirely unexpected kind: an idea. Inattentive during class one day, Harry gets called on by the teacher, who wants to know what has a long tail and revolves around the sun every 77 years. Harry has no idea. But he answers "a planet." After all, he knows that planets revolve around the sun, and this thing revolves around the sun. So this thing should be a planet.

The class laughs. The answer, of course, is Halley's comet. The lesson is over and all disperse. But Harry is puzzled. How come his reasoning didn't work? And then he has an idea:

> A sentence can't be reversed. If you put the last part of a sentence first, it'll no longer be true. For example, take the sentence 'All oaks are trees.' If you turn it around, it becomes 'All trees are oaks.' But that's false.

Now Harry understands why he messed up on the comet question: All planets rotate around the sun, but not all things that rotate around the sun are planets. Harry goes on to realize that sometimes sentences can be reversed, to apply his discoveries in other contexts, and to investigate thinking in other ways.

A novel about reasoning! Of course, you admit to yourself, it's not all *that* interesting. But still . . .

And then you find that the *real* action rotates around the class discussion, just as Halley's comet and planets rotate around the sun. The teacher keeps bringing up these puzzles. What is it to make a discovery, anyway? What's the difference between discovery and invention? This idea of Harry's is a principle of logic, so what are such principles like and what are they good for? And so on. The teacher presses everyone to participate, listen to, and respect one another's ideas. And give *reasons*. Really makes you think!

The Philosophy

The philosophy of Philosophy for Children finds its inspiration from as far back as Socrates and as recently as a straightforward observation about children. Matthew Lipman argues that human beings have been thinking for hundreds of thousands of years. But, with the Greek philosophers, people began thinking *about thinking*. No other discipline, Lipman urges, incarnates as much of a rich tradition in thinking about thinking as philosophy.

Philosophy, yes . . . but for children? Here, Lipman makes an observation crucial to the style of his program. Youngsters, he avers, are naturally interested in philosophical questions. Much of the playful language of children is essentially philosophical in nature, although whimsical and passing, rather than pursued with vigor and depth. Children play on concepts and words all the time, and ask vexing questions like "How high is up." They notice that you can keep asking "why" and wonder how far back one can push back the "why" of something. Forever? And how could it possibly stop?

With these points in mind, Lipman finds the teaching of philosophy to children a peerless approach to cultivating youngsters' minds. In philosophical discussion organized around a rich source (*Harry Stottlemeier's Discovery* was written to be such a source), students can pursue a large number of aspirations related to better thinking: more attention to logic and the rules of logic, readier exploration of alternatives and other points of view, ways of inspecting and testing the truth of claims, valuing of open-mindedness and other points of view, and much more. At the same time, students can be led through discussion toward a deeper understanding of key concepts: law, morals, discovery, science, and so on.

Lipman contrasts Philosophy for Children with other typical approaches to the teaching of thinking. Philosophy for Children does not attempt to teach thinking strategies point blank, as many programs do. Rather, the teacher and the books involve children in systematic thinking about thinking—and about other things. In the course of this, some explicit strategies and criteria (such as Harry's discovery) emerge. Philosophy for Children also does not attempt to integrate the teaching of thinking into other subject matters, such as science or literature. Rather, it has its *own* subject matter, philosophy, ideally suited to the enterprise.

The Design

Philosophy for Children is taught as a separate course, during its own class period. The first course Lipman developed, designed for fifth and sixth grade, focuses on the previously mentioned book *Harry Stottlemeier's Discovery*, a ninety-page book including a number of brief chapters each easily read in a few minutes. The book recounts Harry's intellectual and social adventures in quite ordinary circumstances, with a good deal of social interaction among Harry, parents, and other students and friends. There are moments of excitement and woe. In the course of the story, matters not only of logic but of other sides of thinking come up explicitly or implicitly.

The teacher works from a teacher's manual that offers a number of questions to use with each chapter of the book. The teaching style emphasizes group conversation almost entirely, focusing on the questions and fostering a community of inquiry. The teacher's role is to stimulate and manage the discussions, rather like Socrates. The teacher poses puzzles or draws them from youngsters, calls for reasons, seeks other points of view, and in general pushes the discussion further and deeper. The discussion process leads students to advance arguments and evidence, formulate distinctions, search for alternative ideas, and so on.

Each chapter brings forward several leading ideas and through the vignettes it offers creates an occasion for discussing them. Some of the ideas get focal attention in the novel, while others come up in a more secondary or tacit way. Here are some of the leading ideas from *Harry Stottlemeier's Discovery*.

The process of inquiry • Figuring things out • Styles of thinking • Contradiction • Causes and effects • Discovery and invention • Inductive reasoning • What is a generalization? • What is a possibility? • Explanations, descriptions

---

Harry Stottlemeier's Discovery is a single element in one of the most elaborately developed programs available for cultivating thinking. A number of other books and courses extend the program in several directions. For example, *Lisa: Reasoning in Ethics* suits grades seven to nine. *Elsie*, for grades K through two, focuses on making distinctions. *Pixie*, for grades three and four, concerns reasoning in language. Like *Harry Stottlemeier*, these other books provide narrative settings in which philosophical issues and ideas arise explicitly and implicitly, in ways suited to the focus of the course—ethics, science, social studies, or something else. As with *Harry Stottlemeier*, a teacher's guide helps the teacher to organize discussion around the chapters of the books.

Plainly, *Harry Stottlemeier* and the other components of Philosophy for Children address the thinking defaults identified in the previous chapter. Philosophy for Children lays great emphasis on reflectiveness, discouraging hasty thinking. The traditional philosophical concern with precision in the making of distinctions and the formulation of issues speaks to the problem of fuzzy thinking. Attention to fairness, the generating of options, and consideration of diverse points of view addresses narrow thinking. General ways of keeping the discussion on track speak to sprawling thinking, although this is perhaps the default least treated.

The Success

Several investigators have looked at the impact of the Philosophy for Children program, usually focusing on *Harry Stottlemeier's Discovery*. In general, gains have been found on various tests of reasoning and on reading scores.

One of the most elaborate studies was conducted by the well-known Educational Testing Service of Princeton, New Jersey. It involved a two-year experiment with some 200 students in the Philosophy for Children program and 200 in a control group. The investigators tested for several different kinds of impact:

1. Significant improvement in any or all of the three areas of reasoning treated in the Philosophy for Children program:
   a. drawing formal inferences and identifying fallacies
   b. discovering alternatives and possibilities
   c. providing reasons and explanations
2. Significant improvement in ideational fluency or productivity
3. Significant improvement in academic readiness as measured by teacher assessments
4. Significant improvement in basic skill (reading and mathematics) performance

The findings were positive on all these fronts. Of course, improvement could be expected in the control students on such measures simply as a result of maturation and two years of schooling. However, the Philosophy for Children students showed significantly greater gains than the other youngsters. The positive findings on the reading and mathematics measures demonstrated transfer of learning, since these subject matters were not directly addressed in the Philosophy for Children Program itself. Intelligence can be taught by Philosophy for Children.

Teaching Content and Thinking Together

All the interventions discussed so far take the form of separate courses. Students gather regularly for a focused period of instruction on thinking. This was the natural option for a first wave of efforts to cultivate students' intelligence. To tune up students' writing skills, we teach courses in writing. To orient students to the physical world, we teach courses in geography. Courses in thinking make the same kind of sense.

However, in recent years a different approach has emerged, combining the teaching of content with the teaching of thinking. The idea is that instruction in the subject matters offers ample opportunity to introduce important thinking practices as well. Teaching the subject matters in a thoughtful way is only one step in that direction. Research suggests that instruction needs to give thinking as well as content point-blank attention in order to advance students' reflective intelligence.

In fact, exponents of this approach see a natural partnership between subject-matter instruction and the teaching of thinking. On the one hand, studies tell us that in most classrooms students learn content in a rather rote and routine way. More emphasis on thinking with and through the content being learned would ensure better retention, understanding, and active use of subject-matter knowledge, as argued in my recent *Smart Schools*. On the other hand, the learning of better thinking practices benefits from diverse concrete contexts—for instance, the several subject matters. So instruction in the subject matters and the teaching of thinking make a good marriage, each benefitting the other.

Sometimes this approach is called *infusion*—infusing the teaching of thinking into subject-matter learning. Ideally, I would describe several infusion approaches in this chapter in the same style as the separate courses profiled earlier. However, there is a data gap to be acknowledged. Much more recent than any of the programs discussed here, the infusion approach has not yet received the sustained attention of researchers conducting formal studies of impact. So instead of the full treatment, I will spend one section exploring the character of the infusion approach, one of great promise despite the current lack of data. This has been an area of special interest for me and my colleagues for several years—although not to the exclusion of separate courses—so I will draw first upon our work from the programs *The Thinking Classroom, Thinking Connections,* and *Knowledge as Design.*

Frost's Meaning

One challenge of bringing thinking and subject-matter instruction together is convey a sense of the styles of thinking indigenous to different disciplines. For example, every discipline has its own way of grounding claims in evidence. In literary studies, people generally look to the text itself for reasons in support of an interpretation. What points in the text sustain an interpretation? Are there any points that conflict? In contrast, in scientific inquiry people read the book of nature for answers, making predictions based on a hypothesis and checking to see whether the predictions hold.

This and similar aspects of a discipline are what might be called higher-order knowledge about the discipline. This means knowledge not about the facts and skills but about how the discipline works as a pattern and practice of thinking. In a book developed by Shari Tishman, Eileen Jay, and me, *The Thinking Classroom*, we include a pair of chapters on higher-order knowledge showing how content instruction can bring it alive for students. One sample activity looks to Robert Frost's well-known poem "Stopping by Woods on a Snowy Evening." To many, this poem seems to express a kind of death wish, a will to be done with life's labyrinth of obligations. Such a mood radiates darkly from the last verse: "The woods are lovely, dark, and deep / But I have promises to keep / And miles to go before I sleep, / And miles to go before I sleep." Frost himself denied this erudite interpretation, claiming the poem simply described stopping by the woods on a snowy evening.

What would it mean to look at Frost's poem through the logical lenses of different disciplines? In *The Thinking Classroom*, we outline a scenario where the teacher, Dorothy Bear, asks her students to write about the death-wish interpretation from three different perspectives. One is literary: What evidence can they find in the poem that supports or challenges the death-wish interpretation? Another is historical: What evidence can they find from Frost's life and times consonant with such an interpretation? (Ms. Bear would of course provide them with some helpful sources.) The third is scientific: Consider the hypothesis that the poem invites a death-wish interpretation from people. What study might you do to test that hypothesis? After the students have written their responses, Ms. Bear leads a class discussion and constructs a compare-and-contrast chart not only to probe the soundness of the death-wish interpretation from different perspectives but to throw into contrast the kinds of evidence sought by the three disciplines.

Darwin's Dispositions

Another pair of chapters of *The Thinking Classroom* turns to thinking dispositions. A thinking disposition is a tendency, habit, or commitment toward thinking in a certain way, for instance the disposition to be open minded, the disposition to think in an imaginative, adventurous way, or the disposition to seek out evidence. While cultivating reflective intelligence certainly involves developing learners' thinking skills, dispositions need attention too. People can become reasonably skilled at an activity, like swimming or selling or thinking, without being especially disposed to engage in it. Someone might be an able swimmer but a reluctant one or an able thinker but a lazy one. Teaching intelligence means not just building skills but fostering the thinking dispositions that muster people's energies toward good thinking.

A sample activity from *The Thinking Classroom* pictures Mr. Tonnelli teaching his eighth-grade students a unit on Darwin. This year, he decides he wants them to build an appreciation not only of Darwin's theory but of his zest for inquiry and attention to evidence. Maybe some of it will rub off on them! He begins by having the class read a brief description of Darwin's five-year voyage on the *Beagle* and his subsequent work puzzling over data he had gathered and theories that might explain it. The description highlights Darwin's persistence, his care, his survey of many explanations, and more. Mr. Tonnelli asks his students to put into their own words some of the traits that made Darwin a good scientist. Following their responses, he creates a list on the blackboard, including items like "Don't give up! Ask lots of questions! Be critical!" These are in effect thinking dispositions. Then Mr. Tonnelli asks them to form small groups and explore interpretations for some of Darwin's original data, which he gives them. As they do so, they are to try to put into practice the dispositions listed on the blackboard.

Newton's Thumbtack

One of the perennial challenges of science education is to get students to wear the principle-colored glasses of science. Whereas scientific principles play out their implications moment to moment in the world around us, students tend to see science more as equations in textbooks than as patterns of events that touch their lives.

A few years ago, in a book called *Knowledge as Design,* I developed a thinking-oriented approach to subject-matter learning that helps to build disciplinary understanding and also to relate disciplinary concepts to the everyday world of purpose and action. A version of it also appears as part of the infusion program *Thinking Connections.* The approach asks students to analyze the things and ideas they are studying as designs— structures adapted to purposes. Students use explicit design questions— What are the purposes? What is the structure? What are the arguments (for each part of the structure)? And more. For instance, the Preamble to the Constitution of the United States is a structure adapted to a set of purposes. Look at it this way and you can figure out how it works. The purposes include introducing the document, summarizing some of its key points, and emphasizing a spirit of unity. Many structural features of this elegantly crafted paragraph support those purposes. For instance, the opening "We the people" sends an emphatic message of unity. The choice of the term ordain in "do ordain and establish this constitution" lends a ministerial color to the preamble.

But what about principle-colored glasses for science? One can, for instance, engage students in thinking about a thumbtack from the standpoint of physics. The purpose of a thumbtack is clear enough: holding paper and other light thin objects on cork or wood surfaces. The structure that lets thumbtacks do this handy job is a microcosm of physics that students can get at through some fiddling with thumb tacks and thinking. To compress the story a bit, the thumbtack is a pressure transformer: The broad head allows you to apply your thumb forcefully without cutting yourself (imagine trying to push a nail with its small head into a wall). The point, however, concentrates all that force onto a much smaller surface area—the area of the point itself— yielding a very high pressure that can penetrate a cork or even a wood surface. The tapered point of the tack also brings another principle of physics into play: the inclined plane, one of the basic machines. The tapered point pushes aside cork or wood fibers with much more force than the force applied by the thumb, because of the inclined plane effect. In this and other ways, the thumbtack is a little miracle of practical physics.

Truman's Decision

Many others besides my colleagues and me have developed approaches to infusing the teaching of thinking into subject matter instruction. For instance, Robert Swartz, a philosopher well-known in the thinking skills movement and a good friend as well, has designed many sample lessons with his partner Sandra Parks, showing how subject-matter instruction and the teaching of thinking can merge. The following example draws on their *Infusing the Teaching of Critical and Creative Thinking into Secondary Instruction,* which provides not only many model lessons but also a framework for designing and teaching infusion lessons that teachers in a number of school districts are using.

One such lesson concerns an especially basic and practical kind of thinking—decision making—and a pivotal decision in history, Harry Truman's okay for the first and only nuclear attack in history, the bombing of Hiroshima and Nagasaki. At first blush, students are confidently critical of Truman's choice. But it is not so simple as that. In their lesson, Robert Swartz and Sandra Parks introduce historical evidence about the military circumstances toward the end of World War II, evidence that Truman considered. They engage students in rethinking Truman's decision with a basic decision-making strategy part of which goes as follows.

- Options: What can I do?
- Consequences: What will happen if you take this option?
- Support: Why do you think each consequence will occur?
- Value: How important is the consequence? Why?

As students work through the lesson, they generate alternatives to a nuclear attack such as: Demonstrate the bomb, mount subversive activities, continue conventional bombings, use chemical weapons, invade Japan. Investigating particular options further, they generate consequences. For instance, negative consequences for "invade Japan" might include heavy U.S. casualties, high dollar cost, environmental damage, loss of public support at home, and more. Each consequence positive or negative in turn calls for support to justify the reality of that consequence and an assessment of the importance of the consequence.

Throughout this process, quotes from writings about the military situation inform students' thinking. Both American and Japanese authors are represented. As the logic of circumstances unfolds, students discover a complex situation and a cautious president approving a step with reluctance because of a number of practical considerations. Whatever our ultimate feelings about Truman's judgment, it was neither hasty nor foolish. In the end, students come to a better appreciation of how people shape history through the decisions they make. Just as important, they get an introduction to a decision-making strategy useful in any context of complex decision making.

Other Approaches

There are of course many other approaches to making the development of thinking a presence in subject-matter instruction. Without attempting anything like a review, let me mention three more to give the flavor.

John Barell, a professor at Montclair State College, has worked closely with teachers for many years around fostering thinking through subject-matter instruction. His 1991 book *Teaching for Thoughtfulness* gains inspiration through a prescient quote from a tenth grade student named Emily who points up some dilemmas of schools as they are. In part, Emily says:

> I guess I could call myself smart. I mean I can usually get good grades. Sometimes I worry though, that I'm not equipped to achieve what I want, that I'm just a tape recorder repeating back what I've heard. It scares me . . . I do my work, but I don't have the motivation. I've done well on Iowa and PSAT tests but they are always multiple choice. I worry that once I'm out of school and people don't keep handing me information with questions and scantron sheets I'll be lost.

This opening sally typifies the from-the-trenches tales that inform *Teaching for Thoughtfulness.* Later chapters provide a perspective and an array of techniques that treat the assessment of students' thinking, problem solving, the use of imagination, the development of metacognition, and more.

Howard Gardner, Robert Sternberg, and their colleagues have developed a program called PIFS, an acronym for Practical Intelligence for Schools. PIFS recognizes that students need more than traditional academic skills: They need practical coping skills around reading, writing, solving problems, capitalizing on their strengths to overcome weaknesses, and so on. With this in mind, PIFS offers a mix of separate and infused learning experiences. The PIFS approach highlights building students' understanding of five themes: knowing why (what's the point of this technique, this topic, this homework); knowing self (what are my strengths and weaknesses and how to deal with them); knowing differences (what are the different demands of different subject matters and assignments); knowing process (what are the steps, the strategies); and reflection (examine your work, self-assess, rework).

Finally, the visual arts have been sadly neglected in primary and secondary education in recent years. In a short 1994 book, *The Intelligent Eye*, I explore how looking at art can be a powerful occasion for developing thinking dispositions. Far from being a force fit, looking at art thoughtfully, deeply, and critically provides an unusually conducive setting for cultivating thinking. Works of art present a physical presence to respond to, hold attention, and usually connect to important human themes. The approach capitalizes on an analogy between looking and thinking to counter the four defaults of thinking highlighted earlier: hasty, narrow, fuzzy, and sprawling thinking. Examining any work of art from a Rembrandt etching to an Andy Warhol soup can, you can give time to looking and thinking; make your looking broad and adventurous and make your thinking broad and adventurous; make your looking clear and deep and make your thinking clear and deep; make your looking organized, and make your thinking organized.

I hope that the vignettes above catch something of the spirit and substance of teaching thinking in and through the subject matters, an approach very different from the stand-alone courses that make up the larger part of this chapter. The natural question at this point asks: Which is better?

Answers do not come easily here. First of all, as I emphasized earlier, hardly any data speak to the impact of the infusion approach. Of the programs mentioned above, only PIFS has undergone a formal pretest-posttest evaluation, with positive results. So as far as proof goes, the jury is still out and will probably be out for some time. Second, the most plausible answer to "which is better" says "both are better." Robert Ennis, another philosopher influential in the critical-thinking movement, has argued persuasively for this sensible position. If we can do two things: give better thinking practices focused attention at certain times and also work those same practices into the teaching of the subject matters, this will certainly tune up students' thinking more than either alone.

However, it's often the case that school resources cannot support a double-barreled intervention. When the choice must be made, in my judgment the answer depends on nuances of the approach. Both separate course and infusion approaches can be effective, but each has its traps. Often separate courses stand in isolation from subject-matter applications and even from everyday life applications outside of school. For separate courses to be effective, one must teach for transfer of learning, helping students to connect up the course's concepts and skills to diverse settings. The next chapter looks more deeply into the challenge of transfer.

On the other hand, often efforts to infuse the teaching of thinking into subject-matter instruction get lost amidst the many agendas and busy schedules of conventional instruction. The infusion becomes a token presence that accomplishes little. For infusion to be effective, it must play a frequent and conspicuous role in the treatment of subject-matter content. But when infusion gets beyond tokenism, it can be a powerful force for educating minds. Intelligence can be taught by infusing the teaching of thinking into subject-matter instruction.

Should We Be Satisfied?

The bumblebee flies. As Arthur Whimbey said, intelligence can be taught. Not only the programs reviewed over the last several pages, but numerous other programs and laboratory studies in diverse styles and settings demonstrate the possibility. To update the answer to one of the mindware questions:

MWQ #2. Can people learn more intelligence? Yes, in a number of ways:

- By creating a culture of thoughtfulness, along with allied concepts and techniques, as in *Philosophy for Children.*
- By fostering mental management and cultivating careful systematic thinking, as in *Instrumental Enrichment.*
- By teaching strategies and allied concepts, as in *CoRT* and *Instrumental Enrichment.*
- By infusing the teaching of strategies and mental management into subject-matter instruction.

Of course, such initiatives do not always succeed. Sometimes there is no discernable difference between the learners participating in a learning experience designed to build students' reflective intelligence and the control group that receives no special treatment. However, success by one measure or another occurs often enough to establish the principle.

But none of this warrants total satisfaction with what these programs have accomplished. None of this means that the challenge posed by those persistent intelligence traps is solved. On the contrary, with a firm hold on the principle that intelligence can be taught, it's appropriate to acknowledge the limits in the track record so far.

A pragmatic version of the question is this: If the programs reviewed actually succeed in teaching intelligence, why have they not swept the world? There are a number of answers.

Controversy. The notion of teaching thinking has been controversial in several ways. First of all, as Part I of this book emphasized, many psychologists and laypersons alike see intelligence as a matter of IQ and a fixed genetic endowment. So they believe that people cannot learn to think better. Second, other psychologists have argued that good thinking depends mostly on the acquisition of knowledge and processes appropriate to the subject matter or context in question, treating what I have called experiential intelligence as the one key to the main door. Hearing of this view, educators often feel reluctant to mount separate courses that try to teach general kinds of thinking, although they may look more positively on the infusion approach. Third, a question of values enters the picture. Many parents appear to be more concerned with the acquisition of factual knowledge and basic skills than with students learning to think. Indeed, in the late 1970s, the theme of "back to the basics" became an educational watchword and a slogan against efforts to cultivate students' thinking abilities. Of course, the belief that thinking depends on genetically determined IQ reinforces such a leaning. Finally, even if we do view the teaching of thinking as possible and worth doing, there still are contrasting philosophies about how to do it. Notice how different the programs reviewed are from one another, even though all in one way or another address the defaults. With so much controversy in the air, it's understandable that only a few teachers and schools make the attempt.

Implementation challenges. Furthermore, it has to be said that many of the approaches to teaching intelligence—both those discussed here and others—are by no means easy to implement in full, rich, and careful ways. For example, the Philosophy for Children program relies a great deal on the Socratic art of the teacher. Matthew Lipman himself acknowledges that it is not easy to train teachers to play the required role. Feuerstein's Instrumental Enrichment program requires extensive training for the mediators who work with learners and, when applied in the intended way, involves a relatively low student-teacher ratio.

The difficulty of educational change. No matter whether the program in question is one designed to cultivate intelligence, introduce cooperative learning, enhance student understanding, or advance moral values, introduction of changes in educational practices at any level—elementary, high school, or college—is a difficult undertaking for a host of reasons. School schedules are crowded, curricula are overburdened with agendas, teachers have limited time to develop new skills, much of conventional testing has a facts-and-routines orientation that works against innovation, special interest groups sometimes mount barriers, and more. However, none of this is reason for despair. There are approaches to educational innovation that show promise. To understand all this better, readers are encouraged to consult my recent *Smart Schools* and other sources listed in the bibliography of this book.

Modest impact. Another reason why programs like this have not swept the world is that they rarely achieve dramatic impact. If any of them reliably increased IQ by twenty-five points in ways that persisted and with accompanying changes in a whole spectrum of cognitive performances, or if any of them reliably improved student performance by a couple of letter grades, more attention would be paid.

However, the fact is that for the most part the impact is more modest. Students score a few points better on certain tests, reading scores go up a little, math problem solving improves somewhat, some science concepts are better understood, grades go up a little. All of this is definitely worthwhile from the standpoint of the individuals involved and the society to which they will contribute, but is not exciting enough to capture wide-scale commitment to fostering reflective intelligence in a climate where many agendas compete for attention.

What will happen, then? I see two possibilities. First of all, the moderate success of these and other initiatives in the same spirit may get captured in more efficient forms and folded into normal educational practice. People will emerge from schooling with more mindware and somewhat better cognitive functioning than before. I think that at least this much can and will happen in the long run, as other educational innovations of moderate advantage have gradually been assimilated into routine practice—for example, more effective ways of teaching reading and writing.

The other possibility is that much more powerful ways of teaching intelligence will be discovered, with a much more transformative impact on many facets of learners' thinking, even IQ gains of half a standard deviation or more. This might take no more than persistent application over the course of years of many of the approaches that have already been developed! The simple factor of time-on-task should not be neglected. Remember that students are not expected to master complex challenges like reading or writing in a few lessons. The same holds for the many sides of reflective intelligence, whether they are taught in separate courses or through infusion into the handling of the regular subject matters. Currently, it is rare that a student experiences more than one such intervention for a few weeks. There is little chance to gauge cumulative impact.

Beyond the prospects of cumulative impact, it is possible that newer ways of enhancing intelligence, fundamentally more powerful, will emerge from current work. I have high hopes for more attention to students' thinking dispositions—roughly, the emotional and motivational side of thinking. I also have high hopes for approaches to instruction that recognize kinds of thinking as realms of know-how that one can learn one's way around. The first two chapters of Part III explore these concepts.

Whatever the future holds, at least this can be said with some confidence: The science of learnable intelligence is young yet. New perspectives are still emerging and inspiring new instructional approaches. The terrain, far from mapped and settled, lies fecund with possibility. Intelligence can be taught, to a modest but worthwhile degree at least. How far we can go remains an alluring mystery.

9

The Great Debate

Once upon a time, a wise and beneficent leader in a remote country anticipated aggression from a territory-hungry neighbor nation. Recognizing that the neighbor had more military might, the leader concluded that his people would have to out-think, not overpower, the enemy. Undistinguished in its military armament and generals, the country did have one remarkable asset: the reigning world chess master, undefeated for more than twenty years. "Aha," the leader said to himself, "we'll recruit this keen intellect, sharpened so long on the whetstone of chess. Teach him some politics and military theory. And then outmaneuver the enemy with the help of his genius!"

Fanciful, to be sure. But consider the leader's plan for a moment. Is it disastrously naive, possibly helpful, or a pretty good bet? Within the discipline of psychology and across three decades, very different voices might be heard sizing up the chances of the chess master. One says, "Basically, the chess master plays chess well because he knows the moves of the game well. There's no reason at all why that knowledge should carry over powerfully to political or military matters." Another voice counters: "Well, there are analogies to be mined between chess and matters of political and military strategy. Control of the center, for example—that's a principle important in chess, but also in politics and war." Still another voice emphasizes not the transferrable aspects of

211

chess skill but general problem-solving abilities: "Above all, a chess player is a problem solver. Someone who needs to plan ahead, explore alternatives, size up strategic options, just as a politician or military tactician does. So we might expect a lot from the chess master."

Which of these voices speaks with the most wisdom? Or must another voice altogether be heard delivering some more complicated opinion?

At any rate, these rival voices certainly echo two familiar ideas: experiential intelligence and reflective intelligence. The most skeptical voice emphasizes how specific to chess the chess master's great skill is—mostly a matter of accumulated experiential intelligence in chess. The middle-of-the-roader acknowledges the importance of chess knowledge but urges that useful military principles can be generalized out of it. This voice believes that perhaps, by exercising reflective intelligence, the chess master might make some fruitful connections. The third voice, not skeptical at all, sees the chess master's skill as largely a matter of reflective intelligence—planning ahead, exploring alternatives, and so forth. While the tale of the beleaguered kingdom is a fantasy, these same voices can be heard today reacting to the idea of learnable reflective intelligence.

I have written with some enthusiasm about a theory of learnable intelligence. In previous chapters, I have outlined parts of such a theory, emphasizing how people can learn mindware. But make no mistake about it: A great debate continues between champions of reflective intelligence and champions of experiential intelligence. The most skeptical about reflective intelligence say that high-level intellectual functioning depends profoundly on experiential intelligence (the old guard says neural intelligence); reflective intelligence offers little. They do not use the language of neural, experiential, and reflective intelligence, which is my argot, but that is the gist of their critique. Then there are other voices that articulate a mixed view or an unalloyed positive view.

It is time to hear from the skeptics. Their forum may seem oddly placed, right after a chapter averring that reflective intelligence can be taught. But actually, the more skeptical skeptics would not be very impressed by the kinds of results laid out in the previous chapter or similar results from other settings. These skeptics would view the impacts of such interventions as minor and passing. They would acknowledge that skills in focused areas such as reading or mathematical problem solving might be taught. But they would see those skills as rather specialized, narrow in their application, hardly elevating a learner's intelligence in any general sense. It's important to understand why the skeptics would say this and how to assess their position.

I will argue that the more skeptical skeptics are mistaken but that they have important points to make, points that need to be respected in order to formulate a sound theory of learnable intelligence. The end of the chapter will bring us back to the mythical kingdom with its precious resource, the chess champion of the world for twenty years, appraising the promise of the king's plan: Can he make a brilliant military strategist of his chess master? Or had he better look for another way out?

Before the Fall:
The Golden Age of General Strategies

Life used to be easy for champions of reflective intelligence! Around 1960, it was widely thought that good problem solving and other intellectual performances depended mostly on general strategies. The strategies worked with whatever database of knowledge happened to be needed. Besides IQ, true intellectual ability resided in the general strategies, with the database an incidental necessity. So by learning general strategies, people might come to think better. Moreover, by incorporating general strategies in computer programs, programmers might create machines that in limited but meaningful senses could think.

What kindled this enthusiastic view of strategies, making for a golden age of hope and aspiration? And what went wrong?

One who stoked the fire was the mathematician Gyorgy Polya, with his analysis of mathematical problem solving. Polya stepped outside the typical pursuits of mathematicians to ask not what theorems might be proved, but how mathematicians thought. What made for good mathematical process, not just sound, insightful products? As mentioned in Chapter 4, Polya identified a number of heuristics—his word for strategies—that mathematicians use to solve a problem or prove a theorem. Among these were strategies like: Try to divide a problem into subproblems that you can address one at a time; represent the problem in a diagram or graph; invent a simpler version of the same problem, solve that, and use what you have learned to tackle the more difficult problem.

Polya made a persuasive case for his vision of mathematical problem solving and theorem proving. His publications included numerous examples of mathematical problem solving, illustrating how heuristics could help. It is worth adding a personal testimonial to Polya's insights as well. I became involved in psychology only after completing my doctoral degree in the areas of mathematics and artificial intelligence. I did not encounter Polya's work until after my student days. However, curious about Polya's analysis, I set my mind to addressing some mathematics problems—and paying attention to how I approached them. Was I using any of the heuristics Polya wrote about?

Polya's insight proved compelling! I could easily find in my own practices as a mathematical problem solver and theorem prover many of the strategies that Polya had pointed out. I was pretty good at mathematics, but I had never realized how much that depended on a repertoire of heuristics that I had picked up one place or another or invented for myself. It is not that these heuristic moves were unconscious. Rather, I had not recognized them and singled them out for what they were because they were all part of the larger enterprise of mathematics for me, all mixed in with knowledge of mathematics concepts.

Much as it impressed me later, Polya's analysis impressed a number of people in his day. Here was a strategically oriented account of an unquestionably challenging intellectual activity. Moreover, many of Polya's strategies seemed just as relevant to common-sense everyday problems as to math—including the three heuristics mentioned above. Perhaps good thinking was a matter of good strategies.

More sparkle for the Golden Age of General Strategies came from one of the most exciting areas of research of the times, artificial intelligence or AI as it is called for short. With improvements in computer hardware and computer languages, researchers began to investigate the possibility of machine intelligence, computers programmed to tackle intellectually challenging tasks such as playing chess, proving theorems in mathematics, or identifying the objects seen through the electronic eye of a video camera.

The General Problem Solver was one outstanding example. Developed around 1957 by Alan Newell, J. P. Shaw, and Herbert Simon, this computer program relied on a flexible strategy called means-end analysis. To set the program up for a particular problem, you input information about a beginning state, one or more acceptable end states (the goals), and allowable operations on states, all in a compact notation. Many simple puzzles and problems in logic were easily cast into this form. The General Problem Solver's challenge was to find a sequence of operations that transformed the initial state into any one of the end states.

To make this a little more concrete, a favorite demonstration example was the well-known missionaries-and-cannibals problem. There are three missionaries and three cannibals on one side of the river. The task is to get them across the river in a boat that can only hold two people at a time. The missionaries are safe so long as they are never outnumbered by the cannibals on the near or far side of the river or when the boat pulls up to the near or far side. How can the cannibals and missionaries cross?

In the idiom of the General Problem Solver, the initial state is all six on the near side of the river. The end state is all six on the far side of the river. The allowable operations are safe trips: any boat trip from the near to far or far to near sides that does not leave the missionaries outnumbered. The General Problem Solver's job was to seek a sequence of safe trips that moves everyone to the far side.

The General Problem Solver worked by comparing and contrasting the beginning and goal states, seeking an operation to reduce the contrast—a means that would bring the beginning state closer to the end state, hence means-end analysis. In the case of the missionaries and cannibals problem, reducing the contrast means getting more people safely to the far side. After executing an operation (a safe trip for our sample problem), the program would seek another operation to reduce the contrast yet further, and so on. If, as commonly happens, the program encountered a cul-de-sac where no further direct progress was possible, the program would back up and try another sequence of operations. For example, working on the missionaries and cannibals problem, the program would find that, to avoid a cul-de-sac, at one point it has to do an operation that momentarily moves much further from the goal: Two of the travelers actually have to go back to the first side. It seems odd to have to move away from the goal momentarily. But only in that way could the missionaries be kept safe all the time.

There were other more sophisticated features too. But this suffices to illustrate the general point: Problem-solving power seemed to lie in some rather general principles like means-end analysis, systematically applied to whatever the relevant database of knowledge happened to be.

In those days, a host of factors bolstered the idea that good thinking depended largely on a repertoire of rather general heuristic knowledge: the interesting data that resulted, the connection with the belief in the value of analytic ability, the economy and elegance of the view, the ease with which computer simulations could test it. Many strategies were identified for problem solving, memorizing, inventive thinking, decision making, general mental management, and so on.

As to the specific knowledge of chess, mathematics, or some other domain, it was not thought to be very important. Of course, one had to have it. But there really was not much to it beyond a few rules in the case of chess, a few axioms in the case of mathematical systems, and so on. There did not seem to be enough to know to make the knowledge component very central to thinking ability.

But the golden age could not last. Even in those days, certain results in the literature gave warning that all was not well with this picture of general strategies driving intellectual performance. In the years to come, a wave of compelling findings would cast profound doubt on the centrality of general ability in human thinking, particularly ability based on strategies.

Not, of course, that reflective intelligence as explored in this book consists entirely of strategies. Many other factors figure in reflective intelligence, as already emphasized: attitudes, values, conceptual systems, and so on. However, psychology was not thinking much beyond strategies when all this happened, so strategies bore the brunt of skepticism. The gathering force of contrary findings fell neatly into three parts: the argument from expertise, the argument from weak methods, and the argument from transfer.

The Argument from Expertise

The phenomenon of expertise is already familiar, first as a challenge to the classic general intelligence view in Chapter 4, and again in Chapter 7, where the pattern-driven nature of human cognition helped to explain the thinking defaults. The investigation of expertise has played a supportive role in the discussion, helping to fill in a broad picture of neural, experiential, and reflective intelligence.

However, many involved in the study of expertise have taken the findings quite differently. They have seen a fundamental challenge to the whole notion of powerful general strategies or other general elements in thinking.

Some of the relevant findings are worth recalling briefly. It all began with the study of expert play in chess, that quintessential intellectual undertaking. While chess might seem like a game of pure general reasoning skills (you can see the pieces and know the rules; all you have to do is to think ahead), research revealed that chess expertise reflects a large knowledge base of patterns that come up often in chess play. Chess masters recognize these patterns reflexively. Their high quality of play depends on it.

As mentioned earlier, similar research has been done in a number of fields, for example playing the Japanese game Go, physics problem solving, mathematical problem solving, computer programming, representational art, and medical diagnosis. Always the same pattern emerges. High levels of performance reflect a vast knowledge base rather reflexively evoked.

A couple of the most startling results about expertise have yet to be mentioned. In their work on chess play, researchers William Chase and Herbert Simon used certain assumptions to estimate the size of a grandmaster chess player's repertoire of chess patterns. They put the figure at about 50,000! "Not so unbelievable," they averred. This is roughly the vocabulary an extremely literate person in English might have, and grandmaster level chess players are as literate as you can get in chess. Since then, their estimate has been challenged, but it stands as an imposing testimony to the degree to which expert performance might be memory dependent.

The second as yet unmentioned feature of work on expertise concerns the time it takes to accumulate a strong knowledge base. Biographical investigations suggest that real expertise requires at least ten years to build up. It takes that much time living within a discipline to stock your memory bank. The figure holds even for prodigious individuals, like Mozart. Yes, Mozart started young. But major honored works by Mozart still did not begin to emerge until Mozart was around sixteen years old, twelve years after he began his involvement in music.

With findings like these as a backdrop, it is easy to see why some scholars might view the prospects of teaching general thinking skills skeptically. Good thinking in a domain takes years to attain, and for understandable reasons—the need to build up that crucial library of patterns. Such a view leaves little play for general thinking strategies that might be acquired with a few hours or weeks of practice. That's just not the way the mind works! Or so the story goes.

On the Other Hand: When We Face the Unfamiliar

However, in some investigators' views including my own, cracks began to appear in the granite edifice of the research on expertise. One of the most intriguing fissures concerns what happens when experts in a discipline face problems that fall within the discipline, but are not routine.

For instance, researcher John Clement, working at the University of Massachusetts, Amherst, examined experts' responses to atypical problems in physics. His results were provocative. As in other research on expertise, Clement found that the experts certainly used their rich physics knowledge base, trying to see the deep structure of the problems and deploying foundational principles like conservation of energy. However, because Clement's unusual problems did not yield to the most straightforward approaches, the experts also applied many general strategies.

For example, the experts faced with an unfamiliar problem would often:

- Resort to analogies with systems they understood better.
- Search for potential misanalogies in the analogy.
- Refer to intuitive mental models based on visual and kinesthetic intuition to try to understand what would happen in the problem situation.
- Investigate the problem situation with extreme case arguments, probing what would happen if various masses, distances, velocities, or other measures were pushed to zero or infinity.
- Construct a simpler problem of the same sort, in hopes of solving that and importing the solution to the original problem.

Moves like these remind us of Polya's general strategies for math. Also, Clement found that not all experts successfully solved the nonstandard physics problems he posed, problems no more complex than conventional problems except for their novelty.

What do Clement's findings teach us about the argument from expertise? First and foremost, they warn against the kind of either-or thinking the argument has fallen into. During the Golden Age, people were saying, "It's general strategies that account for good thinking." Then expertise came along, and people argued, "The big knowledge base explains good thinking. So it's not general strategies." But Clement's research, and other research in like spirit, demonstrate a point entirely in accordance with Polya's earlier insights: General strategies work hand in hand with expert knowledge to solve problems. The general strategies are not a substitute for knowledge, but neither is the knowledge a substitute for general strategies.

Furthermore, general strategies become particularly important when the thinker cannot fall back on repertoire entirely, because there are unusual aspects to the problem. Moreover, as argued at the end of Chapter 7, unfamiliar circumstances cannot be viewed as an uninteresting special case. Life is full of novelty and near-novelty. People engage in myriad pursuits intermittently (filing taxes, having wills made, getting married, asking for a raise) without the time to accumulate expertise. Also, schooling and other situations that involve constant extensive learning constantly present novelty by definition. Even if general strategies only figure importantly in not-entirely-familiar situations, that would be plenty of reason to welcome their contribution.

Further affirmation of the idea of general strategies comes in terms almost paradoxical if we think of expertise as expertise in particular domains like physics, history, or skiing. John Bruer in *Schools for Thought*, his 1993 synthesis about instructional innovations based on cognitive science, recognizes a kind of expertise that helps learners to develop expertise in specialized domains. He writes of "intelligent novices." These are people who learn effectively in situations where they lack much initial knowledge because they have expertise as learners. By way of example, he offers a set of learning abilities exercised by John Bransford, himself a noted cognitive psychologist, during a study that used him as a subject learning physics from a textbook with the help of an expert physicist:

(1) Awareness of the difference between understanding and memorizing material and knowledge of which mental strategies to use in each case
(2) Ability to recognize which parts of the text were difficult, which dictated where to start reading and how much time to spend
(3) Awareness of the need to take problems and examples from the text, order them randomly, and then try to solve them
(4) Knowing when he didn't understand, so he could seek help from the expert
(5) Knowing when the expert's explanations solve his immediate learning problem

In similar spirit, Carl Bereiter and Marlene Scardamalia in *Surpassing Ourselves*, a 1993 revisionary examination of the research on expertise, write of "expertlike novices" and "expert learners" in contrast with "nonexpert learners." They itemize some of the traits that distinguish the expert and nonexpert learner: Expert learners recognize that it's hard to tell what's important as you start to study an area. They err on the side of assuming things are important, while nonexpert learners make subjective judgments of importance and ignore items that do not stand out. For another contrast, expert learners recognize that their initial understanding is likely to be simplistic and watch out for complications. Nonexpert learners quickly construct simplistic interpretations and retain them even when problems come up.

The Argument from Weak Methods

I mentioned earlier how research in the area of artificial intelligence (AI) generated high hopes for a science of heuristics relevant to both machine and human cognition. As work continued beyond the glory days of the sixties, a difficulty gradually emerged. Yes, one could provide computers with general repertoires of strategies suitable for tackling a variety of problems of the missionaries and cannibals sort. Moreover, one could program computers in more specialized ways to perform creditably on more authentically challenging problems, for example chess play.

But it proved difficult to get beyond a certain point. The more general programs never managed to handle more than puzzle problems and elementary logic theorems. The more specialized programs never managed to achieve true master status. For example, although many computer chess programs cheaply available for desktop computers could easily beat most amateur chess players, master players could easily beat not only them but the best that extremely powerful mainframe computers can do. Of course, the chess programs are getting better. Eventually, a machine intelligence may be chess master of the world. But it has not happened yet—and in the sixties such an eventuality was thought to be not so far away.

Gradually, AI researchers began to lay their bets differently as they tried to construct powerful artificial intelligence systems. Taking a lesson from both progress on chess-playing computers and the research on expertise, many AI researchers turned to developing expert systems. Such computer systems seek to simulate the intelligence of an expert through a massive domain-specific knowledge base in areas such as medical diagnosis. A number of successes were achieved. Just as in the case of chess, expert systems programs usually fall short of the best the human experts can do. However, a human expert is not always available. As with the General Problem Solver, these expert systems use a number of general inference techniques. But the AI community's sense of where the strength lay had shifted: The large knowledge base held the key, not the inference techniques.

So what did researches think then of strategies that had seemed so promising in the heyday of the General Problem Solver? The AI community came to refer to general heuristics such as means-end analysis as weak methods. Investigators spoke of the power-generality tradeoff; the more general the method, the weaker the method. When new to a domain, all a computer or a human could do was deploy general weak methods that turned out weak results. Real power in problem solving emerged over time, they said, as application of weak methods created the opportunity to learn and store up the particular moves in the domain, building the rich database of an expert. Or, in the case of some expert systems, one would directly program the knowledge base.

Although the notion that general strategies were weak came mostly from AI research, little happened in the psychological community to make a countercase. On the contrary, a number of investigators sought to teach Polya's heuristics for mathematical problem solving without much success. Students exhibited just exactly the difficulties expected, given the results of the research on expertise. They did not know what to do with the strategies. They understood the strategies in broad terms but did not seem to understand the mathematics well enough to apply them in the rather complex and context-sensitive ways required. Context-specific knowledge, much more than general strategies, looked to be the bottleneck.

On The Other Hand: When Weak Methods Are Strong

The phrase "weak methods" does a lot of mischief. It makes the sweeping claim that general methods (divide a problem into parts, and such) are always weak. A better question would be not whether such methods are weak but *when, or in comparison to what?* When a person or computer has abundant knowledge resources directly germane to the problem, general methods look weak by comparison. After all, there is nothing like knowing the answer, or knowing so much about the particulars that you can easily get to the answer.

However, when a person does not have immediately relevant specific knowledge, the specific knowledge the person does have is even weaker than supposedly weak methods. Nothing can be done with it as it stands! Maybe, for instance, you do not know just the right formula for a physics problem. To be sure, you recall other formulas that might pertain, but how? Or maybe you have a flat tire and don't know how to handle the jack on your new car. To be sure, you've handled other different jacks in the past and that knowledge might pertain, but how? Or maybe you have to hire a house painters. You don't know how to find candidates or check their qualifications. Yes, you've dealt with somewhat similar situations that might pertain, but how?

As in Clement's research, mentioned in the previous section, general strategies can help a person to connect up specific knowledge that does not quite fit an unfamiliar situation. Applying general strategies (for instance, making analogies, trial and error, or reasoning backward from the result you want) to the formulas you do remember, the jacks you've struggled with before, the hiring you've accomplished in the past, you probably can connect your knowledge up to the problem at hand. When this happens, general methods save the day, hardly a performance deserving the label "weak."

When strategies are taught to students in ways that bring them into effective contact with a previously existing knowledge base, they can function powerfully by enabling learners to use that knowledge base more flexibly. While I remarked above that early efforts to teach Polya's heuristics had not been very successful, remember from Chapter 4 that Berkeley researcher Alan Schoenfeld, adopting more sophisticated instructional techniques, eventually managed to teach Polya-like heuristics with considerable impact. He did this with students who already knew a great deal of mathematics but lacked problem-solving finesse. For these students, the bottleneck was less lack of knowledge and more lack of problem-solving strategies, so problem-solving strategies made the difference. Again, not a weak contribution.

In artificial intelligence, although work has continued on expert systems, investigators have also returned to the challenge of producing more general models of mind. Two systems in particular, one called ACT* developed by John Anderson of Carnegie-Mellon University, and another called SOAR, developed by Allen Newell, also of Carnegie-Mellon and one of the inventors of the General Problem Solver, are rather well known. Both offer general models of cognitive processing. Both are learning systems that learn by trying to solve problems. Given a new class of problems, they commence by applying general methods. As they work, they search for and store shortcuts in the solution process and so gradually build up a repertoire of domain-specific chunks, much as human beings do, through extended experience.

The way SOAR works, for example, somewhat resembles Clement's physicists facing unfamiliar kinds of physics problems. SOAR tries the specific moves built into its library through experience. However, if SOAR encounters an impasse, as it is called, where the specialized techniques do not work, SOAR resorts to more general methods.

In summary, the weak methods argument against general thinking strategies seems to be an overgeneralization from the fact that general strategies are weak compared to specific, directly applicable knowledge. To offer an analogy, calling general thinking strategies weak is a little like calling a car's sparkplugs weak, because it is the combustion of the gasoline that pushes the car along. But the presence and timing of the spark is critical to ignite the gasoline. The gasoline will burn by itself, once set off, but setting it off at the right time requires some mechanical and electronic finesse. Likewise, experiential intelligence can be counted on to perform its pattern recognition and knowledge supply functions . . . but only if it gets set off in the right direction. The sparkplug needed to do the job is very often some kind of prod from reflective intelligence.

The Argument from Transfer

Transfer is a key notion in the psychology of learning. Transfer occurs when a person applies knowledge or skills acquired from some earlier context in a new context. For example, should the chess master in our opening story succeed in using some of his chess-honed skills on the battlefield, that would be transfer. More prosaically, when a person applies mathematics skills acquired in school in the supermarket, or drives a rented truck during a move using skills developed through car driving, this is transfer.

Psychologists draw a broad distinction between near transfer and far transfer. Near transfer means applying the same knowledge or skill in very similar circumstances, whereas far transfer implies a big leap. For the chess master, carrying over the notion of control of the center from chess to political or military settings would count as far transfer. Not only are political and military settings quite different in general from chess despite its underlying military metaphor, but the meaning of center plays out differently. In chess, it is the center area of the board. In the military context, center might mean a center of command, communications, munitions, or supply, for example. Any of these would make tempting targets.

In the Golden Age of General Strategies, some psychologists and educators presumed that experience with any intellectually rigorous pursuit would build thinking skills and strategies of great generality. Learning the logic imbedded in algebra or in Latin should, for example, yield improved scores on standard IQ tests or better learning in other seemingly unrelated fields. Similarly, learning to program computers in powerful languages such as LISP (popular for AI research) or LOGO (designed by Seymour Papert of M.I.T. and colleagues as an accessible computer language for children) should improve students' reasoning and planning abilities.

However, the track record of far transfer has not been good. A variety of investigations, initiated as far back as the turn of the century, has shown little far transfer from the study of intellectually rigorous subject matters. Early in the twentieth century, E. L. Thorndike reported experiments, some on a large scale, showing that training in such fields as Latin and mathematics had no measurable influence on other cognitive functions, helping to dispel a then-prevalent belief in the training of the mind's faculties.

Many studies since have yielded similar results. Such studies suggest, for example, that training on one version of a logical problem has little if any effect on solving a retelling of the problem in a very different way, with different trappings but the same underlying structure. People simply fail to recognize the connection between the one version and the other, and so do not carry over any tricks of the trade from the first to the second. Studies have also shown that becoming literate, but without schooling, does not improve mastery of general cognitive skills. Findings from research on the cognitive impact of instruction in computer programming generally have been negative. Directly relevant to the teaching of thinking, in at least some studies, children taught general context-independent strategies showed no clear benefits outside the specific domains in which they were taught.

The results on transfer add up to a serious assault on the prospects of general thinking strategies. Insofar as performance in a domain like Latin or programming does involve general strategies, it appears that they do not transfer very well. Indeed, even when directly taught, they may not transfer. What hope is there for cultivating reflective intelligence given the barrier of transfer?

On the Other Hand: When Transfer Happens

In trend, the research on transfer indeed paints a negative picture. It suggests that our cognitive clockwork simply does not incline very much to transfer. But plain common sense says, "Wait a minute." When faced with novel situations, people routinely try to apply knowledge, skills, and specific strategies from other, more familiar areas. In fact, people not uncommonly ignore the novelty in a situation, assimilating it into well-rehearsed habits and mindlessly bringing to bear inappropriate knowledge and skill, yielding negative transfer. Although not of the best sort, this is truly transfer.

Skeptical of the idea that transfer comes hard, Berkeley cognitive psychologist Ann Brown initiated a series of studies pursuing the possibility that the prospects for transfer were much greater than the literature in general suggested. She worked with preschool children and ideas like stacking objects to climb on in order to reach something or mimicry as a defense mechanism in animals. She showed through laboratory and classroom research that fruitful transfer to new problems does take place, even among three- and four year olds, when learners are shown how problems resemble each other; learners' attention is directed to the similar goals of comparable problems; the learners are familiar with the problem areas; examples are accompanied with rules, particularly when the latter are formulated by the learners themselves; and, perhaps most important, learning takes place in a social context that encourages learners to spell out principles, explanations, and justifications.

Brown's results, and other results as well, argue that transfer occurs readily under the right conditions. My colleague Gavriel Salomon and I evolved a theory a few years ago about the mechanisms of transfer and the "when" of transfer—when it occurred and when it did not. We pointed out two distinct mechanisms of transfer, the low road and the high road. Low road transfer occurs when perceptual similarities of one situation to another trigger the making of a connection. For example, having driven a car for much of your life, you rent a truck. The familiar steering wheel, windshield, seat, and so on, evoke all your old driving habits, and those habits more or less fit the need (where they do not quite fit you will have a bit of trouble).

Low road transfer is pattern driven. It depends on abundant practice with the skill or knowledge in question, to set up the perceptual triggering. It is a phenomenon of experiential intelligence. In consequence, there is not much far low road transfer. The pattern-bound character of experiential intelligence gets in the way. Far low road transfer can occur when the same skill gets practiced over a variety of circumstances, gradually stretching from one context to another until it achieves high generality. But the low road mechanism does not serve us nearly as well for far transfer as for near transfer.

Low road transfer contrasts with high road transfer, something much more a matter of reflective intelligence. High road transfer depends on learners' deliberate mindful abstraction of a principle. The tale of the chess master that opened this chapter asks for high road transfer from chess to military strategy. When a psychologist thinks of the mind as a computer and tries to construct a computerlike model of thinking, a business person applies ideas about business management to participating in a church group, or a teacher compares the human circulatory system to the water system of a city, all are attempting useful high road transfers.

In high road transfer, people sometimes abstract principles in advance, keeping them in mind in anticipation of appropriate opportunities for application. For instance, students studying statistics try to get a fix on the kinds of situations to which the general rules might apply. Alternatively, sometimes people face a new problem, ask themselves what they might know that could help, and rummage around in their past learnings for something that somehow connects. For instance, puzzled by a problem in your house of fuses blowing frequently, you might cast about for anything you know that might apply. Notice the contrast with the low road mechanism of automatic perceptual triggering. Here the thinker actively, reflectively seeks connections.

The low road–high road framework helps to explain both the generally negative findings on transfer and the positive exceptions. In the negative cases, the conditions have not favored either low road or high road transfer. As to low road transfer, often the studies sought far transfer (difficult to achieve by the low road) and the skill or knowledge to be transferred was not very well learned in the first place (not setting up the pattern-recognition trigger). For instance, several efforts to build students' thinking skills by teaching programming aspired to far transfer, but the students never learned programming itself very well in the first place.

As to the negative findings and high road transfer, nothing about the circumstances encouraged the kind of mindful, effortful connection making that high road transfer requires. For instance, in the computer programming studies where transfer failed, nothing prompted the students to try to abstract general principles from what they were learning. On the other hand, in Ann Brown's and others' studies that demonstrated worthwhile transfer, either attention to extensive diverse practice or emphasis on mindful abstraction or both appear.

One case in point is an investigation conducted by Philip Adey and Michael Shayer in England, developers of a program called CASE, Cognitive Acceleration Through Science Education. Working in eight schools every two weeks for two years, they substituted a lesson in cognitive development for students' regular science lessons. The CASE lessons highlighted patterns of thinking like control of variables, reflecting the developmental theories of the well-known French psychologist Jean Piaget. The overall approach emphasized creating puzzling situations that challenged prior conceptions, fostering metacognition, and bridging from one context to another. The authors investigated the impact of CASE one and two years after the students completed the instruction. The measures included standard achievement tests in science, mathematics, and English. They found that the intervention significantly boosted performance in a number of the students, although not all, even after a delay of two years. The authors concluded that they achieved long-term far transfer of cognitive abilities.

The first moral of this tale is simply that the readings on the prospects of transfer have been deceptively negative. Transfer can occur abundantly, providing the circumstances activate either the low road or the high road mechanism. The second moral, however, is that transfer is not a free lunch. People cannot be expected to routinely and spontaneously transfer whatever may be transferrable from Latin, programming, mathematics, literary criticism, or other thought-demanding areas of study. Transfer needs point-blank attention. In particular, the effective teaching of general thinking strategies demands plenty of work on high road transfer with its emphasis on active, reflective connection making.

The Case for Reflective Intelligence

How stands the great debate? The community of psychologists have had a trio of reasons to look skeptically on any theory of learnable intelligence highlighting reflective intelligence—the argument from expertise, the argument from weak methods, and the argument from transfer. However, in my view, and in the view of many other psychologists (more, I believe, than a few years ago), these three reasons do not make the negative case they at first seem to. To sum up with the first mindware question:

MWQ #1. What mechanisms underlie intelligence? Experiential intelligence, which yields expertise, does not suffice to account for the range of intelligent behavior. In particular:

- Expertise does not in itself provide for good thinking when the tasks are novel; people need reflective intelligence to help them connect their experiential intelligence with the less familiar, even within a familiar domain. Also, in many important activities people cannot expect to develop real expertise; reflective intelligence must serve in combination with a much-less-than-expert fund of knowledge. To use the language of Chapter 7, experiential intelligence may be the 90-percent solution but that leaves a 10-percent problem, and a high level of reflective intelligence is the 10-percent solution.
- Weak methods on a second look are misnamed. The general methods that have sometimes been called weak by artificial intelligence researchers prove strong and essential ingredients in many situations.
- As to transfer, it is not so hard to come by as reputed. Transfer will occur, given care to set up the conditions on which it thrives—the abundant diverse practice needed for low road transfer or the mindful abstraction needed for high road transfer.

These counterarguments against the arguments from expertise, weak methods, and transfer are not meant to be dismissive. On the contrary, the arguments from expertise, weak methods, and transfer teach us a great deal about the nature and needs of reflective intelligence. The argument from expertise establishes the profound and thoroughgoing role of context-specific knowledge in sophisticated thinking. Indeed, this line of research motivated my concept of experiential intelligence. The argument from weak methods helps us recognize that one cannot expect mindware to substitute for directly applicable context-specific knowledge. There's no substitute for knowing, as the saying goes. Finally, the argument from transfer warns that transfer is not to be taken for granted. Generality and widespread applicability of reflective intelligence do not occur automatically, just because in principle a person is doing something general. The bridging from one context to another has to be sought and prompted.

Which brings us back to the puzzle of the chess master that opened this chapter. Recall the king's ingenious plan—to recruit a citizen of his country, the world chess champion of over twenty years, into a new role as military leader. The king hoped a quick introduction to matters military and political would retool his chess master for war. The master's tactical genius, so obvious in chess, would defend the threatened kingdom. With the arguments from expertise, weak methods, and transfer spelled out, and the general idea of learnable intelligence in mind, what are the chess master's prospects?

In part, an answer depends on knowing more about the chess master. Does he already think a lot in terms of general principles (control the center—any center) rather than entirely contextualized principles (control the middle squares of the chess board)? How reflective is he in general about chess and other activities? Does he tend to do what high road transfer calls for: mindfully abstract principles from particulars? Or, in contrast, is he a gifted intuitive player of chess, with an enormous fund of experience but little predilection to reflect and generalize? Depending on the answers to such questions, one might forecast his chances as ranging from "No way!" to "There's some hope."

It would be irresponsible to stoke the king's optimism very high, however. While the new science of learnable intelligence says that the chess master might carry over considerable tactical knowledge from chess to matters military if his character and other conditions are right, the fact remains that military campaigns are another area of experiential intelligence. However helpful the chess master's general tactical knowledge in getting him off to a running start, however quickly the chess master would outdistance someone studying military tactics without the chess background, however much the chess master's reflective intelligence might allow him to make more creative use of the same classic battles that the general on the other side has also reviewed, the fact of the matter still remains that the chess master will be a relative beginner. While recruiting the chess master for the mission, the king had better hedge his bets and set about making strong alliances with friendly neighbors!

Of course, this cautious reading of the chess master's chances is not at all a lackluster appraisal of learnable intelligence. It is simply a recognition that learnable intelligence involves both experiential and reflective intelligence, the former rather context bound and the second much more general. It is simply a recognition that reflective and experiential intelligence make a partnership. In demanding circumstances, neither partner works very well alone.

Part III

What the Mind Is Made Of

10

The Right Stuff

On July 20, 1969, like so many others, I stayed up late to watch on television a human being set foot on the moon for the first time. To this day, it remains one of my most vivid memories, a rare moment where folks all over the world participated in a collective frisson of unity and adventure.

That moment has an indelible association in my mind with the *right stuff*. This phrase, the title of Tom Wolfe's energetic history of the dawn of the U.S. space program, names the special quality needed by jet pilots working on the double edge of their skill and modern technology, the kinds of pilots that might make good astronauts. If you did not have the right stuff as a pilot, you could say goodbye to the moon before even getting started.

Having the right stuff is just as important for theories as for astronauts. Theories are high flyers too, often reaching far outside our everyday conception of the world to make sense of phenomena in surprising ways. In particular, a theory about learnable intelligence has to have the right stuff. From the beginning of this book I have been asking what underlies intelligence—what kind of stuff. I have called this the first mindware question, and its number-one position is deserved. For a new awareness of intelligence at work around us in everyday life, for a deeper look into the character of intelligence, for exercising educational,

233

political, workplace, and other opportunities to expand intelligent behavior, nothing but the right stuff will do.

This question about the stuff of intelligence inherently has an onto-logical character. Ontology concerns the nature of what exists. For instance, stones exist in one sense, but numbers such as seven or π exist in quite a different sense, if they can be said to exist at all. You can kick seven stones but not seven in general. You can eat a pie but not π. So what can you do with whatever intelligence is made of? What kind of stuff is it? To ask what the mechanisms of intelligence are is to open our minds to whatever kind of stuff might make up those mechanisms.

Spearman and his followers thought that they had the answer to this ontological question. The stuff of intelligence was mental energy, and Spearman's g was the symptom of its presence. If one of my neighbors proves to be a better decision maker or thinker in other ways than another, it's in good part because the first neighbor has a more abundant supply of this mental energy.

We did away with that notion in Part I. It did not make sense to view intelligence as just a matter of mental energy. It did not even make sense to modernize Spearman's conception and view intelli-gence solely as a matter of neural efficiency—the speed and precision of response of the nervous system. To honor what the research from psychometricians, the findings of investigations of expertise, and the results from studies of the learning of strategies and related matter said, we had to recognize three right stuffs that made up intelligence. Neural intelligence was one kind of stuff, presumably some kind of neural efficiency composed of the speed and precision of information processing in the neural system. Experiential intelligence was another kind of stuff, made of the knowledge we gain through extended lived experience in academic areas like physics or nonacademic areas like raising a family. And reflective intelligence was the third kind of stuff, made of thinking strategies, positive attitudes toward investing one-self in good thinking, and metacognition—awareness and manage-ment of one's own mind. The right stuff was three stuffs, each with a role, all important.

The Right Stuff Question

So far so good. However, in this book we want to get the stuff of learn-able intelligence not just right but *very* right. Let us test how sharp and clear it seems at this point. One way to do that is to ask what might be called the right stuff question:

What's the stuff you get when you get smarter?

We all have experiences from time to time of getting smarter. Perhaps you have been managing personnel problems. You had the insight that people often resent even justly applied authority. You take this to heart and strive for more finesse in dealing with people. You have gotten smarter about handling those problems. This is an advance in what I called experiential intelligence: You have developed more insight and know-how in a specialized area.

Or perhaps you have just worked through a major decision: whether to take a new part-time job and drop a previous one. You discovered that early on you were trapped by your own feeling that you had to make a binding commitment: yes or no, make the change or not. Yet there were too many uncertainties. Finally recognizing this, you negotiated an arrangement for a trial period. You would keep both jobs for four weeks, something you could manage all right. That would tell you more than hours of analyzing the prospects. Generalizing from this, you make a rule for yourself—try to find a way to test the waters. This is an advance in what I called reflective intelligence: You have developed a principle of thinking. What makes this reflective, not experiential intelligence is that it is specifically *about* thinking, not about personnel problems or about job switching. It concerns how to deal well with decisions.

Now picture yourself pondering these experiences. Or ponder a similar experience you have had recently where in some sense you got smarter. Ask the right stuff question: What's the stuff you get when you get smarter? Principles, ideas, to be sure. But more generally, what? The idea of experiential intelligence says experience, but that answer wins the prize for vagueness. The idea of reflective intelligence says strategies, positive attitudes, metacognition; but these ideas also seem fuzzy. Although the notions of experiential and reflective intelligence broadly circumscribe what stuff you get when you get smarter, they still leave it rather out of focus.

Let us see what some answers might sound like that are a little more in focus. Here are three different views worth considering. Each has something to recommend it.

- *The strength metaphor.* Maybe getting smarter is a matter of acquiring mental strength. Perhaps as you exercise your mind by solving problems and facing other mental challenges, in some sense your thinking gets stronger. The stuff you get is a kind of mental strength.
- *The process metaphor.* Maybe getting smarter is a matter of acquiring more and better organized mental processes. Certainly learning thinking strategies sounds like acquiring new processes, and metacognition—monitoring and managing your thinking—seems like a process. So the stuff you get is processes and better process organization.
- *The expertise metaphor.* Maybe getting smarter is a matter of acquiring expertise. When you gain insights about managing people, you acquire expertise in doing so, and this boosts your experiential intelligence. When you arrive at decision-making principles like the one mentioned above, you acquire expertise about thinking, which expands your reflective intelligence. So the stuff you get is expertise.

All of these ways of answering the right stuff question have some plausibility. But I want to argue that they all fall well short of the mark. I want to replace all these metaphors with yet a fourth, the really right stuff:

- *The geographical metaphor.* Getting smarter is a matter of coming to know your way around different situations (experiential intelligence) and coming to know your way around decision making, problem solving, learning with understanding, and other important kinds of thinking (reflective intelligence). The stuff you get is very diverse—strategies, habits, concepts, beliefs, values, and more—but it's all part of knowing your way around.

Why all this hard work to construct a better metaphor for answering the right stuff question? There are two motives. First of all, getting the right stuff right is part of the scientific enterprise. It's part of understanding how something works, in this case how your and my learnable intelligence works. So section by section, I want to argue that we need to get beyond the idea of mental strength, beyond the idea of mental processes, and beyond the idea of expertise. None of these are right enough, although they get successively closer.

The second motive has a more practical turn. What we think about the right stuff of learnable intelligence writes a prescription for how we ought to cultivate it in ourselves and in others. If we think the right stuff is some kind of mental strength, we should look to mental exercise to improve it. If we think the right stuff is processes, we should try to identify the key processes, make them more efficient when we have them, and acquire them when we do not. If we think the right stuff is a kind of expertise, then we need to remember that experts do not just act—they understand what they are doing and why, which helps them to do it better. So we need to develop knowledge and understanding.

And what if we think that the right stuff is knowing your way around? What does that say about how we should go about getting smarter? I will save the answer to that until later. For the moment, I hope I have said enough to make the case that it matters. We want a good answer to the right stuff question not just for the sake of being right but also for the sake of being effective.

Beyond Mental Strength

The notion of mental strength that one can build has little presence in professional psychological research. But it is very much a part of our folk psychology, with a strong showing in everyday speech and a platform in the marketplace of popular books on thinking. Much of our everyday language about the mind echoes a strength metaphor. Books promise to increase your *brainpower*, plainly treating intelligence as a kind of strength. We hear of mental calisthenics. We admire *strong* thinkers and aspire to become more *powerful* thinkers.

The efforts to teach thinking discussed in Chapter 8 might be seen through the lens of mental strength. Teaching specific strategies for broad-mindedness, creativity, or analysis of evidence might amount to providing the learner with the exercise bars and pulleys needed to strengthen his or her brainpower—a gym full of Nautilus equipment for the mind. At least potentially, the mind possesses a number of powers— the powers to think about several sides of a situation, brainstorm creatively, seek evidence vigorously and view it critically, and so on. Appropriate exercise might amplify these powers, making them stronger, more precise, and more efficient. Emphasis on self-monitoring and a critical perspective could be understood as the kind of character-building rigor that goes with athletic training.

To caricature it a bit, this general notion can be called a mental muscle theory of reflective intelligence. It offers one answer to "what stuff do you get when you get smarter?" The mental muscle theory treats mind and body in much the same way. Just as your biceps and triceps allow improvement through exercise, so with the muscles of the mind.

So does the strength metaphor—the mental muscle theory—work? Unfortunately, it does not. First of all there is a problem of principle. The mental muscle theory only matches the state of the art in cultivating reflective intelligence in a rough way. To be sure, most approaches to improving intelligence provide abundant exercise. But they overwhelmingly emphasize mental organization, equipping learners with concepts and strategies that help them to restructure their thinking in a more effective manner.

But perhaps the seeming importance of mental organization is misleading. Could it be that what really counts is sheer practice? Unfortunately for the mental muscles theory, there is direct evidence against the notion that practice alone dramatically increases reflective intelligence. Indeed, practice on intellectual tasks may not improve performance at all!

One study in point comes from the research of mathematician-psychologist Alan Schoenfeld, who has investigated extensively the teaching of heuristics (strategies) for mathematical problem solving. (see Chapter 4). In one of Schoenfeld's experiments, a number of sample problems were presented with discussion of how to solve them *and* explicit articulation of the relevant strategies. In addition, the teacher provided extensive practice on problem sets. Students participating in a control condition received exactly the same sample problems and solution explanations, but without explicit mention of the strategies. The control students also worked through the same problem sets.

The students who heard explicit mention of the strategies performed substantially better on a problem-solving posttest. The control group students did not improve at all, despite doing the same practice problems as the treatment students. Moreover, Schoenfeld gathered from both groups of students think-aloud explanations of their approach to some of the posttest problems. He discovered that solving the harder problems, in both groups, depended on using the sorts of strategies that had been made explicit for the treatment group. In other words, the gains in the group explicitly exposed to the strategies were entirely and specifically attributable to the reorganizing impact of the strategies on the students' cognitions.

Other findings to the same effect appear elsewhere in the literature on the teaching of cognitive skills. For another example mentioned briefly in Chapter 4, psychologists Annemarie Palincsar and Ann Brown developed an approach to strategic reading called reciprocal teaching. They sought an instructional method that would help poor readers to perform better, understanding and retaining more of what they read. As part of their research, they contrasted different teaching methodologies. All engaged the students in reading sample materials and discussing them in much the same way. In one variation, the strategies were made explicit and the children practiced their use. In another, the teacher interacted with the students around the same sample texts, using the same sorts of questions, and encouraged the students to participate in the same style, but without calling the questions strategies or drawing explicit attention to them. The students in the explicit group gained substantially on reading measures, whereas the students in the tacit practice-only group gained not at all.

Such findings make a powerful case against a strength metaphor for reflective intelligence. Mental strength is the wrong stuff, not the right stuff. These findings do not, of course, say that practice is irrelevant. Naturally, learners need practice in order to get used to new ways of directing their thinking. However, the studies that show no impact of pure practice approaches tell us that practice does not lie at the heart of the matter. Accordingly, mental strength does not give us a good answer to the right stuff question.

Beyond Mental Processes

If the mental strength metaphor will not do, perhaps the mental process metaphor serves up the right stuff. Broadly, the process metaphor suggests that better thinking depends on better cognitive processes. For instance, a good decision maker would have a better bundle of processes for searching for options. The decision maker would find more and more imaginative options. The good decision maker in a family dispute would not just think "for" or "against" but think of options like this:

- putting a moratorium on the problem until people cool down
- compromising, starting with a clean slate but a new policy
- asking a friend or relative to arbitrate
- insisting on the point at hand but making a concession on something else
- and so on

From a process perspective, this crop of possibilities occurs because of the good decision maker's process repertoire. The decision maker questions assumptions, deliberately seeks more options, seeks intermediate resolutions between "for" and "against," looks to past experience for options, and in general monitors his or her progress in cultivating a greater range of choices. All this involves cognitive processes.

The process metaphor has much in its favor. By and large, successful efforts to boost reflective intelligence have highlighted strategies that help learners acquire new procedures and reorganize old ones to make them more effective. So the process view makes sense in terms of successful instruction.

Also, most analyses of mental functioning developed by cognitive scientists emphasize process. The pages of psychology books are filled with illustrations that show how information flows from one kind of process to another: Here information gets encoded, next it's classified, next it joins with other information to form a more complex and meaningful structure. Stages of processing are the watchword in many analyses of cognition. Often the metaphor of the mind as a computer lurks in the background, and sometimes squats boldly in the foreground. As computers execute programs, so do human beings execute procedures in their minds, sometimes deliberately and often automatically. These procedures carry out the various information processing operations needed to accomplish tasks. There can be no doubt that the process metaphor provides a promising candidate for answering "What stuff do you get when you get smarter?"

Bucking the trend, I want to challenge the process metaphor's claim to the turf of reflective intelligence. Processes are okay up to a point, but they are not nearly enough to give a good picture of how reflective intelligence works. The right stuff is something rather different—a matter of knowing your way around.

Kinds of Knowing

Just as psychologists have struggled to make sense of how the mind works using their tools, so have philosophers. One of the useful distinctions was initially articulated by Oxford philosopher Gilbert Ryle and examined further by others such as my colleagues Israel Scheffler and Vernon Howard. They contrast "knowing that" with "knowing how." You know *that* your phone number is 555-5555, but you know *how* to dial a phone. You know *that* your birthday is August 5, but you know *how* to have a party. Knowing *that* such-and-such depends on having propositions in storage, information stockpiled. Knowing *how* is a matter of being able to do something, given the means and opportunity.

Knowing that and knowing how are quite different. Sometimes we know that, but not how. We know that we should administer cardiopulmonary resuscitation but regrettably do not know how. Sometimes we know how but not that. For instance, we know how to speak our native language, but do not know that we are using relative clauses or subjunctive tenses. It may not matter if you are just communicating as usual, but it may be you are trying to teach others to speak the language. And sometimes, of course, knowing that helps us to know how. You know that the book you seek is somewhere on the lower shelf, which helps you to know how to find it.

Psychologists developing models of thinking and learning have adopted a somewhat related nomenclature, declarative versus procedural knowledge. Declarative knowledge concerns facts, pieces of information. It corresponds roughly to knowing that. Procedural knowledge concerns how to do things. It corresponds roughly to knowing how, to having appropriate information and mental processes at your fingertips to enable you to do things. Like the philosopher Ryle, many cognitive psychologists have warned that it simply will not do to think of knowledge as solely declarative and learning as solely the acquisition of information. Knowledge is often procedural—how to do things—and learning a matter of acquiring ways of doing things.

Speaking of different kinds of knowing is a powerful move to make. It reminds us of the richness available in our everyday vocabulary to make important distinctions about the nature of knowledge. My colleague Vernon Howard, writing about learning and knowing, has discussed other kinds of knowing to clarify what happens when we learn. For instance, he reminds us of the common phrases "knowing what it is to" and "knowing what it is like to." If you have spent a while in Tokyo, you know what it is to be in Tokyo. If you have never been in Tokyo but have spent time in a similar city, you know what it is like to be in Tokyo. Howard highlights how singing instructors in effect make use of this in helping learners to catch on to vocal maneuvers. They use various tricks to get learners to produce a target sound just once, so that they will know what it is, and analogies to evoke a sense of the target sound so that learners will know what it is like. In drawing our attention to more kinds of knowing than knowing that and knowing how, Vernon Howard demonstrates the richness of our everyday language in reflecting different kinds of knowing.

Let me take inspiration from Gilbert Ryle, Israel Scheffler, Vernon Howard, and others who have found this a useful move and draw another kind of knowing from our everyday vocabulary—knowing your way around. I want to argue that there is power in this everyday notion of knowing your way around. It offers us a much richer conception of what we know when we think well—what we know when we have reflective intelligence—than the notion of mental processes or indeed the notion of know-how. The kind of knowledge you have when you know your way around, that's the answer to the right stuff question.

Knowing Your Way Around Harvard Square

What does knowing your way around really mean? Let us begin with an actual if modest piece of geography. For many years, I have worked in Harvard Square of Cambridge, Massachusetts, and for several years I lived in Harvard Square. I know my way around Harvard Square.

One thing this means is that I can find my way from one familiar place to another: from the buildings of the Harvard Graduate School of Education to Wordsworth's, a book store, from Wordsworth's to Holyoke Center, a building full of Harvard offices, from Holyoke Center to CD paradise at Tower Records or HMV. But knowing my way around Harvard Square involves much more than having a fixed repertoire of routes. I can plan new routes to suit the occasion because I have a bird's eye view of where things are. Besides sheer information, values and feelings figure prominently too: I know the places I like and don't like, and the places I like sometimes. I know where to sit when I want coffee and a quiet chat, and where to sit for coffee and the stimulation of a crowd if that's my mood.

From this single example, it's clear that knowing your way around involves a number of psychological processes—the process metaphor is partly right. But it also involves factual knowledge, mental images, values, feelings, and flexible composition of all these into new patterns of action to suit the occasion. In fact, such flexible composition of new patterns of action is very much a part of the connotation of knowing your way around.

Another way of analyzing knowing your way around Harvard Square is to say that it is an area of expertise. I have expertise about Harvard Square. Recall how Chapters 4 and 9 emphasized the role of knowledge and experience in human thinking. To a much greater extent than had been realized, thinking depended on local knowledge, information specific to the context, like my knowledge of Harvard Square. In focusing on knowing your way around, I am resurrecting the idea of expertise. However, later in the chapter I want to draw several distinctions between the idea of expertise as usually understood and the notion of knowing your way around as developed here.

While my familiarity with Harvard Square is a thoroughly geographical case of knowing your way around, the concept easily extends to more abstract activities. It makes perfect sense to speak of people who know their way around the inside of an automobile engine, or the stock market, or nuclear physics. Dentists know their way around your mouth and doctors know their way around your body. Heart surgeons know their way around your heart. Hackers know their way around computers and computer networks.

What we have here in knowing your way around is a concrete concept metaphorically extended—knowing your way around a region extrapolated to knowing your way around any area of human activity. This kind of metaphorical extension should not surprise us. It is a commonplace human trick in making sense of the world. As George Lakoff and Mark Johnson point up in their *Metaphors We Live By*, much of our abstract language finds its roots in concrete physical metaphors. For instance, we speak of *taking a stand* when we commit ourselves to a position. We speak of *finding grounds* when we look for evidence. And we speak of knowing our way around when we are talking about abstract things as well as geographical regions like Harvard Square. Such metaphorical extensions of the concrete are often powerful, and the notion of knowing your way around is no exception.

In fact, you may have recognized that knowing your way around sounds a lot like experiential intelligence, the kind of intelligence you get through extended experience in an area. That's right. Knowing your way around is a way of talking about experiential intelligence, a way of naming what you get when you have extended experience in an area. The extended experience of me around Harvard Square, dentists around teeth, doctors around human bodies, heart surgeons around the heart, and hackers around computers leads them all to know their way around those things.

Knowing Your Way Around Thinking

Knowing your way around gives us a good metaphor for talking about experiential intelligence. But here is a surprise: It also gives us a good metaphor for talking about reflective intelligence. The notion of knowing your way around easily extends to kinds of thinking. Just as it makes sense to speak of knowing your way around an automobile engine or the stock market, it makes sense to speak of knowing your way around decision making or solving math problems or reading strategically or any number of other thought-demanding activities. It may seem odd that the same metaphor of knowing you way around works for both experiential and reflective intelligence. What this means for the relation between reflective and experiential intelligence I will get to later. For now, let us continue to explore the idea. Let me show how well knowing your way around applies to thinking.

Let us look at decision making as a case in point. First of all, it turns out that youngsters recognize decision making as an important area of cognition. They know it's something to be reckoned with. My colleague Shari Tishman has undertaken studies of what children recognize as thinking challenges. The fifth-grade children in her research identified decision making as one of two kinds of thinking challenges that stand out most for them (the other was understanding something). Recognizing decision making as an important area of thinking, youngsters have begun to learn their way around it. They have some ideas about how to handle decision making. They see decision making as resolving conflicting options and approach resolving the dilemma by weighing the advantages and disadvantages. In later work with sixth graders, Tishman collected remarks like the following:

> I think about if it is a good thing or a bad thing to do. I ask will it hurt you or someone else. Will your mother ground you if she found out?
>
> When I make a decision, I look at the good points of my decision and the bad points. If there are more good points that I can think of, I say I do it. But if there are more bad points, then it must be the wrong thing to do.

Beyond weighing advantages and disadvantages, their basic idea is to "try harder" to think about the decision facing them. However, youngsters of this age have a relatively undeveloped conception of how to try harder. It's mostly a matter of pushing yourself to persist and concentrate. Tishman calls this a "force and focus" conception of mind.

Knowing your way around decision making is something that inevitably expands with age and experience. Adults have an impressive grab bag of tactics for trying harder. A few times, I have asked groups of adults a simple question: When you are facing a tough decision, what do you know about how to handle it? People invariably have a lot to say. They mention points such as:

- Give it time.
- See how your feelings about it change.
- Don't give way to a false sense of urgency.
- Talk to a friend.
- Talk to someone who's "been there."
- Seclude yourself.
- Ask yourself when you really need to decide. Can you buy time?
- Ask yourself whether you have to decide at all.
- Ask yourself who else the decision affects.
- Ask if it's your decision or really others' too.
- Brainstorm.
- Make a pro-con list.
- Figure out what your most important goals are.
- Make a list of factors to think about.
- Be objective.
- Trust your feelings.
- Get more information.
- Check your information.
- Look for a way to have your cake and eat it too.
- Consider the consequences of different options.
- Use your imagination: What would this option be like?
- Try out an option to see what it's like.
- Figure out how to try an option without commitment.
- Ask yourself whether you can back out later. How costly would it be?

In other words, adults quite unsurprisingly know their way around decision making to a significant extent. This does not mean that most adults are excellent decision makers; this list pools advice from a number of individuals and, as discussed in earlier chapters, people neglect important aspects of decision making, as of other kinds of thinking. But they are not babes in the woods of decision making, either.

The above list suggests that knowing your way around decision making involves a lot more knowledge than knowing your phone number, address, social security number, or even the dates of the presidents. And the same holds for any area of thinking. Another case in point is reasoning in order to reach sound beliefs and conclusions. My colleague Raymond Nickerson wrote a 1986 book entitled *Reflections on Reasoning* that, he avows in the introduction, is neither a textbook nor a prescription but "a collection of thoughts regarding various aspects of reasoning and what it means to reason well." In effect, the book offers a compendium of what it is to know your way around reasoning. The compendium includes basic concepts like truth, reason, logic, imply, infer, deduce; forms of logical argument, how to analyze them, how to evaluate them, and how to represent them; ways of misleading and misrepresenting so as to persuade; common fallacies such as *ad hominem* argument or appeal to tradition, or stereotyping; and rules of thumb for cultivating better reasoning in oneself. Several dozen concepts, distinctions, strategies, pitfalls, and prescriptions figure in Nickerson's panorama of the terrain of reasoning. As with knowing your way around Harvard Square, there is a lot to know.

Another colleague, Robert Weber, has mapped some of the moves that figure in human invention in a 1992 book provocatively entitled *Forks, Phonographs, and Hot-Air Balloons.* Weber catalogs strategies that seem to have figured over and over again in human invention from the stone-age knife to the laser. For instance, one basic move is a "join," a combination of two or more things as in the Swiss army knife. Of course, not all joins would be useful. I remember years ago running acorss an advertisement for a refrigerator with an audiotape deck installed, a dubious join indeed. Weber urges that one rule of thumb is to combine just those tools or ideas that are used in the same context, for instance a protractor with a ruler along the flat edge. Although the tapedeck built into the refrigerator might sometimes prove handy for music or leaving messages, basically it seems to violate this principle. Another of Weber's guidelines is to combine tools or ideas that are inverses of one another. For instance, the ordinary claw hammer includes the hammer part for driving nails and the claw part for pulling them out. Discussing numerous other operations besides joins, Weber makes the case that invention calls upon a number of often tacit patterns that allow people to generate promising ideas. This does not mean that inventors run through a mental library of patterns deliberately. But plausibly they have a feel for the kinds of patterns that prove fruitful again and again. Invention, like Harvard Square, is something you can know your way around.

Back to Beyond Mental Processes

Recall that our aim was to pit the geographical metaphor against the process metaphor. After taking a look at what knowing your way around decision making is like, how does a process account of decision making compare with the geographical metaphor? Why would I say that knowing your way around is a better way to characterize decision-making ability than talk of cognitive processes? A number of reasons come forward:

- Decision making involves not only processes and strategies but knowledge of various kinds: knowledge of who might help, of how one's feelings change with time, of how others might have a stake, of the importance of checking information, and so on.
- Decision making involves feelings in plenty—caution, perseverance, a spirit of imagination, worry, and so on.
- Decision making involves a conceptual system, highlighting concepts such as options, consequences, goals, pros and cons, factors, objectivity, information, and so on.
- Decision making involves tacit beliefs about the way the world works and the mind works, beliefs such as "You can't really know until you try it" or "The best options are often the imaginative ones you don't see right away."
- Decision making involves values and standards, for instance the values of being thorough or being imaginative or trusting your feelings or taking into account others' needs.

It would not be hard to make the list longer, but this is enough to draw a moral. The process metaphor leaves a lot out. To put it in ontological terms—a question of the "stuff" of reflective intelligence—the process metaphor is ontologically sparse. The process metaphor does not recognize at all, or downplays dramatically, the many kinds of stuff that figure importantly in our knowing our way around decision making or other kinds of thinking, stuff like concepts, feelings, beliefs, values, and knowledge of various kinds. In contrast, knowing your way around is a roomy notion that welcomes a range of kinds of mental stuff and honors their role in informing how people think.

Arguably this is not entirely fair to the process metaphor. A champion of the notion of cognitive processes could complain: "Of course all that's important. Just because I put cognitive processes in the center doesn't mean that I exclude a role for all those other things." This is true. And it's also true that the process metaphor has provided cognitive science with a valuable tool that has yielded a number of provocative theories. At the same time, when we look at the character of our knowledge of decision making, it does not seem any more centered on process than on values or knowledge or concepts. It seems an intricate mix, with cognitive processes playing an important role alongside other important roles played by other kinds of stuff. And remember what's at stake: not just getting the theory right, although that is part of it, but finding the best approach to cultivating reflective intelligence. If we think of it as a bunch of cognitive processes we do one thing; if we think of it as an ensemble of different kinds of stuff encompassed by the metaphor knowing your way around, we might do something quite different.

Beyond Expertise

So what stuff do you get when you get smarter? The right stuff of reflective intelligence looks to be whatever goes into knowing your way around decision making and other kinds of thinking. This right stuff of course has multiple natures, not one. It is processes, strategies, feelings, images, sensitivities, virtually any kind of stuff that supports our acting reflectively. When people learn to be generally more intelligent, they learn their way around thinking.

But if knowing your way around points to the right stuff, is it new stuff? Why not just say that it's a kind of expertise—not expertise about skiing or carpentry or chemistry, but expertise about thinking? Certainly if knowing your way around resembles anything, it resembles the science of expertise developed by psychologists over the last three decades. Recall from Chapters 4 and 9 that A. D. de Groot, Herbert Simon, and William Chase looked into the cognitive processes of expert chess players. Following their lead, other investigators examined such areas of expertise as physics problem solving, mathematical problem solving, computer programming, and medical diagnosis. A number of common patterns emerged. Most tellingly, good thinking in such areas depended greatly on a rich knowledge base developed over a number of years. Expert chess players truly know their way around a chess board. Expert diagnosticians truly know their way around the ills of the human body.

Taking a cue from the experts on expertise, someone might say that reflective intelligence is a matter of expertise as well—expertise about decision making, problem solving, and so on. Expertise, knowing your way around: It all boils down to the same thing.

This is a very sensible observation. However, just as I do not think the idea of cognitive processes does justice to the richness of reflective intelligence, I do not think that the idea of expertise does either. In fact, I do not think that the idea of expertise even does justice to experiential intelligence, although the notion of experiential intelligence builds on the research about expertise.

In other words, expertise has got to go. It just does not offer a good answer to the right stuff question, not as a model of reflective intelligence and not even as a model of experiential intelligence. To see why, let us look more closely at knowing your way around, coming back to expertise a little later.

The World of Realms

The idea of knowing your way around illuminates experiential intelligence, giving us a sense of knowing richer than just knowing that and knowing how. But a further question comes up: When you know your way around horse racing or horticulture, the harpsichord or hypnotism, what is it that you know your way around? These areas of activity of course. But what should one call them in general? It's useful to have a general name and the chosen name is *realms*.

Any topic or area of activity people can come to know their way around constitutes a realm. Ballroom dancing is a realm. Carburetor repair is a realm. So are quantum mechanics, kite flying, weight lifting, reading classic mystery whodunits, English literature of the nineteenth century, arbitration, public speaking, collecting butterflies, and, of course, getting around Harvard Square.

The idea of knowing your way around also illuminates reflective intelligence. There too, it makes sense to speak of realms. Familiar thinking realms that we can know our way around include decision making, remembering and memorizing, everyday problem solving, problem solving in math and science, reasoning and argument, and many more. Less commonplace and more specialized realms of thinking include formal deductive logic, statistical reasoning, legal argument, criminal investigation, invention in the sense of inventors like Thomas Edison or Edwin Land (founder of Polaroid, developer of instant photography), or literary criticism. The next chapter offers a more careful look at what realms of thinking we ought to attend to and how they relate to one another.

Another question of nomenclature: When you know your way around a realm, what makes up that knowing? To be sure, strategies, processes, beliefs, values, and so on, all the stuff referred to before. But what to call such stuff in general? When you know your way around horse racing or horticulture, playing the harpsichord or hypnotism, let us call what goes into your knowing your way around that realm your *realm knowledge.* I mean knowledge here in a deliberately broad and eclectic sense, open to everything relevant whether or not it cleaves close to what is usually meant by the term knowledge.

With the ideas of realms, realm knowledge, and knowing your way around to work with, let us take a deeper look at what realms are like and how realm knowledge helps us to think and act. I will mix examples from experiential intelligence—specific realms like polo playing, child care, and physics—and examples from reflective intelligence—realms like decision making, strategic planning, and diagnostic reasoning. The clearer a vision we get about how realm knowledge helps to think and act, the narrower the usual idea of expertise appears, and the plainer the need to get beyond expertise.

The ABCs of Realms

By definition, realm knowledge includes all manner of stuff, the result of a deliberate open-immigration policy for a richer ontology of mind. It welcomes values, commitments, inklings, whims, insights, understandings, bafflements, curiosities, anything that might make up part of our knowing our way around. Still, a little organization amid the panoply of mental resources would be welcome. To make some order of the chaos, let me speak of the ABCs of a realm. A stands for action system, B stands for belief system, including values, standards, and felt beliefs, and C stands for conceptual system. Any realm has all three. Together, they make up the realm knowledge with which we work, by which we know our way around.

Since I write this passage on the day after Thanksgiving, dining makes a good example. Dining is of course a realm, like any activity we pursue much at all. We know our way around dining. But what is that realm knowledge like?

A *for Action System.I>* A *number of actions figure in the action system around dining, for instance:*
- The physical routines of manipulating knife, fork, and spoon.
- The social routines of eating together, asking for the salt, taking the portion closest to us, keeping our elbows off the table.
- Strategic routines such as pacing your eating on Thanksgiving.
- Characteristic patterns of dining such as appetizer, main course, dessert.
- Customs that accompany eating, such as making small talk.

B *for Belief System.* We hold a smorgasbord of beliefs, values, and feelings concerning dining that inform and motivate our dining action system. For instance, beliefs and values commonly include:
- It's appropriate to eat with table utensils, not with your fingers, and use them correctly.
- Good manners as our society sees them are called for at the dining table.
- In our health-conscious culture, the health value of low salt, low fat, low calories, and fiber.
- Our personal knowledge of what we do and do not enjoy—pecan pie yes, boiled cabbage no.
- What foods are morally or religiously appropriate—for some, beef yes, pork no.
- What foods suit what occasions—turkey for Thanksgiving, popcorn for movies.
- What foods other people we know like.
- If you eat a lot quickly, you'll feel bloated.

C *for Conceptual System.* Dining involves a platefull of concepts important for the acquisition and expression of beliefs and actions such as mentioned above, for instance:
- Specific food concepts such as steak, celery, and rhubarb
- Food types such as meat, vegetables, fruits

- Cooking methods such as fried, broiled, boiled.
- Eating utensils such as knives, forks, and spoons.
- Health concepts such as fat content, calories, salt content.
- General and specific concepts involved in good conduct, such as manners, customs, eating with utensils versus fingers, elbows and places to put them.

So the ABCs provide a simple way of charting some of what goes into knowing your way around the realm of dining, or of any realm. Do the ABCs work for kinds of thinking as well, exposing the ontological richness of our realm knowledge about kinds of thinking? Decision making was discussed earlier and it's too easy to translate what was said into the ABCs, so let us take a different example. Consider a very familiar and sometimes very important domain of thinking: memorizing. People who know their way around memorizing have their ABCs straight:

A for Action System. The actions people carry out to memorize often run along these lines:
  - Rehearsing.
  - Organizing a grab-bag of ideas into categories.
  - Finding links to something you already know.
  - Making up visual associations.
  - Stopping trying to remember something, in the belief that it will come to you later.
  - Testing yourself and concentrating on what you miss.

B for Belief System. Some beliefs, values, and feelings about memorizing that back up the above actions include:
  - Rehearsal aids memory.
  - When I organize something for myself, that helps me remember it.
  - When I relate new ideas to something I already know, that helps me remember them.
  - Visual associations help me remember things.
  - My memory is good or not so good.
  - I can help myself to remember things by tricks like leaving notes for myself.
  - When something is on the tip of my tongue, I will probably remember it a little later.

C *for Conceptual System.* Concepts that figure importantly in the above belief and action systems include:

- Memory
- Rehearsal
- Association
- Image
- Organization
- Forgetting
- Having something on the tip of your tongue

By and large, research underwrites the worth of these beliefs and action patterns. For instance, the feeling that information hangs on the tip of your tongue is no illusion: Laboratory studies show that when people have this feeling, they can answer broad questions about what they can't remember—for instance, what's the first letter—with much better than chance accuracy. This means that you actually have information in storage that you cannot fully access. For another instance, rehearsal is key. But rehearsal alone is much less effective than rehearsal combined with other memory strategies like organizing ideas or making up visual associations. The idea of memory strategies has a long and venerable history. For instance, the Greeks used a tactic for memorizing called the method of loci. This involves associating facts to be remembered with positions in a familiar physical setting, such as nooks and crannies around your house.

What does this look at the ABCs of dining or memorizing tell us? Three points stand out. First and foremost, such lists are like tips of icebergs. You could interview almost anyone at length about the subtleties of their knowledge of dining, and beyond what you would hear lies their unconscious knowledge, embodied in habits and tacit assumptions. The same can be said for people who have cultivated memorizing and accumulated a lot of realm knowledge there.

Second, the As, Bs, and Cs are intertwined. For example, a strategy of memorizing by forming visual associations (part of the action system) rests on the user's belief that this technique indeed locks information into memory (part of the belief system). This belief in turn depends for its formulation on a conceptual system involving such concepts as memory, image, and association (part of the conceptual system).

Third, within the action, belief, and conceptual systems, people employ many different kinds of mental representations: the words by which things are named, our mental images of different memory techniques, feelings of confidence or doubt, and so on. To repeat a refrain, stuff comes in many different kinds. The ontology is complex and rich.

Realms in All Sizes

To get an even better picture of realms, it's interesting to ask what sizes they come in. While realms like dining apply across many occasions and settings, some realms are remarkably small and specialized. Consider for a moment a small gem of a realm called shoe tying. Does it make to sense to say you know your way around shoe tying? At first thought, it's tempting to answer in the negative: Something like tying shoes seems too small to know one's way around. However, a little pondering reveals all the earmarks of a full-fledged realm. Most people know a surprising amount about shoe tying.

In fact, the ABCs that mark any realm provide a good test of the question. Is there a conceptual system around shoe tying? To be sure, and here are some of the concepts in it: shoe, laces, eyes, bow knots, granny knots, tied, untied. There is also a belief system. Here are some of the beliefs: that laces keep your shoes on, that untied laces put you at risk of tripping, that tight laces can be uncomfortable, that shoelaces eventually wear down and break. Finally, there is an action system, its centerpiece the act of tying your shoes. Note that shoe tying is nothing to take for granted: Children require considerable time and effort to learn the trick. Besides that, a number of other actions are part of the action system: rethreading shoelaces when an end slips out of an eye, tightening them, loosening them, installing a new shoelace, repairing a broken shoelace by tying it back together.

How small can realms get? Is the least twitch of your finger a realm? When you reach for your left shoe to put it on, are you exercising a reach-for-your-left-shoe realm? Of course not. Such a small chunk of behavior fails the ABC test. To be sure, there is an action—reaching for the shoe. But there are no beliefs or concepts specific to that action. Basically, the full ABCs that mark a realm develop around activities that we both recognize as distinct and deal with repeatedly over time. These may be small realms like shoe tying, sifting flour, or skipping stones, but they must have enough of a distinct identity to accumulate ABCs.

If realms in general can be large or small, the same holds of realms of thinking specifically. Some realms of thinking such as decision making or memorizing have high generality: They apply to innumerable occasions of greatly varied character. Other realms of thinking bristle with specialization and match far fewer situations in life, although they can be very powerful when they fit the situation. For instance, the use of statistics to test and support conclusions is a specialized realm. It's powerful when we have quantitative information about frequencies of events and want to make predictions or test hypotheses. But these supportive circumstances only occur from time to time. Likewise, formal deductive reasoning is a realm one can know one's way around. However, except in certain formal disciplines such as mathematics, there is rarely an occasion to use the full paraphernalia of formal deductive reasoning.

If something as innocuous as shoe tying is a realm, this tells us right away that our lives overflow with realms. The innumerable small affairs of life all constitute tiny realms over which we gain considerable control. We know our way around getting dressed in the morning, wrapping gift packages, telling time by using a clock, or house cleaning. Just through the course of normal living and learning, we become masters of minutiae.

The principle holds for realms of thinking too. General decision-making ABCs aside, there are dozens of particular kinds of decision making with which people have experience. If you go to movies a lot, you come to know your way around choosing what movies to go to. You have your personal criteria, your information sources such as newspaper reviews or friends, your favorite theaters and times of the week. Likewise, people come to know their way around choosing what clothes to wear, selecting dishes in a restaurant, enjoying a vacation, or selecting socks.

How Realms Are Born and Grow

As an infant, you knew nothing about dining or decision making. Now you do. What happened in between? Where did these realms or any realm come from?

The ABCs of a realm develop around any repeated and identified activity. When day after day your parents made a big deal about dining—eating the right foods, handling utensils correctly, and so on—you began to develop ABCs around dining. When you learned words like decision, discovered that decisions were challenging, and recognized that again and again in different contexts you faced these things called decisions, you began to develop ABCs around decision making. At first your ideas were simple: looking at the pros and cons and trying harder when decisions proved challenging. Over time they became more sophisticated.

Some realms have limited growth potential. There is only so much one can learn about tying shoes, unless one has some special role such as a shoelace designer. But other realms afford endless opportunities for broadening and deepening. The philosopher of education Israel Scheffler marks out this distinction with the term *critical skills*. By these he means open-ended realms that present endless invitations to further mastery. You may finish learning to tie your shoes, but you never finish learning to play chess, write essays, play soccer, program computers, negotiate agreements, or appreciate Mozart. There is always more if you care to invest.

In their 1993 book *Surpassing Ourselves*, cognitive psychologists Carl Bereiter and Marlene Scardamalia introduce a lovely term for continuously expanding mastery in a realm. They write of "progressive problem solving." The learner who approaches an activity like chess, soccer, or child-rearing in this spirit recognizes further challenges, accepts them, and strives to find ways of dealing with them. There results an ongoing process of knowledge-building, an ever richer ensemble of ABCs in the realm in question.

Bereiter and Scardamalia point out that mere participation in an activity gives no guarantee of increasing mastery. People play politics or bridge, manage personnel or paper flow in offices for decades without getting better in any fundamental way. Because we are tired, because we lack good models of better ways, because there are few rewards for doing better, we simply stop investing ourselves in further learning in a realm. Even as we feel satisfied with one, we may be pushing ahead in another realm, through need or fascination or stubbornness or the habit of striving. For you, getting better at bridge may be permanent project, for me perhaps getting better at writing. Whatever our long-term learning projects are, they are the arenas in which we practice progressive problem solving. With the phrase knowing your way around in mind, I like to say *learning your way around*. So long as you sustain progressive problem solving, you learn your way around further and your mastery of a realm expands.

How Realms Work Together

With this tide of realms around, it becomes evident that they mix and merge in complicated ways. Some realms are special cases of other realms: As just noted, there are many specialized realms of decision making in everyday life—selecting movies or stocks, for instance—along with general realm knowledge of decision making. Some realms sit inside other realms as subroutines, so to speak: Handling a hammer is a subrealm of the carpentry realm. Many realms intersect with one another, sharing concepts, beliefs, and patterns of action while having their distinct characters: Thinking realms such as decision making and planning share concepts such as options and consequences, beliefs such as the worth of investing mental effort, and actions such as brainstorming. Moreover, people make decisions about plans and plan to make decisions. Nonetheless, decision making is not just the same thing as planning. Each has its distinctive emphasis, despite overlaps.

With this crazy quilt of overlapping realms, it's important to ask how our realm knowledge from various realms combines to yield coherent behavior. There is no one storyline here. Acting out of realm knowledge is not so neat as playing out the pattern for long division on an arithmetic test. However, several broad generalizations seem reasonable:

A well-developed specialized realm dominates more general realms that might serve instead. Consider a specialized realm of decision making like deciding what clothing to wear. Typically, we make decisions about clothes relying on personal habits, preferences, and considerations—a warm day, a casual occasion, a rough job to do outdoors—with little or no recourse to the general ABCs of decision making.

In circumstances of high stakes or novelty, more general realm knowledge may be brought into play. Occasionally, when a clothing decision carries higher stakes, we may take a more expansive approach. For instance, a teenager preparing for an important date may thoroughly explore clothing options in a much more strategic way than for himself or herself alone.

For another example, as mentioned in Chapter 9, research on expertise shows that when problem solvers in areas such as physics face novel problems, then they behave in a less routine way. They call upon general problem-solving tactics such as developing analogies or conducting mental experiments to augment their detailed expert knowledge of physics.

When a specialized realm is not well-developed, more general realms guide our action and help us to develop it. If you have never bought a car, new or used, you are likely to approach the task using realm knowledge from your general decision-making realm. If your general decision-making practices have a casual character, you may try out a few vehicles, gather impressions, talk to friends. If you are particularly systematic in your mindset, you may also make lists of options, identify pros and cons, calculate costs carefully, and so on. In the process of choosing a car, you develop experience about how to tackle that kind of task. The next time you buy a car, that specialized knowledge will guide you as much as your general realm knowledge of decision making. After several car-buying experiences, you may even establish an effective routine that makes little contact with your general decision-making realm.

Also, more general realms develop out of specialized realms. Where do general realms come from? People cannot have experience with decision making in general, only decision making in particular cases! Or take the realm of human relations. People do not partake of human relationships in general, only in particular—with this or that parent, sister, friend, enemy, teacher, and so on. Sometimes, of course, someone teaches us parts of a general realm: A parent may emphasize thinking about the consequences in decision-making situations or treating others with respect in social situations. However, to a considerable extent, it seems clear that general realms arise out of more specialized realms through a process of abstraction. People end up with ideas about how to handle decisions through having faced and worked through a diversity of decisions in distinctive contexts. People end up with a repertoire of social skills through experience with a number of particular relationships.

To be sure, many of us may not make these generalizations with ideal frequency and scope. Indeed, all this relates to the discussion of transfer of learning in Chapter 9, where it had to be acknowledge that transfer often comes hard. Nonetheless, people do end up with general ideas about decision making, relating to others, and numerous other realms of behavior in everyday life.

Multiple realms characteristically contribute simultaneously to the same behavior. So far, I have highlighted relations of specialization and generalization between realms. But of course realms are often complementary, informing the same action simultaneously from their distinctive standpoints. As I type this sentence, my realms of typing, which is a physical skill; language use, which is a well-routinized linguistic skill;

text organization, which involves a variety of matters about sentence and paragraph structure, style and so on; and knowledge of argument and evidence, which is a kind of thinking skill, conspire together to generate a string of words on the page that fits comfortably with the strings that come before and after and constitutes a coherent message. When you simply walk down the street from one place to another, you simultaneously exercise realms having to do with basic motor control and with your geographical locale and destination. In general, most actions represent the coalescence of multiple realms that simultaneously modulate our behavior. No realm is an island.

Finally, people often carry out multiple behaviors at the same time, guided by multiple realms. Almost every week, I meet with a colleague to lunch and advance joint writing projects. We find ourselves simultaneously wielding utensils, appreciating food, listening, debating, making jokes. All these enterprises end up woven together in the fabric of the whole experience with little subjective sense of effort. All normal human beings adroitly join threads from diverse realms, a virtuosity so commonplace that it goes unnoticed.

If we mix and match realms so much in everyday life, where does one realm end and another begin? How can they be told apart? Basically, you can count two areas of activity as separate realms if they do not need one another. For instance, during those lunches I am using silverware and debating an issue at the same time, but the two activities have nothing to do with one another intrinsically. Often I use silverware without saying a word, and other times I manage to debate without a fork in my hand. The fact that we artfully mix activities does not mean that they merge indistinguishably together.

Now, with this firmer fix on realms and how they work, it's time to go back and appraise the limits of expertise.

Back to Beyond Expertise

Remember the reason for this tour through realms, realm knowledge, and knowing your way around. The goal was to size up the concept of expertise. Does the idea of expertise as developed by psychologists honor all of what we mean by knowing your way around something? In other words, is expertise about particular areas of endeavor an adequate account of experiential intelligence, and is expertise about kinds of thinking an adequate account of reflective intelligence?

I don't think so. To be sure, the ideas of knowing your way around and expertise resemble one another, but less like red delicious and yellow delicious apples and more like apples and oranges. Although apples and oranges share fruithood, they are not the same thing, and although knowing your way around and expertise share many attributes, they are not the same thing either. So let us contrast the theory of expertise as discussed in Chapters 4 and 9 with "realm theory."

Realm Theory (Knowing Your Way Around)	The Theory Of Expertise
Ontology, the kinds of "stuff"	
Realms have a complex ontology, highlighting values, standards, feelings, inklings, intuitions, images, as well as knowledge of facts and processes.	While writings on expertise do not exclude such stuff, they emphasize propositional and procedural knowledge.
Affect	
Realms honor the affective and dispositional side of behavior.	The notion of expertise downplays the affective and dispositional side of behavior.
Size	
Realm theory acknowledges realms of all sizes from shoe tieing to geology.	Discussions of expertise normally focus on large realms—geology, physics, chess.
Generality	
Realm theory makes room for very abstract general realms such as decision making, problem solving, or getting along with people. Of course, there are very specific realms too.	Writings on expertise usually emphasize the highly contextualized and situated nature of behavior: People don't learn generalities but ways of coping with particular contexts.
The richness of generality	
Realms like decision making, problem solving, or getting along with people are rich, complex, and empowering, not sparse and weak.	The writings on expertise tend to imply that very general knowledge is sparse—a few general rules without much leverage.

Overlap, interaction	
Realms overlap and interact in complex ways that allow us to deal with situations that involve very different kinds of knowledge flexibly and effectively.	Discussions of expertise tend to treat areas of expertise as disjoint, like physics, medicine, and chess.
How action happens	
Realm theory says that action emerges from realm knowledge through a complex coalescence of multiple levels of generality.	The picture painted of how expertise yields action is often more linear: The productions in a production system fire to yield automatic but competent behavior.
How learning happens	
Realm theory pictures learning the ABCs of a realm as a matter of learning your way around, or progressive problem solving, with the accumulation of routines but also with an emphasis on constantly reaching beyond where you are.	The theory of expertise in its standard form views learining as a matter of problem solving and knowledge compilation that yields a large repertoire of reflexively evoked routines.

Arguably, all this treats the rich tradition of research on expertise a little shabbily. Certainly the research on expertise has informed us greatly about the workings of the human mind. Moreover, certainly many authors writing about expertise have emphasized some of the cautions advanced above. For example, earlier I mentioned *Surpassing Ourselves* by Carl Bereiter and Marlene Scardamalia. These authors offer a revisionary synthesis of the research on expertise, raising many of the same concerns that I have and construing expertise much more broadly than usual with great insight. So why don't I just say "expertise?" Why all the fuss?

The reason for the fuss is that sometimes it's not enough to use the old metaphor with attached caveats, qualifications, and footnotes. Sometimes we need a new metaphor, that anchors our understanding in a new place. This is how I feel about understanding intelligence. Yes, one could use a patched-up version of the expertise metaphor. But the notion of expertise carries a lot of baggage listed on the right side of the chart above. I think we need a new metaphor that recognizes abstract realms like decision making, that emphasizes progressive problem solving as a mode of learning as much as automatization of routines, that acknowledges explicitly how attitudes, concepts, beliefs, values, and so on are involved. Knowing your way around is such a metaphor. It's clearer and truer to the nature of experiential and reflective intelligence and more suggestive of how to go about getting them. It's closer to the right stuff.

How Experiential and Reflective Intelligence Relate

Once again: What stuff do you get when you get smarter? I asked this question at the outset and by now have come around to a firm answer: The stuff you get is whatever stuff goes into knowing your way around.

One odd feature of this answer is that it comes out the same for experiential intelligence and reflective intelligence. You gain experiential intelligence when you learn your way around specific areas of activity like shoe tying or geology. And you gain reflective intelligence when you learn your way around different kinds of thinking like decision making or problem solving or more specialized thinking endeavors like legal argument or doing mathematical proofs.

How can this be? Why do experiential intelligence and reflective intelligence come out sounding so much alike? After spending so much time distinguishing them, do we reach the conclusion that they are virtually identical twins, hardly worth distinguishing after all?

Twins they are; but fraternal, not identical. They are twins in that they share an explanation in terms of realm theory and knowing your way around. They are twins in that the ABCs of action, belief, and conceptual systems are important to both. Reflective intelligence is like experiential intelligence in that reflective intelligence, of course, requires experience—not just learning a set of concepts, precepts, and practices but living with them, working through them, making them one's own.

Despite all that, reflective intelligence contrasts in a simple and stark way with experiential intelligence. The difference turns on what reflective intelligence is about. Reflective intelligence specifically concerns the good use of the mind, the artful deployment of our faculties of thinking, within disciplines like physics, accountancy, or auto repair and across disciplines in more general categories like decision making. Experiential intelligence about, say, accountancy grants you a rich knowledge base for handling routine problems but does not of itself make you a reflective accountant, one with mindful distance from the books and numbers. Experiential intelligence about, say, relating to people equips you for day to day human relations nicely but does not make you a reflective manager of your relationships. Being about *thinking as such* in its more general and more specialized forms is just exactly what makes reflective intelligence unique.

If this still seems odd, it's worth reaching back to a metaphor used in Chapter 5. I compared reflective intelligence to a river boat pilot, who knows the river, sees far in all directions, and steers the way. To say reflective intelligence is just like experiential intelligence resembles saying that a pilot is just a member of the crew. True, a pilot is a member of the crew, but not *just*. The pilot's position and role make the pilot very special. It's the same with reflective intelligence. Knowing your way around thinking—reflective intelligence—is not just any case of knowing your way around something but a special one with profound consequences for how intelligently you function in the world.

All this leads to another pass at the answer to the first mindware question, updating what has stood since Chapter 5. In particular:

MWQ #1. What mechanisms underlie intelligence?

- *Neural intelligence.* This remains unrevised—neurological speed and precision, in considerable part genetically determined, with different neural structures implicated for different aspects of intelligence, for instance linguistic versus visual-imagistic intelligence.
- *Experiential intelligence.* Recall that the notion of experiential intelligence sprang largely from the research on expertise. Experiential intelligence acknowledges the importance of context-specific knowledge accumulated through experience in guiding intelligent behavior. With realm theory and the idea of knowing your way around, we have a better way of characterizing experiential intelligence than the theory of expertise, at least in its narrower form. Experiential intelligence amounts to realm knowledge—knowing your way around the various settings and contexts where you need to function.

- *Reflective intelligence.* Previously I profiled reflective intelligence as a matter of strategies, positive attitudes, and metacognition. That remains true as far as it goes. But realm theory teaches us that reflective intelligence involves far more than these three. In ABC terms, strategies and metacognition are just two aspects of an action system that involves much more. Positive attitudes about thinking are just one part of a belief system that involves much more. And none of the three directly touches C for the conceptual system. The bottom line is this: Reflective intelligence is best conceived as realm knowledge with ABCs about different kinds of thinking.

Along with this revised answer to the first mindware question comes a revised answer to the second:

MWQ #2. Can people learn more intelligence?

- Yes. Over the years, through instruction, watching others, coping with problems, and in innumerable other ways, people develop realm knowledge in realms where it's needed, accumulating specific and somewhat generalized action patterns, beliefs and feelings, and concepts (the ABCs) and thus end up knowing their way around various realms more or less well—acquiring experiential intelligence.
- To put a name to this learning process, one might speak of *learning your way around.* People come to know their way around by progressively earning their way around. Bereiter and Scardamalia refer to this as progressive problem solving.
- With appropriate instruction or mentors, and with high-order generalizations about thinking in particular contexts, people attain realm knowledge of various general categories of thinking. They learn their way around thinking, developing sophisticated reflective intelligence.

All this helps us to understand how reflective intelligence emerges in individuals and cultures. The potential for reflective intelligence lies implicit in the power of the human mind to build realm knowledge around virtually any topic—gardening, weaving, politics, or what have you. That power, applied to the mind and thinking over the individual's life span and through cultural transmission, begins to generate realms of thinking—knowing your way around thinking itself. In learning our way around thinking, we lift ourselves by our own intellectual bootstraps and position ourselves for more intelligent behavior across the range of endeavors we undertake.

This has immediate implications for formal and informal instruction toward better thinking. If you view reflective intelligence as processes, you teach some strategies. You encourage people to be metacognitive, monitoring and managing their thinking. You focus on A, the action system. However, if you recognize the full ABCs of realm knowledge, you realize that beliefs and values and complex conceptual systems need cultivating as well. Moreover, you appreciate the richly textured kinds of experiences needed for learning one's way around. The whole vision of how to teach intelligence becomes more intricate, nuanced, and challenging—but much more realistic too.

11

Mapping the Mindscape

Old maps are fossils of inquiry. Just as the fossils of biological organisms reveal our organic ancestry, old maps reveal the ancestry of our knowledge of geography. They remind us how little we once knew.

I remember recently seeing an old map of South America that made bygone geographical mysteries very explicit. The eastern coast of South American presented a profile like that on contemporary maps. But the western coast appeared just slightly to the left of the eastern coast, making the whole continent look like a long piece of linguini. The mapmaker clearly did not know what lay to the west and adopted an expediency, sketching in a west coast a little to the left of the east coast. It was sheer guesswork.

In today's world, replete with Mercator projections and globes and satellite photos, we enjoy the luxury of knowing the lay of the land—and the seas—and forget what it was like not to be well-oriented on the face of the earth. We forget that for the larger part of human history people had no idea what lands and seas occupied the larger part of the world around them. We forget the importance of what might be called the navigator's query, the simple and so terribly important question "What's where?"

While a long history of exploration and technological development has provided us with a thorough answer to the navigator's query as far as the surface of our planet goes, the navigator's query lives on in other domains—what's where on Jupiter or at the far edge of the universe, for instance. The navigator's query takes on a much more cerebral sense with the geographical analogy introduced in the last chapter. To view reflective intelligence as made up of realms of thinking such as decision making, problem solving, and remembering is to raise a cognitive version of the navigator's query. It becomes important to ask, "What's where?" What are the important realms of thinking—the continents and subcontinents so to speak—and where are they positioned relative to one another by the measure of whatever kinds of relationships have significance for realms of thinking?

The navigator's query for realms of thinking is of course just one version of a question asked over and over again by numerous scholars probing the nature of intelligence. Recall from chapter 4 that Horn and Cattell highlighted the two main divisions of crystallized intelligence (based on your accumulated knowledge, as when you take a vocabulary test) and fluid intelligence (your ability to cope with novel, abstract, complex reasoning tasks). Guilford proposed 150 separate components of intelligence. Gardner argued for seven distinct kinds of intelligence. Feuerstein advanced three complementary aspects of intelligence—input, elaboration, and output—with a variety of subprocesses for each. The list could easily be extended and in fact I will return to several theories of the organization of intelligence and examine them more closely. The point here is simply that questing after the components of intelligence and their relations to one another is a venerable enterprise, and an essential one in the quest to figure out how the mind works and make it work better.

The basic distinction between neural intelligence, intuitive intelligence, and reflective intelligence highlighted in Parts I and II provides the beginnings of my answer: a broad initial partition of intelligence into three interactive components, the major continents of cognition so to speak. But the real focus of this book falls on one of those—reflective intelligence—and the realms of thinking that make it up. If the navigator's query asks what's where, then what is the answer for realms of thinking?

The answer is worth chasing for the same two reasons that we wanted the right stuff. First of all, toward building a science of learnable intelligence, it's important to get the story of thinking straight, or as straight as possible. Second is the practical side of the matter. If we have a clear vision of what the important realms of reflective intelligence are and how they relate to one another, then we are in a much better position to cultivate mindware in ourselves and others. The navigator's query is no whim: Navigators need to navigate. And so do we all need to navigate through the realms of reflective intelligence that support our best thinking.

The navigator's query is a head breaker. Any reasonable answer needs to face up to the messy variety of thinking. Plainly, different realms of thinking can be *very* different from one another. Knowing your way around decision making is one thing, but knowing your way around syllogistic reasoning is a much more technical and formal thing, knowing your way around used car buying (a specialized variant of decision making) is a much more knowledge-intensive thing with a large helping of human relations folded in for dealing with salespeople, knowing your way around creative thinking is a much more general thing than decision making, but important to decision making. Realms of thinking seem to come in all shapes and sizes—continents, subcontinents, archipelagos, islands. The navigator's query appears daunting indeed.

We recognize some realms of thinking as everyday thinking challenges, matters that come up all the time—decision making, problem solving, explanation, or remembering for instance. It will help to get some insight into where these realms of thinking come from and what makes them stand out.

Mirrors of Mystery

Consider God's thinking. An omnipotent being, God would of course be very good at thinking. God would in the most ultimate sense know his, or her, way around thinking. However, as a being not only omnipotent but omniscient, God would have little reason to think. Why think when you know? Why ponder the mysteries of the atom when you know the mysteries of the atom—in fact, you put the atom together in the first place, with far more care than a thousand Swiss watchmakers. Why puzzle over what will happen next when you stand apart from time and know what will happen next?

There is a clue here about when we think: We think when we do not know, or we are not sure. It is the mystery of how atoms work or what will happen next that makes such topics suitable candidates for thinking about. Thinking, in other words, is a kind of mirror of not knowing, a mirror of the mystery in our lives.

This is obvious enough as far as it goes, but perhaps the same principle extends to different kinds of thinking. Perhaps each realm of thinking reflects a kind of not-knowing in our lives. Perhaps each realm of thinking is a mirror of mystery, a complement to and hopeful remedy for a particular kind of unknown.

To explore what sense this makes, let us construct a kind of fantasy. If God is too smart and knowledgeable to illustrate the challenges of thinking, it makes sense to turn to someone more ordinary. I'm thinking of the beleaguered pilgrim of John Bunyan's *The Pilgrim's Progress*. Writing in 1678 for the edification of all, Bunyan, a Puritan preacher, described his pilgrim's painful progress from the City of Destruction toward the Celestial City, avoiding hazards such as the Slough of Despond, Vanity Fair, and the Plain Called Ease. To be sure, we are not all progressing toward salvation as Bunyan saw it, but we are all Pilgrims headed somewhere. We all have long-term and often lofty aims we would like to achieve, with the pathway to those aims unmarked and beset with hazards.

Consider then Pilgrim, any Pilgrim, loose in a world and striving for something precious. Far from omniscient and omnipotent, Pilgrim nonetheless has resolve. So Pilgrim sets out on the quest.

Pilgrim encounters a fork in the road and wonders which way to go to make progress toward that distant goal. Pilgrim has to cope with a decision. In general, the world presents us with forks in the road, branch points, occasions when we could go one of at least two ways. You can study this topic or that, accept this job or another, invest in this stock or a different stock or no stock, go to one or another set of in-laws for Thanksgiving, work over the weekend or take a break, or indeed accept this faith or that or another. "Which way now" is a pervasive mystery that every pilgrim encounters all the time. Around that mystery, we construct the realm of decision making, with action, belief and feeling, and conceptual systems (ABCs) that help us to deal with it. Some of the decisions we need to make may be as much or more decisions of the heart as decisions of the mind. But that too is something we know our way around, if we know our way around the realm of decision making.

Pilgrim does know his or her way around decision making, let us say. One bit of lore Pilgrim knows says it's smart to cast about for other paths besides the obvious ones. With a little effort, Pilgrim detects a third. Then Pilgrim focuses on comparing the three: Which would serve best? To figure out the best bet, Pilgrim sees the need to predict what lies down each path. In general, when the world presents us with alternative possibilities, it often happens that the outcomes are something of a mystery. The future does not stand before us like the later chapters of a book, ready to be read if we care to peek ahead. You do not know what life will be like with a potential marriage partner in five years, you do not know how your employer will react when you propose restructuring the office, you do not know what a foreign leader will do when you, a career diplomat, explain current policy in one way or in another. Around the mystery of the future, we construct the realm of prediction, a set of ABCs to help us foretell the future as best we can.

As Pilgrim tries to predict what lies down the three paths, the first path seems familiar. Has Pilgrim taken it before? Pilgrim tries to draw from memory information about the first path. In general, we often forecast the future by remembering the past: We have been here or somewhere very like here before. But minds do not operate like tape recorders and remembering the past can be a problem in itself. You are not sure what you read a year ago about investment in tin mining, you think that your shoe size is 11B as you place a catalog order, but maybe not, you wonder whether it was today that you were supposed to complete that report. Around the mystery of the past we have experienced, we construct the realm of remembering, a set of ABCs to help us recall what we have experienced before and to help us recall better later what we are experiencing now.

Pilgrim forecasts the course of the first path from memory. But the second path Pilgrim does not remember. Pilgrim has not traversed it or anything like it. However, Pilgrim can see the beginning of the path down to the first turn— the Northeasterly direction, the dry vegetation, the stretches of ledge stained with yellow-green lichens. If Pilgrim understands how the world works, Pilgrim may be able to predict something of the character and destination of the second path. In general, we often forecast the future by understanding how the world works, what causal and other forces figure in its structure. However, to deploy such an understanding, we have to build it in the first place. The world does not wear its deep structure on its sleeve. To forecast whether your friend will slip away with you for an intimate weekend on Cape Cod, you have to understand your friend's psychology. To estimate your chances of winning a hand of poker, you have to understand something about probabilities and about your opponents' flair for bluffing. To size up whether it is safe to undertake the design of a more efficient species of nitrogen-fixing bacteria through recombinant DNA engineering, you have to understand the hazards of mutant organisms. In general, around the mystery of the world's deep operating principles, we construct the realm of understanding and explanation, a set of ABCs to help us come to causal and other kinds of understandings of the world.

While Pilgrim's saga could go on for some time, this opening episode suffices to draw some basic morals.

- *Realms of thinking are indeed mirrors of mystery.* Major kinds of thinking identified in our concepts and language—decision making, predicting, remembering, understanding and more—correspond directly to kinds of mysteries people encounter over and over again—choice-points and which to choose, the unknown future, the hard-to-remember past, the puzzle of the way the world works underneath.
- *These mysteries arise naturally as one strives to act effectively in the world.* Pilgrim or you or I run into decision points. They arise naturally in almost any real physical environment or for that matter any intellectual environment. The mystery of the future occurs inevitably, because the future does not present itself for us to read off, and so on.
- *These mysteries reflect the nature of the world* and *the nature of the mind.* Choice points and the unknown character of the future are a part of the world as seen by any pilgrim. Limitations in memory are a characteristic of the mind. A mystery can arise from either or both together.
- *As one mystery leads to another, so one realm of thinking leads on to another.* A choice point may lead on to a problem of prediction, if one cannot see the end of each path from where one stands. A problem of prediction may lead on to a problem of remembering, if one's past experience applies. And so on.

For a final point, the mirrors-of-mystery principle applies not only to whole realms of thinking like decision making or remembering but to the ABCs within those realms. What goes into knowing our way around a kind of thinking inevitably and appropriately reflects the exact character of the mystery.

Take for example looking for further options as part of decision making. Why is this simple tactic important for Pilgrim or any of us? Because the world does not generally present all the options clearly marked out as such. If the world worked like one of those mazes in puzzle books, there would be no need for a find-the-options step in decision making.

All the options would be obvious: You either go straight, or left, or right, or back.

But the world does not work like puzzle-book mazes. While we recognize a decision-making situation through encountering a choice, very often there are options worth considering besides those that faced us with a decision, options not yet seen. Since we are dealing with archetypal tales such as the Pilgrim's, here is another. Remember the beginning of Jack and the Beanstalk, with Jack taking the cow to town to sell. A trader approaches Jack offering him three magic beans for the cow. Jack says yes! His options as he saw them were yes or no, and he made his choice. But suppose you were Jack. Consider the wealth of choices you have: Ask about what the beans will do, ask for evidence that they will do it, ask to test one bean on a trial basis before relinquishing the cow, ask for credentials from this fellow, ask where to find previously swapped beans to see what good work they did, and so on. Sure, it's just a fairy tale and Jack lucks out as the story continues. Nonetheless, that moment in the story is a study in impulsive decision making—the tendency to be hasty, the first of our four defaults, won that round. No wonder mom was mad when Jack got home. Unfortunately, it's all too easy to take the obvious options as the only options. All of us are Jack at one time or another.

In other words, an options-finding step in decision making mirrors the mystery of the not-yet-seen. Moreover, an idea-finding technique like formal brainstorming, with its rules for deferring criticism, piggybacking on other ideas and letting imagination run free, recognizes that the mystery of the not-yet-seen has as much to do with the mind as it does the world. Sometimes people do not see what is there to be seen not because the world conceals it but because the way they are thinking about the world conceals it. Jack fixates on the lure of the magic beans. Nothing else penetrates. In general, the mysteries people face reflect both the nature of the world and the nature of the mind, especially the mind's easy fall into any of the four defaults of hasty, narrow, fuzzy, and sprawling thinking. Mirrors of mystery that they are, the realms of thinking named with names like decision making or remembering have double roots in the puzzles of the world and the puzzles of the mind.

In a very broad way, this notion of mirrors of mystery offers a partial answer to the navigator's query, what's where. The whats to be found—the important realms of thinking—are just those that correspond to major mysteries that arise as we attempt to act effectively in the world.

The Soul of Intelligence

So far it sounds like the "what" side of the navigator's what's where question earns a thoroughly technical cold-blooded answer. The whats that matter to reflective intelligence are realms of thinking like decision making and problem solving that people learn their way around, some people more than others. Reflective intelligence amounts to a kind of *savoir*.

Charles Darwin, along with many other great thinkers, teaches us otherwise. A charming anecdote about the young Darwin testifies to the passionate roots of his creative thinking. Darwin developed a special enthusiasm for the study of beetles. One day he was excited to find an unusual beetle in a field, one worth taking home for careful study. Darwin lacked any handy container in which to transport the beetle. So he popped the beetle in his mouth and ran home with the insect safely preserved there.

One way of looking at this remarkable act of mind highlights creative problem solving. Darwin saw the problem: Find a container to hold the beetle. He thought flexibly about what was containerlike: hollow in the center, walls on all sides. He discovered something handy with the necessary properties—his mouth. Darwin's solution shows the opposite of what psychologists interested in problem solving call functional fixedness. People tend to see things only in their usual functions; combs are for combing hair, hammers are for hammering, and mouths are for talking and eating. Creative thinking often involves finding unusual functions for things with conventional functions, just what Darwin did. Presumably Darwin benefitted from a good intuitive or perhaps explicit sense of the realm of problem solving. He knew his way around and took advantage of it.

However, this account of the matter does not do justice to the sheer enthusiasm of Darwin for his inquiries, the kind of enthusiasm that would let you carry a beetle home in your mouth and not think anything of it. Darwin's beetle reminds us of the importance of passion and commitment in thinking.

This theme has emerged from time to time in earlier chapters. For instance, I noted in Chapter 7 philosopher Israel Scheffler's treatment of what he calls the cognitive emotions. Scheffler emphasizes that all too commonly emotions are seen as the antagonists of reason. On the contrary, he urges, all depends on what emotions you have in mind and how they are directed. Some emotions, Scheffler avers, are in fact distinctively cognitive: They specifically serve the enterprise of thinking and understanding. Emotions such as curiosity and the love of truth are cases in point. Not to take such matters into account in answering the navigator's what's where question is to leave out the very soul of reflective intelligence.

Thinking Dispositions

The discipline of philosophy offers a useful way to talk about what might be called the motivational side of thinking: the notion of *thinking dispositions.* I've mentioned dispositions in passing before, but now let me focus on them. In general, a psychological disposition is a tendency to behave in a certain manner. Suppose a stranger comes to your door on a hot summer day, lost and asking directions. Would you be suspicious and talk through the keyhole? Would you be welcoming and offer a glass of lemonade? Probably somewhere in between these extremes, but whatever your leaning, it signals the presence of a disposition. On weekends, do you rise with the sun or sleep in late? What are you disposed to do, that is, what's your disposition?

Dispositions shape our lives. They are the proclivities that lead us in one direction rather than another within the freedom of action that we have. A thinking disposition is simply a disposition about thinking specifically. For instance, the person who works next to you may be closed-minded, suspicious of and uneasy with new ideas, just as if they were strangers, as you know all too well from coffee-break conversations about kids, health care, and office politics. Another co-worker may be open-minded, welcoming of new ideas. Closed-mindedness and open-mindedness alike are thinking dispositions, broad trends that show up in people's patterns of thinking.

A number of philosophers and psychologists have underscored the importance of thinking dispositions. Robert Ennis, a philosopher well-known for his work on the assessment of thinking, emphasizes the importance of dispositions alongside skills or abilities. Philosopher Richard Paul has something very dispositional in mind when he writes of the importance of strong-sense critical thinking. If you are a strong-sense critical thinker, you show a genuine commitment to broad-mindedness and thinking across multiple frames of reference. A weak-sense critical thinker displays high technical skill with the mechanics of reasoning, but lacks the commitment. The cognitive psychologist Jonathan

Baron offers an analysis of thinking that highlights the concept of dispositions. My colleagues Shari Tishman and Eileen Jay and I have recently offered an analysis of intelligence giving dispositions a central place, about which I'll say more later.

For all of these authors and more, the appeal of the concept of dispositions emerges from a fundamental point of logic: Skills are not enough. However technically adroit a person may be at problem solving, decision making, reasoning, or building explanations, what does it matter unless the person invests himself or herself energetically in these and other kinds of thinking on occasions that invite it? The problem is commonplace. Who does not have a son or daughter, brother or sister, cousin or uncle, smart potentially but reluctant to make much of that ability? What matter if a senator or salesperson, a lawyer or lobbyist is cognitively capable of appreciating the implications of new ideas unless they muster the energy and attention to understand and act? Skills may suffice to do well on a test that demands thinking, but out there in the real world skillful thinking without the dispositions to match does not eventuate in intelligent behavior. Dispositions as much as strategic understanding and know-how are critical to intelligent behavior. They are part of intelligence.

Here it's worth recalling again the four thinking defaults highlighted in Chapter 7, the tendencies toward hasty, narrow, fuzzy, and sprawling thinking. As the term *tendencies* reveals, each of these amounts to a negative thinking disposition. When I tend to choose this new suit over that one hastily, I behave less intelligently. When I'm tempted to dismiss my son's request to go off for a weekend with friends without hearing the details, I'm drawn to narrow thinking and less intelligent behavior. When I listen to the commercial that says, "No other brand did better" and take it as a plus without asking myself, "What if all brands did equally well?" I'm giving in to fuzzy thinking and behaving less intelligently. When I get totally tangled up in a conversation about what kinds of insurance to purchase without charting out the options and pros and cons carefully, my sprawling thinking leaves me behaving less intelligently.

Chapter 7 did not call hasty, narrow, fuzzy, and sprawling dispositions because I had not explained the concept. But dispositions they are. Recall that these dispositions arise out of the pattern-driven character of experiential intelligence, which creates an evolutionary double bind: Effective up to a point, pattern-driven thinking often subverts the work of reflective intelligence in situations of novelty, unusual complexity, or risk. Further sources of this quartet of negative thinking dispositions included ego defence, problems of limited short-term memory, and other quirks of cognition.

Although greater strategic knowledge of good thinking practices can help to combat these negative thinking dispositions, the whole notion of dispositions suggests that we need something more than technique. In effect, set a disposition to catch a disposition. Because negative thinking dispositions harry us, we need positive thinking dispositions to counter them.

A Taste of Empiricism

Research on thinking has given far more attention to knowledge and technique than to dispositions. Nonetheless, several lines of research point clearly to an important role for thinking dispositions. For example, psychologist Carol Dweck and her colleagues have developed a provocative line of research on what she calls entity learners versus incremental learners. The distinction concerns what might be called learning style. Entity learners believe that you either get it or you don't. When they do not understand something fairly quickly, they tend to conclude that they cannot and relinquish the effort. Incremental learners, in contrast, see learning something with understanding as a process that demands repeated effort to build an understanding gradually. When initially baffled, they tend to persist. Although Carol Dweck does not cast this contrast in the idiom of dispositions, notice its dispositional character. The difference between entity and incremental learners lies in how they invest their effort, not in what they are cognitively capable of in a technical sense. In fact, entity learners can be very bright—but still, early quitters when the intellectual road gets rough.

Peter and Noreen Facione of Santa Clara University have conducted investigations of thinking dispositions and their role in the critical thinking movement. Facione discovered that among people involved in the critical thinking movement there was less agreement about the place of dispositions than about the place of abilities, and considerable confusion as to which dispositions were central. However, Facione was convinced of the importance of dispositions. Using factor-analytic techniques, he determined a set of seven general thinking dispositions he takes to be particularly important: (1) truth-seeking, (2) open-mindedness, (3) analyticity, (4) systematicity, (5) self-confidence, (6) inquisitiveness, and (7) maturity.

Shari Tishman, Eileen Jay, and I have made a particular study of dispositions over the past several years. One of our concerns has been to demonstrate the genuine contribution that dispositions make to intelligent behavior. For example, several experiments confirm a finding of mine mentioned earlier and affirmed by other investigators as well: Faced with a decision or a question of belief, people focus overwhelmingly on evidence favoring their learning and neglect evidence on the other side of the case. They exhibit what was earlier called my-side bias. My-side bias is an unfortunate thinking disposition, one that works against intelligent behavior in many settings. The problem reflects dispositions rather than abilities, because the same research shows that people are quite capable of thinking much more deeply about the other side of the case than they usually do.

We also worked out a taxonomy of general thinking dispositions that seems well-justified by the existing literature. The scheme involves seven, the dispositions toward (1) broad and adventurous thinking, (2) sustained intellectual curiosity, (3) clarifying and seeking understanding, (4) being planful and strategic, (5) being intellectually careful, (6) seeking and evaluating reasons, and (7) metacognitive self-management (monitoring and guiding your own thinking). Although the labels are different, there is considerable overlap with Facione's list even though we developed our list before learning of his work. I employ an adaptation of this list of seven later as part of a chart of key realms of thinking.

In general, this research has affirmed our belief that dispositions play a crucial role in intelligent behavior. To bring forward the phrase once more, they are the soul of intelligence, without which the understanding and know-how does little good.

The Complex Causes of Dispositions

It's natural to think of a disposition as a single psychological force. The disposition to think broadly and adventurously, for instance, could be envisioned as a kind of steady trade wind that fills the sails of a person's thinking and urges it in a creative direction.

However, this picture of dispositions as unitary felt forces in our cognitive lives is somewhat misleading. It's plain that a single disposition has multiple causes, multiple contributing factors that generate and sustain it.

One important distinction concerns sensitivity and inclination. To be disposed to think broadly on appropriate occasions, you need to be sensitive to those occasions. You need to be alert to the earmarks of situations that call for broad thinking. Such situations are diverse. They include various circumstances of problem solving, decision making, investigating, and so on, where the imaginative exploration of possibilities is particularly likely to pay off.

One of my favorite tales of everyday creativity concerns a colleague who found himself and his holiday companions unpacking the goodies for wine and cheese out in the country—with no knife to cut the cheese. So he cut it with a credit card. Now the natural thing to do was to accept the situation—no knife—and do the best you could breaking up the cheese by hand. But he recognized the circumstances as a puzzle situation: conventional solution blocked. When conventional solutions are blocked, or when the obvious solutions all have distinct downsides, or when the stakes are high even though the obvious solutions seem serviceable, all these are signals the sensitive thinker will pick up toward shaking off assumptions and seeking a new angle.

However, sensitivity in itself does not deliver without the inclination to go with it. It would do little good for my colleague to notice an opportunity for clever thinking about cheese cutting if he didn't care enough to bother. Likewise, you may notice an occasion where you might think broadly and imaginatively, but simply feel comfortable with things as they are, reluctant to put up with the hassles that a different way of managing the circumstances would bring. Indeed, such feelings are quite understandable and natural.

If sensitivity to occasion and inclination to follow through are important aspects of a disposition, then these in turn each have complex roots in the psychological mechanisms of the mind. Sensitivity will certainly depend on a person's repertoire of concepts and beliefs—what discriminations the person readily makes and what beliefs the person holds about the kinds of situations that are likely to arise. Inclination will depend on values and standards about what is important and what is practical. Inclination will also depend on habits of mind—the habit of meeting puzzles head on, for instance, like my colleague facing the uncut and seemingly uncuttable cheese.

Michael Pressley, a long-time investigator of how students learn strategies, and several colleagues identify in a 1989 paper a number of factors that influence whether students actually invest themselves in thinking. They note that people have different styles: The impulsive or high-anxiety student is less likely to sustain a systematic approach to an intellectual challenge. Beliefs that people hold can undermine invest-ment. For instance, some students think that people with good memo-ries benefit from photographic memories, and against that standard there's nothing one can do. Students also hold broad and pervasive beliefs attributing achievement to personal effort, or innate ability, or luck, or task characteristics, or good instruction. Depending on the mix, people may be much more or much less sensitive to thinking opportuni-ties and inclined to try to meet their challenges.

Earlier I wrote of dispositions as the passionate side of thinking and the soul of intelligence. All this is roughly true but not precisely true. Certain-ly dispositions have a strongly emotional character. But a single disposi-tion is not a single emotion nor entirely a matter of emotions. As this dis-cussion of sensitivities, inclinations, and underlying styles and beliefs shows, dispositions are complex phenomena, not just simple feelings.

Dispositions Are Realms

One way to honor the complexity of dispositions is to recognize that dis-positions are thinking realms. More general than such realms of think-ing as decision making or explanation, dispositions nonetheless have all the characteristics of realms.

One test of this proposal remembers that you know your way around realms. Are dispositions something you can know your way around? Consider the disposition to think broadly and adventurously. This does seem to be a kind of thinking you can know your way around. You can know how to brainstorm, recognize the worth of challenging assump-tions, eagerly expose yourself to new ideas, strive to see the implications of new ideas you encounter, exercise caution about functional fixedness and other traps that narrow our vision.

And where would this realm knowledge come from? You are more likely to have it if a parent, teacher, or colleague has been a good model of it—if for instance your mother surprised you with the way she outma-neuvered your father to get the house painted, used an old water tank for a planter, and found a tricky back route that saved time. You are more likely to have the realm knowledge if your profession encourages it. For instance, artists, designers, and advertising people are expected to be inventive. But however you start out, the disposition to think broadly and adventurously can be cultivated—you can learn your way around it.

Or consider the disposition to sound thinking, that is, thinking that reaches outcomes well-justified in terms of evidence, logic, coherence, pragmatic payoff, and so on. You can be sensitive to the need for evidence, remain alert to the relevance as well as the truth of propositions, recognize how context influences functionality, observe principles of logic and good reasoning, and so on, all part of knowing your way around this disposition. You are more likely to have this realm knowledge if a friend or mentor makes plain what it is like by his or her own conduct—if for instance a teacher impressed you with his concern for getting facts about the Gulf War right, his skepticism about early newspaper accounts, his alertness to inconsistencies between one source and another. You are likely to have more of this disposition of your profession encourages it. For example, academic professions in general put a high premium on matters of evidence, argument, and solid conclusions. But whatever your circumstances, the disposition toward sound thinking can be nourished—you can learn your way around sound thinking.

If general dispositions like the disposition to broad thinking or the disposition to sound thinking pass the knowing-your-way-around test for realmhood, they also pass the ABC test. Each involves an action system, a belief system, and a conceptual system. For example, broad thinking calls upon action patterns like brainstorming and assumption finding, beliefs in the presence and worth of unusual ideas yet unseen, and concepts such as creativity, imagination, assumption, constraint, intuition, exploration, open-mindedness, and so on. Sound thinking calls upon action patterns like argument and reasoning, belief in the reliability and importance of various tests of soundness, and concepts like reason, evidence, consequence, context, implication, function, and so on.

Finally, dispositions also pass the mirror-of-mystery test. Dispositions correspond to very general mysteries people encounter as they try to cope with the world in a thoughtful way. The disposition to think in a broad imaginative way corresponds to the fact that often opportunities worth pursuing and solutions to problems take forms not immediately obvious and very different from what one would expect. Cutting cheese with a credit card, for instance. Or for a loftier example fastening things together with material that works like woodland burrs—Velcro. In a more mundane, less surprising universe, the disposition to think in a broad way would not be adaptive; in our universe it is. Likewise, the disposition to think in a sound way corresponds to the fact that our universe does not make either truth or workability obvious. To be sure of our beliefs and confident of the utility of our plans and artifacts, we have to test them out in various ways.

Of course to say that thinking dispositions are realms is not to say that all realms are dispositional. Many specialized realms of thinking do not involve the momentum and commitment of dispositions. I may know my way around formal deductive logic, for instance, but this does not mean that I have a disposition to work through syllogisms at every opportunity. Nor does anything seem to be missing if I am matter of fact about formal logic rather than passionately committed to its exercise. In contrast, if I know my way around broad imaginative thinking or sound thinking in a technical sense, but don't care, then something assuredly is missing. Such general aspects of the practice of thinking cannot be viewed in so matter of fact a way. To gain their benefits requires a certain felt dedication to them, a commitment to their importance, a concern with attending to them—in short, a disposition.

The Mind's Ladder

What is the difference between shopping for a birthday present and making a decision? Immediately the question seems odd. Shopping for a birthday present is an occasion of decision making. When you buy a birthday present, inevitably you make a decision, whether you think of yourself as doing so or not. Even if you get just what the person in question asked for, you still have made a decision, the decision to follow through on the request.

If it's odd to ask after the difference between birthday shopping and decision making, it's straightforward to ask after the difference between the realm of birthday shopping and the realm of decision making. Birthday shopping in particular and decision making in general are realms that sit at two very different levels of generality. I might know my way around birthday shopping in particular, including elements of choice that go into effective selection of presents, and not know may way around decision making in general very well. Alternatively, I might know my way around decision making in general very well, but not know my way around the special nuances of the kind of decision making involved in shopping for birthday presents. However, if I do know my way around decision making well, this general knowledge will at least help me sort out the challenge of shopping for birthday presents in particular, even if I have a lot to learn about the fine art of doing so.

All this brings us back to the navigator's query. The navigator, recall, asks what's where? So far, I have focused mostly on whats, highlighting the way categories of thinking like decision making or sound thinking constitute realms that mirror mysteries people face when they think and guide their thinking in useful directions. The where side of the question asks how these categories relate to one another. The relation between birthday shopping and decision making suggests a primary organizing relationship that clarifies the daunting variety of realms of thinking. The key relationship is generality-specificity.

In fact, the many kinds of realms discussed can be arranged on a kind of ladder of generality. At the top and most general level appears a set of key thinking dispositions. Anchoring the bottom are very specific areas of decision making or problem solving like buying a used car. In between come other realms roughly ordered by generality. The resulting ladder of generality might look something like this, a hierarchy of realms of thinking that answers the where as well as the what side of the navigator's query:

The Ladder of Generality

Level 1: *Dispositional Realms (Thinking Dispositions)*
Clear • Broad • Deep • Sound • Curious • Strategic • Aware

Level 2: *Challenge Realms (Basic Thinking Challenges)*
Decision making • Justification • Explanation • Evaluation • Remembering • Problem solving • Problem finding • Representation • Design • Prediction • Planning • Learning

Level 3: *Tool Realms (Techniques That Support Thinking)*
Brainstorming • Graphic organizers • Pro-con lists • Concept maps • Stepwise strategies • Etc.

Level 4: *Technical Realms (Technical Resources For Thinking)*
Formal deduction • Systems thinking • Taxonomies • Game theory • Probability/statistics • Etc.

Level 5: *Field Realms (Thinking Tuned to Fields, Professions)*
Law • Business • Physics • Mathematics • History • The Arts • Etc.

Level 6: *Situational Realms (Somewhat Specific Thinking Situations)*
Purchase decisions • Conflict resolution • Negotiation • Policy making • Managing emotion • Etc.

Level 7: *Contextual Realms (Specific Contexts of Thinking)*
Used car buying • House design • Career choice • Treaty negotiation • Trip plannning • Etc.

Each level on the ladder of generality deserves a few words of explanation.

Level 1: Dispositional Realms

These are dispositions like the disposition to broad thinking or to sound thinking that steer thinking as a whole in fruitful directions. As argued earlier, all of these dispositions are also realms, with action, belief, and conceptual systems. Thus one can speak of dispositions or more specifically of dispositional realms. Seven general dispositions are offered as core—the dispositions to clear, broad, deep, sound, curious, strategic, and aware thinking. These are a slight revision of the taxonomy of dispositions developed by Eileen Jay, Shari Tishman, and me awhile ago and mentioned in the previous section, to make the dispositions a little more general. To expand on the meaning of each:

Clear. The disposition toward thinking that is clear, coherent, precise, specific, and well-organized.

Broad. The disposition toward thinking that is broad, adventurous, flexible, independent. Respect for and appreciation of other perspectives through tolerance, openmindedness, and empathy. The disposition to seek and find connections.

Deep. The disposition to understand deeply, to seek underlying unities in the form of laws, theories, frameworks and principles, to fathom the causes and other governing factors of ideas, things, and events.

Sound. The disposition toward thinking that is accurate, thorough, fair, knowledgeable, logical, and well-supported by evidence. Concern with truth, judiciousness, relevance, and functionality, in the sense of the functionality of a sound design.

Curious. The disposition toward thinking that is curious, questioning, probing, inquisitive. The disposition to find out about things and to persist in inquiry.

Strategic. The disposition toward thinking that is strategic and planful in style, and that uses stock thinking strategies, graphic organizers, and other devices to sustain effective organization.

Aware. The disposition toward thinking that is metacognitive, aware of itself, critical of its own patterns and progress, and that edits its own practices. This includes awareness of affective dimensions of

thinking—the clues feelings provide us with, how emotions stimulate or stifle a link of thought.

Quite possibly one could add to this list. Certainly one can distinguish
subdispositions, for instance partitioning *sound* or *broad* into multiple
senses. However, here it seems most useful to advance relatively global
dispositions. People whose thinking shows a lively presence of these dispositions are fine thinkers indeed.

One oddity of such a list of core dispositions deserves comment:
They do not always seem to be consistent with one another. For example, sometimes in the midst of broad, flexible, creative thinking it may
be best not to worry too much about sound, logical evidence. What to
make of this? The answer is that it is a fact about human cognition and
indeed the good management of thinking. To say that each of these is
an important thinking disposition is not to say that all should or can
shape our thinking simultaneously, but simply that all should be lively
forces at work in the weave of thinking.

This leads naturally into another question: Where do critical thinking and creative thinking sit on the mind's ladder? The dispositional
realms offer a reasonable answer. Roughly, critical thinking corresponds
to sound and clear thinking, and creative thinking corresponds to deep
and broad thinking, each with their associated ABCs of action, belief,
and conceptual systems.

It's important to recognize that neither creative nor critical thinking
stands well by itself. Good creative thinking always involves a measure
of critical thinking, else it would simply be foolish. Good critical thinking always involves a measure of creative thinking, else it would be narrow. The two need one another. Many authors have highlighted this
interdependence, and Matthew Lipman, developer of the Philosophy
for Children program discussed in Chapter 8, offers a particularly lucid
account in his 1991 book, *Thinking in Education*.

Another warning: The ideas of critical and creative thinking are rather
fuzzy in their everyday usage. This is particularly true of critical thinking.
While Lipman and some other authors view critical thinking as something like clear and sound thinking, still other authors treat critical thinking as a very broad concept that includes creative thinking as a special
case. In this more umbrella sense, critical thinking means something like
clear, broad, deep, sound, etc. thinking all at once. Because of such ambi-
guities, I will not use the term critical thinking much.

Level 2: Challenge Realms

These are very basic realms of thinking that reflect mysteries of a distinctly structural character as people strive to function thoughtfully in almost any setting, the kinds of mysteries Pilgrim encountered a few pages ago. Each realm corresponds to a basic thinking challenge: decision making, problem solving, remembering, and so on—with an associated product of thought: decisions, solutions, recollections, and so on.

As with the core dispositions listed above, I suggest these as core realms of particular importance for the development of thinking. Others might be added to the list, but these at least are fundamental. Here is a brief sketch of each highlighting the mystery it reflects.

Decision making. Knowing your way around the making of decisions, a category of thinking reflecting the fact that people constantly encounter branch points where they must choose between alternative courses of action, and often find other alternatives than the obvious ones.

Problem solving. Knowing your way around reaching solutions to informal and/or formal (logical and mathematical) problems, a category of thinking responsive to the fact that people constantly encounter gaps, situations where they want to get from A to B but see no immediate path and have to find one.

Justification. Knowing your way around devising justifications for the truth or falsity of propositions, a category of thinking reflecting the fact that the world does not make plain what is true and that one can easily be mistaken.

Explanation. Knowing your way around constructing explanations for things and events, a category of thinking respecting the fact that the world does not easily reveal its order; to predict events, as well as to understand things that puzzle us, we need to generate theories, models, and conceptions that explain. Explanation usually looks to causes, form-fits-function relationships (as in fish fins) and governing principles (Newton's laws).

Remembering. Knowing your way around memorizing and remembering, a category of thinking reflecting the fact that human memories do not work like tape recorders; without attention to memorizing and recalling information, forgetting and misremembering happen all too often.

Problem finding. Knowing your way around detecting and defining informal and/or formal problems in an area of interest, teasing out the enigmas, gaps, and opportunities and formulating them in ways that foster inquiry and invention.

Design. Knowing your way around the design of physical objects as well as procedures and other systems, a category of thinking reflecting the fact that people need tools and devices to get things done in the world.

Planning. Knowing your way around the formulation of plans for how to proceed or for how to construct something, reflecting the fact that we cannot always plunge in to good effect—we need to think ahead and envision what things might be like or how they might go.

Evaluation. Knowing your way around the evaluation of things and ideas by way of criteria and judgment, reflecting the fact that the value of something in a given context is often not transparent.

Representation. Knowing your way around the verbal description of things and events, or their representation in other ways, reflecting the fact that people cannot retain or transmit all the information needed without the help of representations.

Prediction. Knowing your way around arriving at sound predictions about what will happen, a category of thinking recognizing that in decision making, problem solving, and like situations one has to forecast the likely consequences of actions.

Learning. Knowing your way around the learning of new information, concepts, and skills. This goes beyond remembering in its concern with learning for understanding, arranging for feedback, assuring sufficient practice of skills, and so on.

This survey of challenge realms poses a couple of puzzles. One puzzle asks, "Are these realms really separate? Sometimes in the middle of making a decision I might have to think out a prediction of something, for instance the consequences of one of my options. And sometimes in the middle of making a prediction, I might have to think out a decision, for instance deciding which of two possible predictions is most likely. It looks as though the basic thinking challenges are all tangled up in one another!"

My answer to this puzzle is that the challenge realms are distinct. Each challenge realm has ABCs—abilities, beliefs and feelings, and concepts—

somewhat distinctive to it. For example, the concept of options belongs particularly to the realm of decision making. The ABCs of a challenge realm guide the basic approach a person takes when engaged in that process.

However, while engaged in a thinking process, a person often encounters subproblems that require a different process. In making a decision, one often faces a subproblem of making a prediction; in making a prediction, one often runs across a subproblem of making a decision. In effect, the basic thinking challenges call upon one another to solve subproblems generated as they play out their own agendas.

I promised two puzzles and here is the second, a puzzle touched on in earlier chapters but worth revisiting: "Do I really need to know my way around a process like remembering or decision making? Don't people usually remember or decide quite spontaneously, without a lot of fuss?"

The answer to this puzzle is yes, we usually do just remember or decide quite spontaneously. The same holds for the other processes; for instance, we solve many problems spontaneously and generate many explanations or evaluations spontaneously. All this occurs because of experiential intelligence, what I've called the 90-percent solution because most of the time (90-percent was simply an expressive way of putting it), we remember, decide, and carry out other thinking tasks in a highly contextual and intuitive manner to good effect. But most of the time is not nearly enough to keep us out of trouble and realize our full potential. All too often, contextual intuitive thinking without reflective intelligence falls prey to the four thinking defaults or other hazards. Knowing your way around basic thinking challenges becomes crucial.

Level 3: Tool Realms

These realms involve knowing your way around tools and strategies that support the kinds of thinking called for by the dispositional and challenge realms. There are innumerable useful tool realms and the list offered is not at all intended to be complete. Here are a few comments on some tool realms, for the sake of clarifying the idea.

> *Brainstorming.* A basic technique for generating diverse imaginative ideas, useful in broad thinking of any sort.
> *Pro-con lists* Pro-con lists are a simple basic organizing tool for evaluation.
> *Stepwise strategies.* Many kinds of thinking are supported by stepwise

strategies involving anywhere from three to a dozen steps. Followed in an orderly fashion, a stepwise strategy for decision making, problem solving, or another kind of thinking fosters an orderly approach, although it does not entirely capture the richness and nuances of the realm.

Graphic organizers. These are any graphic layouts (such as Venn diagrams) that make plain relationships among ideas, allowing people to think on paper.

Concept maps. This is a particular style of graphic organization, where ideas, telegraphically stated, are connected by lines indicating various logical relationships.

Level 4: Technical Realms

These realms involve technical kinds of thinking utilizing logical, mathematical, scientific, or linguistic systems appropriate for some thinking challenges, especially in technical fields. The variety of technical realms is endless, of course. The contrast with tool realms is rough: Technical realms can be considered more technically oriented tool realms. Some examples include:

Formal deduction. This is the machinery of deductive logic, as used in mathematics and some philosophical, scientific, and other applications.

Taxonomies. Taxonomies are formal descriptive systems that strive to classify everything within their scope comprehensively and uniquely, as in the taxonomy of plants and animals.

Probability/statistics. Reasoning with probabilities is a powerful tool in many scientific, economic, and indeed political contexts. Statistics provide a descriptive system for profiling trends and a theory of sampling suitable for establishing general claims about trends through experiment.

Systems thinking. This perspective allows analyzing social, biological, electronic, and other systems in terms of general system properties like input, output, feedback loops, escalation and de-escalation phenomena, and so on.

Game theory. This theory allows analyzing competitive situations in terms of payoffs and probabilities, in order to optimize choices of action.

Level 5: Field Realms

These realms concern thinking within particular fields or professions like law, business, mathematics, or the arts. Dispositional, challenge, and other thinking realms take on more specialized forms within fields and professions, reflecting their particular demands. Instead of discussing this field by field, it's more illuminating to make some comparisons across fields.

While justification as a general thinking realm always involves a pattern of evidence and argument, different fields characteristically call for distinctive kinds of evidence and argument. For instance, formal deductive proof figures centrally in establishing mathematical conclusions, whereas in physics empirical evidence holds sway. In the law, the foundations of evidence lie in information about the case at hand, the written law, and historical precedents of its interpretation. In the creative arts, evidence emanates from the discerning judgment of cultivated eyes and ears rather than deductive proof or experimental findings.

In the same spirit, the ways decisions are made, problems are solved, important information is represented, and things are planned or explained vary from field to field, despite family resemblances that come with the realm in question. For example, making a plan in any field involves constructing some kind of compact schematic representation of something to be realized later (a building, a book, a dance) but the form the plan takes (diagrams, notes, sketches, mental images), the kinds of judgments one has to make (how convenient and presentable the building will be, how readable and informative the book, how engaging and inventive the dance), and like matters vary from field to field. If you are a good planner in general, that quality will help you to organize your planning in any field. But to do a really good job, you need to know your way around the particular turns of thinking appropriate to the field.

Level 6: Situational Realms

These are realms that involve somewhat specific thinking situations that nonetheless recur in a variety of different contexts. For instance, purchase decisions range from personal minor purchases like paperback books to major purchases like cars and homes to corporate purchases such as the acquisition of a building or another company. Often they are special cases of more general realms—purchase decisions are of course a special case of decision making—but they have their own distinctive character and considerations.

Purchase decisions. Despite their variety, a number of common factors figure in purchase decisions: questions of purchase options, good evaluative information, fair price, value received, durability of goods or services, investment value, and so on.

Negotiation. Many situations from personal to corporate to international involve negotiating arrangements. Negotiation involves characteristic dilemmas of rigid principled stands and a competitive rather than a cooperative approach. The work of Roger Fisher and William Ury on negotiating from interest provides a remedy. (See chapter 13)

Managing emotion. Anticipating one's own and others' feelings, dealing with them, and expressing and reading emotions well is an area of thinking that comes up in many home, business, and other situations. Psychologists Peter Salovey and John Mayer term this emotional intelligence. Sometimes it involves constraining emotions, for instance holding in anger, and at other times cultivating emotions, for instance finding the right mood to support a particular endeavor.

Conflict resolution. Conflict resolution applies to endless circumstances in contemporary life and involves a range of considerations such as defining grievances, de-escalating, building mutual respect and understanding.

Policy making. The formulation and implementation of policies figures importantly in government, management, and even home settings. Characteristic factors involve what the policy aims to accomplish, whether it can win support, whether it's enforceable, and so on.

Level 7: Contextual Realms

These are realms thoroughly imbedded in particular life contexts. While they typically benefit from general dispositional and challenge realms, they introduce innumerable nuances of their own emanating from the particularities of their circumstances. Life is made up of a myriad of contextual realms of thinking.

Here are a few examples, with some notes about the special kinds of knowledge they call for, simply to emphasize that these are not just special cases of more general kinds of thinking but have a character all their own. Contextual realms of thinking in effect sit on the borderline between reflective intelligence and experiential intelligence. They benefit from general reflective considerations but also involve a fund of background knowledge distinctive to each.

> *Used car buying.* This is a kind of decision making that benefits greatly from knowledge of cars, prices, and the behavior of sales people.
>
> *Career choice.* This is also a kind of decision making, with the special challenge that people commonly do not have authentic information about fields as they enter them.
>
> *Trip planning.* This variety of planning involves diverse knowledge about modes of transportation and other needs of travel, including one's personal preferences.
>
> *House design.* This variety of design involves a range of technical knowledge about construction as well as about functional and aesthetically pleasing configurations.
>
> *Treaty negotiation.* This variety of problem solving involves knowledge of others' interests and readiness to negotiate, a sharp sense of politics and a recognition of the human dimensions of negotiation situations.

The Puzzle of the Particular

Here at the bottom of the generality ladder it's timely to visit a puzzle touched on in the last chapter, what one might call the puzzle of the particular. It asks: Since thinking always occurs in a particular context, what need is there for more general realms? To take advantage of the contextual realms just mentioned, when we think we are always thinking about something specific—we are out to buy a used car or sort out a career or plan a trip or whatnot. What need, therefore, to talk about general dispositions like broad or sound thinking or general kinds of thinking like decision making or problem solving?

This is an important question and it seems to me that the question has three important answers. The first answer says that, although people are always thinking within one or another specific realm, they often do not know much about it. For instance, I only choose an initial career or shift careers a very few times in the course of my life. However, if I know my way around decision making—and some other general realms that may be relevant, such as evaluation, prediction, and planning—this will help me to manage in this unfamiliar specific realm. In short, the more general realms serve us when we face novelty. This, recall, is one of the principal functions of reflective intelligence.

The second answer points out that even when someone is familiar with a contextual realm, unfamiliar circumstances may arise. Perhaps I am a careers counselor, very familiar with the dilemmas of career selection when it comes to other people. But all of a sudden, I find myself pondering my own situation. Issues come into play that are new for me: I'm older than most of the people I counsel, I have experience with the world in general and human relations in particular that they do not. My potentials are different from theirs. Although I gain something from my knowledge of career planning, I also find myself turning back to my general resources of good thinking.

The third answer says that when we know a lot, our knowledge of contextual realms can trap us. We behave according to habit and custom, without standing back from the circumstances and seeing another, sounder, approach. We fall prey to the four defaults of hasty, narrow, fuzzy, and sprawling thinking. Familiarity with career planning helps to save me from the obvious traps. I know that I need to take a hard look at my knowledge, talents, and skills, not just turn to what interests me most whatever my knack for it. I know that I have to think about the long haul, not what would be fun to do for six months. But wait . . . I don't want to be hasty or narrow. On second thought, maybe something fun to do for six months is just what I need—if I have a plan for what comes after that.

In the same spirit, remember for instance the findings reviewed in Chapter 6: People more knowledgeable in an area do not necessarily think better in that area. To use our realm knowledge in contextual realms well, we often need to modulate our thinking with the more general realms.

The Shape of the Mindscape

In this chapter, I have assembled a response to our navigator's query what's where? Organized by the three mindware questions, this fuller account of reflective intelligence goes as follows:

MWQ #1. What mechanisms underlie intelligence?

- The whats of reflective intelligence are realms of thinking, ranging from very particular realms like used car shopping to very general realms like the disposition to think in a broad way or a clear way.
- As to the where, realms of thinking can be organized roughly according to their degree of generality, how abstract they are and how broadly they apply across contexts, yielding the seven levels outlined earlier: dispositional realms, challenge realms, tool realms, technical realms, field realms, situational realms, and contextual realms.

MWQ #2. Can people learn more intelligence?

- People can learn considerably more experiential *and* reflective intelligence. In particular, the realms of thinking that make up reflective intelligence, like all realms, are areas of activity that people can learn their way around. They characteristically involve an action system, a belief and feelings system, and a conceptual system. People master them—if and when they do—through instruction, watching others, trying things and reflecting on what happens, making rules for themselves, adopting values, and any other of the many ways that realm knowledge accumulates.
- Having the realms of thinking in focus helps us to think about how to teach them as well. As discussed at the end of the last chapter, this means attending to the ABCs of thinking realms, to the action, belief and feeling, and conceptual systems any target realm depends on, and not just to teaching a few tactics. A section of the last chapter takes up this topic again, envisioning a "metacurriculum" for schools that would complement the conventional curriculum with direct attention to the development of thinking.

MwQ #3. What aspects of intelligence especially need attention?

- Focusing on reflective intelligence, the realms from Level 1 through Level 3—dispositional realms, challenge realms, and tool realms—are especially valuable.
- Level 5, field realms, needs attention for true understanding of school subject matters and, of course, for high-quality professional work. Some students headed toward professional work in a field learn their way around the kinds of thinking called for by the field

without it receiving explicit attention, but dismayingly many seem not to do so in a deep way.

- Also Level 6, situational realms, offers high payoff in everyday contexts because situations such as purchase decisions, negotiation, and managing emotions are so commonplace.
- Technical realms (Level 4: formal deduction, game theory, etc.) are a less important part of people's general knowledge. They are usually learned through specific study in response to specific needs or interests. However, some basics of probability and statistics should be in everyone's repertoire.
- It makes little sense to expect and work for general knowledge of contextual realms (used car buying, etc.) of thinking. There are too many of them and they are too individual. People need to recognize their personal needs and seek experience and help specific to them.

The justification for this conception of reflective intelligence comes from multiple sources: the contemporary research on expertise, with qualifications emphasized in the previous chapter; findings demonstrating the defaults of hasty, narrow, fuzzy, and sprawling thinking; findings demonstrating that strategies and other aids to thinking can help; findings demonstrating the importance of dispositions in mobilizing our thinking resources; and so on. In addition to empirical research, the justification for this model lies in a conceptual analysis of what seems to be involved in good thinking practices—the existence of action systems, belief and feeling systems, and conceptual systems associated with such categories of thinking as decision making or broad thinking in general. These are the earmarks of the realmlike character of the components of reflective intelligence.

This answer to the navigator's query and the three mindware questions is unusual by the measure of contemporary writings on reflective intelligence. It says that reflective intelligence is not just a matter of skills or processes to be strengthened or acquired, but a matter of realms to learn your way around. Reflective intelligence has components that mirror the general kinds of mysteries people encounter when they attempt to cope with the world, and with the limitations of neural and experiential intelligence. Reflective intelligence involves not a simple ontology of processes, as many theories in cognitive psychology would have it, but a complex ontology of processes, beliefs, values, concepts, and so on, characteristic of realm knowledge. Reflective intelligence, far from cool and cerebral, demands the impulse to invest in thinking carried by thinking dispositions. Reflective intelligence depends not on a master program that keeps all in order in the computer of the mind but on a loose mosaic of realms at various levels of generality, intelligent behavior coalescing out of their diverse contributions.

Navigators do not ask the navigator's query for fun—well, not only for fun—but because it matters. Navigators who have a sense of what's where can find their way around better. The same holds for any effort to map the mindscape of reflective intelligence. A good answer should help us find our way around better as managers of our own minds and as cultivators of our own and others' reflective intelligence. It's my hope and belief that the picture presented here offers a truer map of the mindscape, more orienting for us all.

12

How the Map Matters

Through some mental quirk, I have always remembered a few terms from that episode that most school children endure: learning the bones of the human body. Words like tibia, ulna, femur, coccyx, phalanges, and metacarpals swim to the surface of my consciousness every now and then, for no good reason but more like the bubbles of gas that appear in swamp water.

Many a school child has questioned why the bones of the body are something children should know. I certainly do not have an answer to satisfy them. But it is much clearer why the bones of the body are something for *someone* to know—physicians and anatomists for instance. The bones of the body, understood by their names, places, and functions, illustrate one of the most fundamental tactics of science: analyzing the world into its components.

To understand the world, we want to know what it is made of. If the slice of world in question is the human skeletal system, we want to know about the tibia, ulna, and so on, not of course for the sake of the names but for the sake of understanding the system through its parts and how they work together. Likewise, if the slice of the world in question lies at the atomic level, we want to know about electrons, protons, neutrons, mesons, neutrinos and what not. If our concerns are stellar, we seek to carve things up in terms of black holes, neutron stars, white dwarfs, red dwarfs, and blue giants. If it is biology, we slice by structure and genetic relatedness: the animal versus the plant and other kingdoms (*Animalia*), animals with spinal chords versus not (*Chordata*), all the way down to toads versus frogs (*Bufonidae* versus *Ranidae*).

This impulse to find components and their boundaries thrives in studies of human intelligence. It is part of the quest for an answer to the first mindware question: What mechanisms underlie intelligence? The last chapter reported my own mission to map out the countries of reflective intelligence, using realm theory and the ladder of generality. But there are many other cartographers of intelligence. They have made their own maps of intelligence as they saw it, proposing different components with different kinds of boundaries between them. In this chapter, I want to take a look at a few of these other mappers and their maps. I will revisit some mentioned earlier and introduce some new ones as well. The priority goes to breadth, not depth: a brief glimpse of several maps for a panorama of different approaches.

But why bother? Because the aim is to spell out how the map matters—what's at stake in the choice between one map or another. Often, the very possibility of learnable intelligence hangs in the balance. And often, how one might best improve intelligence shifts as you look from one map to the next. Comparing maps, I want to urge that the idea of realms of thinking gives a truer picture of learnable intelligence and a better guide to improving it.

The Reaction Against *g*: Psychometric Boundaries

Statistical techniques offer the best established technical approach to finding the boundaries between components of intelligence. Statistical analysis was Spearman's basis for proposing the unified *g* factor, which reflected people's tendency to score consistently higher or lower across diverse intellectually demanding tasks. However, the technique Spearman developed and used—factor analysis—can be applied in different ways. Instead of a unified *g*, one can build a case for multiple intelligences (Chapter 4).

In this spirit and with other refinements, psychometricians such as Horn, Cattell, and Guilford proposed various components of intelligence. Particularly well known is the Horn-Cattell distinction between fluid intelligence (demanded by novel tasks) and crystallized intelligence (reflecting vocabulary and other kinds of consolidated knowledge). However, Horn also identifies several other important components.

Also well-known, although not as well justified, is Guilford's *Structure of Intellect* model with its 150 different components generated as combinations of five operations applied to any of five kinds of contents to yield any of six kinds of products:

Operations: Cognition, Memory, Evaluation, Convergent Production, Divergent Production
Contents: Behavioral, Visual Figural, Auditory Figural, Symbolic, Semantic
Products: Units, Classes, Relations, Systems, Transformations, Implications

The flavor of Guilford's conception comes through simply by browsing in his terminology and the details will not matter here. Guilford's theory does not reflect a pure psychometric approach but a mix of logical analysis and psychometrics, hence the neat organization of the theory.

What kind of boundary does the psychometric tradition mark out? Basically, the psychometrician looks at people's performance on a wide range of tests and asks whether performances on different tests cluster into groups as measured by correlation coefficients. Perhaps performances on tests A, B, and C closely correlate (that is, people who do well on one tend to do well on them all); and performances on D, E, and F closely correlate. This suggests a boundary between A, B, C on the one hand and D, E, F on the other. The psychometrician will say that A, B, and C reflect an underlying component revealed by the way people perform alike on them; and D, E, and F reveal another underlying component.

If statistics provides the boundaries, what is the underlying nature of the components? Statistics do not give us an answer here; the matter is open to interpretation. The components might correspond to physiological modules in the brain, subroutines in the complex information processing the brain must do, different kinds of symbol systems that the mind manipulates, or something else again.

How It Matters

Comparing intelligences. There is a stark difference between these psychometric maps and the idea of realms of thinking sitting on the ladder of generality. The two hold hardly a term or concept in common and offer very different pictures and accounts of how intelligence works. What to make of this?

The contrast comes from how the boundaries get defined—in the case of the psychometric tradition, by factor analysis, in the case of realm theory and other maps later in this chapter, from recent research on expertise and from efforts to analyze thinking and teach thinking. The psychometric methodology certainly wins points for rigor. Moreover, the psychometric community gets credit for its efforts to go beyond Spearman's *g*, building conceptions of multiple intelligences.

Learnable intelligence. In principle, the psychometric approach says nothing one way or another about the prospects of learnable intelligence. As psychometricians measure it, intelligence might turn out to be learnable or not. However, in practice the methodology of the psychometric approach has a built-in bias against revealing learnable intelligence. The design of tests used in such research characteristically emphasizes extremely general traits of mind, overarching factors like *g* and its principal subfactors. However, realm theory says that learnable intelligence involves somewhat specific knowledge about broad categories of thinking like decision making and explanation as well as narrower categories. At least some of that knowledge would be filtered out by the deliberately abstract context-free and complex tasks often used in intelligence testing, although some of it would be relevant. So the psychometric approach probably underestimates how much we can learn to behave more intelligently.

Intelligence gaps. In keeping with this, my main reservation about the psychometric approach concerns what it leaves out. It makes no natural place for the contemporary work on novice-expert differences that motivated the central place of experiential intelligence in realm theory. Nor does it make a place for the vigorous inquiries into higher order thinking that motivate the inclusion of reflective intelligence. Not only are these not represented as major categories, but there is no real place for them at all in the tight-knit webs of statistical connections.

Another problem with the psychometric approach is its inherent agnosticism about mechanism. The approach identifies components of intelligence without saying anything about what causes those components. Without a causal story, it's not clear what if anything we might do to boost intelligence. In contrast, ideas about neural, experiential, and reflective intelligence provide mechanisms that help to explain intelligent behavior causally and point up possibilities for improving it. Realm theory says that we need to cultivate realm knowledge about important kinds of thinking.

In sum, with full credit for its rigor and refinement, the pure psychometric approach seems short on explanations and recommendations, isolated from other explanatory frameworks in psychology, and inherently unkind to the prospects of learnable intelligence.

Gardner's Multiple Intelligences: Neural and Social Boundaries

The psychometric reactions to classical *g* theory bred several theories of multiple intelligences. But the term multiple intelligence belongs most closely to Howard Gardner and his 1983 book *Frames of Mind*. Chapter 4 took a quick look at Gardner's MI (Multiple Intelligences) theory with its seven proposed intelligences:

Linguistic: Prominent in writers, announcers, actors
Musical: Prominent in musicians, music critics
Spatial: Prominent in painters, sculptors, architects
Logical-mathematical: Prominent in mathematicians, scientists
Bodily-kinesthetic: Prominent in athletes, dancers
Interpersonal: Prominent in clinicians, politicians
Intrapersonal: Prominent when we reflect upon and manage ourselves

What approach did Gardner take to finding the boundaries between different parts of the mind? Critical of the psychometric tradition, Gardner argued for his seven on several nonstatistical grounds. Two of the most important were neural and social. On the neural side, Gardner mustered evidence from studies of brain-damaged patients and the feats of idiot-savants, who, although generally low performers, show prodigious abilities in specialties such as arithmetic computation or piano playing. The evidence, Gardner urged, suggests neurological modules in the brain specialized for linguistic, musical, logical-mathematical, and other kinds of information processing.

However, Gardner warns that such studies do not compel the choice of just those seven intelligences. Besides respecting the neurological evidence, Gardner wanted to partition intelligence along socially meaningful lines. Although Gardner acknowledges that any profession involves a mix of the seven, he chose them in part to reflect the obvious demands of professions and other life roles. Thus, writers, announcers, and actors depend heavily on linguistic intelligence, dancers and athletes on bodily-kinesthetic intelligence, and therapists and politicians on interpersonal intelligence. Gardner's approach illustrates how boundary criteria as remote from one another as neurological and social can conspire fruitfully.

How It Matters

Comparing intelligence. On the surface, Gardner's theory of multiple intelligences resembles realm theory no more than do the psychometric theories just discussed. But there is more kinship than might at first appear. MI theory recognizes both the neural and the experiential contributions to intelligent behavior that are so important in realm theory. As just said, MI theory has a double foundation, on the one hand in studies of brain function and brain damage that represent the neurological contribution, and on the other in consideration of professional development in socially important domains, which honors the contemporary research on expertise and context-specific knowledge. In building his perspective, Gardner provides an eloquent and effective reminder that we should not identify intelligent behavior with testlike or doggedly linguistic or mathematical tasks. Human history and social realities cry out for a much broader view.

Learnable intelligence. Gardner certainly thinks that intelligent behavior in particular domains like music or mathematics can be cultivated by effort and education. However, he is skeptical of the notion of general cross-domain learnable intelligence, arguing emphatically for the context-bound character of intelligent behavior. In his concept of intrapersonal intelligence—one's capacity for self-awareness—Gardner makes modest room for something of the sort. But his hopes for its power and reach are not high.

Intelligence gaps. In keeping with this, my main reservation about MI theory is its disregard for reflective intelligence. I have tried to argue throughout this book that people can come to behave more intelligently in a general way. We can learn our way around important realms of thinking like those charted in the previous chapter. MI theory promises nothing like this.

Mike Anderson's Model: Boundaries Between Information-Processing Mechanisms

In his *Intelligence and Development: A Cognitive Theory*, Mike Anderson offers a fresh synthesis of results on intelligence into a comprehensive theory. Anderson's model resembles recent psychometrically based the-

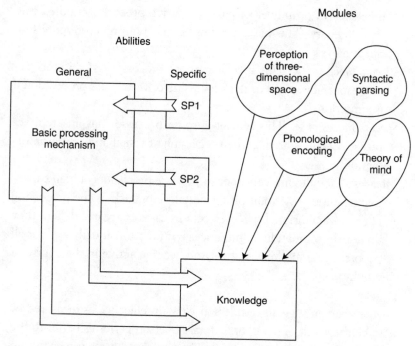

Mike Anderson's diagram of the relationships among the information-processing mechanisms that contribute to intelligence.

ories and Gardner's theory of multiple intelligences in honoring several different kinds of intelligence. However, Anderson sees these kinds in a complex relationship rather different from those discussed earlier.

Anderson's basic strategy for placing boundaries is to partition the mind into different information-processing mechanisms that figure in acquiring information. He "views the brain as a collection of information-processing mechanisms designed to furnish us with information about the world." The best introduction to his vision of intelligence capitalizes on his basic diagram of these mechanisms in relation to one another in the figure above. Let us first consider what the components mean and then touch on some of the arguments for them.

Knowledge. Intelligent performance in real-world situations depends on complex domain-specific knowledge. The mechanisms of intelligence produce that knowledge in the course of years.

Basic processing mechanism. What we call thinking depends on the efficiency of a number of basic cognitive processes bundled into this category. The basic processing mechanism corresponds to Spearman's *g*.

Specific processor 1. This special-purpose processor has an architecture especially suited to the processing of verbal and propositional information.

Specific processor 2. This special-purpose processor has an architecture especially suited to the processing of visual and spatial information.

Modules. Modules are very-special-purpose processors of high capacity fine-tuned by evolution for certain jobs such as the perceiving of three-dimensional space. Except in cases of organic deficit, they do not show individual differences but function equally well for all people. Some modules mature and become active in the course of childhood.

As the diagram suggests, Anderson views intelligence as measured by tests to be the result of a mix of factors. A person performs better to the extent that the person enjoys an efficient basic processing mechanism and good specific processors, has unimpaired modules, has lived long enough so that those modules are active, and has had the range of experiences needed for those several mechanisms to generate the complex knowledge pertinent to dealing with the test. Anderson notes that the same mental age may be achieved by people with quite different patterns of information processing. For instance, comparisons of retarded children with normal children of the same mental age reveal that, although performing at the same level in a rough sense, the retarded children do not perform as well on specific probes of attention, short-term memory, and related basic information processing operations. This presumably signals problems with the mechanisms of knowledge acquisition that account for their achieving the same mental age as the normals later in life.

What leads Anderson to this elaborate map of intelligence? He defines the quest as one for a "minimal cognitive architecture," averring that each element of the map follows upon a body of diverse evidence that demands it. The basic processing mechanism corresponds to the positive manifold discussed in Chapter 2, Spearman's *g* for general intelligence, and the findings relating *g* to reaction time and like measures discussed in Chapter 3. Anderson takes this as evidence that there is indeed a general mechanism that mediates what we call thinking and that this mechanism varies in its efficiency from person to person.

However, Anderson argues, the basic processing mechanism does not suffice to account for the variation in intelligent behavior from person to person. Psychometric studies have detected other patterns of variation, most notably between what might be called linguistic and propositional information processing on the one hand and visual-spatial information processing on the other. On the basis of this and other findings, Anderson proposes two specific processors, each with general computational power but adapted to each of those two kinds of information processing. How do these relate to the basic processing mechanism? Anderson suggests that the specific processors feed algorithms to the basic processing mechanism, which executes them. Thus, knowledge acquisition depends both on effective specific processors that generate good algorithms for challenging situations, and on a basic processing mechanism that carries them out efficiently. Shortfalls at either level can impair performance.

Modules have a rather different character. They are very specialized marvelously efficient computational mechanisms hard-wired by evolution and highly developed in almost everyone. For instance, Anderson emphasizes that even individuals retarded in the sense of IQ handle perception of the visual-spatial world about as well as anyone. Anderson also treats basic aspects of language acquisition such as phonological encoding and syntactic parsing as modules, and suggests that the encoding of causal relationships, the perception of other persons as having their own minds with plans and intentions, and other matters too depend on such modules.

Anderson argues for the reality of modules in part on developmental grounds. The findings of the renowned Swiss psychologist Jean Piaget and of many other developmentalists suggest that children's cognition sits at one level for years and then leaps forward over a period of a few months to sit again for years. Anderson proposes that these shifts involve the maturation of modules in the course of physiological development.

This developmental perspective certainly has lessons to teach us about the nature of intelligence, but most writers on intelligence do not deal with it and by and large neither have I, instead focusing on intelligence in older children and adults. One virtue of Anderson's work is his attention to the growth of intelligence from infancy on.

How It Matters

Comparing intelligences. Anderson's map of intelligence makes for an interesting comparison and contrast with the ones before. As with contemporary psychometric models and with Gardner's MI theory, Anderson's map recognizes several components of intelligence, components with a familiar cast such as linguistic processing or visual-spatial processing. Like most current psychometric models but unlike MI theory, Anderson's theory gives pride of place to *g*. As Spearman held, there is a general factor that influences substantially our cognitive competence. Unlike either psychometric theories or MI theory, Anderson's map of intelligence offers an account in terms of information flow about how the components he identifies relate to one another. Also unlike either, Anderson distinguishes between his special processors 1 and 2 and modules.

Learnable intelligence. Anderson's model says little about the prospects of learnable reflective intelligence. It is simply not intended to treat the phenomena of reflective intelligence. In terms of the trio of neural, experiential, and reflective intelligence, Anderson's map addresses neural intelligence most of all. I do not mean that he articulates mechanisms at the neural level, any more than did Spearman or Jensen. But his model certainly focuses on the hardware of the neural system, the engines of cognition on which all else depends. In formulating mechanisms for the acquisition of knowledge, Anderson honors the importance of experiential intelligence and offers an account of where it comes from.

Intelligence gaps. The detail and sophistication of Anderson's map does not prove, of course, that it outdoes Gardner's or the psychometricians'. His more elaborate conception in turn demands more compelling arguments to justify its specific twists and turns. While Anderson makes a plausible case in his book, there is no need here to reach a final judgment because by and large Anderson's map stands separate from the main concern of this book, reflective intelligence.

Just as Anderson's map has few implications for reflective intelligence one way or another, the realm view of reflective intelligence I've outlined takes a neutral view of Anderson's map and its competitors. So long as people can learn their way around thinking one way or another, whether the way involves Anderson's general and special processors and modules, or Gardner's seven intelligences, or the WERCOF factors, or something else does not matter that much. To put the matter a little glibly, that people learn their way around important kinds of thinking is more important than what neurons they use.

Feuerstein's Model: Boundaries Between Phases

Reuven Feuerstein, one of the pioneers in practical efforts to develop thinking abilities, based his Instrumental Enrichment program (discussed in chapter 8) on an analysis of the thinking problems found in slow learners. Feuerstein organized what he referred to as deficient cognitive functions into three phases reflecting the flow of information through the mind. Here are the three with some sample deficient functions:

Input. Blurred and sweeping perception; unplanned, impulsive, and unsystematic exploratory behavior; impaired temporal orientation. For instance, a child sitting in a math class tracks poorly what's going on, reads haphazardly in different parts of a handout the teacher provides, and runs out of time without finishing the handout.

Elaboration. Impaired problem detection and definition; impaired selection of relevant cues in defining a problem; impaired strategies for hypothesis testing. For instance, the child sees at the end of a story problem about barnyard animals the words "all together" and promptly adds up the numbers in the problem, without carefully ascertaining what the problem asks for.

Output. Egocentric communication; trial and error responses; impaired precision and accuracy in communicating one's response. Called on, the child give the answer 18. Asked "18 what?" the child doesn't know.

This sketch makes Feuerstein's boundary criteria fairly clear. He generalizes observable faults in his impaired learners' handling of subtasks such as exploring a problem, selecting relevant cues, and reporting results. In sorting the list of deficient functions into three phases, Feuerstein neatly organizes everything into intuitively appealing stages of processing.

Note that Feuerstein's deficient functions do not necessarily correspond to anything a psychometrician would identify as a component of intelligence. Feuerstein's boundaries come from the demands of the task! Feuerstein's cognitive functions can be thought of as processes the mind must perform, because tasks require them.

How It Matters

Comparing intelligences. Feuerstein's map of intelligence agrees with realm theory and contrasts with Gardner's MI theory in honoring reflective intelligence. Indeed, his map does not make a specific place for neural or experiential intelligence at all. Instead, it highlights very

308   *What the Mind Is Made of*

general facets of human cognition that can be brought under the individual's executive control, at least to some extent. In this way, Feuerstein offers our first example in this chapter of a somewhat spelled-out mechanism of reflective intelligence: The subprocesses Feuerstein describes tell us point by point what goes sometimes right and sometime wrong with reflective thinking.

Learnable intelligence. The special value of Feuerstein's theory may lie in its invitation to instructional intervention. Remember, Feuerstein has committed himself to the plight and prospects of poor cognitive performers. His three-phase profile of such performers points directly to targets for instructional attention.

Intelligence gaps. Feuerstein's map does not address all the factors it might. First of all, simply from the standpoint of theoretical completeness, the notion of experiential intelligence plays no part in Feuerstein's map, nor does neural intelligence in a specific way, although certainly Feuerstein recognizes neural deficit as one source of problems. Second, while amply addressing the thinking defaults of hasty, fuzzy, and sprawling thinking, Feuerstein pays less up-front attention to narrow thinking, an important category of not-so-intelligent behavior.

Third, Feuerstein's core theory is process centered. The realm view of reflective intelligence recognizes a wide range of other mental entities that figure centrally in intelligent behavior: beliefs, concepts, values, attitudes, dispositions, and so on. In fairness, Feuerstein writes explicitly and emphatically about the importance of such factors; moreover, the building of positive attitudes toward thinking and learning plays a key role in Instrumental Enrichment as an intervention. But these factors do not have much of a presence in his basic map. The essence of realm theory lies in recognizing diverse realms with their complex ontology, a contrast with the process model prominent in Feuerstein's and indeed most other current theories.

Baron's Search-Inference Framework: Boundaries from the Logic of Search

University of Pennsylvania psychologist Jonathan Baron has made an elegant logical analysis of the demands of good thinking. Thinking can be seen as a process of searching for and selecting ideas—ideas concerning solutions, approaches, standards, criticisms, and virtually anything else called for when people think about things. Baron points out that this variety reduces to a mere trio of objectives: "Thinking is, in its most general sense, a method of choosing among potential possibilities, that is, possible actions, beliefs, or personal goals."

Baron boils down his perspective into four processes:

Possibilities. A thinker must search for possibilities. These are possible ways of satisfying the goals at hand, for instance possible actions or beliefs.

Evidence. A thinker must search for evidence that tells how well a possibility serves chosen goals.

Goals. A thinker often has to search for goals, finding subgoals for the goals already at hand, which may be very broad to start with, or revising the original goals in light of circumstances. Once identified, the goals become criteria for selecting among possibilities.

Inference. A thinker must combine evidence to estimate how well the possibilities address the goals.

How well a thinker handles the searches and inference depends on many factors, including information available from memory, external aids such as note pads and information sources, strategies for efficient search, and the thinker's judgments about how much search the situation is worth. Baron notes that both undersearch and oversearch are problems. But people undersearch far more than they oversearch: We tend to explore situations less thoroughly than our own goals recommend!

But how do we gauge whether a person searches too much or too little? Baron offers a clever answer to this: Thinking should help thinkers attain their goals. Too little search, or too much, and our thinking does not do as good a job of this as it might. At first, this answer sounds circular, because goals are one of the items searched for. But of course, thinkers always have some goals as points of departure—including the goals of satisfying primary drives like hunger, survival, and reproduction.

Another important side of Baron's theory is his attention to thinking dispositions as a central concept. Baron draws a distinction between dispositions and cognitive capacities. Roughly, your cognitive capacities are what you can in principle do—for instance, how much information you can hold in short-term memory to work with. Instruction cannot improve capacities, although sometimes you can work around capacity limits, as in using pencil and paper to help with short-term memory. Within the latitude allowed by your capacities, your dispositions determine what you *do* do. Are you disposed to impulsiveness, searching cursorily for possibilities, goals, and evidence? Or are you disposed to compulsiveness, overdoing these searches? Or, more likely, something in between and dependent on the situation? Whatever the answer in a particular case, Baron's view recognizes that our reflective intelligence is a matter of how artfully we think within the boundaries of our capacities.

How It Matters

Comparing intelligences. Like Feuerstein's cognitive functions, Baron's three searches plus inference offer an analysis of task demands. In effect, Baron says that any thinking task implicitly requires this quartet of processes, just as Feuerstein says that any such task requires initial exploration, defining the problem, and so on. Feuerstein's framework is more empirically driven, inspired by multitude of deficits Feuerstein has seen in slow learners. Familiar with the same range of deficits, Baron has chosen a more minimalist logical framework, pared down to only four processes. For Feuerstein, boundaries come from looking at what people do wrong, for Baron by seeking a minimal set of logically sufficient processes.

Learnable intelligence. Baron certainly thinks that we can cultivate reflective intelligence. The four process categories that Baron identifies provide one possible focus for organizing efforts to foster reflective intelligence. The dispositional spin of Baron's analysis accords well with my emphasis on the idea that better reflective intelligence calls for more than just learning the mechanics of good thinking.

Intelligence gaps. Baron does not offer us a full map of human intelligence, nor indeed does he pretend to. His map concerns the kinds of operations demanded by the logic of thinking. Against this map, he gauges how well people follow through on those operations and how they might do better. I endorse the gist of Baron's model. It provides a backdrop against which to discuss the diverse psychological factors that figure in good and not-so-good thinking, including conceptual systems, beliefs, dispositions, and so on.

Sternberg's Triarchic Theory of Intelligence: Boundaries from Context and Subtask

Perhaps the most extensively developed theory of intelligence in recent years is Yale psychologist Robert Sternberg's Triarchic Theory of Intelligence. As the name suggests, Sternberg sees three major sides to intelligence. He calls them the *contextual, experiential,* and *componential* subtheories.

The contextual side of intelligence can also be called practical intelligence. It recognizes people's adaptation to their environments, including social settings. For instance, Sternberg underscores how some people adapt wonderfully well to intellectual settings, such as universities and research laboratories, without being especially creative or strikingly bright in an academic sense. Instead, they function as adroit organizers and artful promoters of themselves. They erect substantial reputations by knowing how to move nimbly in the world they occupy. When we take a critical view of such people, Sternberg notes, we call them operators.

The experiential side of intelligence captures people's ability to cope with novel situations in two ways: insight into the situation and efficient automatization to deal with it better when it recurs. This side of intelligence, Sternberg avers, honors giftedness in the sense of great persons—figures like Einstein and Beethoven who remade fields in fundamental ways. However, high experiential intelligence certainly is not limited to the famous.

Note that Sternberg's experiential category does not mean the same thing as my experiential intelligence. My experiential intelligence—a matter of learning your way around—includes automatization from Sternberg's experiential intelligence and adaption to particular contexts from his contextual intelligence.

The componential side of intelligence deals with people's ability to process information effectively. Sternberg defines a number of components, including metacognitive components that help to steer the cognitive processing.

Notice that Sternberg's componential category is not the same as my reflective intelligence. Yes, the metacomponents from the componential subtheory belong to reflective intelligence. However, some of the performance and knowledge acquisition components in Sternberg's componential subtheory would fall into neural and experiential intelligence. In general, the two frameworks simply put their boundaries in different places.

One can understand Sternberg's triarchic theory better by recognizing familiar ancestors for two of its subtheories. The componential subtheory catches sides of human information processing typically considered by psychometric theories, but with much more attention to mechanism.

The experiential subtheory embraces important aspects of insight and creativity. A fuller feel for Sternberg's triarchic theory follows from seeing some of its elements listed out in more detail:

Sternberg's Triarchic Theory in Outline

I. Contextual or Practical Intelligence: Whatever skills and knowledge are needed for adapting to environments, reshaping them to suit oneself, or indeed selecting new environments where one can thrive.

II. Experiential Intelligence (Orienting to and Automatizing Novelty)
   A. Processes for Dealing With Novelty
      1. Selective encoding: Encoding what information in a situation is relevant
      2. Selective comparison: Interrelating the information with relevant information from memory
      3. Selective combination: Combining all sources of information into a meaningful whole
   B. Automatization (knowledge compilation).

III. Componential Intelligence
   A. Metacomponents or Executive Components—particularly important ones include:
      1. Recognizing that a problem exists
      2. Recognizing the nature of the problem
      3. Selecting a set of lower order (nonexecutive) components for a task
      4. Selecting a strategy for the task that combines the nonexecutive components
      5. Selecting mental representations suitable for the task
      6. Deciding how to allocate attention
      7. Monitoring one's progress
      8. Understanding internal and external feedback about how well you are doing
   B. Performance Components (Called Upon by Metacomponents)—for example:
      1. Encoding a stimulus
      2. Extracting relations between two stimuli or parts of a stimulus
      3. Applying a previously inferred relation to a new situation

C. Knowledge-acquisition Components (which overlap somewhat with experiential intelligence)—for example:
1. Selective encoding
2. Selective comparison
3. Selective combination
4. Sensitivity to contextual cues that convey meaning

What can be said about Sternberg's choice of boundaries? He draws
on an erudite mix of information from many sources to motivate his
scheme. At the top level, the boundaries mark off regions of behavior
neglected by more traditional views. While including the componential
subtheory to represent the kinds of cognitive performances typically
captured by tests as their real-life analogs, Sternberg has added subtheories specifically to reflect performance in and learning from novel contexts, and artful navigation in practical contexts. These boundaries fall
between different contexts of performance. Of course, novel and practical contexts overlap, and the componential mechanisms operate all the
time, serving whatever novel and/or practical contexts demand.

How It Matters

Comparing intelligence. Inside each of Sternberg's subtheories sit boundaries that in a way are like Feuerstein's and Baron's. Basically, Sternberg
looks to logically necessary subprocesses. For example, to tackle a task
at all, at some level you must recognize that a problem exists, encode it,
extract relations, and so on. Like Feuerstein, Sternberg chooses components that often go wrong, opting for an elaborate analysis rather than a
parsimonious one like Baron's. Thus, while Baron's view seems more an
analysis of the logic of thinking-as-search, whether humans or aliens or
computers are doing the thinking, Sternberg's analysis concerns more
specifically the human agent. In contrast with Feuerstein's input-elaboration-output structure, Sternberg offers more of a command hierarchy:
The metacomponents call on other servant processes.

Learnable intelligences. Sternberg champions learnable intelligence.
He believes that the metacomponents, the processes of selective encoding, comparison, and combination, and other features of thinking can
be improved through strategies and practice.

Intelligence gaps. There is much to praise about the triarchic theory.

No other map I know of takes such pains to honor as many themes and subthemes from contemporary psychology. Moreover, the theory steadfastly looks to real-world intelligence, not just the laboratory variety. Sternberg's triarchic theory gives us a fully elaborated mechanism for accounting for intelligent or not-so-intelligent behavior.

Nonetheless, I have some reservations. First of all, the three-way contrast between practical, experiential (in Sternberg's sense), and componential intelligence seems less clear and compelling than the contrast among neural, experiential (my sense), and reflective intelligence. For example, Sternberg's experiential category includes both creativity and efficient automatization, an odd mix. And why should either one be bottled into a category contrasting with practical intelligence?—both are pretty practical. Sternberg has arguments, of course, but the placement seems awkward.

For a second concern, within each subtheory the subcategories look like logically motivated processes masquerading as psychologically reality. For example, I agree that selective encoding, comparison, and combination must figure in cognition. But only in a sense: The mind somehow has to carry out cognitive work that amounts to selective encoding, comparison, and combination. However, this does not mean the mind has separate modules that do those separate jobs. The same worry applies to the Triarchic Theory's long list of metacomponents: Sure, intelligent behavior has to accomplish these things. But that does not mean that each is a separate process in the mind with its own psychological reality.

Finally there is my favorite bugaboo of process. The Triarchic Theory is an ensemble of cognitive processes. It leaves out of the picture many kinds of mental entities like conceptual systems, beliefs, and dispositions. Such "stuff" deserves a place in the sun in a map of intelligence. To be sure, Sternberg knows their importance and credits them in his writings. But this is not the same as giving them a clear place on his official map.

Why Different Maps are Different

Suppose that in 1492, King Ferdinand and Queen Isabella had even more enthusiasm for voyages west than they did. So they funded not only Columbus's voyage but six more. Returning after a couple of years, each captain of the seven expeditions presented the king and queen with a map of the territory discovered—and all the maps were different!

King Ferdinand got annoyed. Maps of the same territory ought to look somewhat the same. Were these captains making up their reports? Had they actually been anyplace? "Let's consider a few beheadings," he said to Queen Isabella. But Isabella said, "Let's consider something else: The West is a big place and maybe their six expeditions ended up looking at different parts of it." And so they argued.

Something like this dilemma comes up around the six maps of intelligence glimpsed in this chapter, plus mine for a seventh. How come they look so different? And who if anyone should be beheaded?

Before scheduling the beheadings, it's worth trying out Isabella's explanation. Are these maps of the same territory? Like what lies west, the mind is a big place. When we speak of intelligence, we take it that we are all talking about the same thing because we say the same word. However, as Part I of this book emphasized, that is not always so. In fact, different expeditions look at very different slices of intelligent behavior. For instance:

- Psychometricians focus on abstract, complex tasks—visual and verbal puzzles of one sort or another. Perhaps more important, they focus on how well people score, extracting statistical trends and relationships. Understandably, they end up with a statistical map of intelligence.
- Much of Feuerstein's work focuses on such tasks too—remember the puzzlelike tasks from Chapter 8. But Feuerstein is interested not just in how well people perform but how they go wrong—how they encode problems poorly, adopt trail-and-error strategies, report results in vague terms, and so on. All this leads to his input-elaboration-output map of the hazards of complex information processing.
- Gardner focuses on conspicuous talent and achievement in domains like writing, music, dance, and mathematics, as well as on neurological deficits. Many of the achievements he highlights might not even be considered intellectually demanding in the usual sense of intellectual—superb dancing for instance. Indeed, Gardner's whole point is to broaden our conceptions of intelligence. This leads to his seven intelligences.

In other words, Isabella's explanation makes good sense. We should not think of the mind as a simple island easily mapped more or less the same way by any expedition, but as more like a continent with different regions that different expeditions chart according to interest and accident.

The region of the mind foregrounded in this book concerns intellectually demanding tasks in the sense of tasks that make you think—whether they are abstract as on IQ tests or concrete as in a dancer or mathematician struggling with a professional problem, envisioning it, defining it, imagining solutions, pursuing possibilities. Also central is not just how well people succeed but how they approach such tasks with success—the knowledge they bring to bear, the concepts they apply, the presumptions they work from, the searches they attempt, and so on. Of the six investigators reviewed in this chapter, Feuerstein, Sternberg, and Baron come closest to the same endeavor. We have all been concerned with what I call reflective intelligence or mindware.

Although the four of us have been looking at something like the same part of the continent, we also have brought home somewhat different maps. What would Isabella have to say about that? One thing she might recognize is that the maps are not as different as they look. In fact, a number of important similarities connect these maps of reflective intelligence. There is recognition of the importance of metacognition (monitoring and regulation of one's thinking), a central role for thinking strategies and their cultivation, identification of typical mishaps in thinking such as failure to search through a broad range of possibilities, and a common commitment to the learnability of intelligence. While one map may be a Mercator projection, another a polar view, and another a globe, the territory underneath is not all that different.

But of course there are some contrasts. I have looked hard at the relation between experiential and reflective intelligence. This led to the notions of knowing your way around and realms. I have looked hard for the elements in play besides cognitive processes—elements like dispositions, concepts, beliefs, values, and so on. This led me to skepticism about a process-centered view and advocacy for the ABCs of realm knowledge, the complex ontology of stuff that underlies our knowing our way around. I have looked hard at how different levels of abstraction seem to figure in our management of our thinking, leading to the different rungs of the mind's ladder. I have tried to urge that seeing things this way helps us to understand learnable intelligence better and tells us much about how to get more of it.

And how to get more of it today and in the decades to come is what I want to turn to now.

13

Mindware and the Millennium

We live on the cusp of millennia, one span of a thousand years meeting another, so inevitably we look forward and look backward. The fact that the local human population of ten-fingered creatures measures time in tens, hundreds, and thousands of years, whereas Martians with seven fingers on each hand certainly would section the clothesline of history very differently, does little to reduce our sense of the pivotal moment.

But perhaps through sheer coincidence, numbers and history do align, because in these days and years there does seem to be some hope of the world coming together in a congenial and coordinated enterprise of human well-being, even as the newspapers are haunted by resurgences of nationalism, imperialism, ethnic hatred, and other ghosts that refuse to go to the grave meekly.

So we look backward and we look forward. An amusing sidelight on the backward looking was the announcement recently by the Moscow Brain Institute about findings concerning the brain of Vladimir Ilich Lenin. As part of the restructuring of the Soviet Union and the lurching democratization of Russia, more openness about such matters became possible. Lenin's brain has lived on as an object of study at the Brain Institute for several decades, laid out in thousands of slices that might reveal a hint of the mind that resided there once. Soviet orthodoxy held

317

that Lenin was a genius, and certainly Lenin was a conspicuously talented mover and shaker. What then did his brain tell us?

In comparison with others, the surface of Lenin's brain was only slightly larger than average. In weight it was much lighter than Ivan Turgenev, the famed Russian 19th Century novelist. Said Oleg Adrianov, director of the institute, "In the anatomical structure of Lenin's brain there is nothing sensational."

There is a lot of looking backwards in this bit of news—looking backwards to a century of disturbing history, the Russian revolution, the First and Second World Wars, Russia's emergence as a dominant power, the nuclear age, the Cold War. And there is looking backwards to a psychology of mind and brain that today seems quaint and even humorous, closer to Mel Brooks' *Young Frankenstein* than to Mary Shelley's pulsing original. There is something naively hopeful about the thought that one might find Lenin's genius such as it was written somehow on the convolutions of his brain, to be read off by peering scientists.

After all, even if one found some differences—and usually such studies do not show much—what would it mean? To make an analogy, imagine noticing that one radio was more powerful and sensitive than another. To find out why, you slice each radio into a thousand sections and closely scrutinize them with a comparative eye. You might discover more of certain substances and configurations in one than the other. Perhaps it would even prove to be the more powerful and sensitive radio that had more of whatever, although you might easily get the opposite result if the more powerful and sensitive radio happened also to have been designed for compactness. If indeed the one with more was also the better, what would those slices really tell you about the nuances of circuitry that made it better? Hardly anything, really.

The physicalist assumption behind many decades of poring over Lenin's brain, the premise that intelligence rests in anatomy, matches well with the spirit of Goddard's list, the set of premises that advocated what amounts to a hereditarian brain-centered view of intelligence. It's all there in the hardware, the brain-centered view says—take a close look at Lenin's brain and you might even see it there.

Such a view might have turned out to be true, but today looking backwards to what has been learned, plainly it is not. Intelligent behavior has at least as much to do with mind as brain, so I have argued through the last dozen chapters. We are in the midst of a slow historical shift from a brain-centered view of intelligence to a mind-centered view, a stately Copernican revolution that allows for the reality and the importance of learnable intelligence.

If sound, and I have argued that it is, such a shift is also terribly important, because we need to be looking forward as well as backward, and intelligence is our future as much as it was our past. Fundamentally, we have nothing else. Except for the neural engine we carry under our skulls, the experiential and reflective intelligence housed by that engine, and the products of past intelligence in the form of an immense support structure of culture and language and artifacts that lets each generation capitalize upon the advances of the previous, we human beings are unimpressive organisms. Other creatures run faster, jump higher, breed quicker, live longer. But no other creature thinks nearly as well or saves up its products of thought for future generations.

The Evolution of Intelligence

Unfortunately, the lesson of the last millennium is that we human beings are not as intelligent as we need to be. Human beings think well enough to get themselves into trouble as a species, something of which no other organism has been capable. Most of the deep problems we face today have emerged as side-effects of advances.

Some of these problems occur because innovation always brings new and unexpected problems. And some occur more because our hearts are not in the right place than because our heads are not on straight. But some of them occur because we are not quite smart enough. We are caught in the evolutionary double bind. The partnership of experiential and reflective intelligence is both our strength and our weakness. Learning our way around new situations with the aid of reflective intelligence, we accumulate knowledge that mostly helps us cope but sometimes in situations of novelty, complexity, and risk overrides reflective intelligence. The problem with the partnership, as with many partnerships, is that it is not quite tight enough.

What is the solution to this seeming evolutionary cul-de-sac? The way out is of course the way forward. The solution is more evolution, not of a biological but a cultural character. As with challenges of literacy and technology, so with the challenge of intelligence—we learn how to handle it better and pass that legacy on to the next generation.

This view of intelligence veers sharply from the notion that intelligence stands or falls on the agility of one's neurons. It is an example of what Austrian biologist Rupert Riedl in his *Biology of Knowledge* calls evolutionary epistemology. By this erudite phrase, Riedl means to say that the stuff of mind—our conscious and self-conscious notions of cause-effect, purpose, similarity, and so on—can be seen as one further stage in a long process of the biological evolution of mind. To use Riedl's own words, "Among its [evolutionary epistemology's] postulates is the view that our conscious cognitive powers are the most recent super-structure in a continuum of cognitive processes as old as life on this planet. . . ."

Although social evolution, like biological evolution, proceeds in fits and starts, explores blind alleys, and sometimes turns back to simpler but well-adapted forms, at least it sets a brisker pace. Over the last decades I see it in action, as matters like creative thinking, critical thinking, and learning to learn get more attention in business, educational, and other settings. But of course the biggest question has to be: What next? What is the future of intelligence? Where do we go from here? If we want to make more of the human mind, what challenges and opportunities flirt with our hunger for more?

While a full answer to that question would swell another book's worth of pages—and mostly with guesses—let me describe four areas for the development of reflective intelligence that especially beckon for development in the near future, partly because the state of the art is where it is and partly because civilization stands where it does. Although by and large I have written from the perspective of a researcher trying to make sense of the nature of intelligence, here I want to pull the practical into the foreground. Here are four valuable aspects of reflective intelligence that we have a collective leg up on—if only we can bring up the other leg and get fully aboard. They are:

- Distributed intelligence, the idea that good thinking depends as much on artifacts, others with whom we think, and the symbol systems that support our thinking as on what we have in our heads.
- Embracing complexity, meeting the challenging of coping with the very high cognitive load inherent in many contemporary situations.
- Dialectical thinking, the kind of thinking that involves cutting across and integrating multiple frames of reference.
- The metacurriculum, a view of education that highlights the importance of full-scale attention to the development of thinking as part and parcel of the teaching of the subject matters.

You will also find running through my exploration of the four a kind of confidence in the worth and destiny of the enterprise. I believe, or I would not have written this book, that the notion of learnable intelligence is a powerful idea. It comes packed with opportunities to understand the human condition better and to better the human condition further.

Distributed Intelligence

Imagine . . .

You sit at a computer looking at an image of an ensemble of buildings. The buildings surround a plaza. You focus on an arch, the gateway to the plaza. A touch of your finger on the keyboard zooms the arch closer. Another touch pulls the viewpoint back and up for a bird's-eye view.

How does it look? Not welcoming enough, you think. Too severe. You need another possibility.

At this very moment, you are collaborating with a colleague half a continent away. Your two computers are slaved together and you have a voice connection too. "I don't know about that arch," you say.

"Just a feeling or can you nail down a reason?" your colleague asks.

"I think I can. The arch is too small in proportion to the circle of buildings. Not generous enough. It gives a cramped feel."

Your colleague agrees, adding "Let me try another option." Your colleague makes a few gestures with a mouse. You track the action, seeing what happens. The image reformats into a version with a larger arch.

"Better," you say. "Definitely better."

It is usual to ask "What is intelligence?" I have been asking that question all the way through this book. But a somewhat different and equally provocative question asks, "*Where* is intelligence?" The usual answer—when the question is asked at all—is that intelligence rests in the heads of individual human beings. Whether intelligence is a matter of neurons or experience or knowing your way around thinking, or all three as argued here, its home lies under your skull.

Oddly enough, this simple and obvious assumption about where intelligence sits can be challenged. I have urged right along that intelligence consists of whatever factors contribute to intelligent behavior. In the above story of two architects designing an arch, consider what some of those factors are. The thinking about alternative arches receives support from a computer-aided design system that realizes the designers' conceptions visually and allows them to manipulate alternatives. This system does not do heavy-duty reasoning for them, but it does provide support for two important cognitive functions: memory and visualization, remembering for them their ideas and displaying their ideas realistically. Second, from a social perspective there are two people at work, operating as a team. The intelligent behavior in question is in an important sense the joint behavior of tandem minds. Finally, they share a language of options, reasons, and so on, that allows them to articulate to themselves and one another where their thinking stands and where they might take it.

All this has the earmarks of a phenomenon that can be called *distributed intelligence*. The basic idea of distributed intelligence says that the resources that support intelligent behavior do not lie solely inside the mind and brain. They typically occur distributed throughout the environment and social system in which we operate.

It's useful to think of intelligence as distributed in three ways:

Physical. We rely on physical artifacts as simple as note pads and as complex as computer-aided design systems and beyond to do various kinds of remembering and computing for us.

Social. We do not typically think solo but in teams where different people bring different abilities to the mix and patterns of collaboration move the general enterprise along.

Symbolic. We do not think in bare thoughts but thoughts clothed in symbol systems, including natural languages with their rich vocabulary of thinking-oriented terms and a variety of notational and graphic symbol systems.

Roy Pea of Northwestern University brought this perspective to my attention a few years ago, formulating a version of it. I have written on it myself, as has my Israeli colleague Gavriel Salomon, who as also edited a book on the theme entitled *Distributed Cognitions*. To try to capture the essence of the idea, I like to contrast person-solo with person-plus. The person-solo is the person functioning with mental resources alone—no pencil, no hand calculator, no partner, and indeed no linguistic or other symbolic resources tuned to the enterprise of thinking specifically, for instance, no terms and concepts like option or reason. Imagine how impaired a thinker this person would be.

The person-plus, in contrast, is the person functioning with such support. The person-plus, not the person-solo, is the typical case. Intelligent behavior is not characteristically the solo dance of a naked brain, but an act that occurs in a somewhat supportive physical, social, and cultural context. Because of that context, the behavior proceeds with more intelligence.

The Future of Distributed Intelligence

The idea of distributed intelligence gives us an outward look to complement the inward look customary in work on intelligence. When enhancing intelligence is the goal, the inward look leads us only to think of training minds of various kinds in various ways. The outward look of distributed intelligence tells us to pay heed to the physical, social, and symbolic setting.

To put this in terms of realm theory, there is such a thing as knowing your way around the use of various physical support systems for thinking, from pencil and paper to spreadsheets to word processors to decision-analysis systems. This is part of reflective intelligence, part of your management of your own thinking. For instance, you can learn your way around the use of concept maps, two- and three-dimensional charts, and outliners. Then there is such a thing as knowing your way around working with others—how to argue fruitfully, to build on others' ideas, to provoke, to listen, to encourage. Finally, there is such a thing as knowing your way around symbolic resources, such as the language of thinking imbedded in every natural language, with its reservoir of terms and concepts like decision, option, reason, evidence, or consequence.

While people do much in this spirit already, from using paper and pencil to employing group brainstorming, it's an ad hoc conglomerate of individually sensible practices. What would it be like to recognize the perspective of distributed intelligence as such and deliberately design whole environments to support intelligent behavior systematically? Imagine a physical environment as supportive of thinking as a good kitchen is of cooking. What would it have? Abundant surfaces to write on, perhaps; computer interfaces supportive of brainstorming, planning, comparing—possibly with graphic organizer programs that help to build concept maps, contrast lists and other useful layouts quickly; ready-at-hand information resources that use associative searches to home in quickly on what you need; easy connectivity with those who might work with you, through electronic mail but also real-time video communication that allows more personal contact-at-a-distance than voice only.

If this sounds technologically heavy, it only concerns physical support for thinking. The human side of the equation enters with social and symbolic support. Human interactions are notoriously messy. Anyone who has sat through a few committee meetings in frustration knows the tendency toward useless drift or the time wasted on minor topics because someone else always has one more thing to say. Anyone with such experience knows that the language of thinking imbedded within any natural language—terms like option, reason, and so on—is not persistently spoken, so meanings and directions blur. People need to learn patterns of collaborative thinking and communicating, part of their reflective intelligence for managing situations where intelligence is socially distributed.

All this is no more than a suggestive sketch of an area that in my view has far to go, but also much to build on. I would hope that the future of distributed intelligence brings a cohesive vision of the importance of the surround in intelligent behavior, the plus part of person-plus.

Embracing Complexity

Imagine . . .

Yesterday you tossed down your notebook in disgust. Too hard to keep track of it all. Too hard to see everything at once! You took advantage of a blank wall in your office, taped up rows of wrapping paper to write on, and began to map out the problem.

In a week, you need to make a series of technical policy recommendations on the overuse of national parks. It's an ecological issue involving dozens of species. It's a political issue. It's an economic issue. It has short-term and long-term aspects. There are issues of legislative precedence. What a mess!

You simply could not keep track of it all as you usually work. You found yourself spending half your time shuffling through papers to find the point you needed to cross-check.

Now, as you lay it all out on the wall, arranged so you can zoom in on anything and glance at it, with important points highlighted so they draw your attention, with arrows connecting one theme and another, now you begin to see it whole.

Maybe, yes, maybe there are some policy options here that the committee would find acceptable. Let's see . . .

———————————

Clearly distributed intelligence has a job to do in this example as well as the previous one. The protagonist of the tale helps thinking along with a large map of the factors involved. However, the real point of the example is not the thinker's solution of papering the wall with diagrams but the nature of the challenge responded to—what I will call cognitive superload.

It was in 1956 that George Miller wrote about the magical number seven plus or minus two. Miller consolidated various research to point up what has come to be recognized as one of the key operating characteristics of human cognition—the cognitive load bottleneck (Chapter 7). People find it difficult to keep track of more than about seven chunks of information at any one time, while they are thinking something through. This bottleneck contributes to the thinking defaults of hasty, narrow, fuzzy, and sprawling thinking.

Most people who have to think a lot solve Miller's problem by way of the physical distribution of intelligence, by thinking on paper or computer, using notes to manage the pinch of short term memory. However, there is a problem beyond the bottleneck Miller identified, one of the same kind but involving many more than seven chunks of information. The thinker puzzling over the national parks policy faces a situation involving more like 70 chunks of information plus or minus 20, or 700 plus or minus 200—not just cognitive load but cognitive superload.

It happens all the time. In hundreds of contemporary settings, people have to deal with truly massive amounts of information at one time, knitting it together to reach decisions and make plans. It happens in social planning, legal cases, military campaigns, public sector policy research and formulation, software systems design, corporate planning, and on and on. All of these and many other settings involve far more cognitive load than Miller dreamed of.

There is a symptom of cognitive superload to watch out for: You are writing things down neatly in well-organized fashion on a sheet or two of paper, and *still* you are confused. It's not a memory problem in the sense of sheer retention of in-process information, not a Millerian seven plus or minus, because your sheets of paper meet that need. It's a problem of organization and access: Where is everything, how do you get at it, and how does it all fit together?

Here is another symptom of cognitive superload in action. Many people will have had this experience. You are participating in a meeting. People are trying to work through a complex issue with many factors and the discussion becomes very confused, flopping around from one issue to another. Then someone suggests a resolution, call it X. Most people think X sounds pretty good (perhaps influenced by the clock) and in five minutes it's settled. But you find yourself sitting there wondering: What about this factor? What about that factor? X doesn't really tie up all the loose ends. The problem of cognitive superload along with other pressures has stampeded most people into a resolution that does not address the factors in play.

How do we get out of such dilemmas? Most of the time, I am afraid, the answer is that we do not. The problem at hand gets solved badly. People take one or another cut at the problem without really accommodating enough information. The cut they take becomes the plan that is pursued for better or for worse, but rarely for the best.

As with the more modest problem Miller identified, cognitive superload exacerbates the thinking defaults, especially the last three. It works to make thinking radically narrow, because there is so much to keep track of that much of it falls away. It works to make thinking fuzzy, because we get confused by the barrage of information. As to sprawling, it foments near chaos, because there is so much to organize we hardly get started on the enterprise.

An emerging science, the science of complex systems, lends even more timeliness to the challenge of embracing complexity. In recent years, a number of scholars have turned toward understanding the behavior of complex systems such as economies, ecologies, weather, the immune system, or animal foraging patterns. While immensely diverse, such complex systems have some common characteristics, among them a tendency for surprising large-scale properties to appear, properties hard to predict from the basic causal rules of small-scale interactions within the system (these properties are usually called *emergent*) and a tendency to function on the edge of chaos, with hints of patterns repeated with variations but far less order than displayed by the orbits of planets or the combinatory behavior of the chemical elements. These and other phenomena of complexity seem quite central to understanding the behavior of the world around us, and our own as well.

The Future of Embracing Complexity

The burgeoning problem of cognitive superload is a characteristic of complex civilization. It is only going to get worse. As it does, better and better ways are needed to cope with and indeed embrace the complexity, drawing information from it. We require some reflective intelligence for dealing with complexity. In the language of realms, we need to know our way around complexity.

Distributed intelligence is part of the solution, the use of physical resources like the wall or a computer database to hold information in an organized way that allows looking for cross-connections. However, the problem of cognitive superload outstrips a problem of information storage. It is a problem of information access.

Partly the challenge is quick retrieval of what is needed when it is needed. Relevant thinking concepts include tagging and indexing information so that it can be looked up rapidly by hand or machine. The dictionary is a modest case in point: You can look up words providing you can guess an approximation to their spelling. Unfortunately, most contexts of cognitive superload require looking up things not by spelling but by some aspect of *meaning*—what something says or implies. Knowing your way around finding things by meaning involves such tactics as categorical and hierarchical classification, taxonomizing, attribute lists, key words, multiple and associative classification.

Beyond retrieval, the challenge is one of effective display of masses of information so that the human eye, our highest capacity information channel, can take it in meaningfully. There is a realm of information display to learn our way around. For instance, researchers at Xerox's Palo Alto Research Center have developed the Information Visualizer, a user interface that helps computer users to sustain an overview and browse through vast amounts of information. The Information Visualizer includes several different ways of representing complex organized information. One format, for example, involves three-dimensional hierarchical trees of Post-It like labels. The user can easily rotate and modify such a tree. Manipulating the tree helps users to get oriented to its layout and navigate more fluently.

Beyond display, there lies the challenge of information consolidation. Not everything is important, and mindware that helps to filter and condense information plays a key role in coping with cognitive superload. Many tactics to know your way around come to mind here—ways of summarizing, prioritizing, and factoring problems into parts for attention one at a time. Artful page or blackboard layouts or computer systems can help to ease systematic efforts to condense and prioritize.

Beyond all these appears the challenge of developing awareness of and tools to deal with the phenomena characteristic of complex systems—emergence, marginally chaotic patterning, and so on. The realm of embracing complexity is spacious and intriguing.

Whatever the technical problems of managing cognitive superload, there is an attitudinal problem as well. In many corporate and government settings, information is viewed as a commodity to be protected rather than shared. Managers lean toward restricted access rather than open access. People know the complexity is there but have no way of getting at it and have to make guesses when they could reason from information. Of course, there are some good motives for protecting information. However, the mindset of hiding information often far outstrips the real necessity. It's bad enough that many contemporary problems are enormously complex without having to grope through them because the information you need has been misered away.

Just like distributed intelligence, the challenge of embracing complexity has been and is being addressed in many specific ways—but for the most part without an overarching vision of its character. In the world of desk-top computers, spreadsheets help to cope with the problem as it arises in budgeting, project planner software as the problem arises in corporate planning, and so on. However, my hope for the future of intelligence is that the problem of cognitive superload will come to be recognized by researchers, product developers, and human resource consultants in a cohesive way in its multiple manifestations, leading to a much more richly developed realm of managing very complex information.

Dialectical Thinking

Imagine . . .

You say, "I understand your position on this Mrs. Franks. I also want us to bring into play here what we could call your interests. What do you concretely need?"

Mrs. Franks looks across at Mr. Evans, her opponent in a contract dispute. "Augustine Construction promised to finish the work by May 11. That's what I want."

You say, "Yes, let me acknowledge that concern. Also, let me explain what I mean by interests. What concretely will happen if the work isn't done by May 11? For instance, what will your costs be and why?"

Turning to Mr. Evans, you add, "You understand, Mr. Evans, this question isn't to favor you. I know your position is that the May 11 date was never actually promised as such. But again, I'm soon going to be asking what your real needs in this situation are."

The consultant in the above exchange is mediating a dispute, using a perspective on negotiation developed by Roger Fisher and William Ury of the Harvard Negotiation Project and popularized through their well-known book *Getting to Yes*. The framework developed by Fisher and Ury begins with the observation that there is a usual way of negotiating— from positions. I have my position and you have yours. We each try to maintain it. We may negotiate in a soft way (ready to compromise) or in a hard way (nonnegotiable demands). Whichever the case, we fall into a pattern of defending the castles of our positions.

Fisher and Ury recommend a shift of perspective called negotiating from interests. As in the above scenario, the aim of negotiating from interests is to get those involved to think about what each really needs—and then to search out resolutions that involve as much mutual satisfaction as possible.

Negotiating from interests rather than positions can be seen as a realm that illustrates dialectical thinking. This is an erudite but not very well defined term for kinds of thinking that stand above the pell-mell of everyday cognition, that look across different systems of reasoning and background assumptions, and that try to synthesize. For instance, negotiating from interests strives for a shift of logic from position-based negotiation to one where people negotiate in terms of their situational needs.

A number of contemporary researchers interested in adult development have investigated dialectical thinking of various kinds. They do not always call it dialectical thinking, but I will here. Some of these researchers have looked to occasions when people attain a systems-level perspective on events in the world that combines simple causal chains into a more comprehensive reasoning system. Families, for instance, can be seen as something like ecological systems, where an action of one party can have ripple effects that trigger another's actions into a spiral of escalating distance—or intimacy. Some of these researchers have looked at problem finding, asking how it is that some ingenious people do not just solve problems but find the problems most worth solving. This may involve a kind of distanced system-level insight into the field in question.

The general view of those exploring dialectical thinking is that conventional creative and critical thinking (brainstorming, pro-con lists, and so on) can only go so far. It lacks the richness of thinking across different patterns of reasoning and linking local patterns of reasoning into larger systemlike relationships. Dialectical thinking represents a further stage or phase in the development of reflective intelligence.

The Future of Dialectical Thinking

As a field of inquiry and even more as a field of instruction, dialectical thinking is young and raw—full of opportunity but relatively unformed. In contrast with most of the research on thinking, much of it specifically addresses adult learners. In contrast with most of the research, it steps away skeptically from the usual involvement with formal tasks that have specific answers (syllogisms and number series problems, for example) or out-and-out inventive tasks (for instance brainstorming or puzzlelike insight problems) in favor of complex open-ended situations. Researchers on dialectical thinking have to some extent deliberately distanced themselves from mainstream inquiry for the sake of a different and perhaps deeper look.

At the same time, their explorations fall comfortably within the province of a realm view of reflective intelligence that highlights knowing your way around. You can know your way around aspects of dialectical thinking. The patterns of dialectical thinking appear in the mental models people have of situations (different visions of what a family is, for instance), reasoning moves that people make (negotiating from positions versus interests), attitudes people hold toward knowledge (how certain it is versus how open to interpretation), and more.

What does the future of dialectical thinking hold? One need is for more comprehensive maps and charts of practical realms of dialectical thinking. Islands of progress appear here. To the work of Fisher and Ury one can add Peter Senge's well-known *The Fifth Discipline*, the title referring to systems thinking. Senge examines the dynamics of typical system-level problems in organizations and industries with their many interacting components, such as: systems often resist change as components react to cancel the effect of perturbations; quick ways out of problems often recreate the problems; and effects of action are often delayed in such systems, leading to taking too much action because nothing seems to be happening.

In his 1994 *The Quark and the Jaguar,* Nobel-prize-winning physicist Murray Gell-Mann explores the emerging theory of complex adaptive systems, a concept that includes such diverse cases as economic systems, the immune system, language systems, and of course the human mind. Among other themes, Gell-Mann probes how complex adaptive systems create or invent. One key concept is basins of attraction. Many systems over time tend to settle into a particular configuration. For example, a ball in a bowl quickly moves to the lowest point. With complex adaptive systems, such as the human mind thinking about a problem, often more than one basin of attraction is available. Imagine how a ball on a muffin tin could settle into any of the various cups. Creative thinking, Gell-Mann emphasizes, often involves escaping one basin of attraction for neighboring basins that have more to offer—for instance by brainstorming, introducing randomness, or considering seemingly crazy or self-contradictory proposals.

Here and there, educational perspectives with an emphasis on systems thinking have emerged as well. The summer 1993 issue the *Systems Dynamics Review* focused on education. An article by Barry Richmand sought to define several thinking skills central to systems thinking. Richmand urged educators to foster what he called dynamic thinking: seeing and deducing complex behavior patterns rather than focusing on and seeking to predict isolated events. He urged attention to closed loop thinking: seeing the world as a set of ongoing interdependent processes rather than as a laundry list of one-way relationships.

Despite such examples, the diverse work on dialectical thinking has been largely descriptive and developmental in character, examining how people think in more and less sophisticated ways, but not how they can be helped toward dialectical thinking. The prospect is exciting, especially because so many contemporary problems of moral and social conflict involve complex systems and colliding frames of reference.

The Metacurriculum

Imagine . . .

You are teaching a social studies class studying famous American women. This week's concerns Amelia Earhart. You say, "We've read how Amelia Earhart disappeared somewhere over the Pacific Ocean in 1937; no remains from a plane crash have ever been found. What a mystery! How can someone just vanish? What do you think—what happened?"

"Maybe her engine blew up," one student suggests.

"Yes," you say, "that's a good theory. We should brainstorm what other theories we can think of. Who has other ideas?"

Another student suggests, "Maybe she had had it, you know, with all the publicity. Maybe she ran away. Maybe she lived on a desert island or in Brazil or something. There were no traces because she hid them!"

Other students come forward with other theories. Soon it makes sense to dip into the question of evidence. You say, "We should ask ourselves what evidence we can find about these theories. Evidence for, and evidence against, 'cause we can't just pat ourselves on the back."

"Well," says one student, "maybe some evidence for the engine blowing up is that nothing was ever found, no remains or anything. The plane blew up, and everything fell into the ocean."

"Yes, good" you affirm, "that's consistent with the plane blowing up. Let's see if it's equally consistent with other theories. Are there other possible reasons for no traces?"

Another student suggests, "What about she was fed up and vanished on purpose. So she hid her plane and everything."

"Yes, that was another theory. That's also consistent with not finding anything. Can we think of any evidence for this theory specifically. For instance, did you read anything suggesting that she was fed up, that she wanted to get away from it all?"

You make a big deal of evidence because you know how easy it is for people to feel comfortable with an idea without evidence—and how easy it is for people to think only of evidence that supports their viewpoint and not evidence that works against it. You ask your students to work in groups, make a plan to look carefully at some details about Earhart's disappearance, and test out some of the theories that have been suggested. As they work, every now and then they have to stop and think about their thinking. Are they keeping focused on the task? Are they accumulating evidence? Have they paid attention to both sides of the case? Afterward, they will report and you will assess their reports.

All this continues over a couple of class periods. By the end, they have learned an amazing amount about Amelia Earhart, her character, and the era. But they still don't know why and how she disappeared. You seize the opportunity for a concluding discussion:

"How close can we come to knowing the past?" you ask. "We don't have time machines. So how do we do the best that we can?" This launches a discussion of how we have to reconstruct the past from evidence—and how often there's more than one way to do it and we can't be sure what happened. You ask your students to think of examples from history and from everyday life.

As one student puts it, "I'm not sure exactly what I did on my birthday six months ago. But I can make a pretty good guess. And I can tell you why it's a good guess."

———————

What if most instruction were like this? What if most instruction in the subject matters had a double agenda—paying attention to the content of the subject matter and also to basic questions like how we know, how can we be sure, and what other possibilities are there? What a difference that would make in the depth and meaningfulness of instruction!

This is just one small sample of a rather grand idea—the *metacurriculum*. The regular curriculum consists of the subject matters of mathematics, English, science, social studies and so on that each child navigates according to ability and interest. But the metacurriculum proposes quite another kind of content with hardly any presence in the typical classroom.

The idea of a metacurriculum begins with a simple point. It's good to have a clear picture of what you want youngsters to learn. That is what a curriculum is for. It says that we want students to learn their way around topics like Amelia Earhart, her adventures, and her disappearance; how fractions work and how they represent real-world situations; the poems of Robert Frost and the way they speak to abiding human concerns; and so on.

The metacurriculum says the same kind of thing. It says that we also want students to learn their way around good thinking. Look to the notion of realms of thinking in its broadest sense, and there you will find the metacurriculum. It includes key terms and concepts about thinking, beliefs about and attitudes toward thinking, and good thinking practices. It includes dispositions like the disposition to think broadly or to think deeply as well as challenge realms like decision making, problem solving, and explanation and tool realms like brainstorming, using concept maps, and writing arguments.

At first blush, uneasy teachers and students might see the metacurriculum as another course or set of courses running alongside the normal curriculum. Where would the time and resources come from? But a parallel strand of instruction is not what I have in mind. As with the Amelia Earhart example, the metacurriculum gets infused into the teaching of the subject matters, regardless of whether there are occasional separate courses that focus on thinking. Toward the end of Chapter 8, I wrote about this seamless joining of learnable intelligence and subject-matter instruction. Here it is again, wrapped in a more ambitious package, not just occasional shots of reflective intelligence but a transformation of education.

One goal of the metacurriculum is to boost students' thinking even as they learn their way around content knowledge. But there is another that directly serves the content curriculum. Developing a feel for how the discipline works as an area of knowledge and inquiry ought to be part of any subject matter instruction. For instance, the Amelia Earhart example is a piece of history, but if you learn only the story of what happened and nothing about how we try to find out what happened, you are missing something. At best, you are likely to think that history is a story with holes—what happened insofar as the facts tell us, with gaps in between like a novel found in a dump with some pages missing. But perhaps the most fundamental fact about history is that the same facts usually let us tell the story in more than one way. That's metacurriculum stuff, and if you don't appreciate it you don't understand history.

In fact, it seems that students often do not understand subject-matter concepts in part because they do not understand how the discipline works as a whole. Here is an example. Many students make endless minor errors in algebra because of false analogies. They often think for instance that the square root of A + B is just the square root of A + the square root of B. Why? Presumably because things like that work elsewhere. For instance, X times A + B is indeed X times A + X times B.

What they seem to forget is that in algebra letters stand in for numbers. Algebra is a generalization of arithmetic. What's okay to do with numbers is okay to do with letters, but only that. You can test out the square root idea with numbers as small as 1 and 1 (and it does not work), but students usually fail to make such checks. It never occurs to them to look to the mother system, numbers. An axiom of the metacurriculum for algebra would certainly be: Numbers are the mother system. Ask mother when you want to be sure. (Often good advice in other situations.)

This is just one example of many that could be given. Although very different from the history example, it's another tip of the same iceberg: the fundamental role of evidence in the disciplines. In every subject matter there are issues of evidence that make up a part of its typically tacit and unattended metacurriculum. Any subject matter deals with truth in some sense, and the kinds of evidence needed to establish truth. In history, evidence stems in good part from the contextually appropriate interpretation of original sources. In science, emphasis falls on the empirical test of experimentation. Formal mathematics demands deductive proof from axioms and previously established theorems. These are all differences in what the ladder of generality called field realms. Unfortunately, conventional instruction hardly touches at all on the distinctive logic of different fields.

Matters of proof and evidence get astoundingly complex when we look to the collisions of values so central to contemporary life and conspicuous in current culture. How to reconcile the interests of industry with those of ecologists? How to reconcile the concerns of developing science (recombinant DNA research for example) with the fears of malicious or stupid uses of dangerous science (an accidentally engineered Frankenstein virus)? Reasoning about such things requires more than scientific or axiomatic methods or the historian's dedication to original sources: It requires some of the resources of dialectical thinking, designed to support reasoning across conflicting value systems.

And that, or anything like it, requires the metacurriculum. Today the metacurriculum hardly exists in most school settings. A few students read between the lines and catch on, acquiring some general feel for reasoning and inquiry in the subject matters they study. Most do not.

The Future of the Metacurriculum

I argued in Chapter 8 that efforts to teach intelligence had been successful—but by and large not dramatic. They had improved intelligence somewhat, but not usually changed people profoundly and for the long term. Why not?

One reason is simply the time and attention it takes. Reflective intelligence involves knowing your way around a lot of realms of thinking. That is not something you learn in a week like memorizing the multiplication tables. Realm theory and the ladder of generality from previous chapters have helped to make clear how much is involved.

To cultivate reflective intelligence on a wide scale, we need a curriculum infused with a metacurriculum. We need explicit recognition that there is much youngsters can learn within and across the subject matters about the good use of their minds. The Amelia Earhart experience could be part of such a program. But just as one swallow does not make a summer, one or even a dozen such episodes will not make youngsters much more intelligent. Educators must create an entire culture of thoughtfulness within classroom settings, where strategies are taught sometimes, attitudes of reflectiveness are modeled by the teacher, values are placed on complex cognition, and so on.

What should be in this metacurriculum? In my recent *Smart Schools: From Training Memories to Educating Minds*, I have discussed the metacurriculum in a more extended way. Since then, my colleagues Shari Tishman and Eileen Jay and I have added some ideas, writing about creating a culture of thinking in school settings in a book called *The Thinking Classroom*. As I see it today, the content of a metacurriculum would draw on key realms of thinking in the ladder of generality.

Dispositional realms. The core dispositional realms, clear, broad, deep, sound, curious, strategic, and aware thinking, in general and as they play out within particular subject matters.

Challenge realms. The core challenge realms, decision making, problem solving, justification, explanation, remembering, problem finding, design, planning, evaluation, representation, prediction, and learning, in general and as they play out within particular subject matters.

Tool realms. A useful kit of tool realms: brainstorming, pro-ing and con-ing, use of concept maps, and so on.

Technical realms. At least thinking with basic probability and statistics.

Field realms. Some sense of the paterns of thinking characteristic of fields studied.

Situational realms. Selected situational realms such as managing emotions, conflict resolution, and negotiation.

Although this list may resurrect the specter of teaching such realms of thinking point blank, my actual image of their proper place involves only a little full frontal instruction, with more emphasis on a continuing presence in the culture of the classroom and the texture of activities and interactions among teachers and students.

These realms comprise a "what" for the metacurriculum. There's also a question of method, the "how." Here we can take a cue from the ABCs of realms, the importance of bridging for transfer discussed in chapter 9, and the central role of assessment in education to create an ABCBA pattern like this, with illustrations from the Earhart example.

A for cultivating an action system around thinking. This means attention to thinking strategies and plans and metacognition. For example, in the Amelia Earhart episode the teacher emphasized brainstorming, group planning, and monitoring the thinking of your group.

B for cultivating beliefs, values, and feelings about thinking. This means attention to the beliefs, values, standards, feelings, and so on, that underwrite good thinking. For example, in the Amelia Earhart episode the teacher entices students to get caught up in the mystery of Amelia Earhart's disappearance and pushes for the importance of evidence.

C for cultivating conceptual systems around thinking. This means attention to the development of the conceptual systems underlying different kinds of thinking. One good way to approach this is to use the right language in context. Thus the teacher in the Amelia Earhart episode employs terms like theory, evidence, and consistent.

B for cultivating bridging (transfer) of what's been learned about thinking as well as content. This means making part of students' learning some explicit connection making between today and tomorrow, this subject and another, school and out-of-school concerns. For instance, the teacher ends the Amelia Earhart experience by exploring the issue of how we can know what happened in the past, drawing historical and personal examples from the students.

A for cultivating assessment that centers on thinking. This means organizing assessments that show students' ability to think with the content they have been learning. For instance, the teacher in the Amelia Earhart episode assesses the reports made by the working groups.

Pursued assiduously, attention to this quintet of concerns creates a culture of thinking in classrooms, a culture that builds students' reflective intelligence across a broad front as well as advancing their understanding of subject-matter content.

Some people believe that full-fledged cultures of thinking already thrive in many thoughtful classrooms around the country. But I believe there are only a few. One often finds generally thoughtful teaching processes that draw out good thinking from children. However, they usually lack explicit attention to the many diverse aspects of thinking that have importance. Research suggests, remember, that explicit articulation of ideas about reflective thinking plays a key role in learners' mastery. Also, one finds classrooms where thinking skills are taught point blank. But those same classrooms may not have a culture of thinking, where matters like respect for others' ideas, a critical concern with evidence, a creative concern with plans and visions, and many other aspects of thinking infiltrate the texture of practices and interactions.

So the most powerful demonstrations of developing reflective intelligence remain to be done. Nothing as modest as a course is enough. Anyone who has worked on the practical side of educational change knows that such transformations face enormous barriers of cultural and institutional inertia. This was discussed briefly at the end of Chapter 8. However, I think the potential rewards are high enough for us to see serious committed efforts to make this happen. When we create classroom cultures where the metacurriculum is both an explicit presence and an implicit part of the texture of the way things are done, then we will be testing the limits of possibility, truly finding out how much reflective intelligence youngsters can learn.

The Artificial Intelligence of Human Beings

Distributed intelligence, embracing complexity, dialectical thinking, the metacurriculum—four themes that sample from the future of intelligence, and every one of them reminds me of Rodin.

Do I mean Rodin the French sculptor? Yes, I do. Although the technicalities of learnable intelligence and realm theory seem remote from the impassioned works of Rodin, a connection begs to be made. On the surface, the connection is the obvious one, to Rodin's famous sculpture *The Thinker*, a cultural icon for intense cogitation. However, the more interesting connection is not that *The Thinker* is thinking but how *The Thinker* sits to do it.

I have always marveled over *The Thinker's* posture—bent forward at the waist, right elbow on his left knee, chin on the back of his right hand. As an experiment, you might like to try it out. Go ahead: Place your right elbow on your *left* knee and prop your head not on your closed fist but on the back of your hand. It's an exceedingly uncomfortable position. You can hardly think in it at all. Whatever other messages it may have, Rodin's *The Thinker* embodies a savvy lesson about the place of artifice of art. *The Thinker* conveys a compeling impression of a human being thinking intensely through a posture quite unsuited to the human body.

Rodin's artifice says a lot about what real thinkers need to do. Rodin exaggerates for the sake of expression, but when we want to work through a tough issue, we often do assume a posture something like that. We know a trick of posture, an artifice, that helps us stay more alert. As Rodin used an artifice to create a compelling work, so do we all have to adopt a range of artifices to make the most of our capacity for thought. Thinking at its best is an artifice—a matter of tricks we try out, concepts we cook up, standards we lay down, images we imagine, beliefs that we formulate, plans we ply, notations we note down, devices we rig up, all in the service of getting the most out of our minds. It's artificial through and through. Every one of the themes in this chapter—distributed intelligence, embracing complexity, dialectical thinking, the metacurriculum—all amount to further artifices that could empower us even more.

I am writing here about what might be called the artificial intelligence of human beings. Thinking at its best is an unnatural act. Of course, artificial intelligence as the term usually is used concerns computers, not human beings. As met briefly in Chapters 6 and 8, artificial intelligence is the science of getting computers to show intelligence behaviors, such as playing chess or proving theorems in mathematics. To speak of the artificial intelligence of human beings is to say something distinctly odd.

But I mean it, quite literally. You see, the natural intelligence of human beings is neural and experiential intelligence with a bit of help from reflective intelligence. We come equipped with our neural systems, well-designed by a billion years of evolution mainly to support experiential intelligence, that accumulation of local knowledge that puts us in a good position to cope with problems and opportunities in context. The trouble is, so much of the time these days we are out of context! We are facing some rather new problem in a rather new setting, or a problem in an old setting that invites a rather new way of thinking about it. We are caught in that evolutionary double bind, where venerable experiential intelligence generates the defaults of hasty, narrow, fuzzy and sprawling thinking, because of the pattern-driven character of experiential intelligence and because of other problems such as the cognitive load bottleneck.

Reflective intelligence in an ascendent role is in a sense unnatural. It's not the way our thoughts easily flow. It counters the pattern-driven momentum of experiential intelligence, dodging the defaults rather than taking a bath in them. Developed reflective intelligence is artificial intelligence—artificial intelligence for human beings. You would not want it all the time because experiential intelligence does a good enough job most of the time. But having it when you need it is probably considerably more important than artificial intelligence for machines.

The artificiality should come as no surprise. Artifice is deep in the human blood and brain. We are creatures of artifice. Most of what surrounds us is artificial. The clothes we wear, the chairs we sit on, the pens we write with, the shoes we walk in are all contrivances of human ingenuity. We routinely extend our physical functioning by artificial means—telescopes and microscopes to amplify our vision, backhoes and bulldozers to amplify our strength, telephones to carry our voices over a distance. No surprise, then, that we should quite spontaneously, without any calculated plot, through a process of cultural evolution that threads through Plato and Aristotle and all the way to today's explorers of learnable intelligence, get artificial about the best use of our own minds.

In fact, an anthropologist would surely say that the artificiality of clothes, chairs, pens, and thinking tactics is not all that artificial for us human beings. It's very much in our nature to create artifices and transmit them culturally, part and parcel of the social evolution I talked about at the beginning of this chapter. To human beings, artifice comes naturally.

In this age of organically grown foods and ecological concerns, the term artificial carries some bad vibes, but realistically the artificial intelligence of human beings offers us a very good kind of artificiality. It need not even feel artificial. Tricks of the trade though much of it may be, mindware can come to function as comfortably and naturally as old shoes—which after all are just as artificial even after they have agreed to get along with your feet as new shoes are before they have agreed to get along with your feet.

There is even a phrase for getting comfortable with something artificial: second nature. When you live with something long enough and take it to heart, then it no longer feels like a contrivance. It's second nature, which feels just as natural as your first nature. In fact, the notions of second nature and knowing your way around are kindred. When you really know your way around—around Harvard Square or the stock market or distributed intelligence or dialectical thinking—its artifice becomes natural. You are at home in the realm.

My long-term hope for the future of reflective intelligence sees people everywhere learning their ways around more and more of it, a common democratically distributed and developed second nature. As the state of the art deepens, as we understand how to set the resources of learnable intelligence in a cultural context of thoughtfulness, as we learn to make up the best mindware and make the best use of it, more intelligent human behavior will become as comfortable and reliable as old shoes, perhaps even in such uncongenial settings as political campaigns and television sitcoms. As we confront the daunting and sometimes dangerous complexities of a new millennium, the more attentive we are to the future of learnable intelligence, the longer and richer our future is likely to be.

Notes

Chapter 1: Telescopes and Intelligence

Goddard's List (pp. 5–7)

The information about and quote from Goddard: Gould (1981), pp. 159–60.

Terman's and Spearman's views: Gould (1981); also see discussion of Spearman's work in the next two chapters.

The caveats about Goddard's list: Evidence and references will be offered throughout the course of this book.

The Revolution We Need (pp. 7–11)

The Rand report on global preparedness: Bikson & Law (1994).

Thinking for a Living: Marshall & Tucker (1992).

"Fewer than four . . .": Marshall & Tucker (1992), p. 67.

"These findings . . .": Marshall & Tucker (1992), p. 67.

Smart Schools: Perkins (1992).

The populist senator: This was Senator Roman Hruska speaking in 1970 of

Richard Nixon's Supreme Court nominee G. Harold Carswell, whose nomination was eventually defeated. Abadinsky (1990).

The Whale Movers: Barry (1990).

The willing student: this experience was related to me by Sharon Bailin, a philosopher concerned with critical and creative thinking.

The Annenberg study: Zuckman (1994).

The March of Folly: Tuchman (1984).

On dysrationalia: Stanovich (1994); the quote is from page 11.

Isn't the Revolution Over Yet? (pp. 15–18)

Beliefs about race and intellectual capacity: Gould (1981).

Attributions of failure to lack of ability: Dweck & Bempechat (1980).

Japanese versus U.S. attitudes toward effort in learning: White (1987).

The Bell Curve: Herrnstein & Murray (1994).

The Affirmative Revolution (pp. 18–19)

Luis Alberto Machado's concept of the revolution of intelligence: Machado (1975).

Chapter 2: The Mind's Apple Falls

Information about Binet throughout this chapter is largely from Gould (1981).

A Number for the Mind (pp. 24–25)

Examples of Binet's tasks for measuring intelligence: Jensen (1980), p. 142.

"One might almost say . . .": Binet quoted in Gould (1981), p. 149.

Stern's innovation that yielded the intelligence quotient: Gould (1981), p. 150.

IQ as calculated today: Brody (1992); Jensen (1980).

Visible Intelligence (pp. 31–34)

"Measurable intelligence is simply . . .": Boring (1923).

Studies of the everyday conception of intelligence by Sternberg and colleagues: Sternberg (1985b); Sternberg, Conway, Ketron, & Bernstein (1981).

The Fundamental Experiment (pp. 34–38)

Descriptions of the fundamental experiment: Brody (1992); Jensen (1980).

The sample tasks: I made these up in the style of typical IQ test items.

The table is a subset of a table from Jensen (1980), p. 215.

Performance on very different intellectually demanding tasks is related: Brody (1992); Jensen (1980).

Relations between IQ, performance in educational settings, and performance in the workplace: Brody (1992), p. 252, 274 and through chapter 9; Herrnstein & Murray (1994), Chapter 3.

IQ more predictive of performance than job-specific measures: Herrnstein & Murray (1994), pp. 63-64.

Inside the Mind's Apple (pp. 38–39)

"What they should learn . . .": Binet as quoted in Gould (1981), p. 154.

Chapter 3: The Empire of IQ

The One and Only Intelligence (pp. 42–47)

Information on Spearman's view is drawn largely from Gould (1981).

"was taken, pending . . ": Spearman, quoted in Gould (1981), p. 266.

"would thus function . . .": Spearman, quoted in Gould (1981), pp. 266-67.

Discussion of Yerkes is based on Gould (1981), p. 192 on.

Mental ages of adults from various national and racial groups: Gould (1981), p. 197.

"it appears that feeblemindedness . . .": statement by Yerkes, quoted in Gould (1981), p. 223.

Information on C. C. Brigham from Gould (1981), p. 24.

"The author presents . . .": Yerkes in the introduction to Brigham's book, quoted in Gould (1981), pp. 224-25.

"I believe those tests . . .": Osborn quoted in Gould (1981), p. 231.

"The general conclusion . . .": Spearman quoted in Gould (1981), pp. 271-2.

Early and misguided efforts to measure intelligence: Gould (1981).

Fast Neurons (pp. 47–53)

Jensen's apparatus is described in Jensen (1980).

Findings about choice reaction time: Carlson & Jensen (1982); Brody (1992), pp. 50-55; Jensen (1980, 1988).

Reservations about Jensen's choice reaction time measures: Longstreth (1984); Brody (1992).

Results about inspection time are reviewed in Brody (1992).

Inspection time in comparison with Jensen's measures: Brody (1992), p. 62-3.

The uncertainty of the neural efficiency interpretation: Brody (1992), Chapter 3.

"at best, plausible": Brody (1992), p. 79.

Your Destiny Written in Your Genes (pp. 53–59)

The cartoon by Charles Addams appeared in *The New Yorker*, May 4, 1981, p. 43.

Findings on genetics and IQ are reviewed in Brody (1992) and Jensen (1980).

Sandra Scarr's argument that opportunity breeds predestination: Scarr (1989).

The limited results from efforts to increase IQ through instruction: Brody (1992), Chapter 9; Herrnstein & Murray (1994), chapter 17; Jensen (1983).

"Taken together . . .": Herrnstein & Murray (1994), p. 399.

Is IQ Fair? (pp. 59–64)

Findings on black versus white IQs are reviewed in Brody (1992), p. 300.

Culture and ethnic bias in tests: Brody (1992), Chapter 10; Jensen (1980), Chapter 9.

Study of impact of eliminating biased items: Gordon (1987).

John Hayes' discussion of ethnic influence on thinking: Hayes (1981), Chapter 11.

Family factors that influence IQ: Hayes (1981), p. 199.

Academic achievement in Jews and non-Jews: Hayes (1981), p. 229; figures from studies by Ladd and Lipset (1975) and Sherman (1965).

"is considered a disgrace . . .": Hayes (1981), p. 230.

Asians' academic success: Hayes (1981), p. 229, referencing Kitano (1976).

General correlation between academic performance and IQ: Brody (1992), p. 252.

Correlation between workplace performance and IQ: Brody (1992), p. 274.

The average IQ of criminals: Herrnstein & Murray (1994), p. 239.

The IQ of the chronically unemployed: Herrnstein & Murray (1994), p. 155.

Brody's warning about the practical import of workplace-IQ correlations: Brody (1992), p. 274.

"The reasons for . . .": Brody (1992), p. 309.

On the IQs of Italian-American children: Ceci (1990), pp. 80-2; Sarason & Doris (1979).

Intelligence as Essence (pp. 64–67)

Stephen Jay Gould's discussion of reification: Gould (1981), Chapter 6.

Chapter 4: The Great IQ Roast

Multiple Intelligences (pp. 70–76)

Thomson's view is discussed in Brody (1992), pp. 10-13 and Jensen (1980), pp. 237-37. An original source is Thomson (1916).

Fluid and crystallized intelligence: Horn (1989a, b); Horn & Cattell (1966). Overview in Brody (1992), pp. 18-26.

WERCOF factors: Horn (1989a).

The complexities of factor analysis around *g*: Horn (1989a); Brody (1992), pp. 13-17, 29-34.

Effects of age on fluid versus crystallized intelligence: Horn (1989a).

Guilford's Structure of Intellect theory: Guilford (1967); Guilford & Hoepfner (1971).

Criticisms of the factor analysis behind Guilford's Structure of Intellect model: e.g., Brody (1992), pp. 29-34; Sternberg (1977).

The Theory of Multiple Intelligences: Gardner (1983).

Criticism of Gardner's Theory of Multiple Intelligences: e.g., Brody (1992), pp. 36-40.

A hierarchical view of intelligence with *g* at the top: Brody (1992), pp. 26, 40; Gustaffson (1988).

Changeable Intelligence (pp. 76–79)

The changeability of IQ over time: Humphreys (1989).

Influences on IQ of vitamin and mineral supplements: Brody (1992), p. 212.

Studies of the impact of family environment: Herrnstein & Murray (1994), p. 422.

Changes of IQ with education between World Wars I and II: Humphreys (1989).

Influence of education on the IQs of Italian-Americans: Sarason & Doris (1979).

Brody's discussion of the influence of education on IQ: Brody (1992), pp. 186-196.

Nearly same-age students with a year more of schooling: Cahan & Cohen (1989).

Intelligence as Expertise (pp. 79–84)

The work of de Groot on chess: de Groot (1965). See also Chase & Simon (1973).

Expertise in computer programming: e.g., Dalbey & Linn (1985); Ehrlich & Soloway (1984).

Expertise in physics problem solving: e.g., Chi, Feltovich, & Glaser (1981); Chi, Glaser, & Rees (1982); Larkin, McDermott, Simon, & Simon (1980a,b).

General review of findings on expertise: Bereiter & Scardamalia (1993); Ericsson & Charness (1994); Ericsson & Smith (1991).

The study of handicapping: Ceci & Liker (1986); Wagner & Sternberg (1986; 1994).

Research on job performance, experience, and IQ: Hunter (1986).

"Contrary to the common belief." Ericsson & Charness (1994), p. 725.

The concept of metacognition: e.g., Flavell (1979, 1981).

Strategies for memorizing: e.g., Baddeley (1982); Higbee (1977).

Problem solving strategies: e.g., Hayes (1981); Polya (1954, 1957).

Metacognition in the early years of life: Olson, Astington, & Harris (1988); Wellman (1990).

Polya's work on heuristics for mathematical problem solving: Polya (1954, 1957).

Schoenfeld's research on teaching mathematical problem solving: Schoenfeld (1979, 1980, 1982, 1985); Schoenfeld & Herrmann (1982).

Research on "reciprocal teaching" of reading skills: Palincsar & Brown (1984, 1988).

Synthesis of results on teaching reading strategies: Haller, Child, & Walberg (1988).

Rules for Reasoning: Nisbett (1993). The study outlined is discussed in Chapter 12.

"People can make . . .": Nisbett (1993), p. 11.

Baron's view of the performance of normal versus retarded children: Baron (1978).

Strategies for simple memory tasks in normal and retarded children: Belmont, Butterfield, & Ferretti (1982).

The importance of self-monitoring for transfer: Belmont, Butterfield, & Ferretti (1982).

Chapter 5: True Intelligence

The New Intelligence (pp. 102–109)

"The complexity of . . .": Salomon (1994).

Most of the points mentioned in this section recall evidence from the last chapter. Only sources not mentioned earlier are cited here.

Impact of teaching strategies on the relation between performance and IQ: Anderson (1992), p. 146.

Influences on IQ of alcohol and lead consumption: Brody (1992), pp. 208-9.

Relation between brain size and IQ: Brody (1992), p. 218.

IQ counts more early in learning something than later: Ericsson & Charness (1994); Jensen (1980), p. 231.

Research showing that greater knowledge does not always yield better reasoning: Kuhn (1991), pp. 240, 262-3.

Pittsburgh studies of reasoning: Means & Voss (in press).

Failure to learn from mere practice and the importance of restructuring: Ericsson & Charness (1994).

How the Three Dimensions Work Together (pp. 109–113)

The role of neurologically based talents in achievement: Gardner (1983).

Focused and polyglot talents: Feldman (1986).

The importance of extensive deliberate practice over dramatic talent: Ericsson & Charness (1994).

The human brain is well-equipped for language and other general functions: a source that directly relates this to models of intelligence is Anderson (1992).

The importance of reflective intelligence in coping with novelty finds evidence in the phenomenon of mindlessness, Langer (1989).

On controlled versus automatic information processing: Schneider & Shiffrin (1977).

The Prospects of Learnable Intelligence (pp. 113–118)

Regarding the limits of conventional educational settings, see among many sources my *Smart Schools*: Perkins (1992).

For settings more conducive to the cultivation of thinking and thoughtful learning, again see Perkins (1992), as well as examples later in this book, especially chapters 8 and 13.

Chapter 6: What's Wrong with My Neighbors' Thinking?

The March of Folly (pp. 126–128)

The March of Folly: Tuchman (1984).

"Pursuit by governments . . .": Tuchman (1984), p. 4.

Conditions of "ideal" folly: Tuchman (1984), p. 5.

Tuchman's discussion of King George's handling of colonial policies: Tuchman (1984), chapter 4.

"Everything one has a right . . .": Benjamin Franklin, quoted in Tuchman (1984), p. 150.

John Wayne Reasoning (pp. 128–130)

Studies of people's respect for a firm position: Baron (1991).

Mindlessness (pp. 130–131).

Mindfulness: Langer (1989).

Experiment with the photocopy machine: Langer (1989), pp. 14–15.

The credit card incident: Langer, 1989, pp. 12-13.

A Study of Everyday Thinking (pp. 131–136)

My research on everyday reasoning: Perkins (1985, 1989); Perkins, Allen, & Hafner (1983); Perkins, Farady, & Bushey (1991).

A Sampler of Other Evidence (136–143)

At Dawn We Slept: Prange (1981).

Thinking in Time: Neustadt & May (1986).

Eyewitness Testimony: Loftus (1979).

The case of Charles Clarck: Loftus (1979), p. 178.

The thinking of judges: Lawrence (1991).

"Maria, an unemployed . . .": Lawrence (1991), p. 73.

Students' problems with reading and writing thoughtfully: for instance, Bereiter

& Scardamalia (1985); Bryson, Bereiter, Scardamalia, & Joram (1991); National Assessment of Educational Progress (1981); Stanovich & Cunningham (1991).

Students' difficulties with story problems: see for instance Schoenfeld (1985); Nesher (1988); Bebout (1990).

Students' confusions about Newtonian concepts: Clement (1982, 1983); McCloskey (1983); Novak (1987); Perkins & Simmons (1988).

People's reactions to mixed evidence: Lord, Ross, & Lepper (1979).

The skills of argument: Kuhn (1991).

" . . . never having considered . . .": Kuhn (1991), p. 267.

Quotes from subjects about school failure: Kuhn (1991), p. 174.

"I wouldn't really . . .": Kuhn (1991), p. 82.

"I would not try . . .": Kuhn (1991), p. 82.

" . . . I could give . . .": Kuhn (1991), p. 80.

Study of decision making: Baron, Granato, Spranca, & Teubal (1993).

"The coach of a . . .": Baron et al. (1993), p. 27.

"You saw . . .": Baron et al. (1993), pp. 31-32.

"Jennifer says . . .": Baron et al. (1993), p. 29.

"The principal . . .": Baron et al. (1993), p. 37.

Chapter 7: The Intelligence Paradox

"Homer himself . . .": Partington (1992), p. 347.

Examples of Homer's nods: Camps (1980), p. 16.

"If we're so dumb. . .": Nisbett & Ross (1980), p. 249.

Is the Paradox Real? (pp. 150–152)

Stich's rebuttals of the notion that people do not reason so badly: Stich (1990).

Stich's rebuttal of the argument from evolution: Stich (1990), Chapter 3.

The issue of impossible ideals: Stich (1990), p. 152.

" . . . it seems simply perverse . . .": Stich (1990), p. 27.

Whether supposedly good thinking is adaptive: Stich (1990), Chapter 6.

Baron's argument for a goal-oriented conception of good thinking: Baron (1985).

Intelligence Traps (pp. 152–154)

Difficulties in syllogistic reasoning: see for instance Falmagne (1975); Johnson-Laird (1983); Markovits (1993); Nisbett (1993).

Confirmation or my-side bias: See for instance Baron (1985); Johnson-Laird (1983); Nisbett & Ross (1980).

Impulsivity: Thurstone (1924).

Cognitive dissonance: Festinger (1957); Festinger & Carlsmith (1959).

Functional fixedness: see for instance Adamson (1952); Dunker (1945).

The four defaults: These were developed through discussion with colleagues Robert Swartz, Beatriz Capdevielle, Shari Tishman, Heidi Goodrich, and others. Bob and I have described them before in Perkins & Swartz (1992).

The Pattern Machine (pp. 154–158)

One eloquent source on the pattern-driven nature of cognition is Margolis (1987).

The pattern-driven character of chess play: de Groot (1965); Chase & Simon (1973).

The pattern-driven character of physics problem solving: Larkin (1982, 1985); Larkin, McDermott, Simon, & Simon (1980a,b).

The notion of knowledge compilation and production systems: see for instance Anderson (1983); Newell (1990).

Intuition as reflecting pattern-driven cognition: see for instance Margolis (1987), Simon (1981).

On connectionism: see for instance McClelland & Rumelhardt (1986).

Newell's argument about the adaptiveness of knowledge compilation: Newell (1990).

Why Homer Thrives (pp. 158–159)

Oral epic: Lord (1974).

The availability and representitiveness heuristics: e.g., Kahneman & Tversky (1972); Tversky & Kahneman (1973, 1974).

Human Inference: Nisbett & Ross (1980). The quote is from page 19.

The Massachusetts Mutual Life Insurance Company survey: Associated Press article in the Boston Globe, Monday, November 21, 1994.

More Causes of Defaults in Thinking (pp. 165–172)

Cognitive emotions: Scheffler (1991).

Descartes' Error: Damasio (1994).

"I began to think . . .": Damasio (1994), p. 51.

The cognitive load bottleneck: Miller (1956).

Good strategies for memorizing: For instance, Baddeley (1982), Higbee (1977).

The reliability of intuitive thinking: see Perkins (1981), Chapter 4.

The coin flipping game and expectation values: Hayes (1981), pp. 162-66.

The Oakland Raiders example: Hayes (1981), p. 172.

The percentage of boy babies problem: Kahneman & Tversky (1972).

"A paradox of the worldly brain . . .": Campbell (1989), p. 35.

"Humans did not . . .": Nisbett & Ross (1980), p. 250.

Chapter 8: Intelligence Can Be Taught

Intelligence Can Be Taught: Whimbey (1975).

Problem Solving and Comprehension: Whimbey & Lochhead (1982).

Reviews of school-based programs to teach thinking: See for example Baron

& Sternberg (1986); Nickerson, Perkins, & Smith (1985); Segal, Chipman, & Glaser (1985).

The Fifth Discipline: Senge (1990).

Six Thinking Hats: de Bono (1986).

Project Intelligence (pp. 179–185)

Sources on Project Intelligence include: Adams (1986, 1989); Bolt, Beranek, and Newman (1983); Herrnstein, Nickerson, Sanchez, & Swets (1986); Nickerson, Perkins, & Smith (1985), pp. 181-87.

The pencil example and approach to creative thinking through design: Perkins & Laserna (1986).

The Bebenians and Tisars example: Adams, Buscaglia, de Sanchez, & Swets (1986).

Evaluation of Project Intelligence: Bolt, Beranek, & Newman (1983); Herrnstein, Nickerson, Sanchez, & Swets (1986).

Reuven Feuerstein's Instrumental Enrichment (pp. 185–191)

Sources on Instrumental Enrichment: Feuerstein (1980); Nickerson, Perkins, & Smith (1985), pp. 148-49; Segal, Chipman, & Glaser (1985), Chapter 1.

The impact of Instrumental Enrichment on less able students: Arbitman-Smith, Haywood & Bransford (1984); Rand, Tannenbaum, & Feuerstein (1979); Feuerstein, Miller, Hoffman, Rand, Mintzker, & Jensen (1981); see the summary in Nickerson, Perkins, & Smith (1985), pp. 155-161.

Impact of Instrumental Enrichment with ordinary students: Blagg (1991).

Edward de Bono's CoRT (pp. 191–195)

Sources on CoRT: de Bono (1973-5, 1983, 1987); Nickerson, Perkins, & Smith (1985), pp. 215-20.

De Bono's evidence of CoRT's efficacy: de Bono (1976), pp. 217-229.

Findings on CoRT from Venezuela: de Sanchez & Astorga (1983).

Studies of CoRT in Australia: Edwards (1991a,b); Edwards & Baldauf (1983, 1987).

Matthew Lipman's Philosophy for Children (pp. 195–200)

Sources on Philosophy for Children: Lipman (1974); Lipman, Sharp, & Oscanyan (1980); Nickerson, Perkins, & Smith (1985), pp. 280-90.

Harry Stottlemeier's Discovery: Lipman (1974).

"A sentence can't be reversed . . .": Lipman (1974), p. 2.

Lisa: Reasoning in Ethics: Lipman (1976).

Pixie: Lipman (1981).

Elsie: Lipman (1987).

General findings on the impact of Philosophy for Children: see the review in Nickerson, Perkins, & Smith (1985), pp. 280-90.

The evaluation by the Educational Testing Service: Summarized in Lipman, Sharp, & Oscanyan (1980), Appendix B. The list of 4 kinds of impact is from page 220.

Teaching Content and Thinking Together (pp. 200–207)

The importance of thinking to content learning: see for instance Perkins (1992).

The notion of infusion: see for instance Swartz & Perkins (1989); Perkins & Swartz (1992).

The Thinking Classroom: Tishman, Perkins, & Jay (1995); the Robert Frost example: Chapter 11.

The Darwin example: Tishman, Perkins, & Jay (1995), Chapter 5.

Knowledge as design: Perkins (1986, 1994a).

Thinking Connections: Learning to think and thinking to learn: Perkins, Goodrich, Tishman & Owen (1993).

The Truman example: Swartz & Parks (in press). For similar examples at the elementary level see Swartz & Parks (1994).

"I guess I could call myself smart:" Barell (1991), p. 3.

Teaching for Thoughtfulness: Barell (1991).

PIFS: Blythe, Gardner, Grimes, Li, Lubart, Sternberg, White, & Williams (1994); Williams, Blythe, White, Li, Sternberg, & Gardner (in press).

The Intelligent Eye: Perkins (1994b).

Ennis's arguments about stand-alone instruction in thinking versus infusion: Ennis (1989). Also see Swartz & Perkins (1989).

Should We Be Satisfied? (pp. 207–210)

The challenge of educational change: see for instance Brown (1991); Fullan (1991); Perkins (1992), Chapter 9; Sarason (1982).

Chapter 9: The Great Debate

This chapter is a revision of an article co-authored by Gavriel Salomon and me (Perkins & Salomon, 1989), published in *Educational Researcher*, Copyright 1989 by the American Educational Research Association, adapted by permission of the publisher.

Before the Fall: The Golden Age of General Strategies (pp. 213–216)

Heuristics for mathematical problem solving: Polya (1954, 1957).

AI and modeling human thinking: Newell & Simon (1972).

The General Problem Solver: Ernst & Newell (1969).

The Argument from Expertise (pp. 216–220)

The repertoire of patterns involved in chess expertise: Chase & Simon (1973).

The time needed to acquire expertise in chess: Chase & Simon (1973).

Time required for Mozart to attain expertise: Hayes (1981), pp. 209-212.

Physics experts solving unfamiliar problems: Clement (1991).

General strategies and knowledge do not substitute for one another: Glaser (1992).

Intelligent novices: Bruer (1993), p. 70.

Expert-like novices, and expert learners in contrast with non-expert learners: Bereiter & Scardamalia (1993), pp. 19, 169-70.

The Argument from Weak Methods (pp. 220–223)

Expert systems: Rich (1983); Wenger (1987).

The power-generality tradeoff and weak methods: Rich (1983); Wenger (1987).

Difficulties teaching Polya's heuristics: Schoenfeld (1985), pp. 71-74.

ACT*: Anderson (1983).

SOAR: Newell (1990).

The Argument from Transfer (pp. 223–229)

Negative findings from early studies of transfer: Thorndike (1923); Thorndike & Woodworth (1901).

Failure to transfer between analogous problems: Simon & Hayes (1977).

Literacy without schooling does not improve general cognitive skills: Scribner & Cole (1981).

The negative trend in findings about transfer from computer programming: e.g., Pea & Kurland (1984a,b); Salomon & Perkins (1987).

Lack of transfer from teaching strategies: Pressley, Snyder, and Cariglia (1987).

Ann Brown's studies of transfer: Brown (1989).

Positive transfer from computer programming can occur: Clements & Gullo (1984).

The low road - high road model of transfer: Perkins & Salomon (1987, 1988); Salomon & Perkins (1989).

The CASE intervention: Adley & Shayer (1993).

Chapter 10: The Right Stuff

Beyond Mental Strength (pp. 237–239)

The importance of explicit strategies: Schoenfeld (1979, 1980).

Explicitness of strategies in reciprocal teaching: Brown & Palincsar (1989).

Beyond Mental Processes (pp. 239–248)

Knowing that and knowing how: Ryle (1949); Howard (1982); Scheffler (1965).

Knowing what it is to, knowing what it is like to: Howard (1992), pp 85–86.

The roots of everyday language in metaphor: Lakoff & Johnson (1980).

What children recognize as thinking challenges: Tishman (1991).

Reflections on Reasoning: Nickerson (1986).

Forks, Phonographs, and Hot-Air Balloons: Weber (1992).

Beyond Expertise (pp. 248–265)

On the tips of the tongue phenomenon, the method of loci, and related memory phenomena, see for instance, Baddeley (1982); Higbee (1977).

Olson and Astington have developed the idea that thinking depends on the development of a language and concepts around thinking: Olson & Astington (1990, 1993); Astington & Olson (1990).

The notion of critical skills: Scheffler (1965).

Surpassing Ourselves: Bereiter & Scardamalia (1993).

Chapter 11: Mapping the Mindscape

The Soul of Intelligence (pp. 274–282)

Sources on dispositions: Baron (1985); Ennis (1986, 1994); Paul (1986, 1990); Perkins, Jay, & Tishman (1993).

Entity versus incremental learners: Chiu, Hong, & Dweck (1994); Dweck & Bempechat (1980); Dweck & Licht (1980).

Factor-analytic determination of a set of key dispositions: Facione & Facione (1992); Sanchez, Reise, Facione, & Facione (1994); Facione, Sanchez, Facione, Gainen (in press).

Evidence for the importance of dispositions and a taxonomy: Perkins, Jay, & Tishman (1993).

Styles and beliefs underlying investment in thinking: Pressley, Goodchild, Fleet, & Zajchowski (1989).

The Mind's Ladder (pp. 282–296)

On awareness of emotions as part of metacognition, see the discussion of emotional intelligence by Salovey & Mayer (1994).

Negotiating from interest: Fisher & Ury (1981).

On emotional intelligence: Salovey & Mayer (1994).

Chapter 12: How the Map Matters

The Reaction Against g: Psychometric Boundaries (pp. 298–301)

The Structure of Intellect theory: Guilford (1967); Guilford & Hoepfner (1971).

Gardner's Multiple Intelligences: Neural and Social Boundaries (pp. 301–302)

The Theory of Multiple Intelligences: Gardner (1983, 1993).

Mike Anderson's Model: Boundaries Between Information-Processing Mechanisms (pp. 302–306)

Anderson's model: Anderson (1992).

"views the brain . . .": Anderson (1992), p. 61.

Retarded and normal children of the same mental age: Anderson (1992), pp. 132-33.

Feuerstein's Model: Boundaries Between Phases (pp. 307–308)

Instrumental Enrichment and the theory behind it: Feuerstein (1980).

Baron's Search-Inference Framework: Boundaries from the Logic of Search (pp. 308–310)

The search-inference framework: Baron (1985).

"Thinking is . . .": Baron (1985), p. 6.

Sternberg's Triarchic Theory of Intelligence: Boundaries from Context and Subtask (pp. 310–317)

The Triarchic Theory: Sternberg (1985a).

Chapter 13: Mindware and the Millennium

Lenin's brain, "In the anatomical . . .": Article in the Boston Globe, Wednesday, January 19, 1994, p. 2.

The Evolution of Intelligence (pp. 319–321)

Evolutionary epistemology: Riedl (1984).

"Among its . . .": Riedl (1984), p. 3.

Distributed Intelligence (pp. 321–324)

On distributed intelligence: Salomon (1993). Pea's analysis: Pea (1993). My analysis: Perkins (1993).

Embracing Complexity (pp. 324–328)

The magic number seven: Miller (1956).

Complex systems: Gell-Mann (1994); Kauffman (1993); Waldrop (1992).

The Information Visualizer: Clarkson (1991).

Dialectical Thinking (pp. 328–332)

Negotiation: Fisher & Ury (1981).

Systems thinking as an aspect of intelligence and human development: e.g., Basseches (1984); Commons, Richards, & Armon (1984); Dorner & Scholkopf (1991); Mines & Kitchener (1986).

Problem finding: Arlin (1975, 1986); Jay & Perkins (in press).

The Fifth Discipline: Senge (1990). In a related spirit, see Stacey (1992).

The Quark and the Jaguar: Gell-Mann (1994). On creativity, see Chapter 17.

Thinking skills for systems thinking: Richmand (1993). See also Draper (1993).

The Metacurriculum (pp. 332–341)

The Amelia Earhart example was developed by my colleague Shari Tishman and added to by my colleague Heidi Goodrich. This version has further adjustments. Another version can be found in Tishman, Perkins, and Jay (1995).

The concept of the metacurriculum: Perkins (1992), Chapter 5; Schwartz & Perkins (1995).

Several elements of the metacurriculum are elaborated in Tishman, Perkins, & Jay (1995).

References

Abadinsky, H. (1990). Voice of the people (letter): Mediocre'a man. *Chicago Tribune*, Wednesday, July 4, p. 12.

Adams, M. J. (Ed.). (1986). *Odyssey: A curriculum for thinking*. Watertown, Massachusetts: Mastery Education.

Adams, M. J. (1989). Thinking skills curricula: Their promise and progress. *Educational Psychologist, 24*(1), 25–77.

Adams, J., Buscaglia, J., de Sanchez, M., & Swets, J. (1986). *Foundations of reasoning* (lesson sequence from *Odyssey: A curriculum for thinking*). Watertown, Massachusetts: Mastery Education.

Adamson, R. E. (1952). Functional fixedness as related to problem solving. *Journal of Experimental Psychology, 44*, 288-291.

Adley, P., & Shayer M. (1993). An exploration of long-term far-transfer effects following an extended intervention program in the high school science curriculum. *Cognition and Instruction II*(1), 1–29.

Anderson, J. R. (1983). *The architecture of cognition*. Cambridge, Massachusetts: Harvard University Press.

Anderson, M. (1992). *Intelligence and development: A cognitive theory*. Cambridge, Massachusetts: Blackwell.

Arbitman-Smith, R., Haywood, H. C., & Bransford, J. D. (1984). Assessing cognitive change. In P. H. Brooks, R. Sperber, & C. McCauley (Eds.), *Learning and cognition in the mentally retarded* (pp. 433–471). Hillsdale, New Jersey: Lawrence Erlbaum Associates.

Arlin, P. (1975). Cognitive development in adulthood: A fifth stage? *Developmental Psychology, 11*(5), 602-606.

Arlin, P. K. (1986). Problem finding and young adult cognition. In R. A. Mines & K. S. Kitchener (Eds.), *Adult cognitive development: Methods and models* (pp. 22–32). New York: Praeger.

Astington, J. W., & Olson, D. R. (1990). Metacognitive and metalinguistic language: Learning to talk about thought. *Applied Psychology: An International Review, 39* (1), 77-87.

Baddeley, A. (1982). *Your memory: A user's guide.* New York: Macmillan.

Barell, J. (1991). *Teaching for thoughtfulness: Classroom strategies to enhance intellectual development.* New York: Longman.

Baron, J. (1978). Intelligence and general strategies. In G. Underwood (Ed.), *Strategies in information processing* (pp. 403-450). London: Academic Press.

Baron, J. (1985). *Rationality and intelligence.* New York: Cambridge University Press.

Baron, J. (1991). Beliefs about thinking. In J. F. Voss, D. N. Perkins, & J. W. Segal (Eds.), *Informal reasoning and education* (pp. 169–186). Hillsdale, New Jersey: Erlbaum.

Baron, J. B., & Sternberg, R. S. (Eds.). (1986). *Teaching thinking skills: Theory and practice.* New York: W. H. Freeman.

Baron, J., Granato, L., Spranca, M., & Teubal, E. (1993). Decision-making biases in children and early adolescents: exploratory studies. *Merrill-Palmer Quarterly, 39*(1), 22-46.

Barry, D. (1990). Boby Yuck. *The Miami Herald,* Sunday, May 20, p. 7.

Basseches, M. (1984). *Dialectical thinking and adult development.* Norwood, New Jersey: Ablex.

Bebout, H. (1990). Children's symbolic representation of addition and subtraction word problems. *Journal for Research in Mathematics Education, 21* (2), 123-131.

Belmont, J. M., Butterfield, E. C., & Ferretti, R. P. (1982). To secure transfer of training instruct self-management skills. In D. K. Detterman & R. J. Sternberg

(Eds.), *How and how much can intelligence be increased?* (pp. 147-154). Norwood, New Jersey: Ablex.

Bereiter, C., & Scardamalia, M. (1985). Cognitive coping strategies and the problem of inert knowledge. In S. S. Chipman, J. W. Segal, & R. Glaser (Eds.), *Thinking and learning skills, Vol. 2: Current research and open questions* (pp. 65-80). Hillsdale, New Jersey: Erlbaum.

Bereiter, C., & Scardamalia, M. (1993). *Surpassing ourselves: An inquiry into the nature and implications of expertise.* Chicago: Open Court.

Bikson, T. K., and Law S. A. (1994). *Global preparedness and human resources: College and corporate perspectives.* Santa Monica, California: Rand Corporation.

Blagg, N. (1991). *Can we teach intelligence? A comprehensive evaluation of Feuerstein's Instrumental Enrichment program.* Hillsdale, New Jersey: Erlbaum

Blythe, T., Gardner, H., Grimes, M., Li, J., Lubart, T., Sternberg, R., White, N., & Williams, W. (1994). *Practical intelligence for school report (unpublished report).* Cambridge, Massachusetts: Harvard Project Zero.

Bolt, Beranek, and Newman. (1983). *Final report, Project Intelligence: The development of procedures to enhance thinking skills.* Cambridge, Massachusetts: Author.

Boring, E. G. (1923). Intelligence as the tests test it. *New Republic, 35,* 35-37.

Brody, N. (1992). *Intelligence.* New York: Academic Press.

Brown, A. L. (1989). Analogical learning and transfer: What develops? In S. Vosniadou & A. Ortony (Eds.), *Similarity and analogical reasoning* (pp. 369-412). New York: Cambridge University Press.

Brown, A. L., & Palincsar, A. S. (1989). Guided, cooperative learning and individual knowledge acquisition. In L. B. Resnick (Ed.), *Knowing, learning, and instruction: Essays in honor of Robert Glaser* (pp.393-451). Hillsdale, NJ: Erlbaum.

Brown, R. G. (1991). *Schools of thought: How the politics of literacy shape thinking in the classroom.* San Francisco: Jossey-Bass.

Bruer, J. T. (1993). *Schools for thought: A science of learning in the classroom.* Cambridge, Massachusetts: MIT Press.

Bryson, M., Bereiter, C., Scardamalia, M., & Joram, E. (1991). Going beyond the problem as given: Problem solving in expert and novice writers. In R. J. Sternberg & P. A. Frensch (Eds.), *Complex problem solving: Principles and mechanisms* (pp. 61-84). Hillsdale, New Jersey: Erlbaum.

Cahan, S., & Cohen, N. (1989). Age versus schooling effects on intelligence development. *Child Development, 60,* 1239-1249.

Campbell, J. (1989). *The improbable machine: What new discoveries in artificial intelligence reveal about the mind.* New York: Simon & Schuster.

Camps, W. A. (1980). *An introduction to Homer.* Oxford: Oxford University Press.

Carlson, J. S., & Jensen, C. M. (1982). Reaction time, movement time, and intelligence: A replication and extension. *Intelligence, 6,* 265-274.

Ceci, S. J. (1990). *On intelligence . . . more or less: A bio-ecological treatise on intellectual development.* Englewood Cliffs, New Jersey: Prentice Hall.

Ceci, S. J., & Liker, J. (1986). A day at the races: A study of IQ, expertise, and cognitive complexity. *Journal of Developmental Psychology: General, 115,* 255-266.

Chase, W. C., & Simon, H. A. (1973). Perception in chess. *Cognitive Psychology, 4,* 55-81.

Chi, M. T. H., Feltovich, P., & Glaser, R. (1981). Categorization and representation of physics problems by experts and novices. *Cognitive Science, 5,* 121-152.

Chi, M. T. H., Glaser, R., & Rees, E. (1982). Expertise in problem solving. In R. J. Sternberg (Ed.), *Advances in the psychology of human intelligence* (pp. 7-75). Hillsdale, New Jersey: Erlbaum.

Chiu, C., Hong, Y., & Dweck, C. S. (1994). Toward an integrative model of personality and intelligence: A general framework and some preliminary steps. In R. J. Sternberg & P. Ruzgis (Eds.), *Personality and intelligence* (pp. 104-134). New York: Cambridge University Press.

Clarkson, M. A. (1991). An easier interface. *Byte, 16*(2), 277-282.

Clement, J. (1982). Students' preconceptions in introductory mechanics. *American Journal of Physics, 50,* 66-71.

Clement, J. (1983). A conceptual model discussed by Galileo and used intuitively by physics students. In D. Gentner & A. L. Stevens (Eds.), *Mental models.* Hillsdale, New Jersey: Erlbaum.

Clement, J. (1991). Nonformal reasoning in experts and in science students: The use of analogies, extreme case and physical intuition. In J. Voss, D. N. Perkins, & J. Segal (Eds.), *Informal Reasoning and Education,* 345-362. Hillsdale, New Jersey: Erlbaum.

Clements, D. H., & Gullo, D. F. (1984). Effects of computer programming on young children's cognition. *Journal of Educational Psychology, 76*(6), 1051-1058.

Collins, A., & Ferguson, W. (1993). Epistemic forms and epistemic games: Structures and strategies to guide inquiry. *Educational Psychologist, 28* (1), 25–42.

Commons, M. L., Richards, F. A., & Armon, C. (Eds.) (1984). *Beyond formal operations: Late adolescent and adult cognitive development.* New York: Praeger.

Dalbey, J., & Linn, M. C. (1985). The demands and requirements of computer programming: A literature review. *Journal of Educational Computing Research, 1,* 253-274.

Damasio, A. R. (1994). *Descartes' Error: Emotion, reason, and the human brain.* New York: G. P. Putnam's Sons.

de Bono, E. (1973-75). *CoRT thinking.* Blandford, Dorset, England: Direct Education Services Limited.

de Bono, E. (1976). *Teaching thinking.* London: Temple Smith.

de Bono, E. (1983). The cognitive research trust (CoRT) thinking program. In W. Maxwell (Ed.), *Thinking: The expanding frontier* (pp. 115-127). Hillsdale, New Jersey: Erlbaum.

de Bono, E. (1986). *Six Thinking Hats.* New York: Viking.

de Bono, E. (1987). *CoRT thinking program. Workcards and teacher's notes.* Chicago: Science Research Associates.

de Groot, A. D. (1965). *Thought and choice in chess.* The Hague: Mouton.

de Sanchez, M. A., & Astorga, M. *Proyecto aprender a pensar: Estudio de sus efectos sobre una muestra de estudiantes venezolanos.* Caracas, Venezuela: Ministerio de Educacion, 1983.

Dorner, D., & Scholkopf, J. (1991). Controlling complex systems; or, expertise as "grandmother's know-how". In K. A. Ericsson & J. Smith (Eds.), *Toward a general theory of expertise: Prospects and limits* (pp. 218–239). New York: Cambridge University Press.

Draper, F. (1993). A proposed sequence for developing systems thinking in a grades 4-12 curriculum. *Systems Dynamics Review, 9*(2), 207-214.

Dunker, K. (1945). On problem solving. *Psychological Monographs, 58* (Whole No. 270).

Dweck, C. S., & Bempechat, J. (1980). Children's theories of intelligence: Consequences for learning. In S. G. Paris, G. M. Olson, & H. W. Stevenson

(Eds.), *Learning and motivation in the classroom* (pp. 239-256). Hillsdale, New Jersey: Erlbaum.

Dweck, C. S., & Licht, B. G. (1980). Learned helplessness and intellectual achievement. In J. Garbar & M. Seligman (Eds.), *Human helplessness*. New York: Academic Press.

Edwards, J. (1991a). The direct teaching of thinking skills. In G. Evans (Ed.), *Learning and teaching cognitive skills* (pp. 87-106). Melbourne: Australian Council for Educational Research.

Edwards, J. (1991b). Research work on the CoRT method. In S. Maclure & P. Davies (Eds.), *Learning to think: Thinking to learn* (pp. 19-30). Oxford: Pergamon Press.

Edwards, J., & Baldauf, R. B., Jr. (1983). Teaching thinking in secondary science. In W. Maxwell (Ed.), *Thinking: The expanding frontier.* Philadelphia: Franklin Institute Press, 129–138.

Edwards, J., & Baldauf, R. B., Jr. (1987). The effects of the CoRT-1 thinking skills program on students. In D. N. Perkins, I. Lochhead, & J. C. Bishop (Eds.), *Thinking: The second international conference* (pp. 453–474). Hillsdale, New Jersey: Erlbaum.

Ehrlich, K., & Soloway, E. (1984). An empirical investigation of the tacit plan knowledge in programming. In J. Thomas & M. L. Schneider (Eds.), *Human Factors in Computer Systems*. Norwood, New Jersey: Ablex.

Ennis, R. H. (1986). A taxonomy of critical thinking dispositions and abilities. In J. B. Baron & R. S. Sternberg (Eds.). *Teaching thinking skills: Theory and practice* (pp. 9-26). New York: W. H. Freeman.

Ennis, R. H. (1989). Critical thinking and subject specificity: clarification and needed research. *Educational Researcher* 18(3), 4–10.

Ennis, R. H. (1994). *Assessing critical thinking dispositions: Theoretical considerations*. Paper presented at the annual meeting of the American Educational Research Association, New Orleans, April 7, 1994.

Ericsson, K. A. & Charness, N. (1994). Expert performance: Its structure and acquisition. *American Psychologist* 49(8), 725–747.

Ericsson, K. A., & Smith, J. (Eds.) (1991). *Toward a general theory of expertise: Prospects and limits*. Cambridge: Cambridge University Press.

Ernst, G. W., & Newell, A. (1969). *GPS: A case study in generality and problem solving*. New York: Academic Press.

Facione, P. A., & Facione, N. C., (1992). *The California critical thinking dispositions inventory*. Millbrae, California: The California Academic Press.

Facione, P. A., Sanchez, C. A., Facione, N. C., & Gainen, J. (in press). The disposition toward critical thinking. *Journal of General Education*.

Falmagne, R. J. (Ed.). (1975). *Reasoning: Representation and process in children and adults*. Hillsdale, New Jersey: Erlbaum.

Feldman, D. H. (1986). *Nature's gambit: Child prodigies and the development of human potential*. New York: Basic Books.

Festinger, L., & Carlsmith, J. M. (1959). Cognitive consequences of forced compliance. *Journal of Abnormal and Social Psychology, 58*, 203-210.

Festinger. L. (1957). *A Theory of cognitive dissonance*. Stanford, California: Stanford University Press.

Feuerstein, R. (1980). *Instrumental enrichment: An intervention program for cognitive modifiability*. Baltimore: University Park Press.

Feuerstein, R., Miller, R., Hoffman, M. B., Rand, Y., Mintzker, Y., & Jensen, M. R. (1981). Cognitive modifiability in adolescence: Cognitive structure and the effects of intervention. *The Journal of Special Education, 15*, 269-286.

Fisher, R., & Ury, W. (1981). *Getting to yes: Negotiating agreement without giving in*. New York: Penguin Books.

Flavell, J. H. (1979). Metacognitions and cognitive monitoring: A new area of child developmental inquiry. *Applied Psychology, 34*, 906-911.

Flavell, J. H. (1981). Cognitive monitoring. In W. P. Dickson (Ed.), *Children's oral communication skills* (pp. 35-60). New York: Academic Press.

Fullan, M. G. (1991). *The new meaning of educational change*. New York: Teachers College Press.

Gardner, H. (1983). *Frames of mind*. New York: Basic Books.

Gardner, H. (1993). *Multiple intelligences: The theory in practice*. New York: Basic Books.

Gell-Mann, M. (1994). *The quark and the jaguar: Adventures in the simple and the complex*. New York: W. H. Freeman.

Glaser, R. (1992). Expert knowledge and processes of thinking. In D. F. Halpern (Ed.), *Enhancing thinking skills in the sciences and mathematics* (pp. 63-75). Hillsdale, New Jersey: Erlbaum.

Gordon, R. A. (1987). Gordon replies to Shepard. In S. Modgil & C. Modgil (Eds.), *Arthur Jensen: Consensus and controversy* (pp. 204–206). New York: Falmer.

Gould, S. J. (1981). *The mismeasure of man.* New York: W. W. Norton.

Guilford, J. P. (1967). *The nature of human intelligence.* New York: McGraw-Hill.

Guilford, J. P., & Hoepfner, R. (1971). *The analysis of intelligence.* New York: McGraw-Hill.

Gustafsson, J. E. (1988). Hierarchical models of individual differences. In R. J. Sternberg (Ed.), *Advances in the psychology of human intelligence* (Vol. 4). Hillsdale, New Jersey: Erlbaum.

Haller, E. P., Child, D. A., & Walberg, H. J. (1988). Can comprehension be taught? A quantitative synthesis of "metacognitive" studies. *Educational Researcher, 17*(5), 5-8.

Hayes, J. R. (1981). *The complete problem solver.* Hillsdale, New Jersey: Erlbaum.

Herrnstein, R. J., & Murray, C. (1994). *The bell curve: Intelligence and class structure in American life.* New York: The Free Press.

Herrnstein, R. J., Nickerson, R. S., Sanchez, M., & Swets, J. A. (1986). Teaching thinking skills. *American Psychologist, 41,* 1279-1289.

Higbee, K, L. (1977). *Your memory: How it works and how to improve it.* Englewood Cliffs, New Jersey: Prentice-Hall.

Horn, J. (1989a). Models of intelligence. In R. Linn (Ed.), *Intelligence: Measurement, theory, and public policy* (pp. 29-73). Chicago: University of Illinois Press.

Horn, J. (1989b). Cognitive diversity: A framework of learning. In P. L. Ackerman, R. J. Sternberg, & R. Glaser (Eds.), *Learning and individual differences: Advances in theory and research* (pp. 61–116). New York: W. H. Freeman.

Horn, J. , & Cattell, R. B. (1966). Refinement and test of the theory of fluid and crystallized intelligence. *Journal of Educational Psychology, 57,* 253-270.

Howard, V. A. (1982). *Artistry: The work of artists.* Indianapolis: Hackett Publishing Company.

Humphreys, L. G. (1989). Intelligence: Three kinds of instability and their consequences for policy. In R. L. Linn (Ed.), *Intelligence: Measurement, theory, and public policy* (pp. 193-216). Chicago: University of Illinois Press.

Hunter, J. E. (1986). Cognitive ability, cognitive aptitudes, job knowledge, and job performance. *Journal of Vocational Behavior, 29,* 340-362.

Jay, E. S., & Perkins, D. N. (in press). Creativity's compass: A review of problem finding. In M. Runco (Ed.), *The creativity research handbook*, Vol. 1. Cresskill, NJ: Hampton Press.

Jensen, A. R. (1980). *Bias in mental testing*. New York: The Free Press.

Jensen, A. R. (1983). The nonmanipulable and effectively manipulable variables of education. *Education and Society, 1*(1), 51-62.

Jensen, A. R. (1988). Psychometric g and mental processing speed on a semantic verification test. *Journal of Personality and Individual Differences, 9*(2), 243-255.

Johnson-Laird, P. N. (1983). *Mental models*. Cambridge, Massachusetts: Harvard University Press.

Kahneman, D., & Tversky, A. (1972). Subjective probability: A judgment of representativeness. *Cognitive Psychology, 3*, 430-454.

Kauffman, S. A. (1993). *The origins of order: Self-organization and selection in evolution*. New York: Oxford University Press.

Kitano, H. H. (1976). *Japanese Americans* (2nd ed.). Englewood Cliffs, New Jersey: Prentice-Hall.

Kuhn, D. (1991). *The skills of argument*. New York: Cambridge University Press.

Ladd, E. C., Jr., & Lipset, S. M. (1975). *The divided academy*. New York: McGraw-Hill.

Lakoff, G., & Johnson, M. (1980). *Metaphors we live by*. Chicago: University of Chicago Press.

Langer, E. J. (1989). *Mindfulness*. Menlo Park, CA: Addison-Wesley.

Larkin, J. H. (1982). The cognition of learning physics. *American Journal of Physics, 49*, 534-541.

Larkin, J. H. (1985). Understanding, Problem Representations, and Skill in Physics. In S. F. Chipman, J. W. Segal, & R. Glaser, (Eds.), *Thinking and learning skills: Vol. 2. Research and open questions* (pp. 141-159). Hillsdale, New Jersey: Erlbaum.

Larkin, J. H., McDermott, J., Simon, D. P., & Simon, H. A. (1980a). Expert and novice performance in solving physics problems. *Science, 208*, 1335-1342.

Larkin, J. H., McDermott, J., Simon, D. P., & Simon, H. A. (1980b). Modes of competence in solving physics problems. *Cognitive Science, 4*, 317-345.

Lawrence, J. A. (1991). Informal reasoning in the judicial system. In J. F. Voss, D. N. Perkins, & J. W. Segal (Eds.), *Informal Reasoning and Education* (pp. 59–82). Hillsdale, New Jersey: Erlbaum.

Lipman, M. (1974). *Harry Stottlemeier's discovery.* Montclair, New Jersey: Institute for the Advancement of Philosophy for children, Montclair State College.

Lipman, M. (1976). *Lisa.* Montclair, New Jersey: Institute for the Advancement of Philosophy for Children, Montclair State College.

Lipman, M., Sharp, A. M., & Oscanyan, F. (1980). *Philosophy in the classroom.* Philadelphia: Temple University Press.

Lipman, M. (1981). *Pixie.* Montclair, New Jersey: First Mountain Foundation for the Institute for the Advancement of Philosophy for Children, Montclair State College.

Lipman, M. (1981). *Elsie.* Montclair, New Jersey: First Mountain Foundation for the Institute for the Advancement of Philosophy for Children, Montclair State College.

Loftus, E. F. (1979). *Eyewitness testimony.* Cambridge, Massachusetts: Harvard University Press.

Longstreth, L. (1984). Jensen's reaction-time investigations of intelligence: A critique. *Intelligence, 8,* 139-160.

Lord, A. B. (1974). *The singer of tales.* New York: Atheneum.

Lord, C. G., Ross, L., & Lepper, M. (1979). Biased assimilation and attitude polarization: The effects of prior theories on subsequently considered evidence. *Journal of Personality and Social Psychology, 37*(11), 2098-2109.

Machado, L. A. (1975). *La revolucion de la inteligencia.* Barcelona: Seix Barral.

Margolis, H. (1987). *Patterns, thinking, and cognition: A theory of judgment.* Chicago: The University of Chicago Press.

Markovits, H. (1993). The development of conditional reasoning: A Piagetian reformulation of mental models theory. *Merrill-Palmer Quarterly, 39*(1), 131-158.

Marshall, R., & Tucker, M., (1992). *Thinking for a living: Education and the wealth of nations.* New York: Basic Books.

McClelland, J. L., & Rumelhardt, D. E. (Eds.). (1986). *Parallel distributed processing: Explorations in the micro-structure of cognition. Vols. I & II.* Cambridge, Massachusetts: MIT Press.

McCloskey, M. (1983). Naive theories of motion. In D. Gentner & A. L. Stevens (Eds.), *Mental models* (pp. 299-324). Hillsdale, New Jersey: Erlbaum.

Means, M. L., & Voss, J. F. (in press). Who reasons well? Two studies of informal reasoning among children of different grade, ability, and knowledge levels. *Cognition and Instruction,* .

Miller, G. A. (1956). The magical number seven, plus or minus two: Some limits on our capacity for processing information. *Psychological Review, 63,* 81-87.

Mines, R. A., Kitchener, K. S. (Eds.). (1986). *Adult cognitive development: Methods and models.* New York: Praeger.

National Assessment of Educational Progress (1981). *Reading, thinking, and writing.* Princeton, New Jersey: Educational Testing Service.

Nesher, P. (1988). Multiplicative school word problems: Theoretical approaches and empirical findings. In M. Behr & J. Hiebert (Eds.), *Number concepts and operations in the middle grades, Volume 2* (pp. 19-40). Hillsdale, New Jersey: Erlbaum.

Neustadt, R. E., & May, E. R. (1986). *Thinking in time: The uses of history for decision-makers.* New York: Free Press.

Newell, A. (1990). *Theories of cognition.* Cambridge, Massachusetts: Harvard University Press.

Newell, A., & Simon, H. (1972). *Human problem solving.* Englewood Cliffs, New Jersey: Prentice-Hall.

Nickerson, R. S. (1986). *Reflections on reasoning.* Hillsdale, New Jersey: Erlbaum.

Nickerson, R. S., Perkins, D. N., & Smith, E. (1985). *The teaching of thinking.* Hillsdale, New Jersey: Erlbaum.

Nisbett, R., & Ross, L. (1980). *Human inference: Strategies and shortcomings of social judgment.* Englewood Cliffs, New Jersey: Prentice-Hall.

Nisbett, R. E. (Ed.) (1993). *Rules for reasoning.* Hillsdale, New Jersey: Erlbaum.

Nisbett, R. E., & Ross, L. (1980). *Human inference: Strategies and shortcomings of social judgment.* Englewood Cliffs, New Jersey: Prentice-Hall.

Novak, J. D. (Ed.) (1987). *The proceedings of the 2nd misconceptions in science and mathematics conference.* Ithaca, New York: Cornell University.

Ohlsson, S. (1993). Abstract schemas. *Educational Psychologist, 28* (1), 51–66.

Olson, D. R., & Astington, J. W. (1993). Thinking about thinking: Learning how to take statements and to hold beliefs. *Educational Psychologist, 28*(1), 7-23.

Olson, D. R., & Astington, J.W. (1990). Talking about text: How literacy contributes to thought. *Journal of Pragmatics, 14* (15), 557-573.

Olson, D. R., Astington, J. W., & Harris, P. L. (1988). *Introduction.* In J. W. Astington, P. L. Harris, & D. R. Olson (Eds.), *Developing theories of mind* (pp. 1-15).
Cambridge, Great Britain: Cambridge University Press.

Palincsar, A. S., & Brown, A. L. (1984). Reciprocal teaching of comprehen-
sion-fostering and comprehension-monitoring activities. *Cognition and Instruction, 1,* 117-175.

Palincsar, A. S., & Brown, A. L. (1988). Teaching and practicing thinking skills
to promote comprehension in the context of group problem solving. *Remedial
and Special Education, 9*(1), 53-59.

Partington, A. (ed.) (1992). *Oxford dictionary of quotations, 4th edition.* Oxford:
Oxford University Press.

Paul, R. (1986). Dialogical thinking: Critical thought essential to the acquisi-
tion of rational knowledge and passions. In J. Baron & R. Sternberg (Eds.),
Teaching thinking skills: Theory and practice (pp. 127-148). New York: W. H.
Freeman.

Paul, R. (1990). *Critical thinking: What every person needs to survive in a rapidly
changing world.* Rohnert Park, California: Center for Critical Thinking and
Moral Critique, Sonoma State University.

Pea, R. D. (1993). Practices of distributed intelligence and designs for education. In G. Salomon (Ed.), *Distributed cognitions* (pp. 47-87). New York: Cambridge University Press.

Pea, R. D., & Kurland, D. M. (1984a). On the cognitive effects of learning
computer programming. *New Ideas in Psychology, 2*(2), 137-168.

Pea, R. D., & Kurland, D. M. (1984b). *Logo programming and the development of
planning skills* (Report no. 16). New York: Bank Street College.

Perkins, D. N. (1981). *The mind's best work.* Cambridge, Massachusetts: Harvard University Press.

Perkins, D. N. (1985). Postprimary education has little impact on informal reasoning. *Journal of Educational Psychology, 77*(5), 562-571.

Perkins, D. N. (1986). *Knowledge as design.* Hillsdale, New Jersey: Erlbaum.

Perkins, D. N. (1989). Reasoning as it is and could be. In D. Topping, D. Crow-
ell, & V. Kobayashi (Eds.), *Thinking: The third international conference* (pp. 175-
194). Hillsdale, New Jersey: Erlbaum.

Perkins, D. N. (1992). *Smart schools: From training memories to educating minds.* New York: The Free Press.

Perkins, D. N., Goodrich, H., Tishman, S., & Owen, J. (1993). *Thinking Connections: Learning to think and thinking to learn.* Menlo Park, California: Addison-Wesley.

Perkins, D. N. (1993). Person plus: A distributed view of thinking and learning. In G. Salomon (Ed.), *Distributed Cognitions* (pp. 88-110). New York: Cambridge University Press.

Perkins, D. N. (1994a). *Knowledge as design: A handbook for critical and creative discussion across the curriculum (with accompanying videotape, production by David Whittier).* Pacific Grove, California: Critical Thinking Press and Software.

Perkins, D. N. (1994b). *The intelligent eye: Learning to think by looking at art.* Santa Monica, California: The Getty Center for Education in the Arts.

Perkins, D. N., & Laserna, C. (1986). *Inventive thinking* (Lesson sequence in *Odyssey: A curriculum for thinking*). Watertown, Massachusetts: Mastery Education.

Perkins, D. N., & Salomon, G. (1987). Transfer and teaching thinking. In D. N. Perkins, J. Lochhead, & J. Bishop (Eds.), *Thinking: The second international conference* (pp. 285-303). Hillsdale, New Jersey: Erlbaum.

Perkins, D. N., & Salomon, G. (1988). Teaching for transfer. *Educational Leadership, 46*(1), 22-32.

Perkins, D. N., & Simmons, R. (1988). Patterns of misunderstanding: An integrative model of misconceptions in science, mathematics, and programming. *Review of Educational Research, 58*(3), 303-326.

Perkins, D. N., & Swartz, R. (1992). The nine basics of teaching thinking. In A. L. Costa, J. Bellanca, R. Fogarty (Eds.), *If minds matter: A foreword to the future* (Vol. 2, pp. 53-69). Palatine, Illinois: Skylight Publishing.

Perkins, D. N., Allen, R., & Hafner, J. (1983). Difficulties in everyday reasoning. In W. Maxwell (Ed.), *Thinking: The frontier expands* (pp. 177-189). Hillsdale, New Jersey: Erlbaum.

Perkins, D. N., Farady, M., & Bushey, B. (1991). Everyday reasoning and the roots of intelligence. In J. Voss, D. N. Perkins, and J. Segal (Eds.), *Informal reasoning* (pp. 83-105). Hillsdale, New Jersey: Erlbaum.

Perkins, D. N., Jay, E., & Tishman, S. (1993). Beyond abilities: A dispositional theory of thinking. *The Merrill-Palmer Quarterly, 39*(1), 1-21.

Polya, G. (1954). *Mathematics and plausible reasoning* (2 vols.). Princeton, New Jersey: Princeton University Press.

Polya, G. (1957). *How to solve it: A new aspect of mathematical method* (2nd ed.). Garden City, New York: Doubleday.

Prange, G. W. (1981). *At dawn we slept: The untold story at Pearl Harbor.* New York: Penguin Books.

Pressley, M., Goodchild, F., Fleet, J., & Zajchowski, R. (1989). The challenges of classroom strategy instruction. *The Elementary School Journal, 89*(3), 301-342.

Pressley, M., Snyder, B. L., & Cariglia-Bull, T. (1987). How can good strategy use be taught to children? Evaluation of six alternative approaches. In S. M. Cormier & J. D. Hagman (Eds.), *Transfer of learning* (pp. 81-120). New York: Academic.

Rand, Y., Tannenbaum, A. J., & Feuerstein, R. (1979). Effects of Instrumental Enrichment on the psychoeducational development of low-functioning adolescents. *Journal of Educational Psychology, 71*, 751-763.

Rich, E. (1983). *Artificial intelligence.* New York: McGraw-Hill.

Richmand, B. (1993). Systems thinking: Critical thinking skills for the 1990s and beyond. *Systems Dynamics Review, 9*(2), 113-133.

Riedl, R. (1984). *Biology of knowledge: The evolutionary basis of reason.* New York: Wiley.

Ryle, G. (1949). *The concept of mind.* London: Hutchinson House.

Salomon, G. (1994, July). A new conception for the future of educational psychology. Presidential address of the Division of Education, Instructional, and School Psychology, The International Congress of Applied Psychology, Madrid, Spain, July, 1994.

Salomon, G. (Ed.) (1993). *Distributed cognitions.* New York: Cambridge University Press.

Salomon, G., & Perkins, D. N. (1987). Transfer of cognitive skills from programming: When and how? *Journal of Educational Computing Research, 3*, 149-169.

Salomon, G., & Perkins, D. N. (1989). Rocky roads to transfer: Rethinking mechanisms of a neglected phenomenon. *Educational Psychologist, 24*(2), 113-142.

Salovey, P., & Mayer, J. D. (1994). Some final thoughts about personality and intelligence. In R. J. Sternberg & P. Ruzgis (Eds.), *Personality and intelligence* (pp. 303–318). New York: Cambridge University Press.

Sanchez, C. A., Reise, S. P., Facione, P. A., & Facione, N. C. (1994). *Personality correlates of critical thinking in college students*. Paper presented at the 102nd annual conference of the American Psychological Association, Los Angeles, California.

Sarason, S. B. (1982). *The culture of the school and the problem of change* (2nd ed.). Boston: Allyn & Bacon.

Sarason, S. B., & Doris, J. (1979). *Educational handicap, public policy, and social history*. New York: Free Press.

Scarr, S. (1989). Protecting general intelligence: Constructs and consequences for interventions. In R. L. Linn (Ed.), *Intelligence: measurement, theory, and public policy* (pp. 74–118). Chicago: University of Illinois Press.

Scheffler, I. (1965). *Conditions of knowledge: An introduction to epistemology and education*. Glenview, IL: Scott, Foresman and Company.

Scheffler, I. (1991). In praise of cognitive emotions. In I. Scheffler, (Ed.), *In praise of cognitive emotions* (pp. 3-17). New York: Routledge.

Schneider, W., & Shiffrin, R. M. (1977). Controlled and automatic human information processing: I. Detection, search, and attention. *Psychological Review, 84*, 1-66.

Schoenfeld, A. H. (1979). Explicit heuristic training as a variable in problem-solving performance. *Journal for Research in Mathematics Education, 10*(3), 173-187.

Schoenfeld, A. H. (1980). Teaching problem-solving skills. *American Mathematical Monthly, 87*, 794-805.

Schoenfeld, A. H. (1982). Measures of problem-solving performance and of problem-solving instruction. *Journal for Research in Mathematics Education, 13*(1), 31-49.

Schoenfeld, A. H. (1985). *Mathematical problem solving*. New York: Academic Press.

Schoenfeld, A. H., & Herrmann, D. J. (1982). Problem perception and knowledge structure in expert and novice mathematical problem solvers. *Journal of Experimental Psychology: Learning, Memory, and Cognition, 8*, 484-494.

Schwab, J. (1978). *Science, curriculum, and liberal education: Selected essays* (I. Westbury & N. J. Wilkof, Eds). Chicago: University of Chicago Press [structure of disciplines].

Schwartz, S., & Perkins, D. N. (1995). Teaching the metacurriculum: A new approach to enhancing subject-matter learning. In D. Perkins, J. Schwartz, M. S. Wiske, & M. M. West (Eds.), *Software goes to school: Teaching for understanding with new technologies* (pp. 255-270). New York: Oxford University Press.

Scribner, S., & Cole, M. (1981). *The psychology of literacy.* Cambridge, Massachusetts: Harvard University Press.

Segal, J. W., Chipman, S. F., & Glaser, R. (Eds.). (1985). *Thinking and learning skills, Volume 1: Relating instruction to research.* Hillsdale, New Jersey: Erlbaum.

Senge, P. (1990). *The fifth discipline: The art and practice of the learning organization.* New York: Doubleday/Currency.

Sherman, C. B. (1965). *The Jew within American society.* Detroit: Wayne State University Press.

Simon, H. A. (1981). *The sciences of the artificial.* Cambridge, Massachusetts: The MIT Press.

Simon, H. A., & Hayes, J. R. (1977). Psychological differences among problem isomorphs. In N. J Castelan, D. B. Pisoni, & G. R. Potts (Eds.), *Cognitive theory* (Vol. 2) (pp. 21-41). Hillsdale, New Jersey: Erlbaum.

Stacey, R. (1992). *Managing the unknowable: Strategic boundaries between order and chaos in organizations.* San Francisco: Jossey-Bass.

Stanovich, K. E. (1994). Dysrationalia as an intuition pump. *Educational Researcher, 23*(4), 11-22.

Stanovich, K. E., & Cunningham, A. E. (1991). Reading as constrained reasoning. In R. J. Sternberg & P. A. Frensch (Eds.), *Complex problem solving: Principles and mechanisms* (pp. 3-60). Hillsdale, New Jersey: Erlbaum.

Sternberg, R. J. (1977). *Intelligence, information processing, and analogical reasoning: The componential analysis of human abilities.* New York: John Wiley & Sons.

Sternberg, R. J. (1985a). *Beyond IQ: A triarchic theory of human intelligence.* New York: Cambridge University Press.

Sternberg, R. J. (1985b). Implicit theories of intelligence, creativity, and wisdom. *Journal of Personality and Social Psychology, 49*(3), 607–627.

Sternberg, R. J., Conway, B. E., Ketron, J. L., & Bernstein, M. (1981). People's conceptions of intelligence. *Journal of Personality and Social Psychology, 41*(1), 37–55.

Stich, S. (1990). *The fragmentation of reason: Preface to a pragmatic theory of cognitive evaluation.* Cambridge, Massachusetts: MIT Press.

Swartz, R., & Parks, S. (1994). *Infusing the teaching of critical and creative thinking into elementary instruction: A lesson design handbook.* Pacific Grove, California: Critical Thinking Press and Software.

Swartz, R., & Parks, S. (in press). *Infusing the teaching of critical and creative thinking into secondary instruction: A lesson design handbook.* Pacific Grove, California: Critical Thinking Press and Software.

Swartz, R. J., & Perkins, D. N. (1989). *Teaching thinking: Issues and approaches.* Pacific Grove, California: Midwest Publications.

Thomson, G. H., (1916). A hierarchy without a general factor. *British Journal of Psychology, 8,* 271-281.

Thorndike, E. L. (1923). The influence of first year Latin upon the ability to read English. *School Sociology, 17,* 165-168.

Thorndike, E. L., & Woodworth, R. S. (1901). The influence of improvement in one mental function upon the efficiency of other functions. *Psychological Review, 8,* 247-261.

Thurstone, L. L. (1924). *The nature of intelligence.* London: Kegan, Paul, Trench, Trubner & Company.

Tishman, S. (1991). *Metacognition and children's concepts of cognition.* Unpublished doctoral dissertation, Harvard University Graduate School of Education, Cambridge.

Tishman, S., Perkins, D. N., & Jay, E. (1995). *The thinking classroom.* Boston: Allyn and Bacon.

Tuchman, B. (1984). *The March of Folly.* New York: Alfred A. Knopf.

Tversky, A., & Kahneman, D. (1973). Availability: A heuristic for judging frequency and probability. *Cognitive Psychology, 5,* 207–232.

Tversky, A., & Kahneman, D. (1974). Judgment under uncertainty: Heuristics and biases. *Science, 185,* 1124–1131.

Wagner, R. K. (1994). Context counts: The case of cognitive-ability testing for job selection. In R. J. Sternberg & R. K. Wagner (Eds.), *Mind in context: Interactionist perspectives on human intelligence* (pp. 133–151). New York: Cambridge University Press.

Wagner, R. K., & Sternberg, R. J. (1986). Tacit knowledge and intelligence in the everyday world. In R. J. Sternberg & R. K. Wagner (Eds.), *Practical Intelligence: Nature and origins of competence in the everyday world* (pp. 51–83). Cambridge: Cambridge University Press.

Waldrop, M. M. (1992). *Complexity: The emerging science at the edge of order and chaos*. New York: Simon & Schuster.

Weber, R. (1992). *Forks, phonographs and hot-air balloons: A field guide to inventive thinking*. New York: Oxford University Press.

Wellman, H. M. (1990). *The child's theory of mind*. Cambridge: MIT Press.

Wenger, E. (1987). *Artificial intelligence and tutoring systems: Computational and cognitive approaches to the communication of knowledge*. Los Altos, California: Morgan Kaufmann.

Whimbey, A. (1975). *Intelligence can be taught*. New York: E. P. Dutton.

Whimbey, A., & Lochhead, J. (1982). *Problem solving and comprehension*. Hillsdale, New Jersey: Erlbaum.

White, M. (1987). *The Japanese educational challenge*. New York: The Free Press.

Williams, W., Blythe, T., White, N., Li, J., Sternberg, R., & Gardner, H. (in press). *Practical intelligence for school handbook*. New York: HarperCollins.

Zuckman, J. (1994). Health reform ads draw criticism. *The Boston Globe*, Tuesday July 26, p. 5.

Index

Gell-Mann, Murray, 331
General intelligence. *See* g factor (general
     intelligence)
General Problem Solver, 214–15, 220–21
Generality ladder, 282–93, 336
Genetics, 42, 53–59, 65, 76, 104
Geographical metaphor for learnable
     intelligence, 236, 242–47, 263–65
George, King, 126–27
Getting to Yes (Fisher and Ury), 329
Global Preparedness and Human Resources
     (Rand Corporation), 7
Goddard, H. H., 5–7, 14, 18, 28–29, 39,
     42, 64, 69, 70, 76, 79, 103, 177, 318
God's thinking, 269–70
Good thinking, 308–10
Gordon, R. A., 60
Gould, Stephen Jay, 44–45, 65
Granato, Laura, 142
Graphic organizers, 289
Guilford, J. P., 73–74, 75, 268, 298–99
Gustaffson, J. E., 76

Haller, E. P., 88
Handicapping for horse racing, 82–83
Harry Stottlemeier's Discovery, 196,
     197–99
Harvard University, 130, 136, 166, 182,
     242–43, 329
Hasty thinking, 153, 160–61, 178,
     189–90, 276
Hayes, John, 60, 170, 171
Heredity. *See* Genetics
Herrnstein, Richard, 17, 57, 61–62, 64,
     101–102, 182
Heuristics, 86–88, 163–64, 213–14, 220,
     222, 238
High road transfer, 225–27
High-stakes thinking in history, 136–37
Higher-order knowledge, 201–202
Hiring, 63, 161
Hiroshima, 204–205
History: folly in, 10, 126–28, 136, 146,
     152, 174; and high-stakes thinking,
     136–36; nuclear bombing of Japan,
     204–205
Homer, 149–50, 158–59
Horace, 149
Horn, John L., 72, 73, 74, 75, 76, 268, 298
Horse racing intelligence, 82–83
How to Solve It (Polya), 86
Howard, Vernon, 166, 240–42
Human Inference (Nisbett and Ross), 163,
     174

Humphreys, Lloyd, 77, 78
Hunter, John E., 83, 106

Identical twin studies, 54–56, 58, 64, 114
Iliad (Homer), 149, 158
Immigrants, 45–46, 63–64
Immune system, 12–13
Improbable Machine, The (Campbell), 173
Impulsivity, 153
Inclination versus sensitivity, 279
Incremental learners, 277
Indians, 63
Information processing, 302–306
Information Visualizer, 327
*Infusing the Teaching of Critical and Cre-
     ative Thinking into Secondary Instruction*
     (Swartz and Parks), 204
Infusion programs, 179, 200–207
Inheritance. *See* Genetics
Inspection time, 50–51, 104
Instrumental Enrichment program: design
     of, 188–90; evaluation of, 190–91; phi-
     losophy of, 187–88, 207, 209, 307; style
     of, 185–86; in Venezuela, 182
Intelligence: Anderson's model of,
     302–306; Baron's search-inference
     framework of, 308–10; Binet's theory
     of, 18, 23–26, 28–29, 38–39, 42, 46,
     65, 70, 113; challenges to classic view
     of, 69–93; changeability of, 76–79;
     chess intelligence, 80–82, 154–55,
     211–12, 216, 217, 220, 228–29; classic
     view of, 5–7, 18, 69–70, 93, 177; and
     complexity, 320, 324–28; consistency
     of, 34–38; crystallized intelligence, 72,
     73, 107, 268, 298; dialectical thinking,
     320, 328–31; and dispositions, 274–82;
     distributed intelligence, 320, 321–24,
     327; evolution of, 319–21; and evolu-
     tionary double bind, 12–13, 160, 339;
     as expertise, 79–85, 106; failures in,
     121–75; Feuerstein's theory of,
     307–308; fluid intelligence, 72, 73, 76,
     79, 268, 298; and fundamental experi-
     ment, 34–38; g factor for general intel-
     ligence, 42–44, 46, 47, 52–53, 64, 65,
     70–73, 75–76, 79, 101, 104–105,
     113–14, 234, 298, 304–305; as geneti-
     cally determined, 6, 42, 53–59, 76,
     104; Goddard's list on, 5–7, 14, 39, 42,
     64, 69, 70, 76, 103, 177, 318; horse
     racing intelligence, 82–83; impact of
     choice of theory of, 99–102; job intelli-
     gence, 83–84; laboratory view of,